A HISTORY
OF BRITAIN
IN 100 MAPS

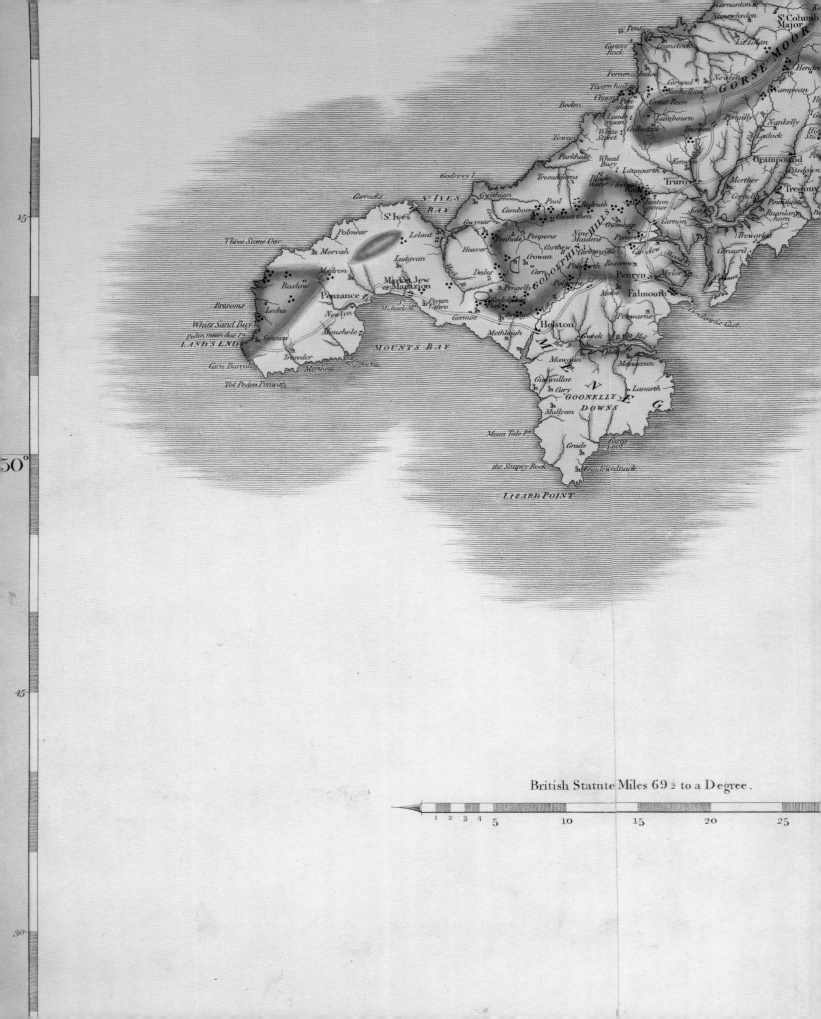

British Statute Miles 69½ to a Degree.

| 1 | 2 | 3 | 4 | 5 | 10 | 15 | 20 | 25 |

St Columb Major
GORSE MOOR
Nanswhyden
Carnanton
Lit. Tolan
Newlyn
Hendra
Carvoal
Nankelly
Nanchellan
Wampican
Pengilly
Carters Rock
Great Reen
Ladock
Pernanzabuloe
Boden
Lambriggan
Trespen
Lambourn
Chiquet
Powan
White Street
Callestick
Kenwin
Grampound
Pitsdown
Parkshate
Wheal Busy
Langarth
Tresaddems
Redruth
Merther
Godrevy I.
St IVES BAY
Black Water
Gwithian
Pool
Sevatk
Truro
Cornelly
Tregony
Gwynar
Camborn
Carnarthen
Nine Maidens
Owenhap
Pengrey
Fenton goose
Pomjogal
Ruganlans horn
St Ives
Lelant
Penhale
Penpons
Kea
Carnon
Polmear
Heaver
Carthew
Carbonelks
Treworl
Morvah
Grovan
Pobsworth
Carn
Dales
GODOLPHIN HILLS
Roserow
Corauril
Madron
Pengelly
Mabe
Carclew
Wood
Mawes
Buslow
Holt
Penryn
Mylor
Ludgvan
Market Jew or Marazion
Peran Uthro
Godolphin Park
Polgrehe
Falmouth
Lecha
Brewons
Penzance
Michaels M.
Germoe
Bulga
Penwarne
Roseland's Cast.
White Sand Bay
Newlyn
Methleigh
Pedenmen due P.
Sennen
Mousole
Helston
Cweek
R. Helf
Helbro
Landsend
Treseder
Carn Barroll
Merthen
Genorna
MOUNTS BAY
M E N E G E
Mawgan
Menaccan
Lanarth
Tol Peden Penwith
Guswalloe
Cury
GOONELLY DOWNS
Mullyan
Mean Tale P.
Grade
Cury 1.002
the Soapey Rock
Landewednack
LIZARD POINT
Thuee Stone Oan
Garrack's

50°
15
45
30

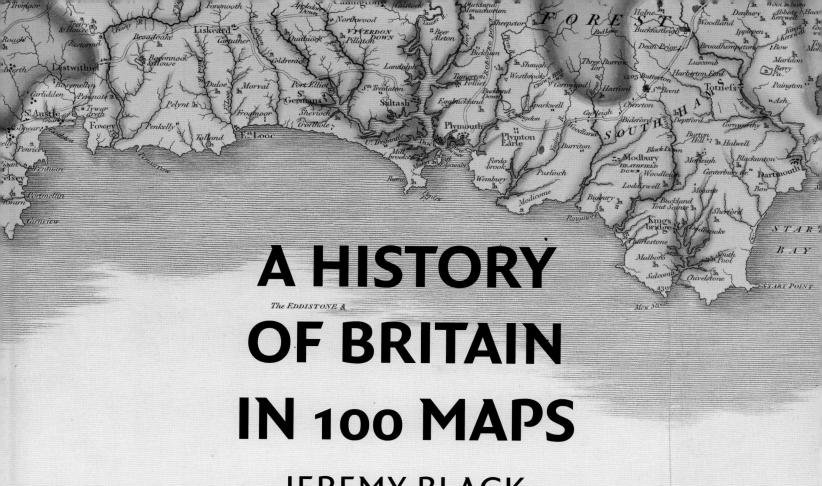

A HISTORY
OF BRITAIN
IN 100 MAPS

JEREMY BLACK

BRITISH LIBRARY

For Bill Gibson

First published in 2022 by
The British Library
96 Euston Road
London NW1 2DB

ISBN 978 0 7123 5471 4

British Library Cataloguing in Publication Data
A catalogue record for this publication is available from the British Library

Edited by Christopher Westhorp
Picture Research by Sally Nicholls
Designed by Karin Fremer

Printed in Italy by L.E.G.O. S.p.A.

PAGE 1 AND PAGES 2–3: Details from William Smith's A *delineation
of the Strata of England and Wales, with part of Scotland...*, 1815.

CONTENTS

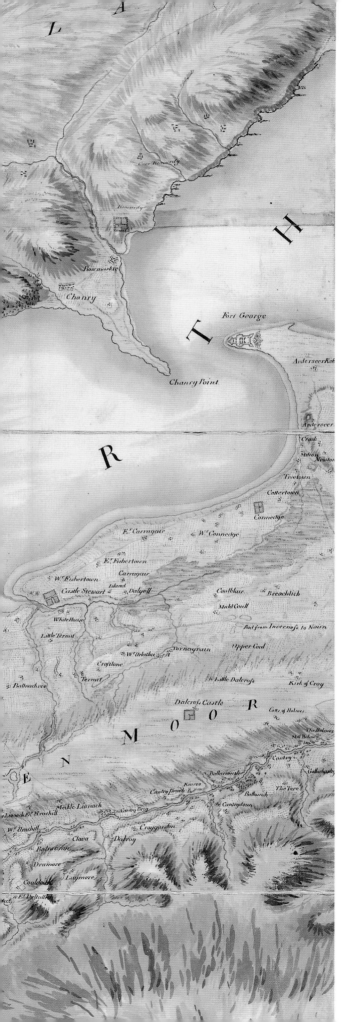

PREFACE

This highly illustrated, yet scholarly, book will provide a history of Britain in 100 maps. In doing so, it will serve two purposes. It will provide both a history of the major themes in British history, notably settlement, environmental change, state formation, ecclesiastical development, industrialisation, urbanisation and modern socio-political developments; and will also offer a history of the mapping of Britain. The text will focus on the major themes, while the 100 maps and their captions will be used both to illustrate this and to provide information on the development and variety of mapping, and the range of what was expected from maps. The selection will cover the historical development of maps in Britain, but the bulk are from the last two centuries when there has been a much greater range of thematic maps and when carto-literacy (the use and understanding of maps) was much further developed. Britain will be the subject of many of the maps, but there will also be a determined engagement with the local and regional dimensions. The caption discussion of the maps will include a consideration of carto-literacy at the time – and thereby of the broader social value of maps. In turn, this dimension will be fed back into the themes of the text. As far as possible, the two will be related and with discussion both ways of influence and example. The organisation will be chronological, as that makes most sense of developments, but during the course of the chronological account there will be references back and forwards in order to create cohesion during the volume.

It is a great pleasure to thank John Lee and his team at British Library Publishing, notably Sally Nicholls and Christopher Westhorp, for their hard work on this topic, and to dedicate this book to Bill Gibson, a good friend of great erudition, style and humanity, and the last is the greatest.

A detail from William Roy's 'The Military Survey of Scotland, 1747–55'. The structure on Culloden Moor labelled 'Little Lionach', south of Culloden House, is believed to be the small, heather-thatched cottage that survives on the battlefield site today, known as Leanach Cottage.

The ariuall of Lambert a
counterfet earle of warick
with Gerald earle of Kildar
and Martine swart a german
against H.7. 1487.

Holyhead

Innys ligod

Presholme Insul

Kirkham

Presto̅ 27   Bra

LANCESTER

Ormeshead
Hilbre Insul

Aberfraw
Bewmaris
Newburgh
Bangor
Aberconwey
Carnarvan
Cast Dalbadern

Caer ferie̅rhod

Newin
Pulheley

Brachipult point

Bradsey Insul

Sidwall Insul

CAR NAR

Cast Dole Jethelan

Harlech
Dolgelle
Barmouth

MERIONIDH

Aberdony

Aberistoyth

Machenllet
Caarnus

S. Aseph
Denbi
Flynt
FLINT

Seteia æst
Wallasie
Weral
Sherwick
Sleghe

Liverpole
Warrington

Flint, 41

Snowdon, 25

Powes land, 8

MO̅ GOMERY

19. Montgom 19.

Pelate, 43

Rosfeaire

Cardigan, 9

CARDIGAN
Cardigan
Lanbeder

New Cast
Trogdern

CEST RIA
Chester
Beston cast

Wrexham
Cast Dinas brane

Dee flu
k. cast

Holt cast

Ruthen cast
Oswester

Blore heath 51

Shro̅wel bury
Newport
Wellinton

Shrowsbury 44

STAF FO
SALO PIA
Lychfel

Bridge north

Mortemers cross 54

RADNOR

Hereforde

Blewith, 25

CAERMAR

The bisshop and his Clarker

Killgarren cast
Newport
Fisscard
S. Davides
Roch cast
Wiston
Narbarth
Flandri

Ramsey Insul

Gresholme Insul

Scalme Insul

Bride bay
Haverfordwe
Marloddton

PENB

Carew
Penbrok

Carmarden, 47

THIN

Milford haven

Wormeshedd point

Henry Earl of Richmond at
milford hauen ariued against
R3 in August 1485.

Lundye Insula

Hartland point

Harton

Stratton

Boscastel

Tintagel cast

Padstow

S. Manga

Broknock, 5

BRECK NOK

GLAMORG IA

Glamorgan, 30

Landai

Ogmore cast

Saint Donces

Crowbridge

Barrey

Flatholmes

Combemarton

Stepholmes

Minhead

MONV METHA

Chepstow

Newport

Caerdyf

Sabrina

Bristoll 10

Axbridge

Wolles

Iffraycombe

Barnestable
Sowthmaylton

Bediford

Chimligh

Holsworthy
Hetherley

Tamarton
Trevena
Camelford
Laun ston

Bodman

EXCESTER

Lydford cast

Chegford

Newton

INTRODUCTION: THE GEOLOGICAL PAST TO MEDIEVAL BRITAIN

Most of British history leaves no record in terms of maps made at the time, but this pre-history to mapping is covered by geological mapping and historical (as opposed to historic) maps. The key event was the breaching of the land bridge between Britain and the mainland of Europe, the Continent, in about 6500BCE. Geological mapping focused on the likely source of raw materials, notably coal, iron and building resources, and was a classic instance both of utilitarian cartography and the degree to which mapping could be both descriptive and anticipatory.

Historical mapping, those maps depicting earlier periods, captures not only the fascination of the past but also its significance as a means to validate claims and identities. In this, maps could serve as a form of exemplary history, and not least for those periods when length of existence itself was regarded as bringing a measure of legitimacy and precedence. This was to be seen for example in attempts to suggest links, or at least parallels, between Roman or Arthurian Britain and later power.

AGE OF THE MAPMAKERS

The long history of the British Isles bestrides two ages of maps. The longest of these ages is that in which the spatial sense of individuals has not come down to us in the form of maps, so that the only maps that are available are later ones, mapping archaeological finds, place name distributions and other indications of earlier ages. Our subject is the second age, the period in which we make maps, and contemporaneous maps record the assumptions, ideas and observations of past ages.

The earlier age, however, survives in that the spatial awareness of people helps to determine their perception – of their immediate environment and of the wider world. Those perceptions long remained particularly important, because even when maps existed most people would never see them or be expected to do so. Instead, maps were mostly for the learned, notably clerics and the wealthy.

Human life in the British Isles during this earlier age developed from being that of hunter-gatherer groups to sophisticated agrarian societies capable of a considerable level of organisation, not least in the construction of sacred sites such as Stonehenge and Avebury. Much of the forest cover was cleared, notably in the Iron Age, and the land put to the plough or used for animal husbandry. A succession of settlers and conquerors repeatedly transformed the political geography of the British Isles, both internally and with reference to the rest of Europe.

A major contrast remained between the islands of Britain (modern England, Scotland and Wales) and Ireland, which was more distant from the Continent and less affected by foreign conquest: the Romans did not rule Ireland or Highland Scotland; the Anglo-Saxons did not settle Ireland, Scotland or Wales; and the Angevin presence was less insistent in Ireland than those of the Tudors and (even more) Stuarts were to be.

THE CHRISTIAN ERA

Yet, whether or not conquered and settled, the British Isles as a whole were converted to Christianity in the first millennium AD/CE, and the religion's spatial imprint provided one form of organisation. Although there was a tension between the comprehensive structure of dioceses and the individual significance of monasteries, they agreed on the universal intercessionary role of the Church. Moreover, the Christian world-view dominated the collective consciousness and the moral code, notably shaping attitudes to sexuality.

Christianity meant a spread of education and literacy, and the beginnings of written law, especially to protect churchmen and their property, as written instruments conveyed rights in land. Society was becoming at least partly institutionalised. The Church was also a means of reintroducing Roman technologies and practices, including reading and writing, both to the parts of early medieval Europe that had lost them, as well as introducing them elsewhere. The Church, as the only institution that spanned the British Isles, was also a major agent encouraging the flourishing of trade and the reintroduction and spread of coinage. Although, initially, a king's baptism was sufficient to 'convert' a whole tribe or kingdom, the baptism of everyone ensured that Christianity also became part of personal and collective identity.

EVERYDAY LIFE

As far as life was concerned, it was far harder and shorter than the average today, with physical toil a more significant factor, and for women as well as men. Women were subordinated to men and expected to defer to them, and in law their husbands represented them. Gender roles were embodied in religious models such as the Virgin Mary and the saints. Women nevertheless played a vital role in the economy, with households being economic units to which women contributed greatly, not least by making clothes and processing food.

Women were not without rights. In the later Anglo-Saxon period there is evidence of their inheriting, holding and bequeathing lands, while married women could control separate property. Aside from the 'enclave' world of the nunnery, individual women also could gain prominence, most obviously as members of royal families, as with Aethelflaed, who ruled English Mercia in 911–18, or Emma, successively the influential wife of Aethelred the Unready and then Cnut. In addition, in Scotland the Pictish royal succession was matrilineal. Furthermore, whatever the superior status and rights of men, relationships within marriage in practice reflected the realities of strength of personality and nature of affection; a pattern that was also true of parent–child relations.

And yet personality and affection operated within a context of differential power and authority, in both gender and class terms. A society of inherited status ensured that many women were treated like chattels or political counters, while the centrality of military activity and ethos left scant independent roles for women. Furthermore,

female behaviour was classified and stereotyped by reference to religion: alongside positive images of the woman as bride, wife and mother, there was a strong negative tradition of the woman as harlot.

The environment and the human ecosystem were only slightly affected by technology. Indeed, patterns of life and death reflected the dominant role of the seasons. Moreover, physical strength and stature were of considerable importance, and wisdom was associated with age. There was no cult of youth or value linked to novelty: these are essentially developments of the last 250 years, and more particularly the last century. The role of heredity in social and political position and economic wealth contributed to a society that was referential and reverential to the past. Inegalitarian social practices and institutions were taken for granted, and were also central to 'politics', an activity restricted to the social elite.

The social structure was very hierarchical, dominated by landlords, who were generally firstborn males who had succeeded their fathers. Although tempered by the rise of lordship and kingship, kinship groups were of considerable importance and had defined legal roles in inheritance and in taking vengeance for hurts to kin members. Kin links were central to the practice of blood feuds. Their context, however, was changed greatly by the extension of royal government, a government that focused on enforcing the law. As a result, royal justice took precedence over blood feuds.

Royal government, however, was affected by disputes over who should be king, a process present from the outset. From the thirteenth century, there also came to be formal restrictions on royal government stemming from an idea of the kingdom as separate to the monarch. This most famously led to the restrictions stipulated in Magna Carta (1215) and, later in the century, to the development of parliamentary processes in England.

Koct...

ara diuidens anglos z pictos olim. chi

Ro
ueluo bure
Sahotes
nicor.

Walle

Crindale | Chinemue

Houu castm.

Werdale | Blac

Ha | B.

ex chu

Horth
W.

kar leolu

tucest!

comitat cestr

marchia Gest a Richemud

Duo brach

Duncimu

Ber
land

Sabna fl. qd z
maredt. tp su
excellucam.

Istei

Alutona

mor

pola ab

Sale
restr

mor cop pund

Ebordai

Be

yol conud.

Heram tra
pincolas su ob ke fluui
z britannia di
se ractitat a
rees origine
urile pmitua
et modiuola
ia pastouil
olas h agri
os z bel
3 (7d)

fon
tes

Pons Burgi

Bu
ge

ventont

Nigo
nia. ep

theo
kestr

pont ker

tulze

uevlau

Dene cas

Smar

Liu

de ser

Bristol
du

luche
feld

Blic

Cliut isqv.

glou
nia
ne
ff

use

Henwere

Ra

dunciu ke

Beal War

traha

Rt

nresiaz
croilas

taun

Diuis. Saresb
Vilto si marleb.

Houge

bestai

legetest.

Len

NORTH

HOLA

Bristol
du

2 Ff

tamer
y se fa
cuut tam
gicut lor z
dan fluui

feren
da

oron

yle. Vultu.

un Jordane

se

Stanf Burg

A.

Bedef

Horham

gra

Horwiu

Bathonia

Midelser.

Vindles

CIA
tho
ver
TIS

Welles traligt

cenobuu
sa albani

Dunestap

Orefod

Suffolk

vunaru

MAPPING THE ROCKS

William Smith, *A delineation of the Strata of England and Wales, with part of Scotland...*, 1815.

The science of geology suggested a new physical geography and history for Britain, which was depicted by William Smith (1769–1839) in a map that became iconic, in part due to its visual appeal. Geological mapping, however, was developed for utilitarian reasons, which was linked to the evolution of mineralogy, in turn related to a dynamic expansion of accessible and useful knowledge. Although the understanding of different strata provided the analytical tool, it was maps that helped transform popular appreciation of the subject. Geology also became an element in the domestic tourism that gathered pace at the close of the eighteenth century, not least with an interest in fossils, for example on the Dorset coast.

Alongside his geological map, with its colour-coded key, Smith produced a stratigraphic table, geological section and county geological maps, collectively intended to form a geological atlas. Smith's map, which was used by George Bellas Greenough when preparing his own geological map of England and Wales for publication by the Geological Society of London (of which he was president) in 1820, was followed by more detailed and sophisticated mapping. Official geological mapping developed in the 1830s, and by 1890 England and Wales had been mapped.

Successive geological maps were an important instance of the development of thematic mapping for utilitarian purposes. These maps were seen as a way to provide information on the location of coal, minerals, building materials and rock strata appropriate for reservoirs or for artesian wells. Older practices such as the use of divining rods were criticised and discarded.

Accompanied by cross-sections, geological surveys offered a form of three-dimensional mapping that appeared to make sense of the surface of the Earth and to enable it to be exploited for human purposes. In Ireland, where Richard Griffith produced pioneering geological maps in the 1830s, the Geological Survey of Ireland, administered as a regional office of the British Geological Survey, was founded in 1845. The Ordnance Survey of Ireland was completed in 1846, and, in an instance of the importance of accurate base maps and of the cumulative nature of information acquisitions, the geologists used the latter's maps for their own field surveys. By 1890, the one-inch-to-the-mile geological map of Ireland was completed in 205 sheets.

There was also a major effort to interpret the discoveries of geology and the very process of geological research, a subject that enjoyed much public attention, so that they did not invalidate the historical framework of theology. To a degree, this effort matched the attempt in Britain to ensure that the counter-revolutionary tendencies of the period were still capable of being aligned with the idea of a belief in progress.

William Buckland, who became Reader of Mineralogy at Oxford in 1813 (and practiced zoophagy, eating the heart of Louis XIV of France to that end), published his proof of the biblical Flood, *Reliquiae Diluvianae, or Observations on the Organic Remains Attesting the Action of A Universal Deluge* (1823). He followed that in 1836 with his own *Bridgewater Treatise*, which sought to use geology and other scientific tools to prove the power of God as shown in the Creation. In *Man as Known to us Theologically and Geologically* (1834), another clergyman, Edward Nares, Regius Professor of Modern History at Oxford from 1813 to 1841, had attempted to reconcile theology and geology – a task different from his need, in 1832, to explain why he had given no lectures for a decade, or, indeed, visited Oxford: Nares blamed the students' lack of interest.

Culturally, this information was mapped onto the psyche, a process seen with engravings of paintings that captured these ideas. For example, the impact of geological thought was apparent at the start of Charles Dickens's novel *Bleak House* (1852–53): 'As much mud in the streets as in the waters had but newly retired from the face of the earth, and it would not be wonderful to meet a Megalosaurus, forty feet long or so, waddling like an elephantine lizard up Holborn Hill' in Central London. Megalosaurus (Great Lizard) was the name Buckland, as president of the Geological Society of London, gave to the giant reptile of which the fossil bones had been found.

The versatile printer of Smith's map, John Cary, reflected the dynamism of the cartographic world. A map-seller, he also produced terrestrial and celestial globes, astronomical books, canal plans and road books and maps, including in 1790 his *Survey of the High Roads from London to Hampton Court* and 25 other places around the metropolis, a volume on the pattern of Ogilby's *Britannia* (of which Cary printed a new edition in 1798) divided into 40 strips covering, for example, London to St Albans in three maps, which was reissued in 1799, 1801 and 1810. Sir Archibald Geikie produced a *Geological Map of Scotland* (1892) that was published by J.G. Bartholomew.

A
DELINEATION
OF THE
STRATA
OF
ENGLAND AND WALES,
WITH PART OF
SCOTLAND;
EXHIBITING
THE COLLIERIES AND MINES,
THE MARSHES AND FEN LANDS ORIGINALLY OVERFLOWED BY THE SEA,
AND THE
VARIETIES OF SOIL
ACCORDING TO THE VARIATIONS IN THE SUBSTRATA,
ILLUSTRATED by the MOST DESCRIPTIVE NAMES
BY W. SMITH.

FIRTH OF FORTH

THE

GERMAN

OCEAN

THE

IRISH SEA

ST. GEORGE'S CHANNEL

CAERNARVON
BAY

CARDIGAN
BAY

THE WASH

EXPLANATION.

RIVER THAMES

BRISTOL CHANNEL

THE ENGLISH CHANNEL

ROCKS IN THE LOCALITY

British Geological Survey, 'Exeter: Solid and Drift Geology', 1995.

For this sheet (325), the original (Old Series) geological survey at the 1:63,360 scale was resurveyed and transferred to the New Series map published in 1899. This was photographically enlarged to the 1:50,000 scale and reprinted in 1986. This map, published in 1995, was based on the resurveying on the 1:10,000 scale in 1982–91. The cross-sections show the general relations of the rocks along the three lines drawn on the map, with a 1:50,000 horizontal scale and a vertical exaggeration by 2.5 times. Magnetic anomaly maps appear at the bottom left and generalised vertical sections at the bottom right. The geological data is printed in colour on a black-and-white background of settlements and roads. This explains the very varied topography of the area, notably Woodbury Common in the southeast, the most westerly of the sandstone commons of Wessex, the Haldon Hill to the southwest, and the alluvial river valleys, especially of the Exe and Clyst, which show up as white. Exeter Cathedral itself reflects material from over two quarries, including volcanic rock quarried two miles west of the River Exe that was also used in the city walls. In east Exeter there were quarries where Heavitree stone, a type of red breccia stone, was quarried from about 1350.

Whereas much of the Southwest has rocks largely of the Devonian (named after Devon) and Carboniferous eras, from about 395 to about 250 million years ago, the eastern area including that depicted in this map is largely composed of Permian strata from about 280 to 230 million years ago, notably breccias, marls and conglomerates. Upper Permian strata are more to the east of the Exe estuary and valley and Lower Permian to their west. Soils are related to underlying strata, but in turn human influence has increased, not only through changes in the water table, but also through deforestation.

The data available for geological mapping increased greatly in the nineteenth century, partly as a result of the British Geological Survey, and more core samples became available as boreholes were drilled. More recently, knowledge also increased from remote sensing, and physical and chemical techniques for age-dating. As a result, knowledge of rock calibration improved. At the same time, a geological map remains a work of inference and therefore uncertainty.

During the twentieth century production techniques for the maps changed, with copperplate engraving replaced first by the use of ink on paper and then on plastic film, subsequently by the use of photomechanical reproduction techniques, and finally by geological cartographic computing, for storage, analysis and presentation.

The British Isles have a very varied geology, topography, climate and natural vegetation. We should be careful about projecting the modern environment onto the past: climate and drainage, even the coastline and water levels, were different. Yet, in simple terms, the bulk of the west and north of Britain is higher and wetter, its soils poorer, and its agriculture pastoral rather than arable: centred on animals, not crops. Much of Ireland is like west and north Britain, although there is less high land. However, there are many exceptions to this general description of the British Isles as a result of a highly complex geological history and of great climatic variations.

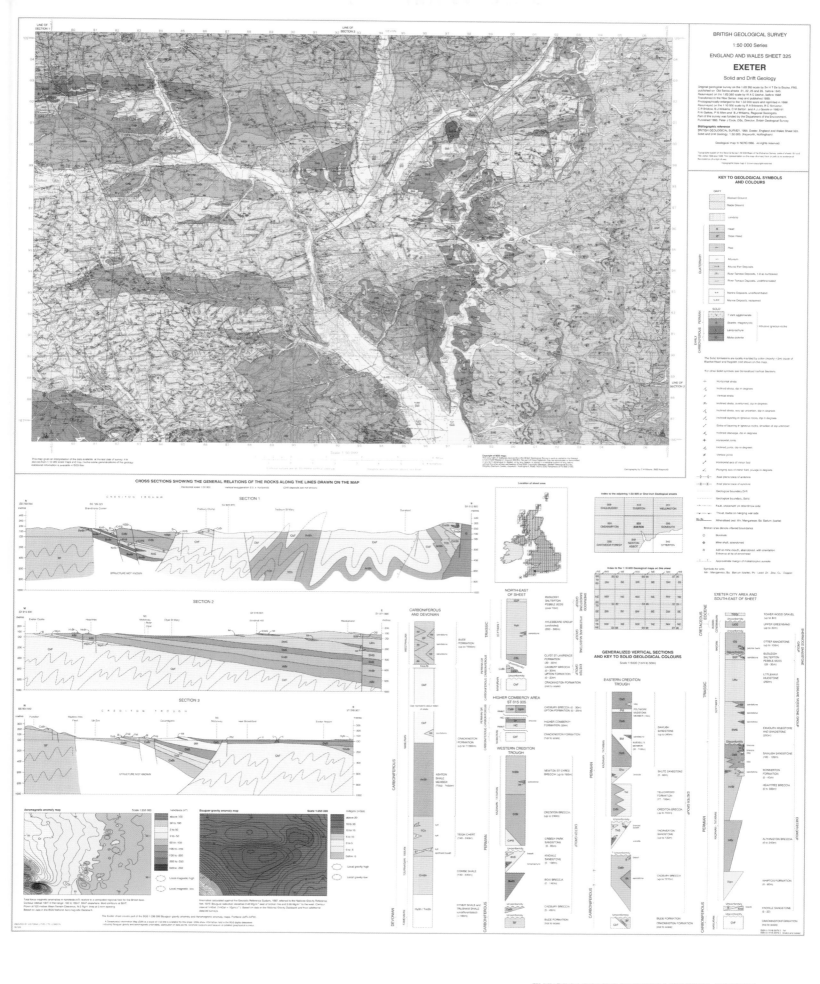

FIGHTING FOR BRITAIN

John Speed, *The Invasions of England and Ireland with all their Civill Warrs since the Conquest*, 1601.

Historical mapping provided a far later way to cover earlier history. Thus, John Speed's *A Prospect of the Most Famous Parts of the World* (1627) included 'A Brief Description of the Civil Wars and Battles fought in England, Wales, and Ireland', illustrated by a double-page black-and-white map drawn in about 1601 of 'The Invasions of England and Ireland, with all their Civill Warrs since the Conquest', a reference to the Norman Conquest of 1066 and including a number of images relevant to the Spanish Armada of 1588. The map was arresting, illustrative and definitely added visual interest to the book, but it suffers in crowdedness through its depiction of events as simultaneous when they were greatly separated in time, indeed by over half a millennium, a traditional device characteristic of early maps, including *mappae mundi*. This crowdedness provided confusion, as the simultaneity was far from relevant. In practice, invasions ensured the strategic importance of the southern and southeastern coasts, notably Dover, because routes to London were crucial, and the Scottish border was far distant.

Simultaneity was also seen with the map of post-Roman England published by Christopher Browne in 1700. In contrast, by 1797 John Andrews, in his *Historical Atlas of England*, provided separate maps of the Ancient Britons, Roman Britain, Saxon England and England at the time of the Danelaw, but nothing later. John Speed's county maps also included historical information, for example sites of battles. Speed's work captured the growing interest in English history from before the sixteenth century, and history that was accompanied by maps. The Anglo-Saxon scholar and cartographer Laurence Nowell (1530–c.70), dean of Lichfield Cathedral, in his 13-section mid-sixteenth-century manuscript map of England and Wales, gave place names in Old English and used Old English letter forms. The Kent antiquarian, mapmaker and Justice of the Peace, William Lambarde (1536–1601), a pupil of Nowell who enjoyed Queen Elizabeth I's favour, not only produced the first English county history, *A Perambulation of Kent* (1576), but also drew a map of the Anglo-Saxon kingdoms. This reflected a marked rise in interest in Anglo-Saxon roots after the break with Rome in the Reformation and notably in early British Christianity.

PRESENTING THE SAXONS

Charles Pearson, 'Saxon England', 1870.

Maps which present Anglo-Saxon spatial views are rare, although Anglo-Saxon awareness of geographical features is shown both in numerous place names and in their settlement geography. Historical geographers have sought to clarify this situation by offering a guide to later perceptions. In his *Historical Maps of England* (1870), Charles Pearson (1830–94) presented geography as playing a direct role in history, but with the physical geography increasingly overcome in recent decades – 'the hills are losing their old influence' – such that it was necessary to understand the new human geography.

The coastline of the Saxon period is used in this map by Pearson, while the emphasis on physical features ensures that variations in territorial boundaries and political hierarchies were not captured. Extensive woodlands are presented in order to explain the direction of settlement, Pearson reflecting that although 'man triumphs over the elements', this triumph was essentially a matter only of the previous half-century.

Pearson, who had already published *The Early and Middle Ages of England* (1861), presented geography at work in the great political divisions of the country's history. Describing the mountains as 'the conservative element ... in our history', Pearson observed that the Roman presence was limited in the upland regions – Southwest England, Wales, Galloway and Lancashire – and that 'it was precisely these parts where the nationality was unbroken, that afterwards sustained the struggle against the Saxon'.

Developing the theme that progress was related to the limitation of royal authority, and linking it with a sense that upland areas were socially conservative and politically reactionary, Pearson argued that in the civil war of Stephen's reign (1135–54), 'the Empress Matilda, who represented the not infrequent combination of legitimate title and an oppressive government', drew her support from the upland west, but Stephen from London 'and the commercial towns of the east'. In the 1260s, 'London and the south and east were with the great constitutional leader [Simon] De Montfort; the north and west sided with the King [Henry III]. In the Wars of the Roses, the Yorkist part, which on the whole was that of good government, received partisans from the same district as De Montfort.' Similar comments were made about the English Civil War of 1642–46

and then for the Jacobite uprising in 1745: '...nowhere, except in the Highlands, could Prince Charles Edward have raised an army; nowhere but in the north-western counties, still only partially civilized, did he find recruits. Our country is so small, that in Cumberland and Westmoreland at least, the hills are losing their old influence.'

In practice, although it is dangerous to adopt a crude socio-economic or geographical determinism in explaining the divisions between the two sides, and it is clear that each had support in every region and social group, it is also true that Parliament's support was strongest in the most economically advanced regions: the south and east of England, many of the large towns, especially London and Bristol, and in industrial areas; while support for Charles in England and Wales was most pronounced in less advanced regions: the north, Wales and the west. Thus, religious and political differences were related to socio-economic situations, although not dependent on them. For example, the Derbyshire lead miners were split. Charles's supporters feared religious, social and political change, and were motivated by concepts of honour and loyalty.

The north and west contain fertile lowlands, such as the central lowlands of Scotland, the Vale of York in Yorkshire and the Vale of Eden in Cumbria; while the south and east include areas of poor fertility, such as the sandy wastes of the Breckland in Suffolk or the hilly greensand of the Weald in Kent. Nevertheless, the essential contrasts in England are between the colder, hillier north and the warmer, lower south, the wetter west and the drier east, and, despite the effects of climate change in the past, these contrasts have been consistent. And there are political consequences. Upland areas such as the Pennines, a range of hills that forms the backbone of northern England, have not generally served as centres of power. Instead, prior to the Roman invasion, hill forts were more numerous in the south and west of England. There were relatively few in the north and east. Some were in the Cheviots and Lothians of southern Scotland, but there were very few indeed in the Pennines proper. For much of English and Scottish history, wealth and influence have been disproportionately present in the south of each country, with the east also being generally more significant than the west.

SAXON ENGLAND

EXPLANATION

Roman Towns .... EOFERWIC

Saxon Towns .... HEORTFORD

PRESENTING THE ROMANS

Claudius Ptolemy, 'Map of Britain', 1511.

The Roman account of Britannia in part survives via the work of Claudius Ptolemy, a Greek scholar (c.100–170 CE) who worked in Alexandria. He never visited Britain and produced no known maps, but left a list of places and coordinates from which later maps were made, including Greek ones in the early fourteenth century. The first manuscript map of Ptolemy's *Geographia* was translated into Latin in about 1415 and the first printed one in about 1462. Thomas Elyot, in *The Boke named the Governour* (1531), encouraged parents to teach history with reference to Ptolemy's maps.

There were relatively few place names on the map, but some tribal names were included (for example, the Cantii, whose principal town was Londinium) as were certain rivers. The alignment of Scotland was seriously flawed, but can be corrected by a repivoting. Agricola, the Roman governor of Britannia from 77 to 84 CE, sent a fleet to survey and map the coast of Scotland in 79 CE. In 83 CE Agricola crossed the Forth and won a notable victory against the Caledoni at Mons Graupius, but part of his army was transferred to the Continent and, partly as a consequence, only the Scottish lowlands were conquered. The Romans could win victories in Aberdeenshire, as Agricola and later Severus did, but retention of territory proved a different matter.

Anglesey (Mona), which the Romans had earlier conquered, is marked, as is Ireland, which they did not attack, although Agricola considered doing so. Ireland, nevertheless, received a small but steady flow of Roman coins and other imported materials, in all likelihood the result of mercenary activity and trade from Irish Sea (Ibernicus Oceanus) ports in western Britain such as Chester. Identification of places mentioned by Ptolemy can be eased by matching names to later counterparts and by linguistic analysis. Comparison with other ancient sources is very helpful, not least because Roman itineraries at the period provide plentiful material on places and the road network. Later research methods for translating ancient into modern coordinates include triangulation and flocking, the latter being a form of data analysis.

The Roman Conquest ensured that links with the Continent were greatly strengthened. Agriculture, much of which centred on Romanised farms or villas, was important and the bulk of the population lived in the countryside. Farming also improved. In the late third and fourth centuries, larger ploughs were introduced and coulters (vertical blades) were added, leading to

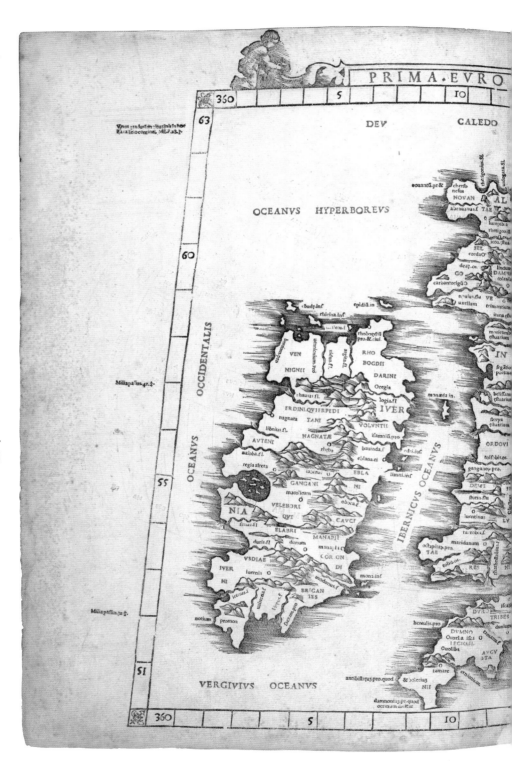

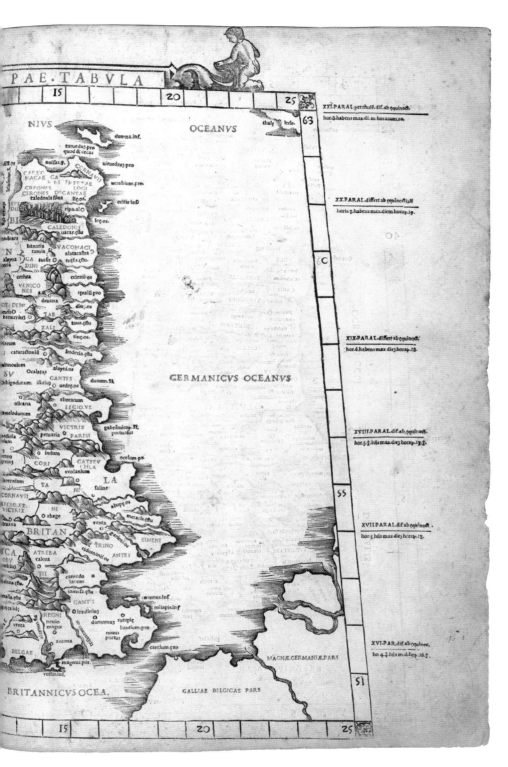

the cutting of deeper furrows, which permitted the working of heavier soils. The introduction of two-handed scythes enabled hay to be cut faster and thus larger quantities to be stored for winter forage. Corn-drying kilns were constructed, and crop rotations were introduced, while animals were overwintered in hay meadows. Animal- or water-powered mills offered significant enhancements in agricultural and industrial productivity.

The greater quantity of archaeological material surviving from the Roman period suggests a society producing and trading far more goods than its Iron Age predecessors. The prosperity of the rural economy underwrote the cost of building numerous villas: large noble houses in the countryside constructed in a Roman style and heated from under the floor by a hypocaust system. Another testimony of the human imprint was the wiping out of the bear in England by the end of the Roman period. Humans were the dominant species. Meanwhile, the clearing of virgin woodland in lowland England continued.

Roman Britain acquired an urban system linked and structured by roads, such as Ermine, Stane and Watling streets and the Fosse Way. Reflecting the quality of Roman engineering, these wide highways were built to a high standard, with stone foundations and gravel surfaces. Towns such as Londinium (London), Verulamium (St Albans), Lindum (Lincoln) and Eboracum (York) were centres of authority, consumption and Roman culture – including, eventually, Christianity. Some towns, usually with 'chester' in their name, emerged alongside Roman fortresses, but others developed as a result of local initiatives by the native elites keen to adopt Roman culture and material life.

Roman religious cults spread, although assimilation with the beliefs of the ancient Britons was important. When Christianity became the state religion in the fourth century CE, this brought more systematic cultural links between England and the Continent, links not shared by non-Roman Scotland. In contrast to Christianity, the pre-Roman Druids, whom the Romans stamped out, and the cults of the Olympian gods which the Romans introduced, had both lacked diocesan structure and doctrinal regulation. The Olympian cults, however, prefigured Christianity in linking England to the Continent.

THE IMPRECISION OF EARLY MAPPING

Priscian, 'World Map', 1025–50.

Acquired in 1598 by Sir Robert Cotton (1571–1631), a key figure in the Elizabethan interest in antiquarianism, this *mappa mundi* ('world map') has been dated to about 1025–50 and was possibly made in Canterbury and based on an updated late-Roman original: it is in a copy of a fifth-century geography manual, Priscian's *Liber Periegesis* ('Book of Geographic Descriptions'), which was based on an earlier work. The British Isles are given a more prominent role than in the later Hereford map (see following pages). Very small, the map understandably cannot offer much accuracy (see detail, below). Wales is presented as an island and Cornwall, the Scilly Isles, the Orkneys, the Channel Islands are all shown; the Southwest has two warriors fighting. Ireland is oriented east–west, with Armagh marked. London and Winchester, the major towns in southern England, are marked, as is Kent, while Strathclyde, which was for a while a separate kingdom until conquered by the Scots in the eleventh century, is distinguished from 'Brittannia' [sic] to the south. The green used elsewhere in the map for mountains is not in evidence for the British Isles.

The period was very much one of unsettled borders, and notably so between England and Scotland. There was no fixed border and Scotland had expanded southwards to overrun Lothian in the tenth century, an achievement confirmed with victory over the Northumbrians at Carham in 1018. Both England and Scotland were ethnically, geographically, economically and culturally diverse. Thus, Scotland included Scots, Picts, the Britons of Strathclyde and the Angles of Lothian.

Communications in the period were relatively primitive, with long-distance bulk transport only economically viable by water. On land, ridge-routes were important. The greater role of bridges is suggested by the extent to which, from the 740s, labour services for bridge-building and repair became an important provision in charters. The map possibly dates from the reign of Cnut (r.1016–35), his sons Harold Harefoot (r.1035–39) and Harthacnut (r.1039–42), or Edward the Confessor (r.1042–66). Cnut ruled because of the success of Danish invasions and the death of his vigorous Anglo-Saxon rival, Edmund Ironside. Cnut sought to rule not as a conqueror, but as a lord of both Danes and non-Danes. He was the king of a number of kingdoms, not a monarch seeking to enlarge one kingdom. Cnut took over an effective governmental system, did what an English monarch was supposed to do as head of state and, unlike the Norman William the Conqueror, did not have to face rebellions. In 1018, Cnut reiterated the legislation of his predecessors. He did not purge the Church, was the benefactor of a number of prominent English monasteries and was not culturally alienated from the Anglo-Saxon world. He made London his military and governmental centre in England. The demographic growth, agrarian expansion and commercial growth of the tenth and eleventh centuries saw the arts of sheep and corn husbandry mastered and there was considerable foreign trade. Cnut's England was more stable than much of western Europe.

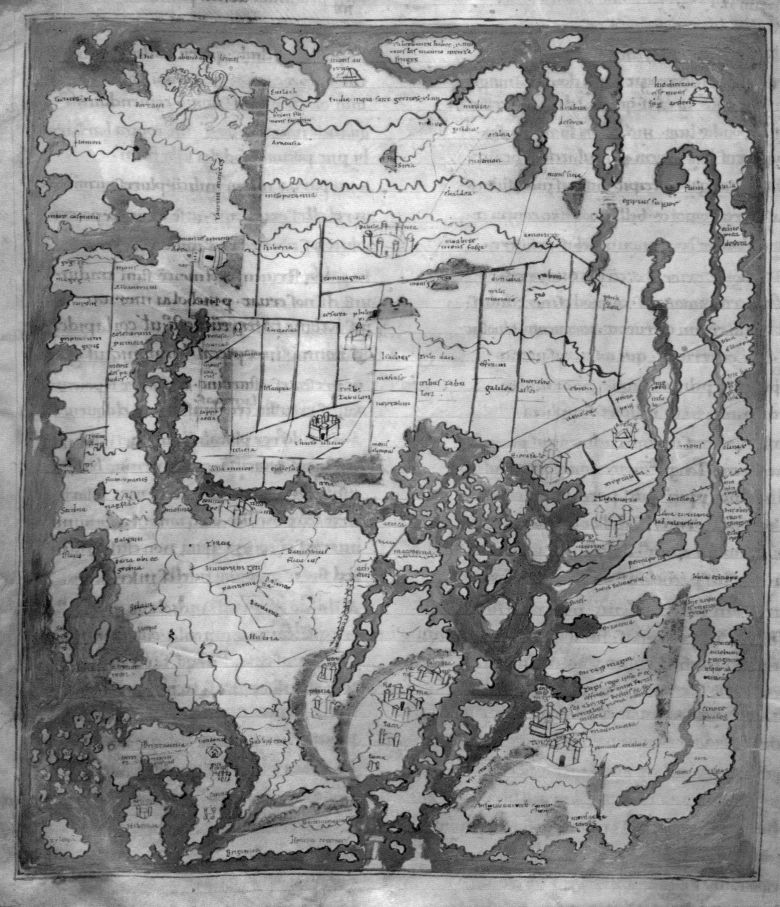

ON THE EDGE OF THE WORLD

Richard of Haldingham, 'Hereford *Mappa Mundi*', c.1300.

The Hereford *Mappa Mundi* ('world map') was made in about 1300, probably in Lincoln, and bears the name of Richard of Haldingham, a canon of Lincoln who entered the household of the bishop of Hereford. The map relates geographical knowledge in a Christian format, offering a combination of belief and first-hand observation. Such maps employed a tripartite internal division, depicting three regions, namely the regions of the world divided between Noah's sons – Asia, Europe and Africa – all contained within a circle [the O], which also suggested the Wheel of Fortune. This theme was to be captured in Shakespeare's *King Lear* (1606): 'I am bound upon a wheel of fire.'

At the apex of the world, outside the frame, Christ in Majesty on the Day of Judgement presides over the world, and the map was probably placed between pictures, or reliefs, of heaven and hell. Christ in Majesty was a certainty above a Creation, the goal and nature of which was clear in God's purpose, but which man could only partly fathom. As the symbol of Creation, the circle acted to contain the ephemeral nature of human activity.

Christian clerics, and particularly those in England, played a significant role in the mapping of the period, as also with the Duchy of Cornwall and, probably, Ebstorf world maps of the same period, the latter possibly by Gervase of Tilbury (1150–1228).

The depiction of the British Isles in the map is one designed to fit the space, and to capture relationships rather than an exact form. This approach throws light on the remark by Roger Bacon, a Franciscan friar who taught at Oxford, who in his *Opus Maius* (c.1268) stated that: '...if one does not understand the physical form of the world, history is apt to become a stale and tasteless crust...'

The British Isles were represented at the lower left of the Hereford map, on the edge of the world, capturing the idea that sailing into the Atlantic was journeying into the unknown. This presentation reflected Classical ideas, rather than the experience and imagination of the medieval period. Indeed, the Norsemen, who in the tenth and eleventh centuries dominated much of the British Isles, had also established bases on the Faroe Islands, Iceland and Greenland, from where they sailed on to North America. Moreover, DNA research on the Icelanders of the period suggests

an important Irish component, probably derived from slaves. The Norse were a major presence in Ireland into the twelfth century, in northwest Scotland until the late thirteenth, and in the Shetlands and Orkneys until 1468–69. This is not an impression created by the map. Nor is there any reference to the westward imagination and experience of the British Isles, which ranged from Irish tales of voyages to St Brendan's Island and other Atlantic islands, to long-range fishing expeditions, notably to Icelandic waters.

The Hereford *Mappa Mundi* very much reflects a Roman and Christian pattern by focusing on cities, which were the centres of government, lay and ecclesiastical, of commerce, and of communications. Thus among the British cities shown are the major English bishoprics of Lincoln and Winchester, with Lincoln, a renowned centre of learning, the most far-flung. Separately, the respective size of the parts of the British Isles are disproportionate, while the River Tweed does not separate Scotland from England in the manner shown. The use of Anglo-Norman as well as Latin in the map indicates that the information offered was for laity as well as clergy.

The British Isles were at an edge of the Christian world, one articulated by the processes of Church government and justice, which centred on Rome, and by pilgrimages, which focused on Jerusalem. In addition, holy orders, notably the Benedictine and Cistercian monks, and the Franciscan and Dominican friars, as well as crusading organisations, in the shape of the Hospitallers and the Templars, all had foreign headquarters, and this further increased a governance and mutual awareness that spanned the Channel. So did British trade, with wool exports to the Low Countries the most important industry, which brought considerable prosperity to East Anglia and Lincolnshire.

The mapping of religious themes also led to some coverage of parts of Britain. The Benedictine monk Thomas Elmham (d. c.1428), in his *Historia monasterii sancti Augustini Cantuaariensis* (*History of St Augustine's monastery, Canterbury*), on which he finished work in 1414, used a plan of the Isle of Thanet to illustrate the legend of Dompneva's hind, whereby the monastery received lands as delineated by the route of a running hind.

MEDIEVAL POWER

Matthew Paris, 'Map of Great Britain', c.1255.

Matthew Paris, a Benedictine monk at the wealthy St Albans' Abbey north of London (an abbey probably founded in 793), produced four versions of a map of Britain in the 1250s. As with the later Gough Map of about 1360 (see pages 32–35), the Paris map appears to have followed the approach of beginning with an outline, partly from a portolan chart and partly from a world map, then inserting information, probably from an itinerary, which was an important form of spatial information and part of the cartographic world. Such maps attempt to present the actual physical appearance of the country rather than to represent the relationship between places in simple schematic diagrams.

The map by Matthew Paris is mainly delineated by its rivers and coastlines on either side of a north–south axis. It is particularly rich in the number of named cities, towns, hills and rivers – more than 250 of them. Panels around the margins of the map identify the nearest land in each direction.

The boundary between England and Scotland is clearly marked by Hadrian's Wall – 73 miles long and built between 122 and 130 by the Emperor Hadrian to mark the Roman Empire's northerly border. Further north is the 39-mile-long Antonine Wall, built in 142–154 for his successor, Antonius Pius. Both walls are shown by Paris schematically as battlemented features. The Antonine Wall was, in fact, a rapidly abandoned ditch-and-turf wall structure, but, even if that distinction was known by Paris, it is unclear how he could best have shown it. At the time of his mapmaking, the walls were of no military or political significance. Scotland under Alexander II (r.1214–48) was stable as a result of the crushing of opposition in Argyll, Caithness and Galloway. In 1237, the Treaty of York fixed the frontier with England, ending Scottish attempts to expand into Northumbria and Cumbria, and Henry III (r.1216–72) abandoned in 1244 the idea of attacking Scotland.

London is acknowledged by Matthew Paris as the largest city by depicting it with the most elaborate towered and battlemented frame surrounding its name, dominating the river. Castles, such as Windsor and Pontefract, both major fortifications, are marked. Windsor was a royal fortress and Pontefract Castle, in Yorkshire, was where the deposed Richard II would be murdered in 1400. Because the Southeast of England has been moved to immediately south of London, with Rochester, Canterbury and Dover all marked accordingly, the Isle of Thanet appears off the south coast, alongside other misplaced islands. Such a mistake was a failure to understand location, but it also captured the idea that Kent was south of London on the route to the Continent.

In northwest Wales, the peaks of Mount Snowdon are roughly indicated and labelled 'Snaudun'. In this period, the area was under Llywelyn, Prince of Gwynedd, who had performed homage to Henry in 1247, when, in addition, all the lands east of the River Conwy went to the king. Having defeated his brothers in 1254–55, Llywelyn set out to restore the earlier dominions of Gwynedd, which brought him into rivalry with Henry's eldest son, Edward, who, in 1254, was granted the Earldom of Chester and the royal lands in Wales. Llywelyn overran northeast Wales in 1256, and central Wales in 1256–57, and invaded South Wales in 1257. Another Welsh ruler, Gruffydd ap Gwenwynwyn of Powys, refused to acknowledge Llywelyn as overlord, and in 1257 sought shelter with Henry III whose advance that year achieved nothing. The fate of Wales was still unclear, but the map provides no clue to this.

Nor are the ambitions of the kings of Scotland to seize the Western Isles brought out: in 1249, Alexander II died en route to invade them; but, after war in 1263–66, notably an indecisive battle at Largs in 1263, and even more the death soon after of king Haakon Haakonsson of Norway, the Western Isles were acquired under the Treaty of Perth. However, Norwegian sovereignty over the Shetlands and Orkneys was confirmed then. Thus, British politics was far more dynamic and uncertain than the map suggested, not that that was Paris's intention.

Le chastel de Doure lentree e la clef de la riche isle de engleter. e au...

paf de Iurnee

labbeie seint augustin

ken[t]

Cantebire. chef de iglises de engletre

Iurnee

lewe de ... aye delwere

Roucestre ki est euesche[s]

MVSEVM
BRITAN
NICVM

Iurnee

La cite de lundf. ki est chef denglere. Brutus ki prime enhabita engleterre la funda. e laie la troie la nuuele.

Westm...

la rue... la grat riue de tamise lambeth

la e. pint entre la iglise sei pol seit mara...

...gate. hougate. Crupelgate. Bissopesgate. Billingesgate. Allegate

Beu...ue... is

Reins

Iurnee

Pois

Seit entin

Iurnee

Seint Richer

Arar

Iurnee

Cuftroil

nee

Iurnee

Cateif

nre dame de Boloine

Witsant port de mer cunt[re] Doure

LONDON AND ITS STRENGTHS

Matthew Paris, 'London to Dover, Itinerary from London to the Holy Land…', 1250–59.

The depiction of London, in a pictogram map, was drawn as part of a road map for pilgrims to Jerusalem. In practice, few would actually have carried it with them on the journey, often using it, instead, as a devotional tool for pious contemplation at home. A verbal navigational guide would be more useful for travellers.

The journey starts from London where pilgrims could visit the shrine of Edward the Confessor (r.1042–66) at Westminster Abbey, which is shown to the right of the drawing. Edward was made a saint in 1161 and his body translated to the abbey two years later. Henry III (r.1216–72) fostered the cult of St Edward and commissioned a life of him from Matthew Paris, whom he knew.

The Tower of London is on the left. The use of Caen stone from Normandy for most of the White Tower, which was intended as palace as well as fortress, reflected the lack of good building stone in the London region. The name appears to have been used after 1240 when Henry III had the structure painted with whitewash. The use of stone was encouraged by the frequency and destructiveness of fire, as in 1212 in which many Londoners were trapped on London Bridge as the fire took hold of the timber buildings on the stone-arched bridge completed in 1209.

The cathedral church of St Paul had been devastated by fire in 1087, its replacement providing an opportunity to create a Romanesque successor to the Anglo-Saxon style, a work that was as expressive of the new Norman order in religion as was the White Tower in military might. Delayed by another fire in the 1130s, the cathedral may not have been completed until the end of that century, and therefore had Gothic as well as Romanesque features. At its total extent of 644 feet, the cathedral was the longest in England, and its timber spire, 520 feet high, exceeded Salisbury's 404-foot spire made of stone. Destroyed by lightning in 1561 and never rebuilt, the spire was only topped in London by the Post Office Tower finished in 1964.

The road map presented a key link between Britain and the Continent: medieval Christendom. This idea of the Christian world led many, notably Richard I, Richard the Lionheart, in 1189–91, to crusade; and it also ensured that the structure of ecclesiastical government was fortified by fresh impulses. The strengthening of papal government from the eleventh century, with the Gregorian reforms, was important. So also was the introduction of new groups, from the Knights Templar to the Friars. However, tension between the Church and the Crown was a growing element, with hostility to what were judged foreign elements in the Church, to popes and prelates seeking to dictate temporal policy, and to the movement of money abroad.

At the same time, the Church helped provide a sense of identity, with parish churches providing a detailed pattern of belonging, as well as the basis for social and cultural activity, notably philanthropy. With churches the venues for weddings, baptisms and burials, the generations were linked. William Fitz Stephen in the 1170s noted 13 conventual churches and 126 parish ones in London and its suburbs, and the buildings, precincts, graveyards and related street patterns imposed a particular order on the city's topography and were very important to local mental mapping.

The linear nature of the route shown, via Rochester and Canterbury to Dover, was appropriate not only for an age when extensive use was made of Roman roads but also for Matthew Paris to be able to fit it into the space available, and in so doing he also captured the role of the journey as a spiritual task. Canterbury is shown as walled, while the castles of Rochester and Dover are depicted. The defensiveness of the state was understandably a key theme, because the French had invaded at the close of John's reign and his son, Henry III, had only gained the throne as the result of the defeat of French invaders, including in a naval battle off Dover in 1217.

London had played a major role in the earlier crisis of 1215, when the barons opposed to John were able to march straight into the city through gates left open for them, although a royal force held onto the Tower and resisted them, until the Tower was transferred to the keeping of the Archbishop of Canterbury. The Lord Mayor of London was one of the 25 men responsible for enforcing Magna Carta, the charter of liberties that John was obliged to sign that year.

Canterbury had become more significant, to pilgrims, because Archbishop Thomas Becket had been murdered in the cathedral in 1170 by four knights seeking to please Henry II, who was angry with Becket's determination to protect the right of appeals by clergy to the papal court rather than the royal courts. Rapidly memorialised with sainthood in 1173, Becket's tomb was soon the focus for pilgrimage, as was to be recorded by Geoffrey Chaucer in his *Canterbury Tales* (c.1387).

A SCEPTRED ISLE

'The Gough Map', *c.*1360

The precise date and the identity of the mapmaker of the Gough Map are unknown, although, based on analysis of the handwriting, it is thought to date from about 1375. At 45 inches by 22 inches the map is large – eight times bigger than that of Matthew Paris (see pages 28–29). It is also unmatched in Europe for the area covered and detail up to its date of production. Research in the 2010s, including high-resolution scans, has suggested different scribal hands and a three-layer map, with the second and third layers both produced by re-inkings and alterations during the fifteenth century. Locally collected regional information appears to have played a role in the updating – being responsible, for example, for the details for Cumbria, notably the number of rivers. (An interactive, searchable Gough Map was also produced as a result of using the modern digital technology.)

The map could also be a copy based on an earlier original, possibly reflecting the interests of Edward I (r.1272–1307), notably his campaigning in Wales and Scotland, although that has been contested. Named after Richard Gough, who bought it in 1774 and bequeathed the map to the Bodleian Library in Oxford in 1809, this was a practical map, possibly produced for administrative use.

England was a remarkably homogenous state by European standards, with an emphasis on the Common Law serving as a way to enhance public power and contributing greatly to the extent to which England was governed. Lords exercised much of their influence through the public courts system rather than private judicial power. This was an important source of political, geographical and social cohesion, and helped ensure that influence over the government was a key dynamic of politics, rather than defiance of it.

The map provided an effective guide to routes and the resulting national and interurban networks, and showed nearly 3,000 miles of red lines, many of which followed Roman routes. Reflecting the quality of Roman engineering and planning, and the lack of any need to consider land ownership, these roads were built straight and to a high standard, with stone foundations and gravel surfaces. From London, Watling Street went to Chester, Ermine Street to York and Stane Street to Chichester, while the Fosse Way went from Lincoln to Exeter. However, rather than roads,

the red lines may indicate routes that transmitted goods, demands, information and innovations in an increasingly economically sophisticated society with networks of exchange providing opportunities for economic specialisation. The amount of money in circulation had markedly increased in the thirteenth century, facilitating credit. In his British Topography (1780), Gough stated that the map could 'justly boast itself the first among us wherein the roads and distances are laid down'.

Across England from the very late twelfth century, fords at major crossing points were replaced by bridges, which increasingly rested on stone arches and were able to accommodate carts. A developing network of regular carriers' routes was instrumental in creating a national transport system. Mercantile credit was crucial to this system.

This stronger emphasis on land routes did not put London at a disadvantage, instead supplementing its position as England's most important port. Indeed, markets and fairs provided key intermediary points in the integration of London with the national economy. From the fifteenth century, Kendal, in distant Cumbria, was served by regular packhorse trains (organised groups of packhorses) moving goods as far as London.

North is to the left of the map. While more islands are shown off the east and south coast than is now the case (for example, Harty off the north Kent coast), fish are marked in the North Sea, and a ship with castellated bow and stern east of the Orkneys. Northern Europe at the top of the map is poorly differentiated, although five towns are indicated, including Sluis, the outpost of Bruges, where in 1340 Edward III (r.1327–77) won a major battle over a French navy.

The significance of rivers in Britain is clearly brought out, and notably so for the Severn. The coastline is better for England than Wales, let alone Scotland. In general, accuracy and detail are far greater than for the Matthew Paris maps, with the settlements usually correctly placed. Wealthy East Anglia (detail, opposite) receives particular attention, and eastern England is presented with more accuracy than western. Tax records reflected the wealth of the Southeast: the new tax valuations required for the lay subsidy of 1334 indicate that the five wealthiest counties per square mile were,

in descending order, Middlesex, Oxfordshire, Norfolk, Bedfordshire and Berkshire. All areas, however, were hit hard by the taxation necessary for war with France and Scotland. London and York were the two cities whose names were written in gold. They were the two centres of government.

The towns are very differently shown, not least with reference to their scale and decoration, those north of Hadrian's Wall lacking dark outlines and the same decorative detail. Aberystwyth appears as a single building.

The map appeared in the aftermath of the plague outbreak known as the Black Death, although probably prior to the Peasants' Revolt of 1381. Like the Great Famine of 1315–17, caused by harvest failure resulting from bad weather, the plague hit population levels that were anyhow under pressure as a result of the impact of earlier expansion on resources, for population growth had outstripped agricultural development. The subsequent attempt to control labour helped produce the breakdown in order known as the Peasants' Revolt, although of course there were no hints of that on the map, which very much reflects a different form of mapping. The settlement hierarchy encoded in the Gough Map has enabled historical geographers to estimate population density and show its major variations.

CASTELLATED SCOTLAND

John Hardyng, 'Map of Scotland...', 1440–50.

Focusing on towns and castles, this manuscript map accompanied a history (*Hardyng's Chronicle*) designed to support the English Crown's claim to Scotland. The map does not provide any guide to the Scottish coastline, but includes the Solway Firth and the rivers Tweed and Forth. Aside from waterways, the map marks a number of major settlements, which are principally represented in terms of castles. The major ecclesiastical centres of Dunfermline (detail, opposite) and Glasgow were marked with churches. The map is oriented with west at the top.

Hardyng (1378–1465) had battle experience at Shrewsbury (1403) and Agincourt (1415) and served Sir Robert Umfraville (c.1363–1437), Keeper of Warkworth Castle and Lord of Redesdale in his frequent campaigning on the Scottish border, including the burning of Roxburgh (1410) and Peebles (1419). After Umfraville's death, Hardyng retired to the Augustinian Priory at Kyme where he wrote his chronicle of English history. Under Henry V (r.1413–22), Hardyng had visited Scotland to investigate the feudal links of Scotland to the English Crown, although he was not above forging documents. James I of Scotland (r.1406–37) was a prisoner of Henry.

Scottish chronicles, such as those of John Fordun, Andrew Wyntoun and Walter Bower, instead presented Scotland as a state with its own independent history defined by hostility to England. Local administration and justice were left to the nobility and some powerful magnates, such as the Earls of Douglas in the Borders and the MacDonalds, Lords of the Isles, in west coast Scotland, wielded great power, the latter able to deploy 10,000 troops in 1411.

This local 'justice' was a politics of kidnapping and sudden executions. Released in 1424, James I gained power in 1425 by overthrowing his cousin, the former regent, Murdac, the 2nd Duke of Albany. Albany and his relatives were seized and beheaded. James then reimposed royal control in the Highlands, before being murdered in his bed in an attempted coup. James II (r.1437–60) faced civil war between aristocratic factions, but in 1452 William, 8th Earl of Douglas, was stabbed to death while under his safe-conduct. James, however, died in 1460 when a wedge blew out of a cannon during the bombardment of English-held Roxburgh Castle.

Scotland was poorer and less populous than England, its agriculture less developed and without an important export comparable to English wool, or later cloth. Scottish government was less sophisticated than that of England and its armies were smaller, but independence was retained. This was one of the many aspects of the period that were important to subsequent developments. They did not make any particular developments inevitable, and the unions of Aragon with Castile, Lithuania with Poland, and Brittany with France, among others, showed that longstanding divisions could be overcome, but maintenance of Scottish independence was important to subsequent developments in the sixteenth century. Conversely, there was to be a union of Crowns in 1603.

Dogge hous

Busshoppes gate Strete

1

THE SIXTEENTH CENTURY

Mapping in the sixteenth-century British Isles was dominated by the output of Tudor England, although Scotland firmly maintained its independence under Stuart kings, while in Ireland the grasp of Tudor England was only confirmed at the very beginning of the seventeenth century. Tudor England, however, had a more powerful state and a more populous, wealthier, society, and each served as the basis for more extensive map production. This production was aided by the new technology of print, which also helped to ensure a greater survival of maps. Map printing began with woodcuts, but rapidly moved over to copper engraving, the incised lines of which proved more effective for providing cartographic detail.

Production was a multi-step procedure entailing cost, labour and the possibility of error: the map image had to be engraved first with the careful incising necessary, the copper plate had to be inked, the maps had to be printed onto paper, and hand-painted colouring was then applied. Copper plates were expensive and deteriorated with use, but could also be stored, reused and updated. Foreign mapmakers, notably from France, Italy and Portugal, were important in this era, but during the reign of Elizabeth I (r.1558–1603) English mapmakers became much more significant. During this period, references to maps increase, and this can be seen in Shakespeare's plays. The popularity of Saxton's county maps encouraged interest in mapping, and from the 1570s estate maps were increasingly drawn to scale.

The sixteenth century was when the medieval continuation broke, and dramatically so with both the nationalisation of the Church, in England under Henry VIII (r.1509–47), and the enforced switch of the national churches to Protestantism. These changes were cause and consequence of a strengthening of government and an increased use of the vernacular (native language), which was very much the case with the culture of print, including maps.

The British remained predominantly rural, although the relative significance of London greatly increased. Religious change did not transform a society in which males, the old and the wealthy were dominant; but it was important in encouraging new values and emphases, not least a decline in that of celibacy in favour of a greater role for marriage, as encapsulated by the clergy. The end of the authority of the universal Church was also followed by the dethroning of its power over intellectual speculation, and the net effect, albeit not always by an easy process, was one of a culture of more freedom of thought and expression. This contributed to the scientific advances of the seventeenth century, the period of the 'Scientific Revolution'.

The sixteenth century also saw economic developments of consequence, notably a rise in population, an increase in coal production and the enclosure of farmland (as part of its more controlled and intensive use). Some of these trends were general, but others were more specific to particular regions and therefore opened up or changed the divisions between regions. This included religious affiliation, with some areas noted for retaining a degree of Catholicism, including Lancashire, west Sussex and Ireland.

FORTRESS ENGLAND

'Map of the Coast of Cornwall and Devon...', 1539–40.

On the pattern of the Saxon Shore fortresses built by the Romans, England's King Henry VIII responded to the alliance in 1538 between Emperor Charles V (ruler, among much else, of the Low Countries and Spain) and Francis I of France, and the consequent fears of invasion, by initiating a costly programme of defences. The gathering of information came first. In February 1539, Henry's leading minister, Thomas Cromwell, ordered a survey of the coast to advise on invasion risks and necessary fortifications – information that was sent to court in the form of sketch plans and text, which were compiled at Greenwich into maps. The risks were highlighted by exaggerating the size of the beaches and reducing that of the cliffs. The defensive measures portrayed included both real and proposed forts, while church towers served both to locate places and, like beacons, to provide heights from which information could be conveyed. This map could have been explained to Henry personally and then annotated to reflect his decisions.

These decisions led to the building, in the 1540s, of a series of fortifications – at Sandgate, Deal and Walmer – on the south coast of England, the 'Castles of the Downs', fortifications that mounted cannon in order to resist both bombardment by warships and attack by invading forces. The fortifications built under Henry were essentially gun platforms. They took the form of a semi-circular multi-gun platform – and that became the standard solution for coastal defence because it permitted engagement with ships from whichever direction they approached and, if not sunk, as they passed. The bastioned enceinte was added during Elizabeth I's reign as part of the anti-invasion measures. The designs of these coastal forts influenced those built by the English in Bermuda in the early seventeenth century.

More generally, the anchorages on the south coast of England – for example, the Solent, Exe, Dart, Plymouth (see detail, right) and the Fal – were protected by fortifications, as with the building of artillery forts at Southsea, Portland, Hurst, Calshot, and at Pendennis and St Mawes at the mouth of the Fal. The defences at Dartmouth were improved, notably with Lamberd's Bulwark in 1545.

In 1588, in response to the threat from the Spanish Armada, and again in 1596, when another Spanish invasion attempt was prepared, there were hasty preparations – cannon were mounted on the walls of Corfe Castle near the Dorset coast and at Portland, Carisbrooke Castle and Pendennis; but there were few strong fortifications and the defences of England primarily rested on the fleet and the army. As the army had limitations, it was the navy that was crucial, and this rested in part on developments under Henry VIII.

THE POWER OF THE TRENT

'Map of the River Trent and its tributaries...', c.1540.

The River Trent in Nottinghamshire, showing both Nottingham and Newark castles. Water power was a key element in the agriculture and industry of Tudor England, and was tapped by the waterwheels in mills. Particularly important for the production of flour, water power was also used for metallurgy, in which it powered bellows and hammers, such as those in the Wealden iron works. Indeed, Shakespeare in *The Tempest* has Prospero refer to Ariel as 'venting thy groans as fast as mill-wheels strike'. Much industry was located in the countryside in part because of the importance of water power provided by fast-flowing rivers.

Rural Britain was dotted with mills, some of which survive, such as the Dunham Massey Sawmill near Manchester, originally used for grinding corn; Houghton Mill near Huntingdon, Cambridgeshire; the Pitstone Windmill near Tring, Hertfordshire; the White Mill near Wimborne, Dorset; and the Nether Alderley Mill in Cheshire. Although not built until 1743, the City Mill in Winchester, Hampshire, was on the site of earlier corn mills on the River Itchen.

The course of the Trent provides the basis for Harry Hotspur's complaint when the division of the country is discussed in 1403 by the three conspirators in Act III, Scene I of Shakespeare's *Henry IV, Part 1* (1597) –

> 'Methinks my moiety [share], north from Burton [on Trent] here,
> In quantity equals not one of yours:'

This leads Hotspur to propose a 'new channel' for the river, so that:

> 'It shall not wind with such a deep indent,
> To rob me of so rich a bottom here.'

But there is no historical evidence of such a discussion.

This map of about 1540 was apparently produced to show that plans to divert the River Trent from Newark's mills would not lessen their productivity. The course of the river and works on it had long been causes of contention, although major changes were not undertaken until the late eighteenth century when two locks were built near Newark where the channel divides.

Similarly, the Earl of Devon's weir over the Exe downstream of Exeter was a major point of disagreement from the thirteenth to the sixteenth centuries because it stopped ships from reaching Exeter and benefitted the rival port of Topsham. In the end, the Exeter Ship Canal was built in 1564–67 to circumvent the now silted-up river channel, which had been reopened after the execution in 1538 of Henry, 1st Marquess of Exeter, who had fallen foul of his former friend Henry VIII.

In the sixteenth century, there was a controversy over a mill weir on the Trent near Shelford Priory between Nottingham and Newark. The priory had been suppressed and the lands given to the Stanhope family. Sir Thomas Stanhope, a key local figure who was an MP and also Sheriff, clashed with another powerful local landowner, Gilbert, Earl of Shrewsbury, which led

to a long diversion channel being dug in 1593 to bypass the mill.

Rivers then – very differently to what a river entails on a modern map – combined to form trading systems that covered much of the country. This was a reflection of the poor quality of the road system, and of the relative ease of moving bulk goods by water. As a result, areas that lacked navigable rivers were at a significant disadvantage.

The vellum map uses pictograms to show distinctive fish weirs, such as the one near Markall Bridge (centre, left), and numerous mills as well as bridges: the importance of rivers focused attention on the latter. In his *Survey of London* (1598), John Stow, while providing a strange view of English geography, proudly compared London to the prospects offered by other rivers:

'This realm has only three principal rivers on which a royal city may be situated: Trent in the north, Severn in the southwest, and Thames in the southeast; of which the Thames, both for the straight course in length reaches furthest into the belly of the land, and for the breadth and stillness of the water, is most navigable up and down the stream: by reason whereof London, standing almost in the middle of that course, is more commodiously served with provision of necessaries than any town standing upon the other two rivers can be, and doth also more easily communicate to the rest of the realm the commodities of her own production and trade.'

ENTRY TO ENGLAND

'Proposals for Dover Harbour', 1552.

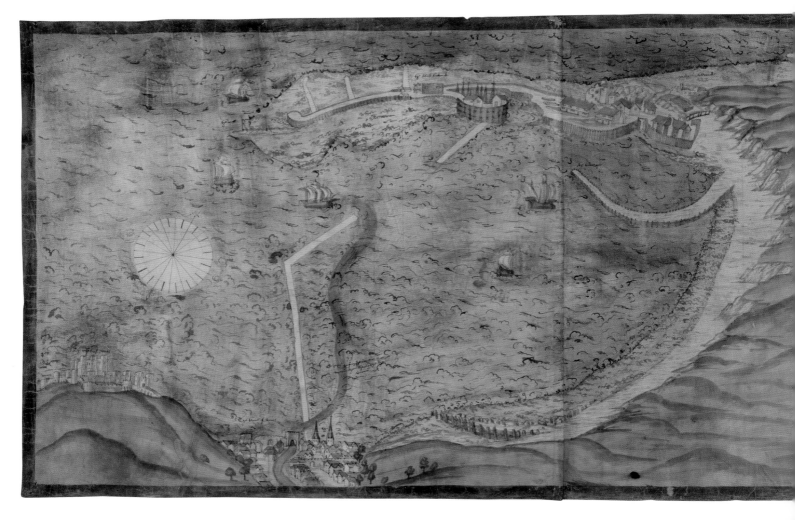

Although the need for harbour works made Dover more expensive, being the shortest crossing it was the most important port for travel to France, and also because Calais, on the opposite shore, was an English port from 1347 until it was captured in a surprise French attack in 1558, thereafter remaining part of France.

Under a thirteenth century royal charter, the Maison Dieu ('House of God') had a financial interest in the port of Dover and therefore an incentive to increase its use. Founded in 1203 by Hubert de Burgh, the Constable of Dover Castle, the hospital of the Mason Dieu existed to provide hospitality to pilgrims en route to Becket's shrine in Canterbury Cathedral, and also to house the poor and ill.

Henry VII (r.1485–1509) gave some money to encourage the building of a new harbour at Dover by Sir John Clark: a harbour with a pier and two fortifications, known as the Wyke, at the southwest side of the bay. *Holinshed's Chronicles* (1577) recorded:

'There was a round tower built by one John Clark, Priest, Master of the Maison Dieu, about the year 1500, at the south-west side of the Bay, which served somewhat to defend the ships from the rage of south-west winds, but especially to moor ships that were tied thereto. Many great rings were fastened to the tower for that purpose, as it may be seen, since it showeth there at this hour, and thereby that part of the Bay was made so pleasant, as ever after that corner of the Bay hath been called, and is at this day, "Little Paradise." Nevertheless, this was thought very insufficient

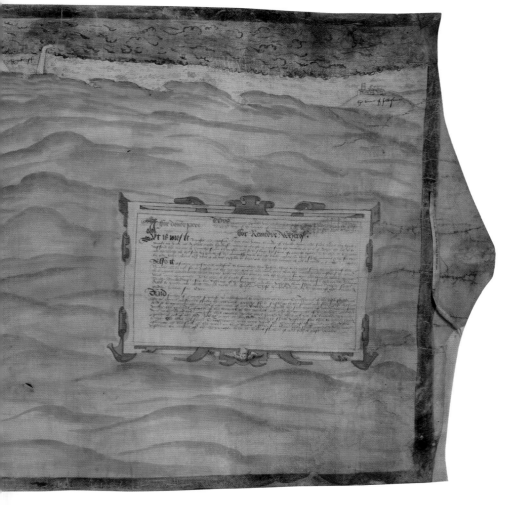

for the number of ships which usually lay for harbour in the Road.'

In 1520 Henry VIII embarked at the harbour at Archcliff in Dover in order to take part in the festivities of the Field of Cloth of Gold, his ultimately unsuccessful meeting with Francis I of France. At that time, the recently installed cannon were available to salute Henry from Clark's Round Tower. The significance of the position was shown by a later visit Henry made as part of his concern about the defences of the south coast from possible attack by France or Spain. He added Moat Bulwark to the defences. Separately, as part of the Protestant Reformation, the Maison Dieu in Dover was surrendered to the Crown in 1544.

Under Edward VI (r.1547–53), the harbour works stopped and the town became increasingly poor, and disorderly, a situation that persisted under Mary (r.1553–58), leading, under Elizabeth I (r.1558–1603), in 1559 to the dispatch of royal commissioners to keep the peace. The corporation lost control when Dover Harbour Board was formed by royal charter in 1606.

This map is one of a number of contemporary plans which, as with many early maps, are of uncertain origin, in terms of authorship, date and accuracy (in this case whether the works planned were attempted or not). The map reflects the idea of a 'Mighty Pier', a 1,400-feet-long stone mole (see detail, left) that Henry VIII had begun, but left unfinished due to cost as well as the difficulty of the task. This plan was abandoned at the end of Henry's reign, but interest revived under Mary, possibly due to war with France.

The map is typical of many of the period in that it is highly pictorial, and, indeed, a fusion of approaches as a result. There is no scale, which would have been a practical problem for those considering it.

HEART OF THE CITY

Frans Franken, 'Copperplate Map of London', c.1559.

A map of London that was based on a survey rather than providing a panoramic view, making it the earliest true map of London. It was created in 15 sections or plates by Flemish artist Frans Franken, or Francken. Although there are no surviving copies of the printed map, three of the original engraved copper printing plates have survived and provide a view of much of the densely built-up heart of the City, showing the areas around Moorfields, the City and St Paul's Cathedral. This Moorfields section shows a bird's-eye view for the layout, while buildings are presented as if viewed from the south. The original map was probably designed for hanging on a wall and is believed to have measured approximately three feet eight inches by seven feet five inches.

Bishopsgate Street is prominent on this section, with two of London's medieval monastic hospitals: St Mary Bethlehem ('Bedlame') and St Mary Spital ('S. Ma Spittel'). What had become known as the Bethlehem Hospital was later abbreviated by Londoners to 'Bethlem', which often became pronounced as 'Bedlam'. By the early 1400s most of the patients had symptoms of mental illness rather than any physical ailment. (In the 1890s an extension to Liverpool Street Station was built on the foundations of the first hospital, which lasted from 1247 to 1676.) The medieval city walls, Moorgate, Bishopsgate and the church of All Hallows-on-the-Wall ('All holyes ni the Wall') can also be seen.

Buildings outside the walls are shown too, including the linear development north along Bishopsgate Street, but the general impression there is of a rapid change to rural activities, with fields and animals. Other activities depicted outside the walls include the laying out of cloth to dry or bleach, and citizens practising archery, part of their civic duty to protect country and city. In reality, many of the dwellings outside the walls would have been the 'mean cottages' or shacks criticised by John Stow In his *Survey of London* (1598), but they have been deemed not worthy of inclusion.

The population of London rose from about 50,000 in 1500 to about 200,000 in 1600, when England's second-largest city, Norwich, had about 15,000 inhabitants.

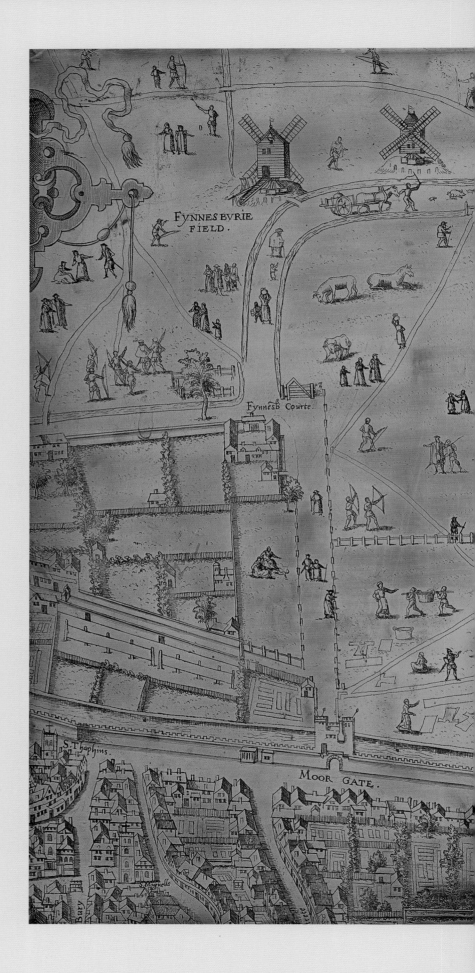

SHORDICH

S. Mª Spittel

THE SPITEL

Dogge hous.

Blak hows

R FIELD.

Bedlame

Bedlam Gate

Giardin di Piero

S. Butolf

All holyes ni the Voall.

BVSSHOPPES GATE.

PAPYE

VNSDICHE.

Busshoppes gate Streete.

WALES MAPPED

Humphrey Llwyd, 'Cambriae Typus...', 1574–92.

The first map of Wales as a separate country also reflected the international links of Britain with the Continent. Born at Foxhall, the family estate in Denbigh in about 1527, and of mixed English and Welsh descent, Humphrey Llwyd, like many talented Welshmen, moved to England for preferment. Educated at Oxford, he was from 1553 until his death in 1568 in the service of Henry, 12th Earl of Arundel, Chancellor of Oxford University, for whom he acted as a physician and also collected books. Elected MP for East Grinstead in 1559, and MP for the Denbigh Boroughs in 1563, Llwyd allegedly helped the legislation for translating the Bible into Welsh, and in 1566–67, on a visit with Arundel to the Continent, he met the great Flemish cartographer Abraham Ortelius in Antwerp.

Subsequently, Llwyd was given a royal stipend to produce a map of Wales for inclusion by Ortelius in his atlas *Theatrum Orbis Terrarum*, which was first published in 1570. Although Llwyd's 'Cambriae Typus' was sent to Ortelius in 1568, it did not appear in print until the 1573 *Additamentum* to the atlas, by when Llwyd was dead. In a letter accompanying the manuscript, Llwyd explained that the map gave the ancient names of rivers, towns, people and places, as well as the modern English names. The coastline lacks accuracy. There is a whale in Cardigan Bay, part of the standard decoration of maps, as in Christopher Saxton's of Cornwall. The whale shown may also be a pun on Wales. Dublin and Bristol are among the non-Welsh cities shown, and in many respects they, plus Chester, Ludlow and Shrewsbury, were among the most important towns for regions of Wales. The map comes with a scale.

Wales was shown as extending to the River Severn, which expressed an antiquarian view, but also the idea that the Marches, which originally were outside the full English governmental system, were part of Wales. The Court of the Council in the Dominion and Principality of Wales and the Marches, usually called the Council of Wales and the Marches, an administrative body based in Ludlow, had been established in 1457, re-established in 1472 and redefined in 1542, with the Marches including Cheshire (until 1569), Shropshire, Herefordshire, Worcestershire and Gloucestershire, in other words more than was shown by Llwyd. Uneasiness about the security situation far from London led the government in 1536–43 to push through union with Wales so that it was assimilated into the English governmental,

parliamentary and legal systems. Parliament was to suspend the Council of Wales and the Marches in 1641.

The Protestant Reformation had more of an immediate effect on the Welsh population than did the administrative changes. Although they were in serious eclipse by this time, the dissolution of monasteries and chantries had an impact on landholding, substantially to the benefit of the local gentry, and also disrupted the fabric of many communities. Education and poor relief were affected. Nevertheless, although enthusiasm for the Reformation was limited and areas of Catholicism remained, there was no equivalent to the opposition to religious change that existed in England, Ireland and Scotland. Indeed, the translation of the Bible into Welsh helped to sustain a sense of national identity. Translations of the Anglican Book of Common Prayer and the New Testament were published in 1567 and William Morgan's readily comprehensible translation of the entire Bible appeared in 1588, although the metropolitan dominance of Britain was such that it had to be printed in London: by law only certain presses could publish Bibles anyway. Thanks to the translation, Welsh could be the official language of public worship and religious life in general, and the clergy had no need to catechise and preach in English. The Welsh language could develop from its medieval oral and manuscript characteristics into a culture of print.

Elizabeth I's reign (1558–1603) was a period of peace, rising population and expanding agriculture in Wales, and the more fertile lands of South Wales ensured that it had the highest population. Denbighshire was also well populated, while upland Radnorshire and Merionethshire had the lowest population. Welsh cattle and sheep were driven to English markets, especially London.

Characteristically for maps presenting large areas in this period, there is no indication of the development of industry in South Wales, where coal production rose and metallurgy developed. Swansea's annual coal exports rose from about 1,800 tons in the 1550s to about 7,700 in 1640. Henry VIII supported iron and lead mining near Llantrisant, while lead mining in Cardiganshire developed subsequently under Elizabeth I. The first copper smelter near Neath, built by the Mines Royal in about 1584, depended on the water power of the Aberdulais Falls; the copper came from Cornwall, an aspect of the maritime economy of the Bristol Channel.

Whereas Wales was heavily fortified with castles in the thirteenth and fourteenth centuries, and they played a major role in the resistance in the rebellion by Owain Glyndŵr (Owen Glendower) in 1400–c.1415, the suppression of that revolt ended Welsh attempts at independence and many of the castles were abandoned or, as with Beaumaris and Conwy, fell into disrepair. Others were enhanced, not with fortifications but with comfortable and splendid internal 'spaces', especially long galleries, as happened at Raglan, Powis and Carew. In the event, some of the castles, such as Harlech, were to be used in the English Civil War, which should more properly be known as the British Civil Wars.

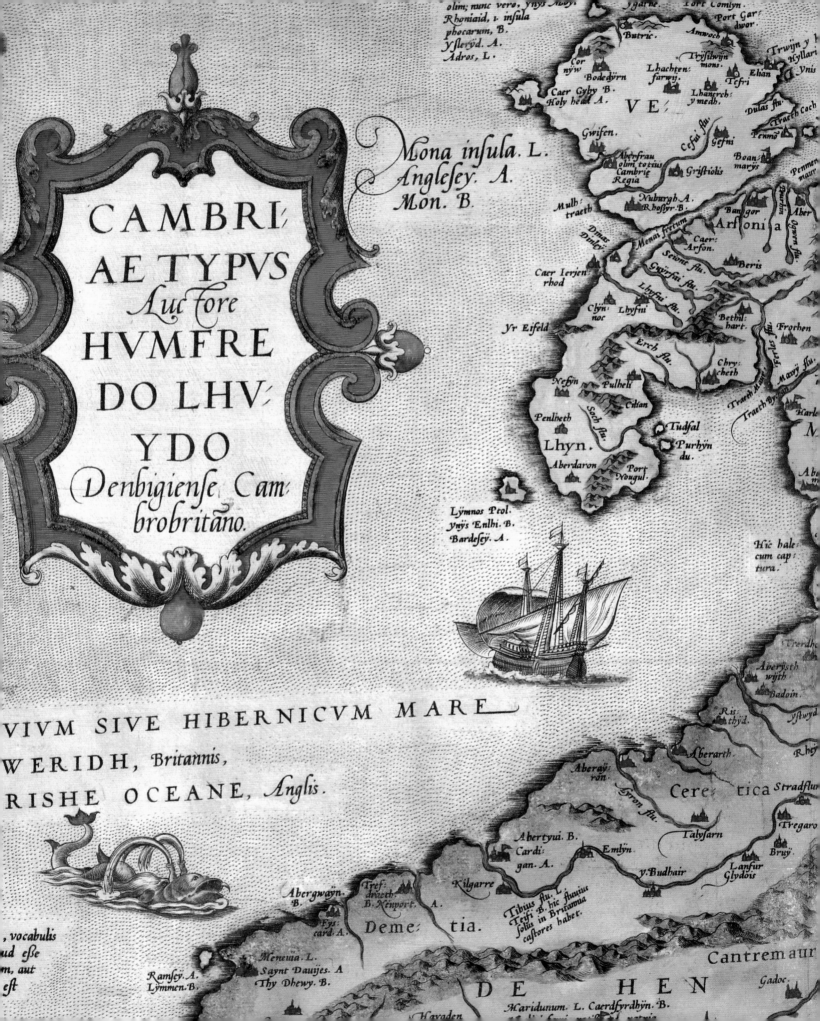

olim; nunc vero, ynys Adoy,
Rhoniaid, i. insula
phocarum, B.
Ysleryd. A.
Adros. L.

Butric

Amwoch

Trysilwyn
mons.

Cor
nyw

Trwijn y
Hyllari

Bodedyrn

Lhachten
farwy.

Tefri

Ehan

Ynis

Caer Gyby B.
Holy head. A.

Lhanerch
ymedh.

Dulas stu.

Traeth Coch

VE

Penmo.

Gwisen.

Cefni stu.

Gefni

Boan
marys

Aberfrau
olim totius
Cambrie
Regia

Penmen
maur

Griftiolis

Arfonia

Mulh
traeth

Nuburgh A.
Rhossyr. B.

Ban
gor

Ogwen stu.

Aber

Dinas
Dinlij

Menai fretum

Caer
Arfon.

Parthin

Mona insula. L.
Anglesey. A.
Mon. B.

Caer Ierjen
rhod

Seiont stu.

Beris

Gwijrfai stu.

Clyn
noc

Lhyfni stu.

Bethu
hart.

Frorhen

Yr Eifeld

Erch stu.

Ferles stu.

Maryi stu.

Chry
cheth

Traeth Mawr

Nefyn

Pulheli

Traeth By

Harle

Penlheth

Sach stu.

Cilian

M.

Lhyn

Tudfal

Purhyn
du.

Abe

Aberdaron

Port
Nongul.

Lymnos Ptol.
ynys Enlhi. B.
Bardesey. A.

Hic hale
cum cap
tura.

Trerdhc

VIVM SIVE HIBERNICVM MARE

Averyth
wijth

WERIDH, Britannis,

Badoin

RISHE OCEANE, Anglis.

Ris
thyd.

Ystwyd

Aberarth

Aberay
ron

Rhej

Cere tica

Stradflur

, vocabulis
ud esse
m, aut
est

Bron stu.

Abertyui. B.
Cardi
gan. A.

Emlyn

y Budhair

Talysarn

Tregaro

Bruy

Lanfur
Glydois

Kilgarre

Abergwaijn.
B.

Tref
draeth
B. Newport. A.

Tibius stu. L.
Teifi B. hic stuuius
solus in Britania
castores habet.

Deme tia

Demetia

Ramsey. A.
Lymmen. B.

Menevia. L.
Saynt Dauijes. A
Thy Dhewy. B.

Maridunum. L. Caerdfyrdhin. B.

DE HEN

Cantremaur

THE MAJESTY OF ANGLIA

Christopher Saxton, 'The Counties of England', 1579.

This impressive map by Christopher Saxton drew upon his county surveys and is the first printed one of the counties of England and Wales. It had flaws, as in the coverage of the neighbouring areas of southern Scotland, eastern Ireland, and the Isle of Man, but showed Wales more accurately than did Humphrey Llwyd's map. The coasts are full of shipping and large sea monsters, providing pictorial detail to complement the land, where 52 counties are differentiated by colour and identified by their Latin names in a numbered index. Differences across England and Wales emerge clearly, as in the scarcity of towns in the Fens and the Breckland.

The map bears the royal arms, and such maps were an aspect of majesty, and a proclamation of the extent of the state and of its unity in and under the Crown. Marcus Gheeraerts the Younger painted Elizabeth I standing on a rendering of the Saxton map, the 1583 printed wall map *Britannia*, and she was also pictured on the title page of Saxton's atlas. War with Spain from 1585 to 1604 was further to foster national consciousness, providing a new focus for the commemoration of national history, notably with the sense of providential support after the defeat of the Spanish Armada in 1588.

Born in about 1542–44 in Yorkshire, the talented Saxton learned surveying and was commissioned to produce county maps by Thomas Seckford MP, a prominent official, whose arms appear below the cartouche, and who was close to Elizabeth's leading minister, Sir William Cecil, Lord Burghley (1520–98), Secretary of State from 1550 to 1553 and 1558 to 1572, and Treasurer from 1572 until his death. The industrious Burghley had a substantial collection of maps, some annotated in his own hand, and was a key patron of Laurence Nowell (1515–76) in his mapping and other scholarly work in the 1560s. Nowell gifted him a map he favoured, *A General Description of England and Ireland with the adjoining coasts*, and he also surveyed the east coast of Ireland. Burghley had manuscript maps, including early proof states of Saxton's printed county maps, bound together in an atlas.

Saxton's surveying was backed by the government. In 1576 the Privy Council instructed the Justices of the Peace and mayors in Wales to give him all assistance in travelling and viewing the principality, while Burghley was sent proof copies of the county maps to which he added his own notes to the margins. Saxton carried out surveys that led to the engraving of 34 county maps, most of which covered a single county, although some covered several, a practice that was criticised. The scale of the maps varied as did the degree of pictorial detail. Woods, bridges and hills were drawn in, as were the fenced-off parks of major landowners, but not roads. The level of accuracy was high, although there were some significant errors, such as the shape of Cornwall, in that the Lizard Peninsula was overly large, a point that was clearer in the county map.

The popularity of Saxton and Saxton-derived maps reflected the desire for images drawn to scale in which crucial physical outlines were precisely marked. The maps also indicated the increased use of uniform conventional symbols to depict natural features – for example, forests and hills.

Although plans of county towns were added, his maps were copied with few, if any, changes for two centuries, largely because the cost and effort of new surveys appeared redundant, not only for commercial reasons but also due to the authority of the Saxton maps. His copper printing plates were reused, but with alterations, for example by William Webb in 1645 and Philip Lea in about 1690. Partly as a result, the maps helped to establish and consolidate the visual image of counties, and to provide pictorial support to the idea of England and Wales as an assembly of those counties.

The significance of the county for local government, justice and the raising of troops, all encouraged this idea. So also did the extent to which the reorganisation of dioceses under Henry VIII in 1540–41 increased the overlap between them and counties: while Westminster did not retain its new status, Chester, Gloucester, Peterborough, Bristol and Oxford did.

Meanwhile, England was becoming more integrated economically, which financed demand elsewhere in the country for London goods and services. The development of Northeastern coal production freed London from dependence on nearby wood and enabled its rising population to rely on a mixture of fuel from a distance and food from nearby.

AULD REEKIE

Georg Braun and Frans Hogenberg, 'Edenburgum, Scotiae Metropolis', 1581.

Georg Braun and Frans Hogenberg's *Civitates Orbis Terrarium*, published in Cologne and Amsterdam in six volumes from 1572 to 1617, provided maps of the cities of the world judged most significant. This copper engraving of Edinburgh was made after a 1574 woodcut by Raphael Holinshead. There is no hint of Leith and the Firth of Forth. The west is dominated by the castle, indicated as 'Castrum puellarum', which means 'castle of the maidens' and perhaps derives from the Pictish era practice of the kings keeping their daughters safe from harm there and educating them in preparation for marriage. It is connected by the High Street or Royal Road, later known as the Royal Mile, which leads via the Church of St Giles to the town gate and Holyrood Abbey. In practice, many in the city lived in insanitary, medieval multi-storey buildings with as many as 12 floors. (The coal-produced smog and noxious smells of human waste in this densely inhabited city gave rise to the city's nickname of Auld Reekie, which means 'Old Smokey' in the Scots dialect.) In Latin on the verso, there was a text by Braun that translates as:

'To the west of the city a mountain with a tall cliff rises up, upon which stands a castle, which is extremely secure due to its natural setting. On the side of the city to the east lies a majestic monastery to the Holy Cross, alongside it a royal palace set within an exceedingly charming garden. There are two large streets in this city, one that is paved with ashlar stone, leading from the Maidens' Castle to the monastery and to the royal palace, and the other is the highway. From the highway running from north to south countless smaller roads branch off, all of which are lined with very tall buildings.'

The city had about 15,000 inhabitants. It had been the dramatic setting for key episodes in mid-century Scottish history, including the successful English siege of 1560 and two murders later that decade: in 1566 David Rizzio, Mary, Queen of Scots' private secretary and favourite, was stabbed to death in Holyrood Palace, and then in 1567 at Kirk o'Field, which was adjacent to the city wall near the Cowgate, her second husband, Henry, Lord Darnley, who was one of those who had killed Rizzio before the pregnant Mary. Followed by her marriage to James, Earl of Bothwell, Darnley's murder helped lead to Mary's overthrow. She was captured and forced to abdicate, escaping in 1568, only to be defeated at Langside and flee to England where Elizabeth I had her imprisoned and in the end, after being convicted of treason, beheaded in 1587.

The enforced abdication of Mary encouraged the expression of ideas about the responsibility of the Crown to the people that eroded the stress authoritarians could put on the duties owed by subjects. This contractual theory of kingship was pushed by the leaders of the Church, not least George Buchanan who became tutor to the infant James VI (r.1567–1625). The king went south in 1603 to claim his new crown as James I in England, a transition managed with far less difficulty than had been anticipated and he stayed in England, except for one visit. Despite James's hopes for a 'union of love', or at least a measure of administrative and economic union between England and Scotland, there was fear in England about the legal and constitutional implications, and because the Westminster Parliament did not want a parliamentary or legal bond, Scotland remained an independent state governed by the Scottish Privy Council.

EDENBVRG.

RURAL TRANSFORMATION

John Darby, 'Map of the Parish of Smallburgh, Norfolk', 1582.

This is one of the first English local maps to be drawn to a consistent scale and is in unusually good condition, probably due to its never having been displayed because of its unfinished state. There is no title, several field name panels are left blank, and some decoration is only in pencil. In addition to these omissions, there is no numerical or alphabetical key to the terrier – the written register of plots that, with the information it contained of acreages, tenants and leases, would have been indispensable for the practical management of the estate.

Smallburgh, 14 miles northeast of Norwich, was a Saxon settlement where much common land was enclosed in the Tudor period. However, some land continued unenclosed and can be seen on the map – for example, the large field on the bottom right (following pages). The map includes pictures of the grazing animals, as well as hunting, a boatman and maids carrying out estate tasks. Norfolk was a major area of food production, with grain, especially barley, shipped from Great Yarmouth, and animals were walked to the London markets. The map also deploys colour to signify land use: from yellow-ochre for arable land and light green for heath or meadow to rich green for pasture and dark green for marshland.

At the same time, there was a far greater need for all-round agricultural production than was to be the case by the late nineteenth century or, still more, today. Thus, the detailed pattern of land use was far more complex and interdependent than might be suggested by references to (upland) pasture and (lowland) arable. At the level of the individual farmstead, and again of the village, there was a degree of self-reliance that is alien to modern farmers. This self-reliance reflected the relative difficulty of food preservation and transport in an age before refrigeration and motor vehicles, as well as the intensity of very local systems of exchange, and the degree to which self- and local-reliance made more economic sense than in the modern age of specialisation through comparative profit margins.

The map was annotated in 1762, a period in which East Anglican agriculture remained highly profitable, the annotations reflecting small alterations in the plot shape as well as the course of the stream. These annotations suggest that the map was still used as a record nearly two centuries after it was drawn. John Darby was a mapmaker between 1582 and 1594 who worked in East Anglia, producing written estate surveys as well as a map

of Blakeney harbour and a plan of Aldeburgh. South is at the top of the map; at the bottom right-hand corner there is a surveyor with a pole, which acts as a scale bar. The scale is one that became commonly used for estate maps – 12 perches (66 yards) to an inch, equivalent to 1:2,376. A perch is a historical measure of length or area, also called a pole or rod.

This period of rising population brought prosperity to the rural economy, but the increase in food prices benefitted principally those who controlled land. Landlords tried to increase the yield of their customary estates or to destroy the system of tenure on customary terms; and only occasionally could tenants combine to resist their landlords in the courts. Entry fines and rents were increased and customary tenants bought out or evicted in order to make way for fixed-term leases. In Norfolk, opposition to landlords, especially their enclosure of common lands, led to a rising in 1549 under the leadership of Robert Kett. The rebels seized Norwich, but were defeated at the battle of Dussindale.

Much of the peasantry lost status, and became little different from poorly paid wage labourers. Indeed, the growing number of paupers and vagrants led in 1572, a decade before this map, to the introduction of a compulsory poor rate, a key step in a series of Poor Laws. Despite this, the situation was bleak, especially for able-bodied men unable to find work.

Economic change, and the impact of the market on food and wages, led to anxiety, which was an aspect of the remoulding of society under the impact of a population increase and the Reformation. For most people there was scant prospect of advancement, and social mobility was therefore to be feared. Economic pressure led to widespread malnutrition among the poor and to much starvation. Most folktales centred on peasant poverty, and in many the desire for an unending source of food played a major role. Malnutrition stunted growth, hit energy levels and reduced resistance to illness. Poor diet encouraged parasitic infection, hepatitis and salmonella. It was not possible to alleviate the situation by imports. In a crisis at the end of the century, death rates rose in the 1590s.

The map was made for Edward, 12th Lord Morley (1550–1618), who had regained possession of his family's lands in 1578. His Catholic father, Henry, 11th Lord Morley (1533–77), had lost them in 1572 when accused of treason. Henry was made

a Knight of the Bath at the coronation of Queen Mary in 1553. East Anglia had strongly backed Mary Tudor in 1553 against the unsuccessful coup by John, 1st Duke of Northumberland, in an attempt to put his daughter-in-law, the Protestant Lady Jane Grey, on the throne. In turn, Henry refused to sign the 1558 Act of Uniformity as Elizabeth expected, and in 1570 he left England, without the permission of Elizabeth, to go to the dominions of Philip II of Spain (formerly Mary's husband), who gave him money in 1574. Henry died in Madrid in 1577, by when relations between Elizabeth and Philip were very poor.

Edward, in contrast, cleaved to the new order and was one of the 36 peers who, in 1587, tried Mary, Queen of Scots for treason. He did not join Edward, Lord Zouche, the sole commissioner who dissented against the conviction and death sentence. East Anglia, meanwhile, became a major centre for Protestantism.

John Darby, 'Map of the Parish of Smallburgh, Norfolk', 1582.

Parish of Beeston

Tunstead

Occidens

Parish

Dilham

TUDOR EXETER

John Hooker, *Isca Damnoniorum, c.1587.*

John Hooker (c.1527–1601) was the first Chamberlain of Exeter, from 1555 until his death, and MP for the city in 1571 and 1586. An antiquarian born in Exeter, he wrote on Devon's history, producing a history of the bishops, as well as an account of the city, and was one of the editors of the second edition of Holinshed's *Chronicles*, which was used by Shakespeare. The map (entitled after the Roman settlement name, Isca Dumnoniorum) captured the small size, with the exception of London, of even the leading cities in the period, and the continued role of the enclosing walls. The castle can also be seen. The bridge at the front was the first across the River Exe, and thereby provided the lowest crossing point, other than by ferry, into south Devon and Cornwall. Fishing, milling and shipping on the river are shown. The bird's-eye view is commonplace in this period.

The chief city for a prosperous agricultural zone, Exeter was also a major centre of textile production that benefitted from the rapidly developing export trade in cloth to the Mediterranean, where there was a growing market for lighter weight 'new draperies'. Exeter had a population of about 8,000. There were disproportionately more large towns in the southern half of England, especially in East Anglia and the Southwest, with the Southeast missing out in large part because of the inhibiting effect of London on the growth of nearby regions, and because it had less industry than those other two regions. The presence of so many towns in the south impacted on not only the economic but also the political importance of the area, because it was largely responsible for the high number of parliamentary boroughs there.

In addition to being the focus for trade, consumption and services, towns were centres of government, lay and ecclesiastical, and Exeter provided both. Urban expansion was a product of the role of towns as centres of manufacturing, trade, government and leisure, although all four were also pursued in the countryside, just as there was much market gardening within town walls, as well as orchards and gardens, the latter particularly for milk. The map does not show the 'three commonjakes' (latrines) the Council agreed to in 1568.

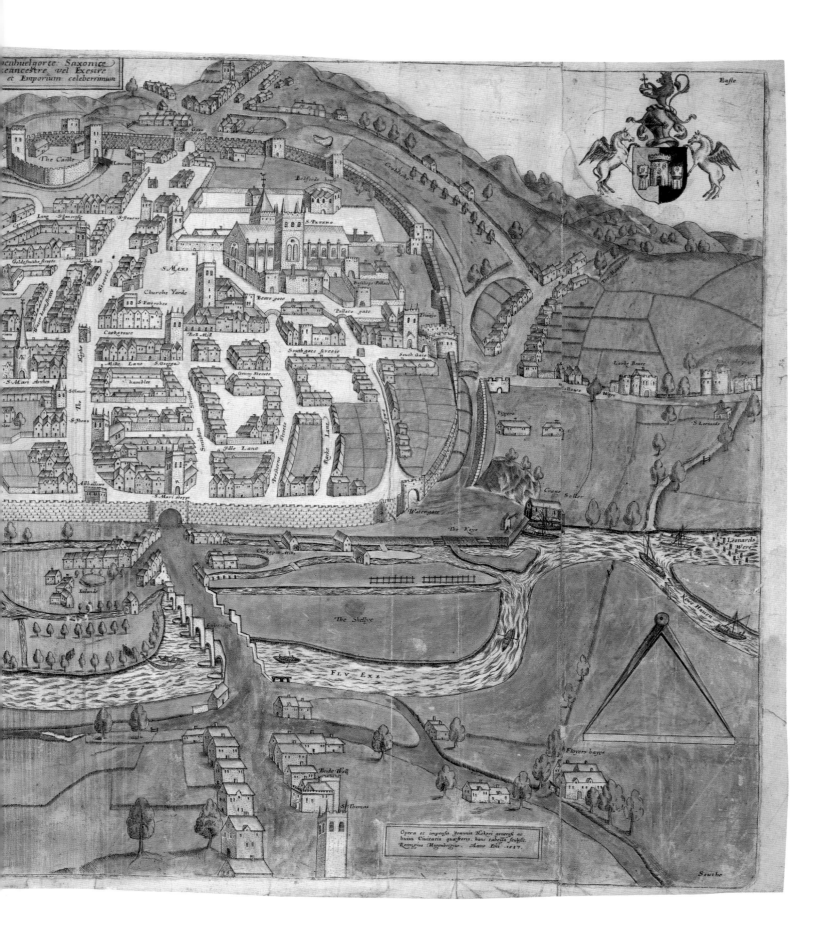

Various labels visible on the map include: The Castle, Bedfforde house, S. Peters, Bisshops Pallace, Churche Yarde, Southgate streete, South Gate, Crabb..., The Shilhye, FLV EXE, The Kaye, Watergate, Crane Seller, S. Leonards Were, New Haven, Bride Well, S. Thomas, Floyers hayes, Easte, Southe

Opera et impensis Ioannis Hokeri generosi ac huius Ciuitatis quaestoris hanc tabellam sculpsit Remigius Hogenbergius Anno Dni 1587

GRANARY OF THE COUNTY

William Sheldon, 'Tapestry Map of
Warwickshire', 1580s.

A tapestry map reflected the variety of mediums that could be used for mapping. But cloth is fragile and this is the only one of the Elizabethan originals to survive complete. William Sheldon (1511–70), a gentleman, made the plans and commissioned a group of Flemish weavers to produce the tapestry at his manor house of Barcheston in Warwickshire. He was the patron of Richard Hicks of Barcheston, former tutor to Sheldon's son, who while visiting Flanders became familiar with tapestry-making, which was seen as a way to provide employment for the poor.

Sheldon was typical of the rising group of property-owners, benefitting from officeholding that helped to provide the cohesion for Tudor England. He served as an MP, a Justice of the Peace and a Sheriff, all for Worcestershire, bought lands made available by the dissolution of the monasteries under Henry VIII, and played an important role in the administration of this process, as well as in the dissolution of the chantries. He may later, under Elizabeth I, have been suspected of Catholic sympathies, but he had given scant sign of them.

Warwickshire, Shakespeare's native county, was heavily wooded, but the part between the River Avon and Edge Hill was described as the 'very granary' of the whole county, with the Vale of Avon also noted for its cattle-grazing, and the limestone belt for its sheep pastures. Most of the Forest of Arden, the setting of As You Like It, was in Warwickshire.

Tapestry was not to be a tradition of mapmaking that developed, in part because it resembled previous practices of medieval mapmaking with their slow and individual practices. In contrast, print offered faster and cheaper map production.

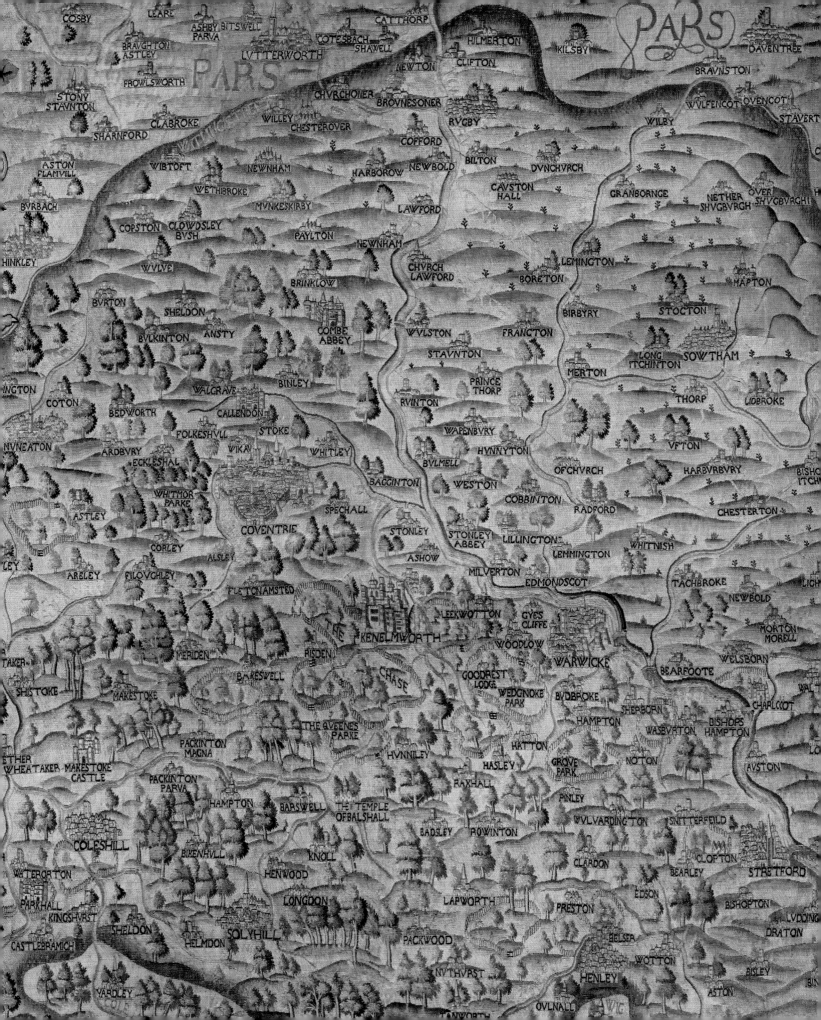

WARWIKSHEAR·SO·NAMID·AS·WEL·BY·THE·SAXONS·AS·OF·VS·AT·THIS
DAYE·IT·IS·DEVIDED·IN·TWO·PARTS·BY·THE·RIVER·AVON·RONNINGE
THROVGH·THE·MIDEST·THE·ON·IS·CALLED·FELDON·THE·OTHER·WOOD
LAND·THE·MOST·MEMORABLE·TOWNES·IN·THE·FELDON·ARE·LEMINGTON
TAKING·THE·NAME·OF·THE·RIVER·LEAM·WHERE·A·SALT·WELL·SPRINGETH
ICHINGTON·AND·HARBVRY·BETWENE·WHICH·TWO·TOWNES·FREMVDVS
THE·SONN·OF·KINGE·OFFA·WAS·SLAYN·A·MAN·OF·SINGVLER·VERTVE
AND·WAS·BVRIED·IN·HIS·FATHERS·PALACE·CALLED·OFCHVRCH
THE·WOODLAND·BEINGE·THE·NORTH·PART·AND·THE·GREATER·WAS
BY·AN·AVNCIENT·NAME·CALLED·ARDEN·WHICH·SIGNIFIETH·A·WOOD
IN·THE·MIDLE·OF·THIS·REGION·STANDETH·COVENTRE·SO·CALLED·OF
THE·COVENTE·OR·MONKES·A·CITIE·IN·TIMES·PASTE·POPVLVS·AND
RICHE·BY·THE·TRADE·OF·CLOTHING·AND·MAKING·OF·CAPPES
NEAR·COVENTRE·ON·THE·EAST·PART·IS·CALED·ON·THE·AVNGIENT·S
SEAT·OF·THE·LORDE·SECRAVE·FROM·WHOM·IT·IS·DESCENDED
TO·THE·BARONS·OF·BARKLEY·BY·TH·MOWBRAIES·DVKES·OF·NORTHFOLK
WESTWARD·FROM·COVENTRE·STANDETH·THE·CASTLE·OF·KENELWO
RTH·COMPASSED·ABOVT·WITH·A·GREAT·POOL·FIRSTE·BIVLDED·BY
IEFFREY·CLINTON·CHAMBERLAYNE·TO·KINGE·HENRE·THE·FIRST
ABOVT·V·MILES·FROM·THENCE·STANDETH·WARWICKE·CALLED·BY
THE·BRITAYNES·CAER·GVARVIC·WHICH·SIGNIFIETH·A·PLACE·OF
DEFENCE·WHEAR·IS·A·CASTLE·OF·GREAT·FORCE·BIVLDED·BY·THE
ROMANES·WILLIAM·THE·CONQVEROR·ORDEYNED·XII·BVRGESSES·IN
WARWICKE·TO·ATTENDE·ON·HIM·IN·HIS·WARRES
NEAR·VNTO·WARWICK·IS·GVYES·CLIFFE·A·PLACE·OF·WONDERFVL
PLEASVRE·WHEAR·GVYE·OF·WARWICKE·BVILDED·A·CHAPPEL
AND·WAS·THERE·BVRIED·READ·W·CAMDEN·HIS·DISCRIPCION·OF·BRI

THAMES DEFENCES

Robert Adams, 'The River Thames from Westminster to Tilbury Hope...', 1588.

Robert Adams (1540–95), Surveyor of the Queen's Works from 1594, was a skilful mapmaker who produced maps of the Spanish Armada crisis of 1588. This map shows the scheme for the defence of the Thames; it has south at the top, and the River Thames runs from Westminster on the right to Tilbury. Lines across the Thames show the position and reach of cannon that could be fired from batteries including 'olde' blockhouses. Two defence booms are also depicted.

Marked as 'A' (see detail, right), a force was gathered at West Tilbury under Robert, Earl of Leicester, Elizabeth I's favourite. Elizabeth's route to that camp on 8 August is shown. In her speech, she stressed her own dedication:

'I am come amongst you ... being resolved, in the midst and heat of battle, to live and die amongst you all, and to lay down for my God, and my kingdom and for my people, my honour and my blood, even in the dust. I know I have the body of a weak and feeble woman, but I have the heart and stomach of a king, and of a king of England too, and think foul scorn that [the Duke of] Parma or [the King of] Spain, or any Prince of Europe should dare to invade the borders of my realm.'

Tilbury was regarded as crucial because, drawing on the example of Spain's knockout blow against Lisbon in 1580, which had led to the conquest of Portugal, there were fears that the Spaniards were aiming directly for London. In particular, there was the possibility of a Spanish force landing on the Essex bank of the Thames. In contrast, most earlier invaders, notably the Romans and the Normans, had landed on the Channel coast and had to fight their way to the Thames, and cross that river – although Denmark's Cnut had aimed straight for London. In practice, the English troops were mostly poorly trained, supplies were limited and the great English strength was at sea. What would have happened had the Spaniards landed is, of course, unknowable, although a landing of 4,000 Spanish troops at Kinsale, Ireland, in October 1601 proved unsuccessful because the force was rapidly besieged by a larger English army, which in January 1602 defeated both the Spaniards and an Irish army that had marched to their relief.

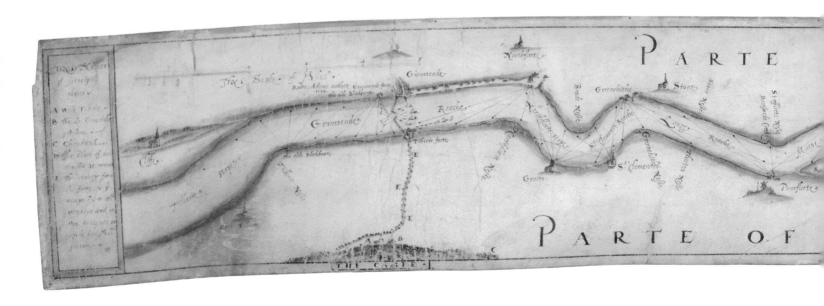

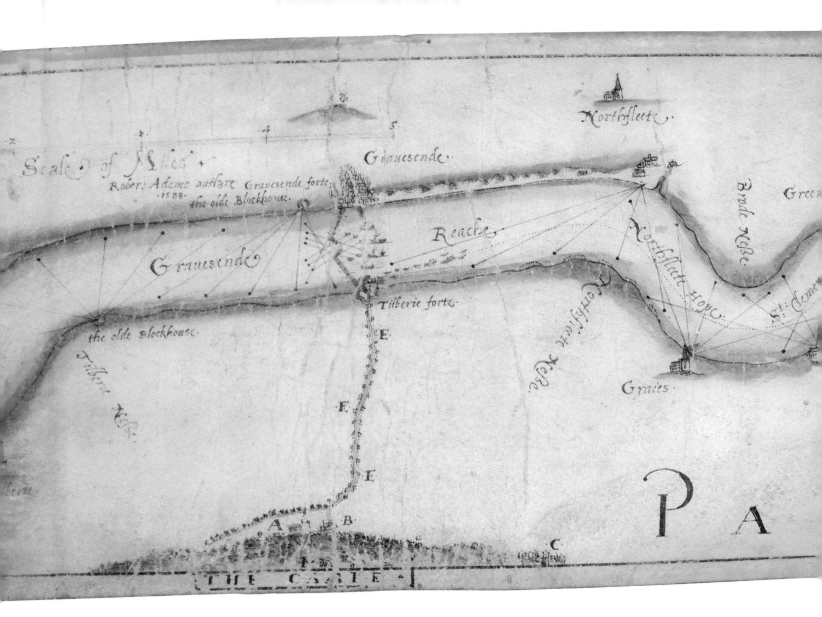

Scale of Miles

Rober: Adams auct fere Grauesende forte
1588   the olde Blockhouse.

Grauesende

Grauesende

the olde Blockhouse

Tilberie Hilse

Graues Reache

Northfleete

Brode Nesse

Gree

Northfleete Hope

St. Cleme

Coalhouse Nesse

Graies

Tilberie forte

E

E

E

A   B

THE CASTE

C

P A

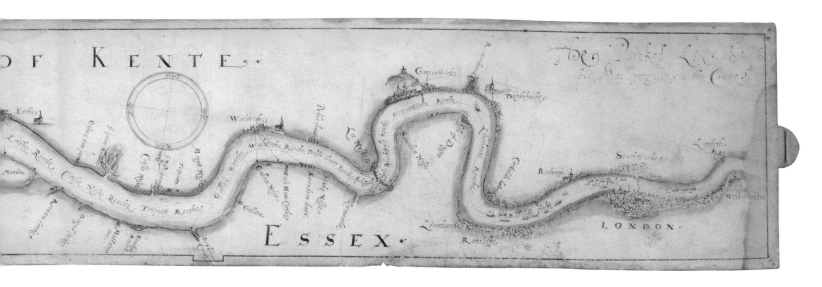

OF KENTE

ESSEX

LONDON

Lambeth

Westminster

A HISTORICAL MANOR

John Walker, 'A Trew Platt of the Manor and Towne of Chellmisforde', 1591.

The nature of individual plots emerges clearly in this map, as does the proximity of the fields. Most sixteenth-century English towns were the size of modern villages. The colours, by 'John Walker Architector', remain vivid, while the pictogram element continues from earlier maps, and the church of St Mary the Virgin and the market-cross or sessions house is drawn in elevation. At a scale of six inches to 96 perches [1:3,168], the map shows field names, the names of tenants, hedges, gates, trees and woodland, water, including the rivers, and it distinguishes demesne, freehold and copyhold holdings. The brown strip in the centre is the High Street (detail, below), with the Middle Row of shopping developed from market stalls that had not been taken down overnight. The central position of the crossing over the River Chelmer is readily apparent. The map was commissioned to illustrate a detailed written survey of the manor of Bishop's Hall. The increasing use of the compass in mapmaking from the late fifteenth century was reflected in a growing tendency to draw local maps with north at the top. Triangulation was introduced and the plane table and the theodolite developed. Walker's map includes a scale bar and dividers.

The Walkers of Hanningfield were an Essex family. John (c.1550–1626) produced a series of local maps, including one in 1615 of Hanningfield for Edward, Lord Bergavenny. John's son, another John, was also a surveyor and mapmaker, with extremely fine lettering as well as his father's use of colour. Such maps proclaimed control. Thus, Sir William Cordell (r.1522–81), the Master of the Rolls and a frequent MP, commissioned in 1580 a survey of his manor of Long Melford, in Suffolk, near the Essex border, a former possession of the abbey of Bury St Edmunds which he had purchased in 1554, and it still hangs in Melford Hall, with every field named.

Essex was a major source of provisions and goods for London, notably grain and, from northwest Essex, meat. Market gardening was focused close to London, with much of Middlesex's woodland cleared accordingly, because of the perishable nature of fresh food combined with transport problems, which were considerable by both land and sea. Pasture land was also located there, both to provide milk and to secure pasturage for animals that had been driven to London for slaughter.

A Trew platt of the manor. And towne of chelmissorde. 1591 By John Walker Architector

North

South

ESte

THE HUNDREDS OF KENT

Philip Symonson, *A New Description of Kent...*, 1596.

Philip Symonson 'of Rochester, gent.,' was Receiver and Paymaster for Rochester Bridge from 1593 to 1598. He produced estate maps on behalf of the very wealthy Rochester Bridge Trust, which had been involved in boundary disputes, and, in 1594, one of Rye harbour for the officials instructed to advise on its improvement. Symonson was elected Mayor of Rochester in 1598, but died that year. There is no known patron for Symonson's county map, but a link to Burghley can be found through the Kent landowner, official, lawyer and historian William Lambarde, also a Warden of Rochester Bridge, who recommended Symonson's work. Lambarde published the first English county history, *A Perambulation of Kent* (1576).

Measuring 31 by 21 inches, the map was drawn at a much larger scale than earlier maps of Kent, which permitted more accuracy and detail. The numbers on the map related to the hundreds (a division of local government) listed on the map's bottom-left quarter. Far more detail is provided than in Saxton's map of Southeast England. The coastline is more accurately depicted, main roads are shown, and whether churches had towers or steeples.

This map, and the series of county maps planned by John Norden (1548–1629), continued the county mapping tradition launched by Saxton. The general trend was to emphasise the need for precision in the portrayal of the crucial physical outlines: coastlines and rivers. Maps drawn to scale were well established. At the same time, the fate of these projects underlined the limited nature of the market, given the popularity of Saxton's work. Norden, a surveyor, planned the *Speculum Britanniae* ('Mirror of Britain'), and a Privy Council order of 1593 instructed Lord Lieutenants to help Norden, who was 'authorised and appointed by Her Majesty to travel through England and Wales to make more perfect descriptions, charts, and maps'. Middlesex was published in 1593 after a draft had been corrected by Burghley, and Hertfordshire five years later. Norden's patron, Burghley, had reiterated his backing in 1594, but the project was to be abandoned, leaving surveys of five other counties in only manuscript form.

As an instance of the dominance of London, Symonson's map was engraved there by Charles Whitwell as two sheets to be joined down the middle, and almost all the surviving specimens carry the added imprint of the London print-seller

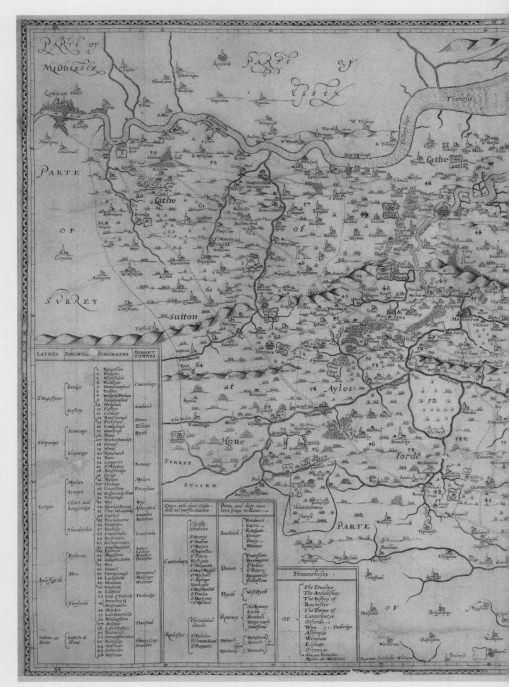

Peter Stern, who embellished the map with inset views of Dover and Rye. Between 1596 and 1775, eight editions were published, including by Peter Stent and Robert Sayer.

Grain was moved to London from Kent, both overland and by sea from ports including Sandwich, which in this period was taking in Protestant refugees from the Low Countries. The immigrants brought improvements to market gardening, including the cultivation of celery. As a result, in the harsh harvests of the 1590s, which of course left no trace in maps, the pressure to serve London led to food shortages elsewhere in much of the Southeast. In comparison to Kent, however, the difficulties of transportation across the Weald ensured that there was no comparable effect in Sussex. West Kent was also an important source of London's wood supply, while Maidstone developed paper-making and brewing for the London market.

Another aspect of the linkage between London and the Southeast was the extent to which the area had the most Protestant parts of the country. London, Kent and Sussex had a disproportionately high number of Protestant martyrs, and the 1554 rebellion against Mary's decision to marry Philip II of Spain, and thus apparently ensure a Catholic succession, focused on Kent.

The 1590s were very difficult years because of an intractable war with Spain and pressure on food supplies. Death rates rose, notably in 1597. There was also a political dimension to social unrest, especially to opposition to the enclosure of common land by landlords. Rumours of rebellion spread and there were preparations for one in Oxfordshire in 1597. The traditional recourse, of action against vagrants and the allocation of stored grain, was matched by attempts to improve the situation, notably by building up stores, passing Poor Laws and reviving legislation against enclosures.

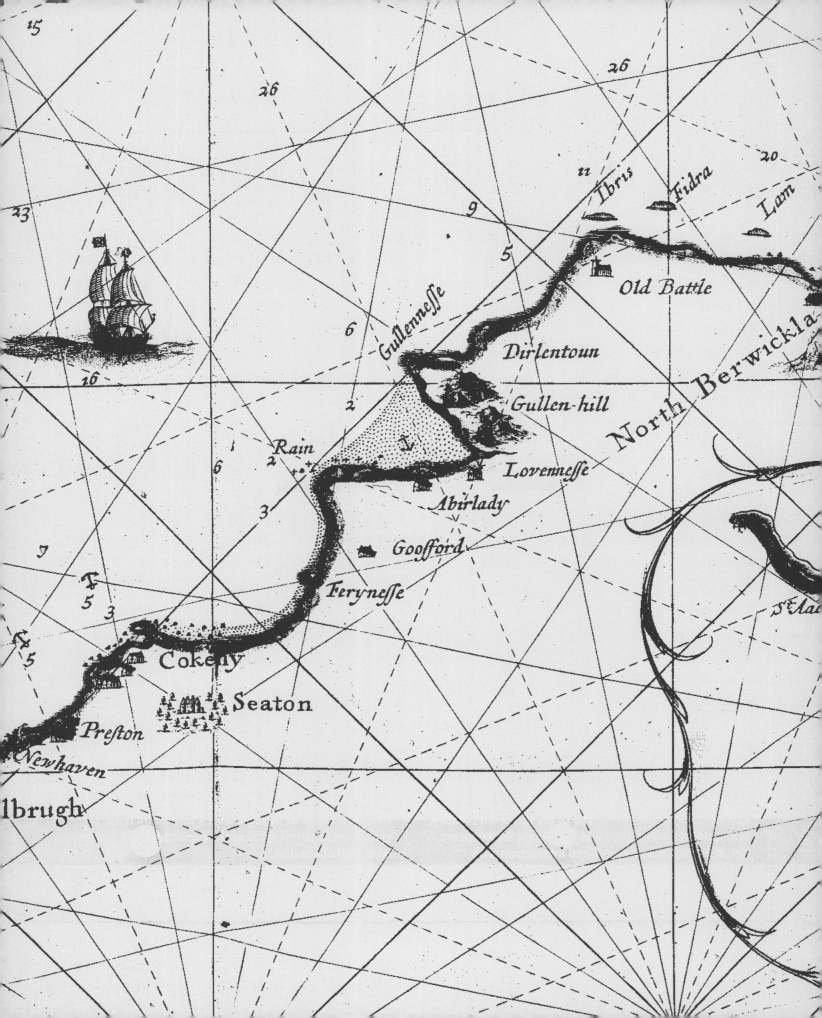

15

26

26

23

16

9

5

11 *Ibris* *Fidra* 20

Lam

Old Battle

Gullenneſſe 6

Dirlentoun

2 *Gullen-hill*

North Berwickla

1 *Rain* 2

6 *Lovenneſſe*

3 *Abirlady*

7 *Gooſford*

5 *Feryneſſe*

3 *St Au*

5 *Cokeny*

Seaton

Preston

Newhaven

lbrugh

2

THE STUART AGE

Civil war and revolution is the dominant impression of the age, and would certainly have been traumatic for contemporaries, with the violence causing very high casualties and much devastation and disruption. This was particularly so in Ireland, but also the case in other parts of the British Isles. The results of the conflict were a dominance of the British Isles by English-based political systems and the eventual victory of a system of limited monarchy in which the Westminster Parliament became a permanent feature of the political system, one further expressed in and established by the union of Scotland with England (and Wales) in 1707, which represented a far deeper relationship than that caused by the personal union of the crowns in 1603.

The period additionally saw the environmental pressures of the 'Little Ice Age', with climate-cooling affecting agricultural yields, while the major population increase of the sixteenth century was followed by stagnation. There was economic development, notably in foreign trade but also in increasing coal production and coal-based industries. Culturally, there was a continuation of the vernacular of the sixteenth century, and notably so with the plays of William Shakespeare. Yet, there was also a continued interaction with Continental culture, and particularly with English Baroque figures such as Christopher Wren, John Dryden and Henry Purcell.

Meanwhile, mapping increased in frequency and type. A changing understanding of sight was significant. Scientific developments undertaken by the Dutch, especially in optics, caused a stress on sight as the sense through which God reveals Creation most clearly to mankind. Greater reliance came to be placed on geographical realism in cartography rather than on the older stylised maps, which did not depend on accurate topographical description. Separately, the numbers of historical and geographical works from the period that are missing their original maps gives us an indication of the level of interest those maps generated, either immediately or in the years that followed.

Initially, a specialised trade in atlases was relatively slow to develop in Britain, certainly in comparison with the Netherlands. Moreover, possibly due to the financial problems affecting the Crown, as well as to the coming of peace in 1604, there was comparatively little government support for mapping. In contrast, the map trade grew rapidly after the Interregnum of 1649–60, with six map- and chart-selling concerns in London by 1660, but about 16 by 1690, with a further increase by 1720 in establishments near the expanding and wealthy West End of London.

SEIZING ULSTER

John Norden, 'A Plott of the Six Escheated Counties of Ulster', c.1610.

Found in the papers of Robert, Earl of Salisbury, Chief Minister of James I at the time, this map by John Norden of six 'escheated' counties, meaning reverted to the Crown, reflects the possibilities for English and Scottish settlers ('planters') created by English victory in the Nine Years' War (not that of 1688–97, but the war otherwise known as Tyrone's Rebellion, from 1594 to 1602–3), a conflict that was more immediately marked by a map of the English siege of Enniskillen (see inset, below). Built in 1428, the castle was captured by English forces in February 1594, with the garrison killed after it had surrendered. From May 1594, the Irish besieged the garrison, defeating a relief force. In May 1595, the garrison surrendered and was then, in turn, killed. The map shows the original capture by Devon-born Captain John Dowdall (c.1545–c.1606) who had moved to Ireland in about 1560, serving in the army and settling in Pilltown, where land had been taken from the Desmond branch of the Fitzgeralds. It depicts Dowdall's forces, cannon, a trebuchet and boats on Lough Erne. His men breached the enclosure wall (bawn) with pick-axes and threatened to blow up the castle. Mapmaker John Thomas presents, in one image, different stages of the operation.

The role of boats in the map reflected the significance of water links and therefore of

positions that guarded them. Thus, in 1595 there was the capture of English-held Blackwater Fort which, built that year, had a similar layout to that at Enniskillen. The defenders were not executed in this case, presumably because they had not killed Irish defenders as had happened at Enniskillen.

Hugh O'Neill, Earl of Tyrone, a Gaelic lord and Catholic whom Dowdall criticised in a letter to Burghley in 1595, raised a substantial army of 10,000 men that was as well armed as the English. The wooded and boggy terrain of Ulster was well suited to guerrilla conflict, and at Clontibert in 1595 O'Neill successfully ambushed an English army. Three years later, at Yellow Ford, another English army was badly battered when attacked on the march, while in 1599, Robert, Earl of Essex, Elizabeth I's arrogant and incompetent favourite, failed to defeat O'Neill, being disgraced as a result. In 1600, the English sent a more effective leader, Charles, Lord Mountjoy, who campaigned in the winter to disrupt O'Neill's logistical system.

English fears of foreign intervention in Ireland were realised in 1601 when Philip III of Spain sent 4,000 troops to Kinsale, a port in southern Ireland, to support the Catholic O'Neill. Mountjoy responded by blockading Kinsale, only for his force to be rapidly weakened by sickness. O'Neill's relieving army decided to attack, only to

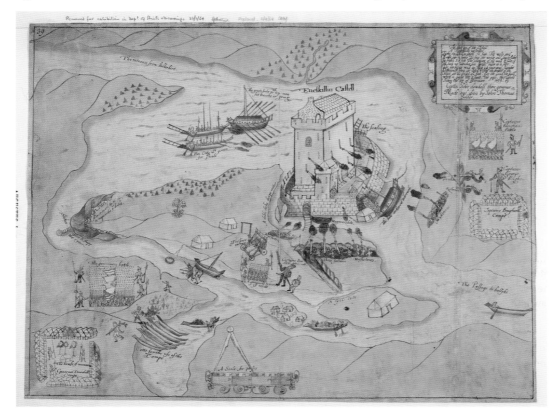

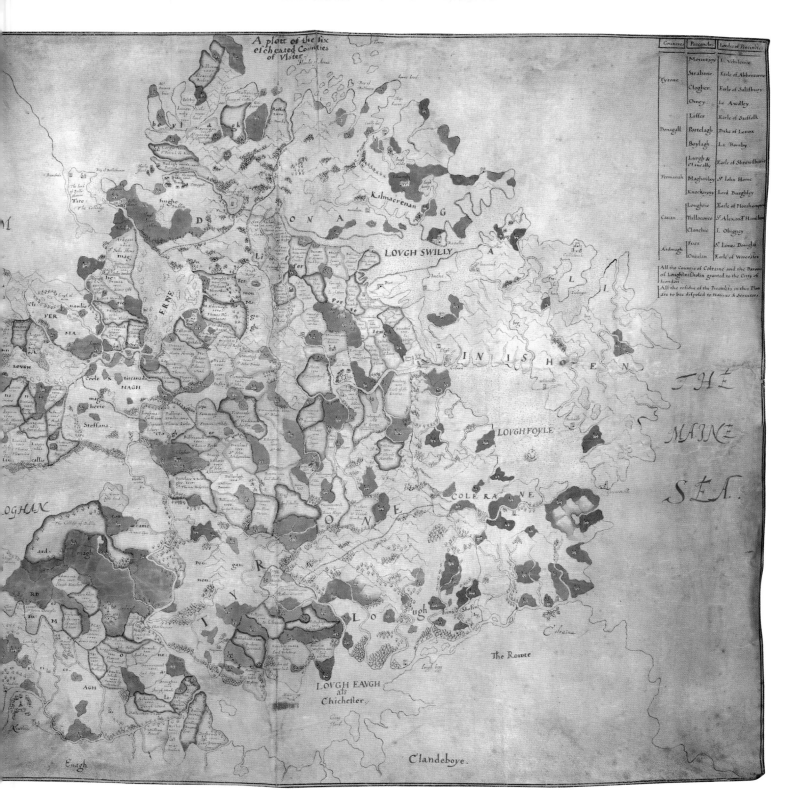

A plott of the six el cheated Counties of Vlster.

Counties	Precincts	Lords of Precincts
	Mountjoy	L. Vchiltrie
Tyrone	Strabane	Earle of Abbercorne
	Clogher	Earle of Salisbury
	Omey	L. Awdley
	Lifter	Earle of Suffolk
Donagall	Portelagh	Duke of Lenox
	Boylagh	L. Barnby
	Lurgh & Clincally	Earle of Shrewsburie
Fermanah	Magheriboy	S John Home
	Knockynyny	Lord Burghley
	Loughtie	Earle of Northampton
Cauan	Tullocoree	S Alexand Hamilton
	Clanchie	L. Obigney
Ardmagh	Foes	S lames Douglas
	Onealan	Earle of Worcester

All the Countie of Colraine and the Baronie of Loughinfholin granted to the Citty of London

All the refidue of the Precincts in this Plott are to bee difposed to Natines & Servitors

LOVGH SWILLY

Kilmacrenan

LOVGH FOYLE

COLE RA NE

THE MAINE SEA.

The Rowte

LOVGH EAVGH als Chichester.

Clandeboye.

mishandle the battle, which was decisively won by Mountjoy. O'Neill was restored to his lands when he submitted in 1603, but the imposition of English law and custom in Ulster led him to flee to Italy in 1607 (the 'flight of the Earls') and much of Ulster (3.8 million acres) was then seized and awarded to Protestant English and Scottish settlers. Other 'plantations' were established further south – for example, in Wexford, Leitrim, Westmeath and Longford, although these had fewer Protestant settlers. Irish discontent over land, religion and political status was to explode in the rising of 1641, a rebellion that launched a decade of bitter conflict at the end of which the position of the Catholics had been much weakened, not least by the loss of much land.

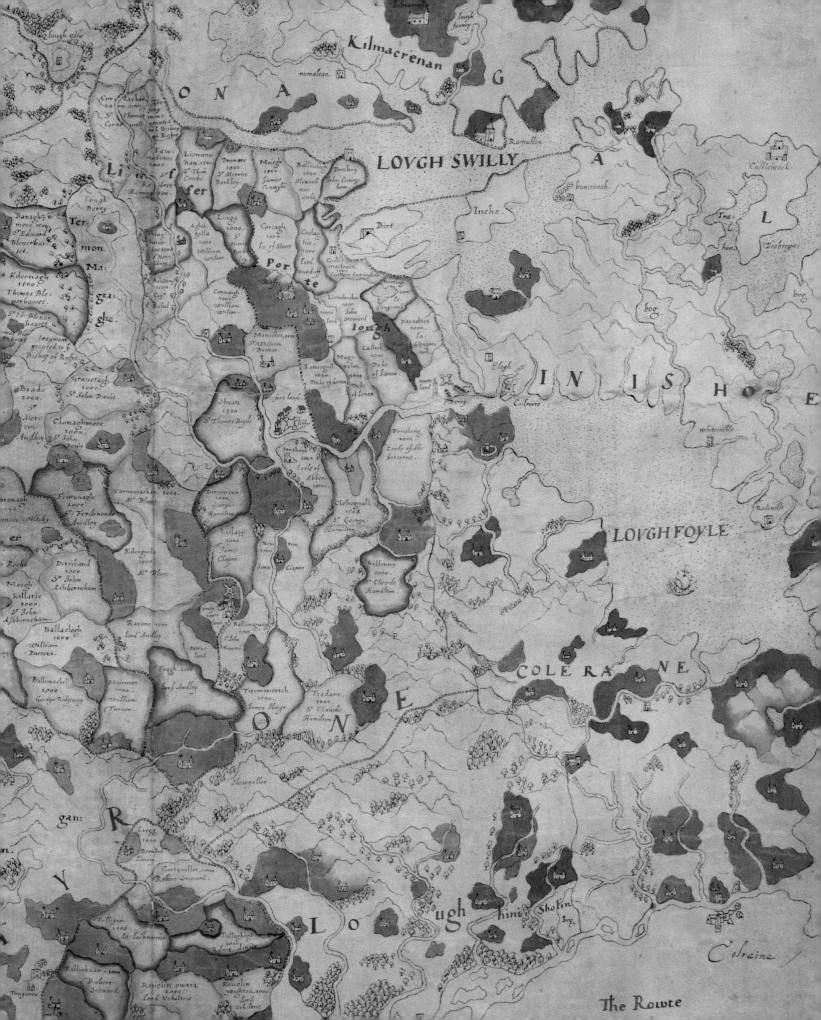

MAPPING AT GROUND LEVEL

'Map of Bassingham', 1629, and Margaret and William Bowles, 'The Mannar of Brainston and part of Nutford...', 1659.

This petition (opposite), in favour of enclosure, by villagers in Bassingham, southwest of Lincoln, complains about the six miles their stock had to walk to the pasture, which 'sore beates theire feete and impoverisheth them', because of the 'cornfields' that were unenclosed open fields. The petition was addressed to Susan, Countess of Warwick (1582–1646), by her 'poore tenants'. The countess was a daughter of Sir Henry Rowe, Lord Mayor of London, and widow of William Holliday, the Chairman of the East India Company, and the second wife of Robert, 2nd Earl of Warwick (1587–1658), a keen exponent of English imperial expansion and a Puritan opponent of Charles I. The common grazing land was at a distance from the village, where 61 households were recorded in 1563. Ditches or 'dreines' were necessary due to the high water table in the flat lands near the River Witham. Indeed, drainage schemes became more significant in England in the 1620s and 1630s, although they also caused dissent, especially in the Fens, due to the potential impact on traditional lifestyles.

The map of Brainston (Bryanston) in Dorset (following pages), near Blandford Forum, presents the type of land use, while the details of tenants and acreage were given in tables, thus showing how maps were part of an information system. The map shows surveyors, of whom William Bowles was one, at work. Surveying was an aspect of control and a source and focus of social tension; it was seen as a tool of landlord control and landlord-directed change, and maps as a means of recording the information. It is believed that Bowles' data was transformed into graphic form by a female mapmaker, Margaret Bowles.

In *The Surveyors Dialogue* (1607) by John Norden, Surveyor to the Duchy of Cornwall, he offered an inclusive view of economic change, 'Surveys are necessarie and profitable both for Lord and Tenant', only to meet with the farmer's claim, 'oftentimes you are the cause that men lose their land'. The surveyor's view – 'the faulty are afraid to be seen ... the innocent need not fear to be looked into' – would have convinced few. The tension between oral and literate traditions was also seen with the idea of the 'estimated acre', the folk equivalent of surveying, which remained legitimate for many, certainly into the eighteenth century, and was usually the preserve of the old men of the parish. In about 1600, Norden had produced an atlas, containing 28 maps, of the Suffolk estates of Sir Michael Stanhope, as well as a reference map for the 28.

Market developments were both regional and national, with regional variations in prices as a result becoming less pronounced. Thus, the enclosure of land in County Durham during the century, so that it could be more easily cultivated and adapted to new agricultural methods, was a response to the rise in population associated with the development of lead and coal mining.

Both maps and references to market development and economic integration provide scant indication of the social unrest arising from economic change, notably enclosure riots, which were frequent. In 1607, over 1,000 rioters in Northamptonshire, Leicestershire and Warwickshire were suppressed by the local gentry, with over 50 killed, including the execution of the ringleaders. The major ringleader, John Reynolds, known as 'Captain Pouch', claimed to have authority from God and the king to destroy enclosures and to have in his pouch the means to protect his followers from harm.

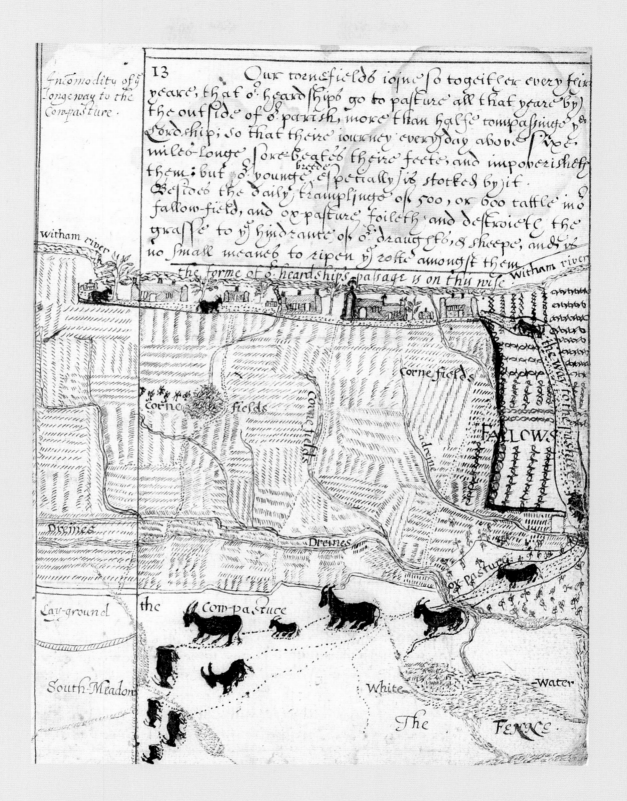

Margaret and William Bowles, 'The Mannar of Brainston and part of Nutford...', 1659.

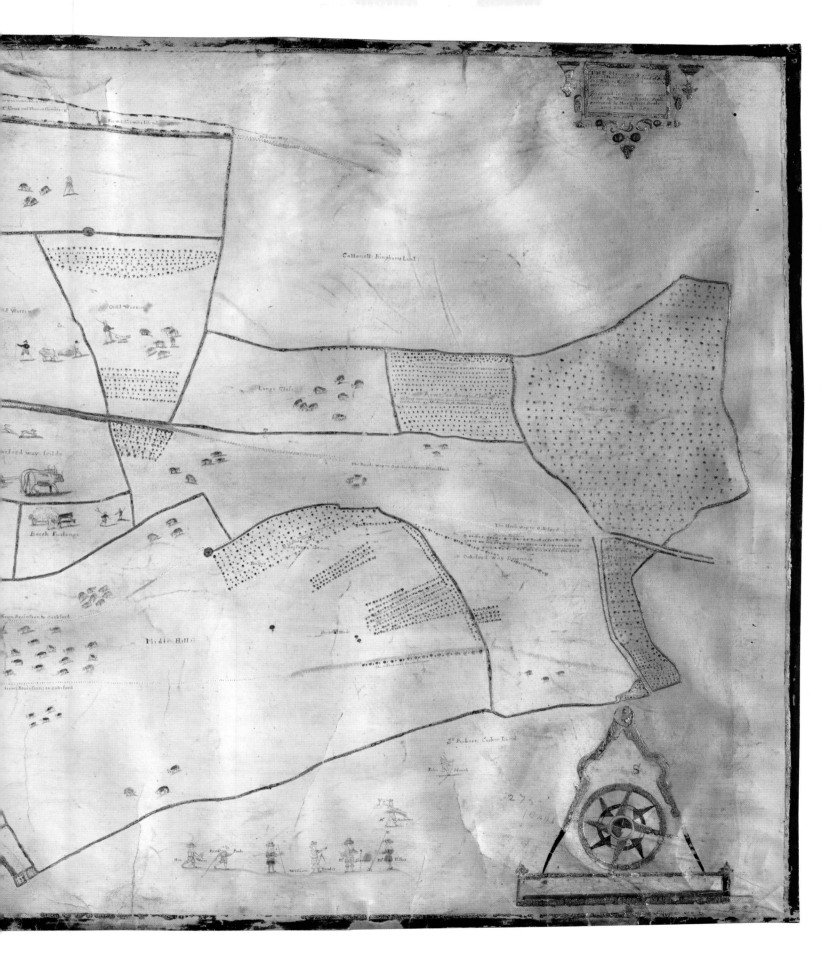

A COUNTRY PLUNGED IN CIVIL WAR

Wenceslaus Hollar, *A True Mapp and Description of the Towne of Plymouth and the Fortifications thereof...*, 1643.

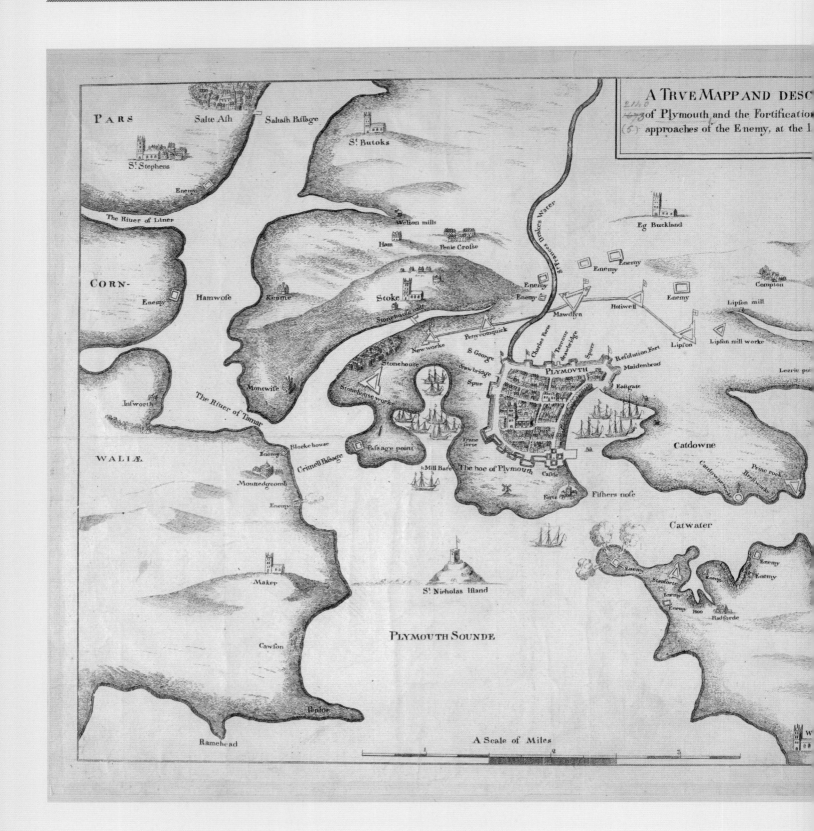

TION OF THE TOWNE
ereof, with the workes and
eige A° 1643

The Leerie

Plymton marie

Saltrum

Beckley

flit mills

Plymstock

Wenceslaus Hollar (1607–77), a Bohemian draughtsman and engraver trained in Frankfurt, became an artist in service to Thomas, Earl of Arundel, accompanying him back to England in 1637, although he also took on other commissions. A Royalist, Hollar was besieged in Basing House before being captured there in 1645. After escaping, he worked in Antwerp then returned to London in 1652. Although he worked actively and produced a career total of over 3,400 drawings and etchings, he died in poverty. His maps included those of warfare on the Continent.

War was a major cause of mapping, and notably so for fortifications and sieges. Thus, a map was produced of the fortifications hastily thrown up round London by Parliament, while other sites were also mapped. Plymouth was the major Parliamentary position in the West Country that, unlike Bristol and Exeter, successfully withstood attack when the Royalists overran most of western England. Bristol was stormed on 26 July 1643, while Exeter, which survived a poorly provisioned Royalist siege in December 1642–January 1643, fell in September 1643.

Hollar's map shows Plymouth within its walls, as well as the new works built to the north in a more modern series of fortifications constructed essentially of packed earth. As with London, these works were designed to keep the Royalists, whose positions are marked as 'Enemy', further from the older walls, which would have been vulnerable to cannon fire. The Parliamentary line also served to protect the anchorages to the east and west of Plymouth, both marked with ships on the map.

Whereas Gloucester held off Royalist siege, thanks in part to supplies brought overland by a Parliamentary army, these ships off Plymouth, as in Parliamentary-held Hull, provided the key supply route for the city. Moreover, Parliamentary warships ensured that the Royalists could not mount amphibious attacks from their positions round 'Plymouth Sounde' (as annotated in the map), including Plymstock, Plympton, Egg Buckland, Tamerton and Mount Edgecumbe, and, in turn, left these positions vulnerable to Parliamentary attack. The siege formally began at the end of September 1643, but was abandoned before Christmas as too formidable a task, and the Royalists relied instead on a blockade that, in the end, failed. Colonel William Ruthven, the commander of the garrison, supported by experienced Scottish mercenaries, provided a vigorous defence.

The major Royalist field armies were defeated at Marston Moor near York on 2 July 1644 and at Naseby in the Midlands on 14 June 1645. These Parliamentary victories took precedence over local struggles. In 1646, the remaining Royalist forces succumbed. Parliamentary victory in England was due to a number of factors, including the backing of the wealthiest parts of the country, the support of the Scots, London, the major ports and the navy, and the religious zeal of some of its followers – Cromwell saw himself as God's chosen instrument, destined to overthrow religious and political tyranny, a potent belief. On the other hand, the Parliamentarians suffered from lacklustre and unsuccessful commanders, such as the Earls of Essex and Manchester and Sir William Waller, the leading generals in 1642–43. Moreover, the Parliamentarians initially had far less effective cavalry than the Royalists. Parliamentary taxation also aroused hostility.

In turn, the Royalists suffered from a lack of resources, from serious internal divisions, from uncertain command, and from only limited support in the areas they controlled. As with the collapse of royal power in 1639–40, the defeat of Charles I owed much to the Scots, and it is not surprising that they played such a major role in the politics of the late 1640s, nor that England only became really stable when the rule of the Commonwealth government in England was forcibly extended to Scotland in the early 1650s, albeit ending with the overthrow of the Interregnum government in 1660 when the army in Scotland under General Monck successfully invaded England, thus preparing the way for the restoration of the Stuart dynasty in the person of Charles II.

MAPPING SCOTLAND

Robert Gordon, 'Scotia regnum cum insulis adjacentibus...', 1654.

Mapping of Scotland had improved in the mid-sixteenth century, when John Elder and Lawrence Nowell both produced maps. More followed in the seventeenth century, and a more accurate depiction of the coastline emerged, although the Highlands remained poorly mapped. The Scottish part of John Speed's map of Britannia (1612) was disproportionate in giving less relative space to the Highlands, especially Caithness and Sutherland in the far north.

Timothy Pont (c.1565–1614), who sought to emulate Saxton, faced a much tougher task in Scotland, where he travelled widely in the 1580s and 1590s. However, whereas in England there existed a pressing commercial opportunity and imperative (in the shape of a buoyant market), in Scotland those were missing, as was comparable government support, and Pont's manuscripts with their identifiable maps were not published in his lifetime. Instead, they proved a basis for the maps of Scotland which appeared in a Dutch work, the 1654 extension of Joan Blaeu's *Atlas Novus*, the sixth volume of Blaeu's *Atlas Maior*. Using the significant image of the hazards of maritime travel, Blaeu presented his role as that of rescuing material that was otherwise at risk of being lost 'like sacred objects from a shipwreck ... deposited with us in the safe harbour of Amsterdam, where we engraved them for the use of posterity, to live again (in case they should perish) in copper', a reference to the engraving of maps.

Blaeu's map of Scotland, as acknowledged, was the original work of Robert Gordon of Straloch (1580–1661), a landowner and scholar, who had completed 'Scotia regnum cum insulis adjacentibus' ('The Kingdom of Scotland with adjacent islands') in 1648 for Charles I. John Adair (1660–1718), Scotland's Geographer Royal, as part of his publicly funded mapping of Scotland from 1681, produced *The Description of the Sea-Coast and Islands of Scotland* (1703), although the intended second part was never published. His unpublished surveying of the coasts included the Orkney and Shetland Islands. However, John Cowley's 'Display of the Coasting Lines of Six Several Maps of North Britain' (1734) highlighted the incompatible nature of map outlines of Scotland. Nevertheless, the spread of mathematical information helped mapping. Thus, the *Edinburgh Courant* in April 1708 advertised: 'Those who desire to learn any of the mathematical sciences ... applied in surveying, gauging, dialling, in measuring heights and distances, and in solving the most useful bases

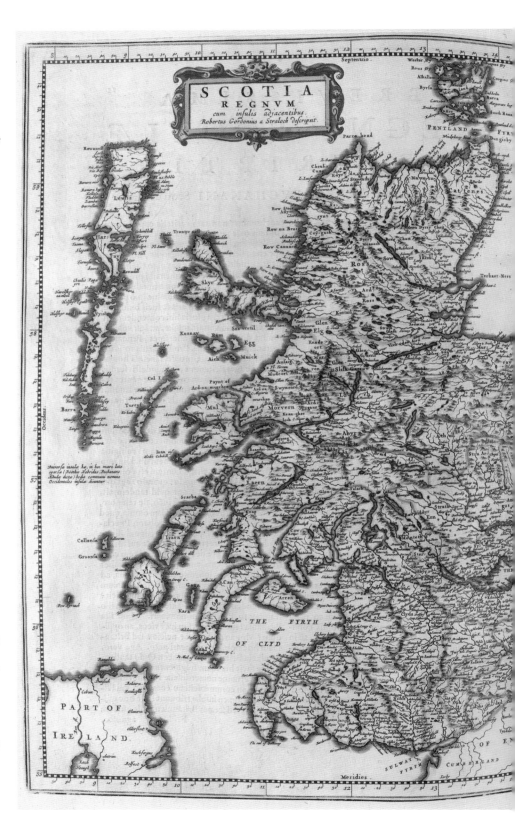

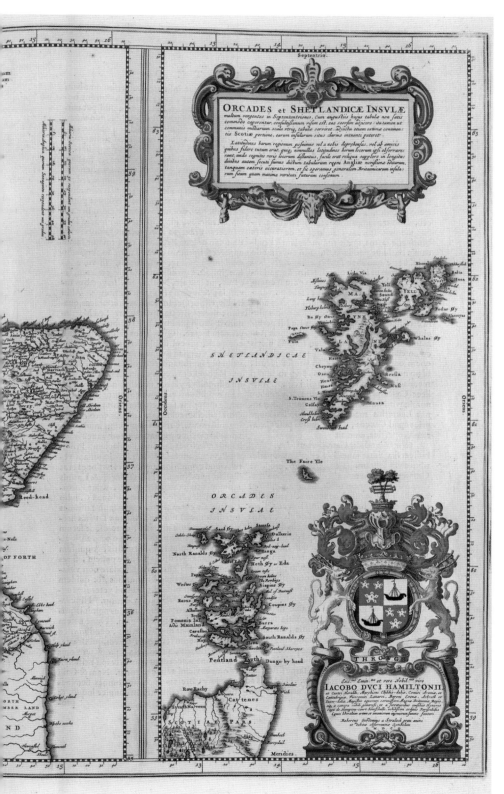

of geography, astronomy and navigation etc. They may be instructed in these....'

Scotland changed as a result of the union of the two crowns in 1603 when James VI of Scotland became James I of England. The country was governed by the Scottish Privy Council and the absentee kingship proved relatively successful. The succession was followed by a firm campaign of repression against the reivers or moss-troopers who dominated the border lands (and many were killed), but the situation in the Highlands among the unruly clans remained troubled. Thus, in the 1630s, Sir William Forbes of Craigievar in Aberdeenshire and his kinsmen at Corse suffered greatly from a Highland brigand band, which in 1636 was captured, hanged, and their heads displayed as a warning. Support by the absentee Charles I (r.1625–49) for a stronger episcopacy and a new liturgy, and a tactless and autocratic handling of Scottish interests and views, led in 1640 to a war in which the English army was defeated. The Scots subsequently successfully intervened in 1644 on the Parliamentarian side in the English Civil War, but the victors of 1646 fell out, and the Scots then invaded England in 1648, only to be defeated at Preston.

Moreover, the conflicts from 1639 to 1746 brought instability to Scotland, where they were experienced as bitter civil wars that reflected and exacerbated sectarian and regional divisions. Oliver Cromwell's decisive victories over Scottish armies at Dunbar (1650) and Worcester (1651), and the successful siege of Dundee by General George Monck (1651), led to the fall of Scotland, the first time it had been conquered. As a result, in 1652, with the Tender of Union, Scotland was declared part of a Commonwealth with England and Ireland. The Scottish Parliament and executive council were abolished, the power of the Scottish nobility was curtailed, and measures were taken to adopt English law. In 1653, Scotland alongside England, Ireland and Wales, was represented in the Parliament, usually known as Barebone's Parliament (after a radical member, 'Praise-God' Barebone), appointed by Cromwell and his council of officers, although the representatives from Scotland and Ireland were mostly Englishmen serving there. A Royalist rising in favour of Charles II in the Highlands in 1653 was defeated the following year.

Soa vretil

Chastel cam- Kilchamerun
Elg L. Coich
L. Ouien
L. Nevish Kilgoan
Kannay Rum Kilmaroy Knode
Egg Arisaig L. Turron Mur ort
Muick Yl. Tirrim Ard Achago
Aich Mudeort Ellan Finan Glen
Slif
Helskyr L. Soel
Houmoir Kilmos Ard na Swyneord L.
Poynt of C. Megarie murchen
Yl. Charn Ard-na-murchen C. Loch Alyn Ard
Taleburg Maddy Col I. Achanadevin Ard torenish gaur Torrychaslet Kilmaille
Kil-Fadrit Calva Killinaig Issuri I. Kildarie Morvern Kean-gher Chowil Lenath
Soa Breccah C. Mul Arrois C. loch C. Nagar Inner-Lo
Eriskey Turryf Gunna Kilimug Kilchren C. Balacheules toir Blairnglerach
Fard Grega Kilthoubil nen Apping Yl. Moun Koryesman
Barra Hildesey Kirkaboi Gomedra Vtua Krcak Lismoir Suno Lieren Ardeurich A
Via Fladda Kilibunt H. Stackir Glen-Coen
Watersa Momich Burg Killoune Dowart Innes Darach
Scarpa Iunga Stafa Killinachor Beandyr-loch Ardchattan Stron-Mial- Glen-
Linga Bach Ardcrost Inneraw lachan Stree
Sandrera Kean-darar Loch Bay C. Dunstaffage C. Eist
Pappa Beach Dunalddss Kilbryd Lochenyell Glen-
Megala Kerrera Kilmore C. Cheulcharn Shyre
Bernera Iona ins. Seil Liggan Inis-Darach Clachan Disert Glen-wrch Gle
Hodie Colmkill Sinn Laern Kilchoan Inis chonel C. Megachan L. Ree
Universæ insulæ hæ, in hoc mari late Kilchoan Inischery C. ort Sonathan Blairevin
sparsæ (Boethio Hebrides, Buchanano Laung Anagra Duning Drumfin Inner-rora Ardgorta
Æbudæ dictæ) hodie communi nomine Scarba C. Chrei- Kennan Duntyn Fincharn Kilorid- Cragon
Occidentales insulæ dicuntur. genes Knap Inerlakan Creigan Kilchaterin Killesn
Owranagiald Knokintaul dail Cow Keanloch gorl
Kilibysa Karswick Kilmort ell Kilnalash gnanan
Collonsa Killouran Iurra Terbaet Kilmgehon Ottyr Skyach Inner L. Aleck Tnerchupil Owrg Achnag's
Gruonsa Ardmeanish Inne Ayse Kildusislan L. Girr Christy Calan Achinbrek vrachy
Kilchomkil Ardart dill Ormsa Batman Poynt Kery Arthus Arehaytes
Kounndel Praoig Kilbarren Levy Herbaet Inerchon Cragon
Yla Kildalchan Ard Fadrik Aldbee Stron Oruk
Ereby Doun Owaig C. Kilchalmac Shibbenes Boot Achindarroch C.
Dow Myrtach Gaga Kilmichel Can- Kilchalmanel Lok of Arren Skelmorly
osfryn Kilean Spersac Brodwick Cumbramejor
Kilchonan Yl. Tegza Baslachantuy Cunnadel C. L. Ranfa Lladda I. Cumbra Bay
Elisdel Kara tyr Sadael Ortrenen Arren Hunterston
Orersa Dawner Poynt Puincors
Kilwhouslan Salt cotts
Kilkeran THE FYRTH Irwing
Raughlin Iofet Ailze Lady yle
Killinlan Elsbery head Ayr
OF CLYD Dan or Ca.
Donanerony Toy Kilbrun Turnbery head Achindren
Dunseek Baltern Ye Mul of Cantyr Ardmillon Car- Minndol
Colran Reedcastle Sanda P. Port Moulin Girvan Cass
Kilochen Dalwharra
Balsallach Trochray
Krokfeley Bargeny rick Balkeny Kirk Boyt
Stenchar Knokfanfa Brodach K. Knokfa
Ardstinchar Carmont Pin horry
Knokdolian Lagans Kirk- G'lash
Knokenrowl patrick
Barlan L.

REBUILDING LONDON

Christopher Wren, 'The London Plan', 1666, and John Gwynn, *A Plan for Rebuilding the City of London*

After the Great Fire in 1666..., 1749.

After the Great Fire of London, which raged for four days in 1666, had destroyed about two-thirds of the City, Christopher Wren (1632–1723), John Evelyn and others produced plans for rebuilding the capital on a layout that broke from the essentially medieval street system. These plans reflected the interest in Baroque-style Continental street plans, as in Paris and Rome, which were seen as modern and their regularity as beneficial.

Wren's plan, presented to Charles II in September 1666, was drawn to a scale of about 435 feet to an inch. While that offered the possibility of some detail, it essentially meant a focus on the general plan for rebuilding, which indeed was what interested both the king and Wren. Initially, Wren had produced a plan only for the section of the City intended for rebuilding, but this was replaced by the plan shown here (below) which covers the entire City and not just the fire-damaged area, which was distinguished by being edged in yellow wash. The surviving streets were

drawn with dotted lines, the churches identified by crosses and the markets by the symbol for Mercury, the Roman god of trading.

In 1749 Wren's drawings were sold and John Gwynn, a founder of the Royal Academy, obtained Wren's rebuilding plan and redrew it (right), with some explanatory comments. Wren proposed a city with two central points: the Royal Exchange, from which ten roads were to radiate, and a piazza in front of St Paul's Cathedral, which was to be the focus of three key routes in the western part of the city. The river was to be faced by a 'Grand Terras'. Robert Hooke and Richard Newcourt each proposed a regular grid. However, resources and will were lacking, and the existing property rights of individuals were one of the chief stumbling blocks to an organised replanning; instead, it was piecemeal. The sole new street was King Street – and from that Queen Street, which created a new route from Guildhall to the Thames. Wren, however, rebuilt 52

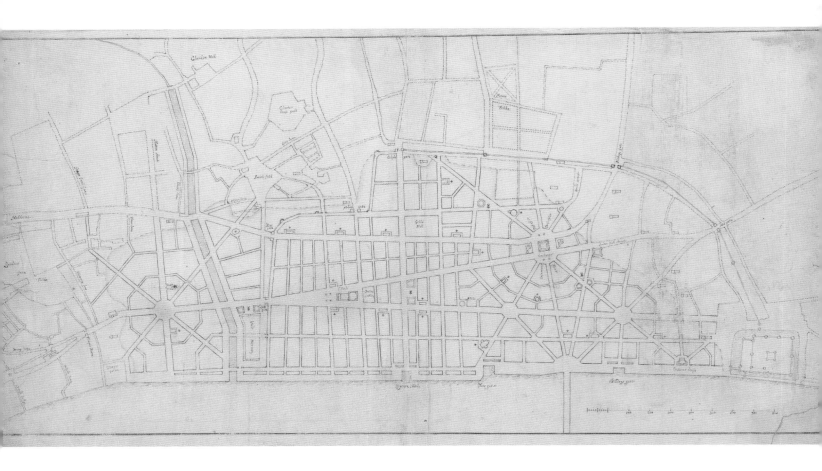

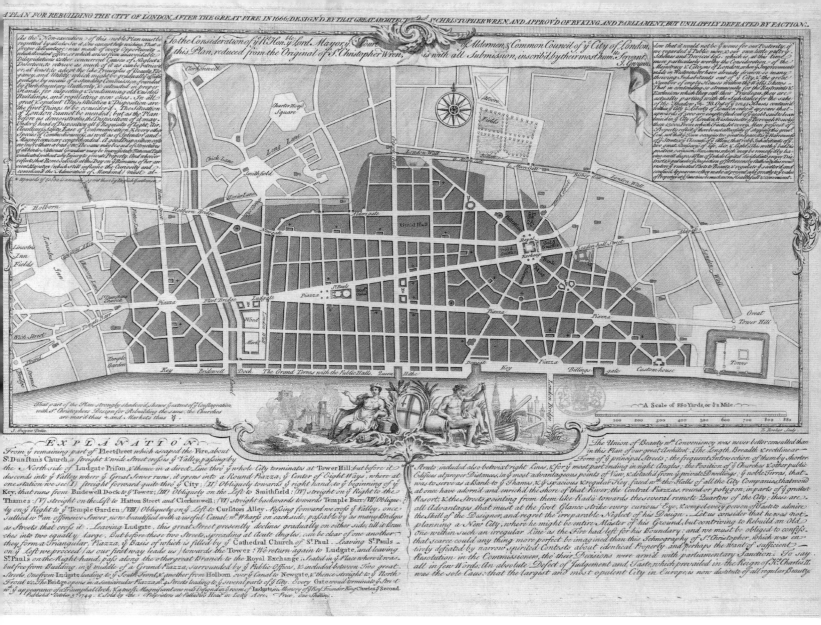

churches in the City, including St Paul's Cathedral, which was finished in 1710. Evelyn's proposal consisted of interconnecting squares and piazzas, as well as the removal of noxious trades from areas of polite habitation, while Wren's showed boulevards and open squares.

The Rebuilding Acts for London of 1667 and 1670 were more restricted in their scope, although they dispensed with the need to use accredited tradesmen (in accordance with guild regulations) and also sought to limit the danger of a new fire by stipulating that a building should have no projecting windows and be at most four storeys' tall. Houses were to be built out of brick and to be uniform in their frontages, and these regulations (seen as modern) acted as the model for large-scale urban building in England. The fire also encouraged the taking out of insurance policies.

Fires went on being a cause of maps. Thus, more than a century after Wren, Thomas Jefferys was to produce 'A Plan of all the Houses, destroyed and damaged by the Great Fire, which begun in Exchange Alley Cornhill, on Friday March 25, 1748', the product of another major London fire. Beyond London, wood and thatch burned readily, and firefighting faced many limitations, and the situation did not change rapidly, with Warwick being hard-hit in 1694. In Devon, Tiverton was badly damaged by fire in 1726, 1730 and, especially, 1731, with the last fire leading to an Act of Parliament that all roofs thereafter should be of lead, slate or tile. Elsewhere in Devon, Crediton lost 460 house s to a single fire in 1743, while much of Honiton had to be rebuilt after fires in 1747 and 1765.

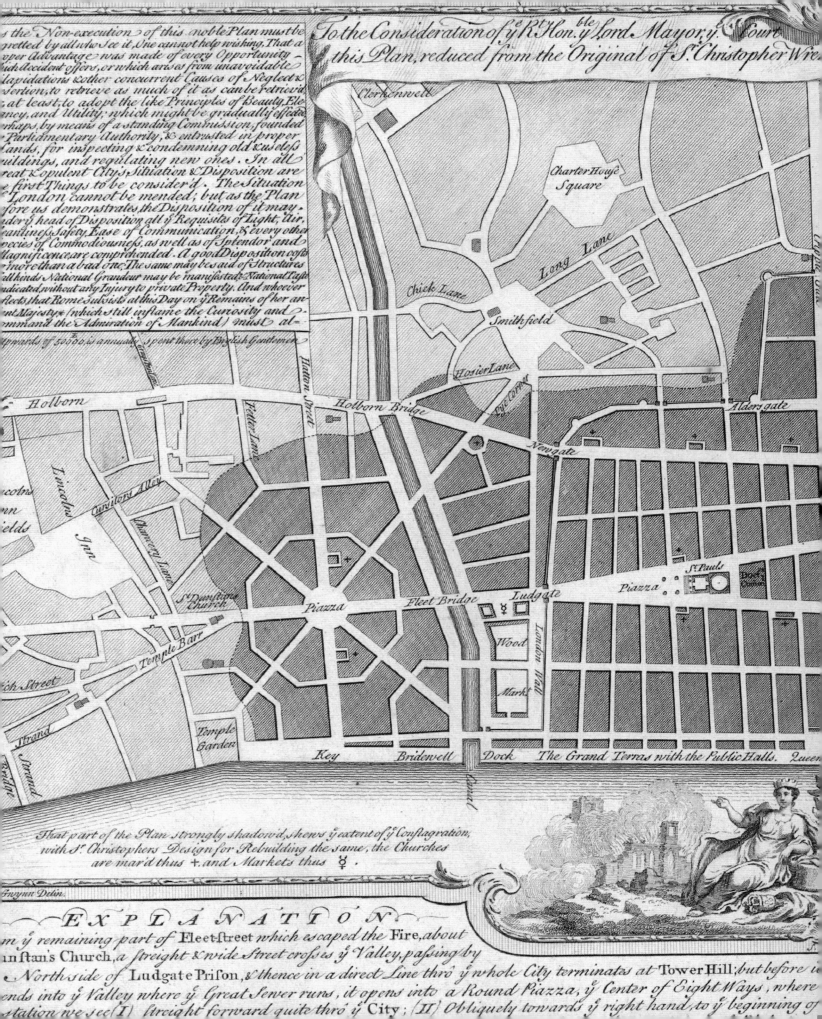

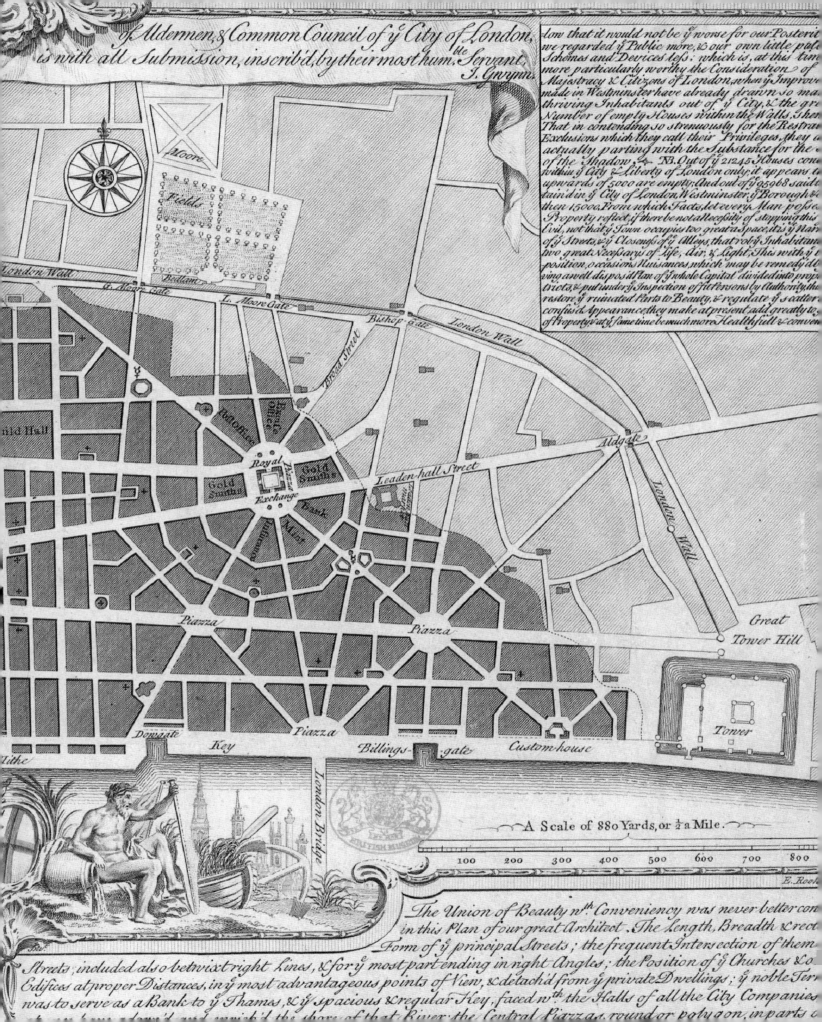

of Aldermen, & Common Council of ꝡ City of London,
is with all Submission, inscrib'd, by their most hum.ble Servant.
J. Gwynn.

low that it would not be ꝡ worse for our Posteri
we regarded ꝡ Public more, & our own little pub
Schemes and Devices less : which is, at this tim
more particularly worthy the Consideration of ꝡ
Magistracy & Citizens of London, when ꝡ Improv
made in Westminster have already drawn so ma
thriving Inhabitants out of ꝡ City, & the gre
Number of empty Houses within the Walls. Then
That in contending so strenuously for the Restrai
Exclusions which they call their Privileges, they a
actually parting with the Substance for the
of the Shadow. — NB. Out of ꝡ 21245 Houses con
within ꝡ City & Liberty of London only, it appears t
upwards of 5000 are empty; And out of ꝡ 95968 said t
tain'd in ꝡ City of London, Westminster, ꝡ Borough &c
then 15000, From which Facts, let every Man posse
Property reflect, if there be not a Necessity of stopping this
Evil, not that ꝡ Town occupies too great a Space, it is ꝡ Narr
of ꝡ Streets, & ꝡ Closeness of ꝡ Alleys, that rob ꝡ Inhabitant
two great Necessarys of Life, Air, & Light. This with ꝡ
position, occasions Nuisances, which may be remedy'd
ving a well dispos'd Plan of ꝡ whole Capital divided into prop
tricts, & put under ꝡ Inspection of fit Persons by Authority, tha
restore ꝡ ruinated Parts to Beauty, & regulate ꝡ scatter
confus'd Appearance, they make at present, add greatly to
of Property, & at ꝡ same time be much more Healthfull & conven

Moore
Fields
Bedlam
G. Moore Gate
L. Moore Gate
Bishop-gate
London Wall
London Wall
Aldgate
London Wall
Broad Street
ild Hall
Post Office
Bank Office
Royal
Exchange
Gold Smiths
Piazza
Gold Smiths
Gold Smiths
Bank
Mint
Leaden-hall Street
Great
Tower Hill
Piazza
Piazza
Piazza
Tower
Downgate
Key
Billings- gate
Custom-house
Tithe
London Bridge

A Scale of 880 Yards, or ½ a Mile.

100   200   300   400   500   600   700   800

E. Roo

The Union of Beauty w.th Conveniency was never better con
in this Plan of our great Architect. The Length, Breadth & rect
Form of ꝡ principal Streets; the frequent Intersection of them

Streets; included also betwixt right Lines, & for ꝡ most part ending in right Angles; the Position of ꝡ Churches & o
Edifices at proper Distances, in ꝡ most advantageous points of View, & detach'd from ꝡ private Dwellings; ꝡ noble Ter
was to serve as a Bank to ꝡ Thames, & ꝡ spacious & regular Key, faced w.th the Halls of all the City Companies

Præcipuæ Civitates	les Villes Principales	Cities
Urbes	les Villes	Townes
Castella	les chasteaux	Castles
Pagi	Villages	Villages
Loca Postarum	le Maison de post	the stages
Divisio Provintarum	division do Provices	doee devid the Shires
Viæ Postarum	signifie les chemins de poste	the Postroades
Numeri litterales Distantiam locorum significantes	les lettres nimbre par toute la carte demonstre combien loing lune place est de l'anstre	the numbers demonst... destance of miles from... place

CERTA Demonstratio per a grandi totam Angliam per Postam secundum, Ordinationem ibidem, septem milliaria in æstate, quinque milliaria in Hyeme in Una hora conficiuntur.

Descriptio viarum Angliæ per postam: LONDINO EDENBURGUM in Scotiam; locorum in quibus renovantur equi; nominorum viarum excurrentium à præcipius civitatibus aliisque Urbibus, Castellis, notis: per signa & Litteras in quamque Provintiam, ut supra notatum incommodum peregrinantium, in prædicto Regno, Manifestata & edita per R. CARR.

UNE parfaicte, demonstration, pour, cheminer de post à post, par tout l' Angleterre; à sept mile chaque heure, an Esté en cincq; en hyver comme de coique vous trouverez; les Ordonnances à touts les maisons de poste.

Description de touts les chemins de poste qui sont en Engletere, de LONDRE jusques à EDENBURG en la Ecoce lieux ou on peut avoir de Schoteana frais, congeur en distance, & leurs noms & chemins de poste, qui de mocede Villes, principalis quils sont cognus par diverses marques & Caractères, comme icy dessus est montre ce que est fort necessaire pour toutes passagiers dans le dit Roy Jaume edidie & signé par R. CARR.

A perfect direction to travel all England by Post seven miles par houre, in the Summer, and five in the Winter, as you will find an order for it in all Post-houses.

A Description of al the postroads in England, from LONDON to EDENBOROUGH in Scotland the stages, distances and names, of miles & the branches from the severall stages, Citties, Chief-Towns and Castles, in each shire and County, to be known by their severall Characters, which are hear bove mentiond which is very neassary for all travellers to know, who do travell in that Kingdom; drawn and perfected by R. CARR.

EEN Perfec... door Engelan... uure in de Se... een order in

Beschryvi... in Engeland... EDENI... Plaetsen al-w... gen, verte ofte... wegen, die v... Steden, Cast... yder Provinti... reykens of Ca... de, 't welck se... soonen in 't ve... bracht en get...

LINKING THE COUNTRY

Captain R. Carr, *A description of al[l] the postroads in England...*, 1668.

Roads were a key element for mapping from the Roman period, as shown by the Peutinger Map (dating to 335–366). The Roman road system in Britain was largely unimproved during the Middle Ages, with the piecemeal efforts of local parishes proving unable to better the situation. However, the system began to change from the late seventeenth century when a network of regular and reliable long-distance wagon services developed in England, while the first turnpike road dated from the 1660s, on part of the Great North Road from London to York: a 1663 Act of Parliament authorised Justices of the Peace in Hertfordshire, Cambridgeshire and Huntingdonshire to take a toll in order to improve the road.

Richard Carr made the map from a draft by James Hicks, the Chief Clerk to the Post Office. The map was organised by and for the purpose of postage; it covered all the postroads, their stages and distances, and advertised that it was possible to travel seven miles an hour in the summer and five in the winter. The royal crest of arms provided authority as, differently, did the scale. The description and key was in (from left to right) Latin, French, English and Dutch, which reflected foreign interest in the country.

The map shows the underlying Roman structure of the communication system, but, like other maps of this type, it does not provide any indication of road quality or indeed of the factors involved, notably the significance of terrain and drainage. The latter led easily to problems with the passability of the roads, which encouraged an emphasis on the major ones. Hills presented more of an effort for the horses pulling carriages, but the real problem, and one difficult to grasp in maps, was that of drainage. Rain caused a particular problem for roads on heavy clay soils, as in south Essex, the Midlands and the Vale of Berkeley in Gloucestershire, or on the greensand of the Weald in Kent, Surrey and Sussex.

Under the Statute for the Mending of Highways (1555), each parish was responsible for road upkeep, but, as the resistance of the surface, usually loose and rough, to bad weather or heavy use was limited, there was a need for frequent repair. Expensive in both materials and manpower, because it could not be mechanised, this duty was generally not adequately carried out. Only the largest of holes were usually filled. In his play *She Stoops to Conquer* (1773), one of Oliver Goldsmith's characters observed of a rural journey (to Quagmire Marsh): 'It's a damn'd long, dark, boggy, dirty, dangerous way.' In December 1782, one Jeremy Lister wrote from Gainsborough in Lincolnshire: 'The roads are exceeding bad, the road towards Lincoln being the only one that is anything tolerable, and that in general is through very deep sand.'

Road construction and maintenance were of limited effectiveness in marshy regions, such as the Fens and the Somerset Levels. Valleys, such as the Avon, Exe, Ouse, Severn, Thames and Trent, were prone to flood, as is still the case. As a result, most land routes sought to follow ridges where the soil was drier and lighter.

Fords were the standard means by which many rivers were crossed, and fording was made more difficult by spring thaws and autumn floods. Having not yet in effect been canalised, as was later repeatedly done in the nineteenth century, most rivers in seventeenth-century Britain were shallower than their modern counterparts and had broader courses with lower banks, and were thus harder to bridge (although not to ford) and far readier to flood. There were no real flood-prevention schemes.

Deficiencies in the road surface so affected carriages that more social engagements were held once the moon was in its brighter waxing phase, because it meant the road surface could be seen more readily at night. Carriages were also affected by springs snapping and by horses bolting. Going up and down steep hills could be particularly difficult and dangerous, and being on the roof of a coach was especially risky. Overturning could be fatal. As a result of the problems of the road system and of the physical limits on what could be moved by cart as opposed to barge, water transport was particularly favoured for the movement of heavy or bulky goods. Thus, cloth was generally taken from Stroud, a major cloth-making centre benefitting from water power, to London by Thames barge from Lechlade.

Road links affected relations within and between regions, with distance setting a bound to experience, and journeys challenging certainty and confidence. Carr's map was an attempt to provide a more optimistic gloss.

1668

ies Go Engles miles, 1s
dutsche mylen.

THE

P SEA

Newport   Oostende
erken

ANDEREN

Princepall esteed
Steden
Casteelen
Dorpen
Post Platschen
de schyding vande Prouencien
de Post Weegen
de chiuerlesteren bewijsen hoe
uerre dat een platsche vanden
anderen leyt

vijsinghe om te reysen
ft, seven Engelsche mijlen par
de vijf in de Winter, gelijck
huysen daer van te vinden is.

n alle de Post-wegen, die
n LONDEN tot
G H in Schotland, de
verfche Paerden kan krij-
en, en haer namen en Poft-
incipale Steden en andere
de Dorpen uyt-fpruyten in
ekendt fijn by verfcheyde
ls hier boven is aenwijfen-
g is voor alle reyfende per-
Koningrijck in 't light ge-
door   R. CARR,

METROPOLIS OF THE WEST

James Millerd, *An Exact Delineation of the Famous Citty of Bristoll and Suburbs*, c.1673 and 1696.

Bristol was a key port, notably for river traffic up the Severn, for commerce in the Bristol Channel, especially to South Wales and North Devon, for trade to Ireland, western Europe, and over the Atlantic. The city was also a major manufacturing centre, particularly of refined sugar (based on imports from the Caribbean produced by slave labour), soap and glass. Regional trade was enhanced, particularly with the River Avon from Bath improved by 1727. The Bristol market was supplied with butter and meat from South Wales, cheese from Cheshire and Somerset, and milk, eggs and poultry from the West Country. A major cultural centre, Bristol was one of the first cities in England with more than one newspaper.

James Millerd was a mercer by trade, a Burgess of the city and in 1696 one of the first elected Assistants of the new body responsible for Bristol's poor. His plan-view map first produced c.1673 was a newly surveyed one that was to form the basis of all maps of Bristol until that of John Rocque in the 1740s. Yet, change was also registered in 'Millerd's map' and it was released in several revised versions. Editions after 1684 show the Cornmarket on the Quay, and 'Corne Market 1684', the year of its erection, is engraved over the structure. This is the 1696 edition because it bears the name 'the Mint 1696', indicating the place where coinage was being struck. From 1697, the 'great house' that had become a 'sugar house' (that is, factory) and then the Mint (for the recoinage of 1696), was the home of Bristol's pioneering Corporation of the Poor: a public workhouse and hospital known often as St Peter's Hospital because it was in St Peter's parish. The establishment of the corporation was an expression of civic responsibility by the city's wealthy merchants to address public concern about the problem of poverty. The term 'great house' was used in Bristol, and elsewhere, to describe the largest mansions of the urban élite, which quite often were adapted to act as sugar or soap manufactures in the seventeenth century.

The map shows the rivers Avon and Frome ('Froome flu'), and the extensive maritime life on the river. The castle had been demolished by the Cromwellian government in 1656, which, in an age-old pattern, opened the way to new buildings on the site. This demolition was part of the widespread 'slighting' or destruction of part or all of fortifications that was important during and after the Civil War and that continued into the 1660s, when the restored Stuart dynasty razed part of the defences of Parliamentary-supporting towns such as Gloucester and Northampton. However, some of Bristol's walls had survived the Royalist storming in 1643 and the sieges; the gated nature of the entrances to the city is clear from the map (Temple gate is visible at the bottom), as is the proximity of the countryside.

Just as with the 1684 and 1696 versions, that of 1728 incorporates new buildings built in the intervening period as well as changes – for example to the name of the 'great house', as well as the demolition of the Corn Markethouse (the Cornmarket referred to above), with the words therefore added 'as it stood before taken down'.

There was no earlier plan of Bristol of any real value to assist Millerd. He also published a perspective view of Bristol taken from the southern heights. Such views remained a key way to present cities, and an aspect of the important continued overlap and interaction of art and cartography.

PLANNING THE ROUTES

John Ogilby, 'The Road from London to King's Lynn', 1675.

John Ogilby (1600–76) was a Scot who ran a dancing school until unfortunately lamed in a fall, when he became a tutor, founded Ireland's first theatre and then had his career derailed by the Irish rising of 1641, whereupon he turned to making money by translating, first Virgil and then Aesop and Homer. The Stuart Restoration in 1660 in the person of Charles II brought Ogilby patronage, while he established a printing press in London, which published atlases among other works. He was appointed Cosmographer by Charles II in 1671, and His Majesty's Cosmographer and Geographic Printer in 1674. The following year there appeared the first volume, *Britannia*, of what was intended to be a multi-volume road atlas, based on surveys sponsored by the king. *Britannia* was a masterpiece that offered detailed mapping of a wholly new order.

Ogilby provided 100 strip maps, with a standard scale of one inch to a mile, and a standard mile of 1,760 yards in place of the frequent use of local measures. The title page shows a surveyor instructing two subordinates pushing Ogilby's 'Wheel Dimensurator', a measuring wheel that showed the distance travelled on a dial. About 7,500 miles of road were surveyed and the maps were supported by 200 pages of text, which included helpful information, notably a summary of the road, distances, facilities and turnings to be avoided. A compass rose aided orientation.

In yet another instance of the overlap of art and cartography, the strips were presented as *trompe l'oeil* scrolls with the tops and bottoms furling over themselves. A decorative cartouche contains a description of the route. The maps, read from bottom left to top right, offered considerable detail, including landmarks, the building material of the bridge, the direction of slope, inns, fords and whether roads were enclosed or open. Woods, a haunt of highwaymen, were shown.

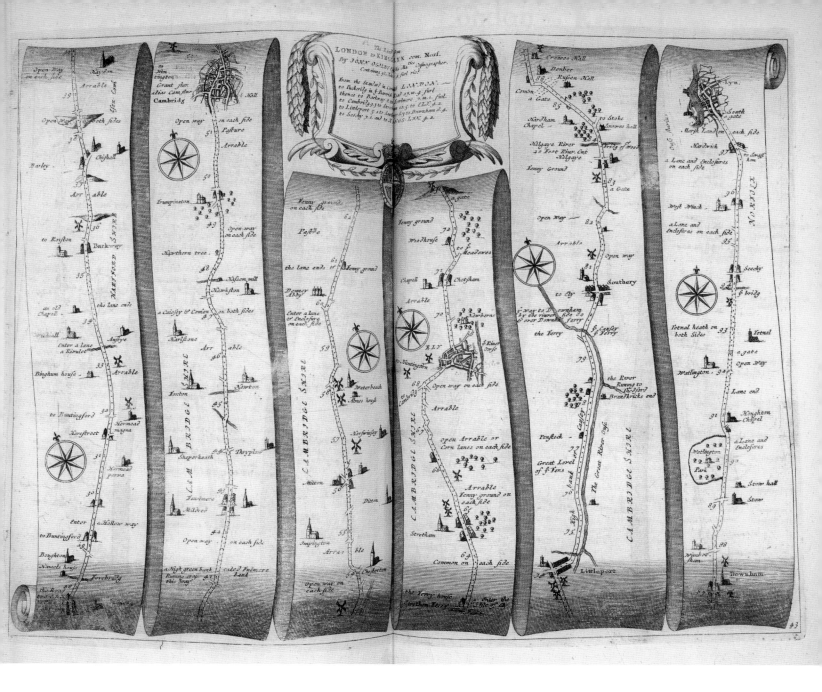

Ogilby had hoped for the project to do more than 22,000 miles of road as well as 25 town plans, but he died before the prospectus could become that developed. *Britannia* sold well, with four editions in the first two years, and pocket-sized versions appeared in 1719, 1720 and 1757. *Britannia Depicta* (1720), engraved by Emanuel Bowen, had the road maps on both sides of the page, which reduced the bulk, and also included small maps of each of the English and Welsh counties.

Other route maps included William Berry's *The Grand Roads of England* (1679), John Seller's *A New Map of the Roads of England* (c.1690) and (pictured opposite) George Willdey's *The Roads of England*

According to Mr Ogilby's Survey (1712). Established in 1680, the Penny Post benefitted from the road system, as did the press, which expanded greatly from the lapsing of the Licensing Act (of newspapers) in 1695. Stagecoaches stopped at inns at each stage of the journey, obtaining fresh horses, and thereby travelling faster. The Ogilby maps demonstrated the salience of London in the system. Although the value of his maps diminished greatly in the mid-eighteenth century as turnpiking became more common, they were a major achievement. Costs depended on whether the maps were hand-coloured or not.

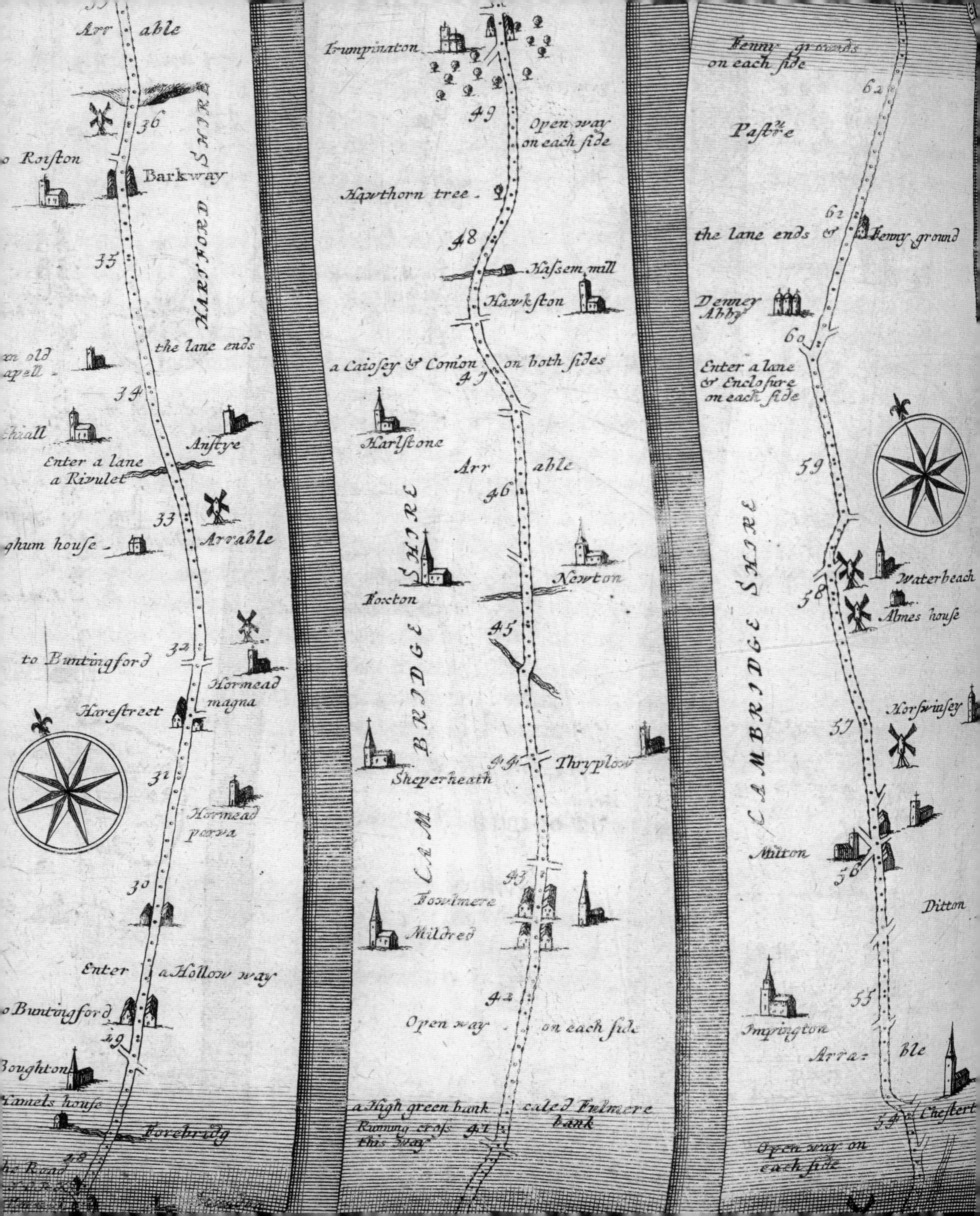

Left strip:

Arr able

🌫 36

o Roiston   Barkway

35

HARTFORD SHIRE

xn old apell

the lane ends

34

chiall   Anstye

Enter a lane a Rivulet

33

ghum house   Arrable

32

to Buntingford   Hormead magna

Harestreet

31

Hormead parva

30

Enter a Hollow way

o Buntingford

29

Boughton

annels house

Forebridg

he Road   28

Middle strip:

Trumpinaton

49

Open way on each fide

Hawthorn tree

48

Kaſſem mill

Hawkston

a Caiofey & Comon on both fides

47

Harlstone

Arr able

46

CAM BRIDGE SHIRE

Foxton   Newton

45

Sheperheath   Thryplow

44

Fowlmere

Mildred

43

42

Open way on each fide

a High green bank caled Trelmere bank

Running crofs this way   41

Right strip:

Fenny grounds on each fide

62

Paſture

the lane ends

62   Fenny ground

Denney Abby

60

Enter a lane & Enclofure on each fide

59

CAMBRIDGE SHIRE

Waterbeach

58

Almes house

Horfwinfey

57

Milton

56

Ditton

Ingrington

55

Arra ble

54   Cheſtert

Open way on each fide

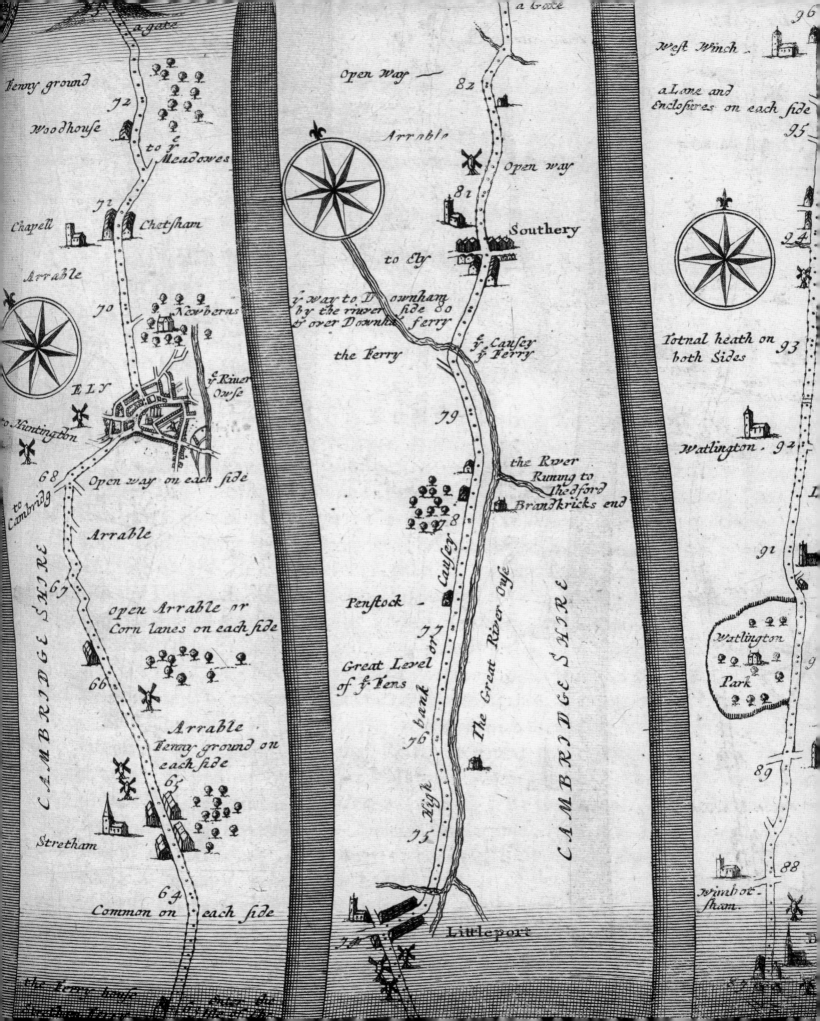

a gate

Fenny ground

Woodhouse

to y^e
Meadowes

72

Chapell   Chetsham

72

Arrable

70   Newberns

ELY   y^e River
Ouse

to Huntington

68   Open way on each side

to Cambridg

Arrable

67

open Arrable or
Corn lanes on each side

66

Arrable
Fenny ground on
each side

65

Stretham

64

Common on each side

the Ferry house

CAMBRIDGESHIRE

Open way

Arrable

Southery

to Ely

ye way to Downham
by the river side
& over Downha ferry

the Ferry   ye Causey
ye Ferry

79

the River
Ruming to
Thedford
Brandkricks end

78

Penstock

Great Level
of ye Fens

The Great River Ouse

High bank or Causey

77

76

75

74

Littleport

CAMBRIDGESHIRE

---

a gate

82

81

West Winch

a Lane and
Enclosures on each side
95

94

Totnal heath on
both Sides   93

Watlington. 92

91

Watlington
Park   9

89

wimbot-
sham.   88

MAPPING THE COASTS

Greenville Collins, 'Edinburgh Firth', 1693.

The sense of mapping as a vital aid to national defence was recognised in England in 1681 when the government appointed a naval officer, Captain Greenville Collins (c.1634–94), commander of the eight-gun yacht HMS *Merlin*, 'to make a survey of the sea coasts of the kingdom by measuring all the sea coasts with a chain and taking all the bearings of all the headlands with their exact latitudes'.

Collins had extensive experience of navigation, including a failed attempt to reach Japan by a northeast passage north of Asia, an attempt that was wrecked off the Arctic Ocean island of Novaya Zemlya. He had also served in the Mediterranean against Algerine privateers (the Barbary Corsairs, operating out of parts of North Africa west of Egypt), who were a major and conspicuous threat to trade, and Collins drew maps on his mission.

Collins lobbied for an improved survey of Britain's coast, not least to rectify mistakes, to provide a centralised system for collecting and disseminating improved maps, and to give himself something to do in the years of peace that began in 1674 and lasted until 1688. The survey, which lasted seven years, had many limitations due to the speed with which it was accomplished, the limited manpower available and the lack of an available comprehensive land survey of the coastline as the basis for a marine survey. More generally, maritime mapping is in part dependent on its land counterpart, both practically in fixing the coastline and what is on it, and functionally in terms of the linking to usage.

Collins's results were published in *Great Britain's Coasting Pilot*, also known as *The English Pilot*, which contained sailing directions, tide tables, coastal views and charts, thus offering a codification of information that hitherto had often been a matter of the local 'secret' knowledge of pilots. The complete work was first published in 1693. From 1683, Collins was allowed to style himself Hydrographer in Ordinary to the King. This chart depicts the Firth of Forth with the adjacent coasts of Fife and Lothian between St Andrew's Bay and Dunbar.

The survey was reprinted frequently in the eighteenth century. The interest in such mapping was utilitarian in an economic sense, as well as military and political. In 1670, Charles II ordered the Council of Plantations, 'to procure maps or charts of all … our plantations abroad, together with the maps … of their respective ports, forts, bays and rivers' – in short, to prepare a cartographic record of empire.

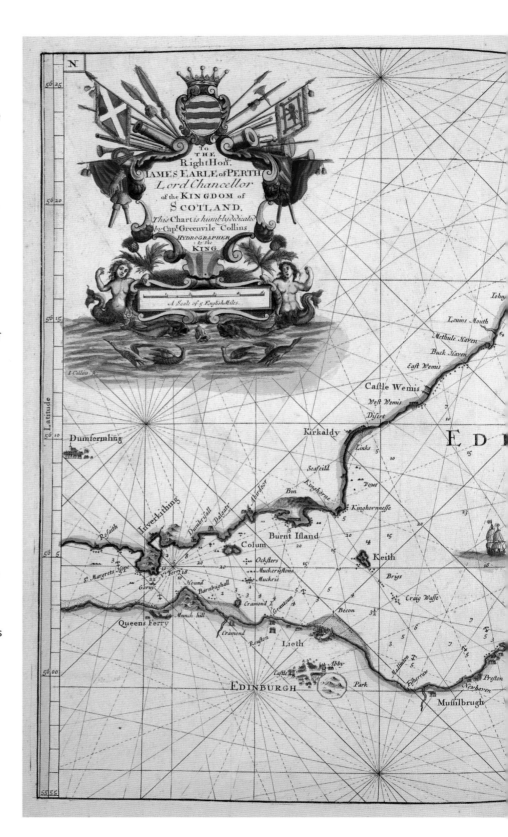

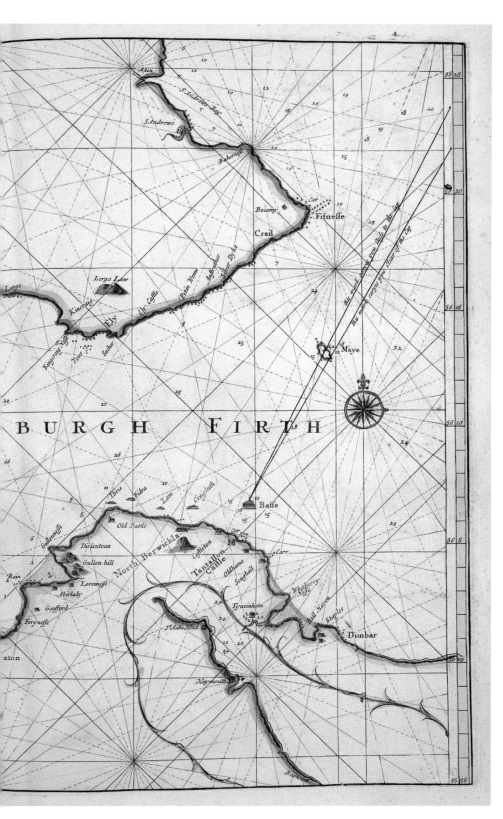

Eventually running to four books encompassing the known globe, numerous editions of *The English Pilot* were published throughout the eighteenth century. Although many of the maps were derivatives of earlier Dutch charts, the work proved enormously popular, not least due to the charts' accompaniment with sailing directions written in English. (English knowledge of foreign languages was limited.) As part of a more general challenge to the Dutch maritime position, the *English Pilot* was a direct and ultimately successful challenge to Dutch hegemony over the sea chart market, which was a crucial one for mariners.

Better charts did not prevent the risks faced by voyagers. Jonathan Wilson, a Cumbrian Quaker and malt dealer, recorded in July 1726:

'I set forward towards Cork ... but I met with contrary wind and was driven into Wales and so after four days came home again and stayed about a week at home and so set sail again and met with contrary winds again and was driven upon the coasts of Ireland near the mountains of Newry ... but after six days at sea got safe and well to Dublin.'

The same year, the *Magnae Britanniae Notitia: or The Present State of Great Britain* declared:

'Great Britain may be justly counted the principal nation for trade in the whole world, and indeed the most proper for trade, being an island which hath many commodious ports and havens, natural products, considerable manufactures, great encouragement from the state for the sake of customs and duties paid, the breeding of seamen, and the increase of shipping, freedom in religion, the pleasure and healthfulness of our clime, the ease and security of our government; all conducing to the encouragement of maritime trade.'

This trade was both coastal and international. For example, the first shipload of Cheshire cheese reached London in 1650, by 1664 more than 14 cheese ships were sailing from the Northwest, and by the 1680s over 50. Return cargoes from London helped to transform the regional economy in the Northwest and elsewhere, and encouraged shipbuilding. In 1698, Peter the Great of Russia came to the Royal Dockyards at Deptford to see shipbuilding in progress, while in 1695–98, Britain's first commercial wet dock was built at Rotherhithe, London.

MAPPING THE ESTATE

Joel Gascoyne, 'The Lanhydrock Estate', 1694–99.

Land surveyors developed appropriate conventions in the way they recorded information so that estate maps from different areas could be compared. The estate map of Cotehele in Cornwall from the 1550s lacks a sense of scale, and is, in part, diagrammatic. In contrast, the maps of Cotehele produced in 1731 and 1784 were more reliable as to scale and distance. This was also true for example of the estate map of 1699 for Baddesley Clinton, the Stourton map of 1725 and George Ingham's 1764 survey map of Kedleston. Charles Bodville Robartes, 2nd Earl of Radnor, owner of the Lanhydrock estate in Cornwall, commissioned Joel Gascoyne's *Land Atlas* of 1694–99, which is a masterpiece of the estate surveyor's work. It depicts over 40,000 acres of the earl's Cornish estates in colour on 258 parchment maps. These provided information on the customary and statute acreage of plots, the definition of boundaries, systems of cultivation and tenement, and field names.

The maps throw much light on land use, notably as arable, commons, meadow and woodland. They also show the infrastructure, notably buildings, industry, roads (including their use), through funnels and swellings, for sorting and processing livestock, towns, trackways and waterways. Names of tenants were listed as were the majority of the neighbouring landowners. The precision offered provided the opportunity to determine and represent the features that constituted a boundary. The gardens at Lanhydrock House itself include a bowling green and flower and kitchen gardens. No documentation, however, survives to clarify the commissioning or use of these beautiful, detailed maps, with their vibrant colour. The maps are generally produced in volumes from west to east.

The display of status was clearly seen in housebuilding. Having bought the estate in 1620, Sir Richard Robartes began building a new house. In 1625 he paid £10,000 to become Baron Robartes of Truro (the baronetcy had been reinvented a few years before by James I as a badge of status and a way to raise money). Earlier, the estate, a manor of the Priory of St Petroc, had been bought by the Glynns of Glynn, a neighbouring estate, taking advantage of the Dissolution of the Monasteries. John, 2nd Baron Robartes of Truro, the leader of the Parliamentarians in Cornwall during the Civil War and a devout Presbyterian, had the plaster ceiling of the Gallery at Lanhydrock ornamented with scenes from the New Testament.

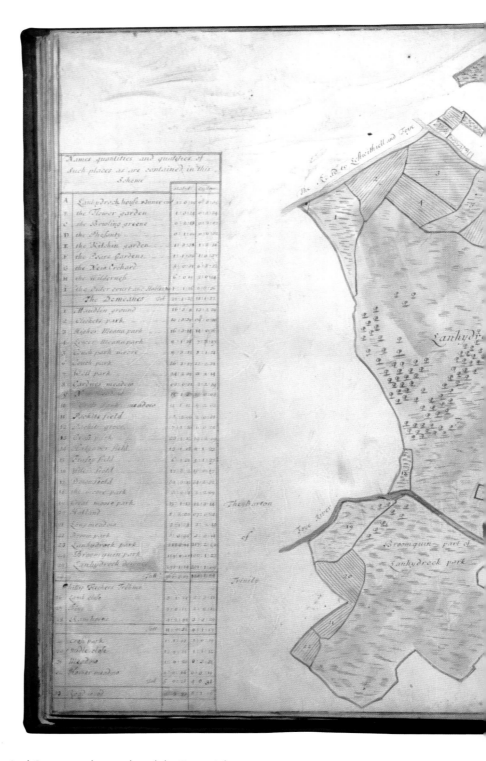

Joel Gascoyne also produced the Stowe Atlas for the Grenville family, as well as a nine-sheet *Map of the County of Cornwall newly Surveyed* (1699). The quality of the mapping was superior to that at the beginning of the century – for example, William Senior's 1610 map of the estate of Hardwick.

Although the Land Surveyors' Club, the forerunner to the Institute of Chartered Surveyors, was not founded until 1834, guides to surveying

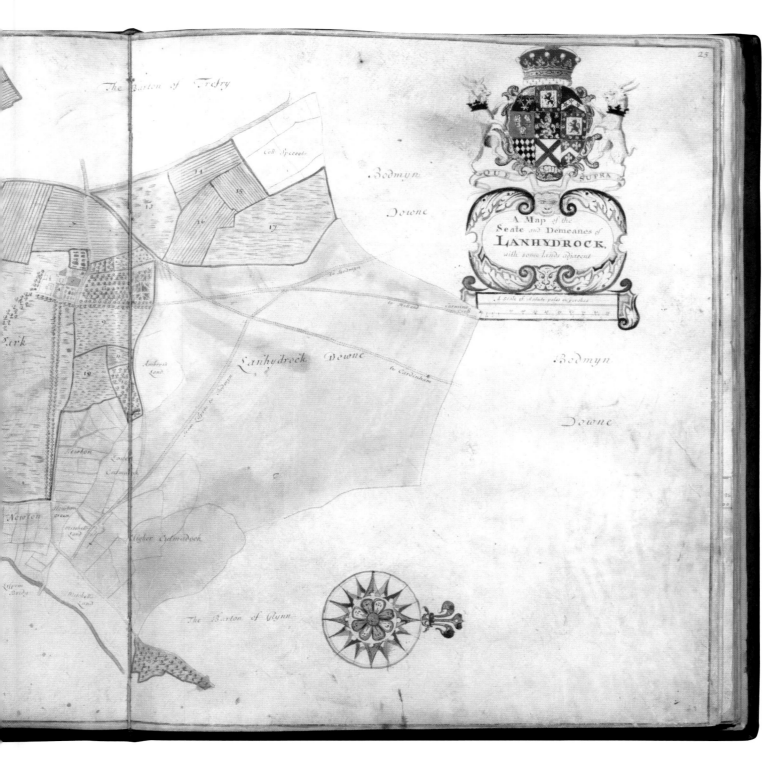

A Map of the Seate and Demeanes of LANHYDROCK, with some Lands adjacent.

appeared much earlier, including William Leybourne's *The Compleat Surveyor* (1685). In *The Duty of a Steward to his Land* (1727), Edward Laurence claimed:

> 'As a steward should know the quantity and quality of every parcel of land occupied by the several tenants, so likewise he should have a map of the whole drawn out in the most perfect method, which may show ... the true figure of every parcel ... so nearly that he may detect any tenant from alienating the least parcel from his lord.'

Land management encouraged a great increase in estate mapping in the eighteenth century. In 1739–42, Wadham College, Oxford, had five maps made of its Essex estates, while in 1736, William Brasier surveyed Mease Place Farm in Harrow for New College, Oxford.

MAPPING IRELAND

Henry Pratt, *A Mapp of the Kingdom of Ireland*, 1708.

Advertised in London for a guinea (£1.05), this was a map that would have helped ministers and civilians alike to follow any fighting that broke out in Ireland; although in 1708 France instead launched an invasion attempt against Scotland that was thwarted in part by poor navigation. Henry Pratt's map is described as 'divided into its provinces, counties, & baronies, and supply'd with many market towns & other places of note omitted in former mapps ... : together with plans of the citys and fortified towns'. Pratt depicts roads and barracks, and his plan of Drogheda includes the nearby 'Battle at the Boyne', the decisive engagement in which William III defeated James II in 1690, pressing on to capture Dublin.

The map also includes an inset locating Ireland in relation to Britain and France. The full title emphasises the research that has gone into the map: 'newly corrected & improvd by actuall observations'. The map is hand-coloured and the scale is in both Irish miles and English miles.

The war in Ireland in 1688–91, which had ended with a total Williamite victory, more generally encouraged mapping in the 1690s, 1700s and early 1710s, notably by Christopher Brownen, Robert Morden, James Moxon, Coronelli, Hubert Jaillot, Herman Moll, William Knight, Henry Chatelain, George Willdey, Charles Price and John Senex.

Following on from William Petty (1685), who had greatly improved on the work of John Speed (1610), Pratt increased the clarity of the cartographic representation of Ireland. Among the number of mapmakers, his work was particularly taken on by Thomas Jefferys (1759), Daniel Beaufort (1792), Aaron Arrowsmith (1811) and Thomas Larcom (1839).

Whereas the Catholics had held 22 per cent of the land in 1688, by 1703 this had fallen to 14 per cent. Catholics in Ireland were prevented from freely acquiring or bequeathing land or property by legislation of 1704 known as the Penal Code; they were also disenfranchised and debarred from all political, military and legal offices, and from Parliament.

The Penal Code was designed essentially to destroy the political and economic power of Catholicism rather than the faith itself, although it was also an attempt to erode Catholic belief and practice. The ability of the Anglican establishment to proselytise in Ireland was limited by its general failure to communicate with a still largely Gaelic-speaking population. In contrast, the Catholic colleges stipulated a knowledge of the language as a requirement for the mission. The Catholic percentage of the population did not diminish, because the Catholic clergy continued their work, sustained by a strong oral culture, the emotional link with a sense of national identity, and by hedgeschool (small, informal, illegal schools) teaching, and in reality serious repression was episodic. If it had been possible to implement the religious clauses of the Penal Code and if a persistent attempt had been made to do so, then Catholicism might have been seriously challenged, although the military forces in the island were not large and the result in 1715 and 1745 might have been Jacobite insurrections (in favour of the Catholic Stuart claimants to the throne) as serious as those in Scotland. Catholic clerics in Ireland in the 1730s still prayed for the Stuart claimant 'James III' and the draconian wartime legislation of 1697, 1703–04 and 1709 was inspired by fears of Catholic disloyalty and links with France. Persecution usually slackened in peacetime, and for most of the century vicious confessional action was infrequent. Nevertheless, longstanding religious grievances helped to exacerbate political disaffection in the 1790s.

On the other hand, the ability of the state to exert control was limited in Ireland as elsewhere, and there was much independent community action and resistance. Thus, smuggling thwarted the Revenue Commissioners, while illegal alcohol production was widespread, as were prison rescues and riotous defiance. From the 1760s, the situation was more disrupted with the emergence in the province of Munster of the Whiteboys, a group that pushed forward agrarian resistance.

3

THE HANOVERIANS

In the introduction to his *Historical Atlas of England* (1797), John Andrews was clear about the value of geographical information: 'Those unacquainted with geography can never form a proper judgment of the facts recorded in history, as they must strike the mind in a confused manner, without order and without connection.' Although very limited in his coverage, Andrews's atlas was very different from the maps of Speed. Decorative details had been reduced as part of a general process in which mapmakers sought to appear scientific, separating maps from their decoration.

Jabez Fisher, a visiting American in 1776 touring the copper-smelting site at White Rock near Swansea established in 1737, was in no doubt that he was seeing change: 'Here are 43 Furnaces constantly in Blast, all employed in their proper departments, and 150 Men who appear like what we might conceive of the Inhabitants of Pandaemonium. The greatest decorum is however preserved; they all move like a Machine.' Earlier, in 1754 Reinhold Angerstein had similarly noted of Coalbrookdale: 'It is amazing how far the art of casting iron has been developed in this place.'

By the early eighteenth century the shock of the new was increasingly apparent in Britain, and as the number and types of maps increased, so it became easier to tell the story of national development through maps. Mid-century was a particular period of change, with the decades 1740–60 seeing Jacobitism definitively crushed, Scotland firmly in the British system, Britain defeating France to become the major Atlantic power, and the start of sustained population and economic growth.

The British state faced major challenges, in the form of the American War of Independence (1775–83) and the French Revolutionary and Napoleonic Wars (1793–1815), but it was able to survive both.

The increase in the scale of mapping already seen in the late seventeenth century continued in the eighteenth and the increasing frequency of publication was to be expected from a growing and more populous society. Alongside maps for particular practical uses, there were also other maps for those who essentially wanted them for visual entertainment, the latter rather like the travel literature of the period, as with Thomas Malton's *Picturesque Tour through the Cities of London and Westminster* (1792).

Geography was regarded as a major adjunct to understanding history and also seen as an important tool to development. Thus, after a visit from England via Berwickshire to Edinburgh and Glasgow in 1760, Joseph Spence wrote of the road programme:

'...they laid a map of the whole country before them; first marked lines of communication from the most considerable towns to the capital, and to one another, for the benefit of commerce and travelling; made a fund of £30,000 by a subscription; and began at once with nine roads from Edinburgh, which are already branched out into above thirty. I went no farther than Glasgow ... all [the roads] very good, and mostly made so within these eight years.'

THE ENGINE OF ECONOMIC GROWTH

James Corbridge, 'Newcastle Upon Tyne', 1723.

James Corbridge was a Norfolk surveyor and cartographer, whose subjects included Norfolk, Suffolk and Great Yarmouth. Newcastle was a source of coal for East Anglia, which may be how Corbridge came to produce this map, which is typical of the town maps of the period by showing roads, walls, gates, markets and halls for various merchant guilds and companies. The border, as again was typical, had a pictogram element, with engravings of the major houses, churches and public buildings. Positioned at the end of the original Tyne Bridge is the central Sandhill area, where the medieval town hall once stood until a Guildhall replaced it in 1655–58. The building was refaced with classical elevations from the 1790s onwards. The Guildhall contains a historic Court Room, a Mayor's Chamber and a main hall known as the Merchant Venturers' Court where inbound or outbound travellers would meet.

The map of Newcastle revealed there had been significant growth in the city since John Speed had mapped it in 1609, as well as a change in the cartography towards a clearer image and a style less dependent on a pictogram format. Isaac Taylor followed the same policy in his map of Wolverhampton in 1750.

Later in the century, most of Newcastle's medieval gates and walls visible in the map were demolished, while new assembly rooms in 1776 were followed by a theatre in 1788. A similar process was seen in other cities.

Newcastle was of considerable significance as the major port for the Northeast of England, which became the key production area for coal, the amount of which shipped from the River Tyne had risen to 400,000 tons by 1625 and over 600,000 tons in 1730. Seventy per cent of this coal went to London in 1682, and King's Lynn and Great Yarmouth, the ports for East Anglia, took half of the rest. When the Scots invaded England in 1644, one of their objectives was to capture the Northeast, and thereby secure coal supplies for their parliamentary allies in London.

The major use for coal was domestic heating, notably in London, which was at a distance from local wood supplies (and coal in any case offered higher calorific value for the bulk). There was also increasing use of coal for manufacture, and by 1700 it was the main fuel in sugar refining, brewing, salt boiling and brick-making. As a result, in part of local coal, Newcastle produced about 40 per cent of all the glass made in England in the seventeenth century. Moreover, sales to national markets brought money and workers into areas that produced coal and increased local demand, especially for food. Newcastle, in 1711, was one of the first cities with more than one newspaper and its papers circulated through the Northeast and into Cumbria, North Yorkshire and southern Scotland.

The Northeast of England accounted for nearly half the national output of coal, which was about three million tons in 1700. East Shropshire, South Yorkshire and South Staffordshire, in that order, all in England, were the next three leading areas of production. Output rose by just over one per cent a year to 5.2 million tons by 1750, and then by more than 2 per cent a year for the rest of the century. This growth was far greater, in absolute and relative terms, than that in any other country.

Coal production helped to make the British economy distinctive, providing a cheap energy economy. This opened up a powerful comparative advantage over Continental economies, where energy remained largely dependent on wood, although, as in Britain, water and wind power were also valuable. By 1750, 61 per cent of all the energy used in England was provided by coal, which was six times more significant than wood, and produced energy equivalent to that from 4.3 million acres of woodland. Even if the figures can be queried, the trend was clear. Coal offered many advantages: it was readily transportable, and certainly more easily so than wood, and notably so in energy equivalence; and thus coal altered the pressures of distance. Coal was also a controllable fuel, especially in comparison with wood, and therefore more useful for manufacturing that required a steady heat. Coal could be mined throughout the year, whereas watermills were affected by ice, flooding and summertime reductions in water flow.

Coal was of limited value without transport, but coal in the company of transport, as with the railways with horse-drawn wagons that took it to the Tyne, could serve as the basis for the creation of buoyant mixed-industrial regions with large pools of labour and demand, and special services. Separately, by raising labour productivity, cheap energy made it easier to pay high wages and thus to sustain demand. The need to move coal acted as a spur for innovation, especially for the construction of canals.

Coal was also crucial for the powering of steam engines, which were potent symbols of a new age. The steam pump demonstrated by

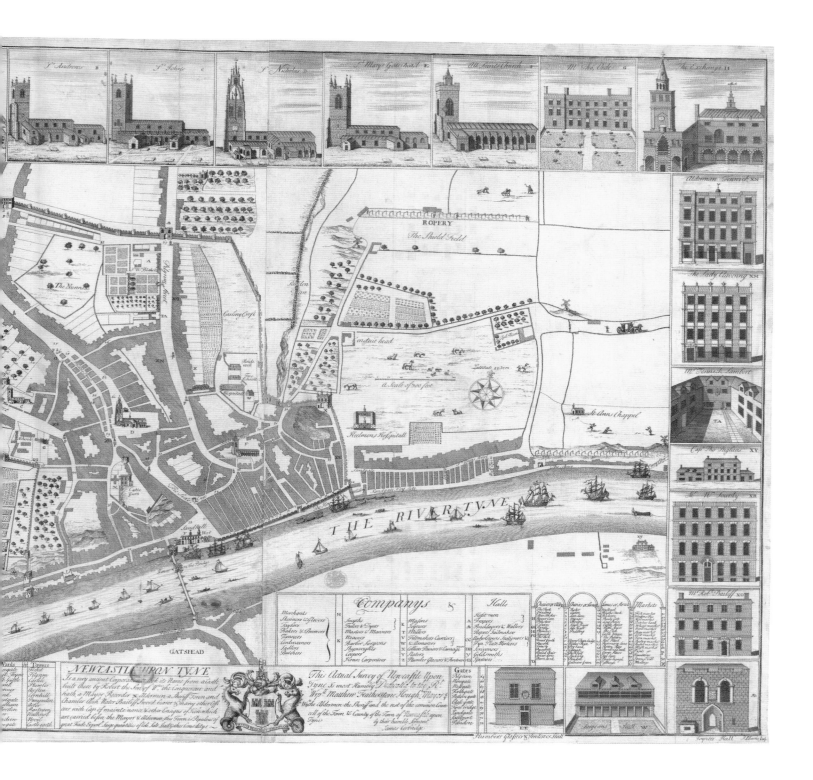

Thomas Savery in 1698 was of little importance, but in 1712 Thomas Newcomen, a Dartmouth ironmonger, produced his Atmospheric Engine, in essence a beam with a cylinder: the injection of water condensed the steam, causing the piston to descend under the weight of the atmosphere, and thus lift the pump rods at the other end of the beam. The piston was returned to the top of the stroke by the weight of the pump rods. Simple compared to what was to come, but also a major change. Successive developments in technology, including in related engineering, were highly significant in the growth of coal-powered industry, but also important was the availability of investment.

A DYNAMIC CAPITAL

John Rocque, *An Exact Survey of ... London,*
Westminster ye Borough of Southwark..., 1746.

French-born Rocque, the son of Huguenot immigrants, began his surveying of London in 1738. He was financed by subscription, including by over 100 peers. His methodology included trigonometrical surveying to build up a lattice of points measured between church steeples, which provided the prominent points. But the differences between those measurements and his detailed ground survey slowed down the project.

The resulting *Plan of the Cities of London and Westminster and Borough of Southwark,* engraved by Rocque's partner, John Pine, and published in 16 printed sheets in 1746, is the most accurate and detailed representation of the eighteenth-century metropolis that exists, with some 5,500 street and place names. Churches were scrupulously recorded, but industrial buildings were not. The map was largely accurate for the most densely developed parts of the city, such as the West End, although many smaller streets and courts were omitted, a contrast that underlines the difficulty that exists still today of mapping historical data precisely. Pictorial detail is present, as with boats on the Thames, but it is limited. The map showed Mayfair under development, the name of the district deriving from a fair held on the site of Shepherd's Market. The Chelsea Water Works' reservoir was also visible. Rocque's map, which was at a scale of 200 feet to an inch (1:2,400), was also used for governmental purposes, for example setting the rates.

Squares such as Hanover Square, laid out between 1717 and 1719, were a key element in the development of the West End. They tended to be public, rather than private, arenas until the 1720s, when the emphasis came to be on exclusivity: open spaces were enclosed, laid out as gardens and restricted to residents – gentrification linked to social exclusion.

Rocque at first described himself as a *dessinateur de jardins* (garden designer) and surveyed the gardens of royalty and the aristocracy, mostly near London. Smaller versions of his plans appeared in a volume of *Vitruvius Britannicus* (1739) dedicated to Frederick, Prince of Wales, whose cartographer he later became. These plans included Claremont and Esher, the seats respectively of Thomas, 1st Duke of Newcastle, and his brother Henry Pelham, key figures in the ministry.

Rocque published a new map of Bristol in 1742 and also surveys on which maps of Bath, Bury St Edmunds, Chester, Chichester, Exeter, Lewes, Shrewsbury and York were based. Rocque was also responsible for maps of Middlesex, Oxford, Berkshire and Buckinghamshire. Between 1755 and 1760, he surveyed the Irish estates of James, 20th Earl of Kildare, producing what became eight volumes of maps. His activity reflected the range of surveying and mapping options available in the dynamic economy of the period.

As the centre of government, the law and consumption, London's equally dominant position in the world of print helped shape views, opinion and fashion. London publications spread designs, while London craftsmen were in demand across the country. Bright provincials such as Thomas Sheraton went to London and had their ideas and talents validated there. The norms of the language were set in London by works such as Charles Vyse's *New London Spelling Book* (1776) and other vogue methods and books, which were, in turn, advertised in provincial newspapers. Talented foreigners also visited London. Josef Haydn

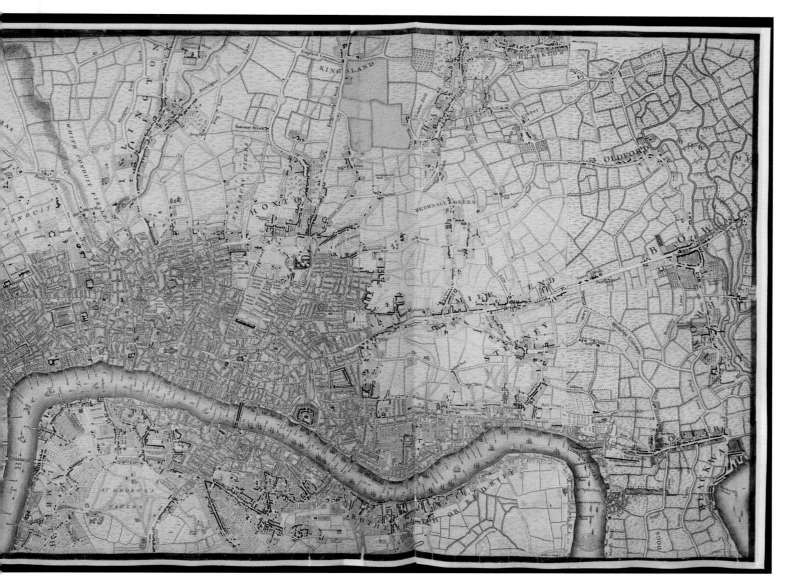

went there in 1791 and 1794 to give 60 successful public concerts for which he wrote his London symphonies. The turnpike and postal systems centred on London, reflecting and sustaining its economic importance. Moreover, London-based insurance companies, such as the Sun Fire Office, and the banks were able to organise business throughout the country.

The city expanded rapidly from over half a million people in 1700 to over a million in 1800. The stock of accommodation available to the bulk of the population declined in quality in the 1720s–50s as buildings deteriorated, and there were few housing starts. Thus, the effective density of population increased, with all that that implied for potential exposure to infection.

The novelist Henry Fielding presented London in terms of a corrupt court and aristocracy, steeped in vice, at its West End and, in contrast, a more acceptable, broader commercial metropolis.

The interplay between the two was a major theme in literature. London, generally understood as the West End, was a setting for villainy for many artists and writers. For example, the snares that bedevil William Booth in Fielding's novel *Amelia* (1751), while in Fielding's *Joseph Andrews*, the lascivious Lady Booby returns to London to devote herself to 'a young Captain of dragoons, together with eternal parties at cards'. In Oliver Goldsmith's play *She Stoops to Conquer*, the countryside people are more honest and balanced than their London counterparts. In 1785, London was described by a visitor of two years earlier as the only place in England where condoms were sold publicly.

Rocque's map of London was, in turn, replaced by Richard Horwood's 32-sheet map, which appeared between 1792 and 1799. Horwood's map, which included street numbers, extended further east than that of Rocque.

PACIFYING THE HIGHLANDS

William Roy, 'The Military Survey of Scotland', 1747–55.

Separate to the British Army, the Board of Ordnance was responsible for artillery and engineering, including the provision of maps. The reorganisation of the Board of Ordnance that followed the 1715–16 Jacobite uprising led to the establishment of a body of 28 engineers as well as an increase in mapping. This mapping was to be important to the attempt to provide a military infrastructure to hold down the Scottish Highlands. Aside from fortifications, the engineers produced road maps that were designed to provide strategic and operational information to help military planning and moves. Mapmaking reflected both need and a perception of weakness. There was certainly a shortage of maps, one that General Hawley regretted during the '45, the rebellion led by Charles Edward Stuart, Bonnie Prince Charlie, that captured Edinburgh and marched as far south in England as Derby. The rebellion culminated in April 1746 at Culloden Moor, subsequently mapped by Roy (opposite).

The military survey of 1747–55 by Lieutenant Colonel David Watson, Deputy Quartermaster-General of the Military District of North Britain for the Board of Ordnance, and William Roy of the Board of Ordnance was a valuable addition, and part of a more general interest in Scottish geography, which included the publication of *Geographia Scotiae* in 1749, as well as maps such as that by James Dorret in 1750. Six surveying parties were employed on the Board of Ordnance project, and the survey was the basis for a map. The works were designed to help in the British government's military response to any future rebellion, and to assist in the process of the governmental reorganisation of the Highlands. This was a key aspect of a longer-term extension of central control that included road-building, in which George Morrison (see following pages) was prominent, and the establishment and improvement of fortified positions, notably the still-impressive Fort George.

The survey covered roads as well as terrain, but the mapmaking instruments available, and the speed of the survey, posed problems of accuracy. The survey itself was unpublished until used in 1805 as the basis for a map by the noted commercial mapmaker Aaron Arrowsmith. This represented a relationship between military

mapping and private entrepreneurship that was less close than that for maritime charts where there was the incentive of the market for merchants.

Born in Scotland in 1726 into a family that produced agents for landowners and thus understood surveying, William Roy (1726–90), once associated with the Board of Ordnance, also sought to improve the mapping of terrain and spherical trigonometry. His investigations with Sir George Shuckburgh (1751–1804), a gentleman-scientist, were published as *Observations made in Savoy to ascertain the Height of Mountains by the Barometer* (1777). Promotion in the army, in which he was commissioned as a lieutenant in 1756, brought Roy to Major General in 1781. He was also promoted in 1783 to be Director and Lieutenant Colonel of the Engineers, a body under the Board of Ordnance.

Roy had been prominent in mapping the south coast of England and its fortifications in 1756 in response to the threat of French invasion. He produced sketch maps to help understand the tactical situation prior to the Battle of Minden in 1759, and played a major role in the early stages of what became the Ordnance Survey, planning the trigonometric stations and establishing their precise latitude, longitude and height.

The defeat of the '45 was followed by a determined attempt to transform Highland society. The clans were disarmed, hereditable jurisdictions abolished and Highland clothes prohibited. The rebellion and its suppression thus gave cause and opportunity for the sort of radical state-directed action against the status quo that was rare in eighteenth-century Britain.

More long-term political changes were also important, with Scotland, like many dependent parts of multiple kingdoms or federal states, losing its capacity for important independent political initiatives. This owed much to Scots themselves, especially the numerous Presbyterians, who were firm opponents of the Stuarts and supporters of the Protestant succession. Scotland retained a different established Church and legal system to England. Scots also took a major role in the developing empire, not least a disproportionate share in the army, while many settled in England but without the tensions arising from Irish migrants.

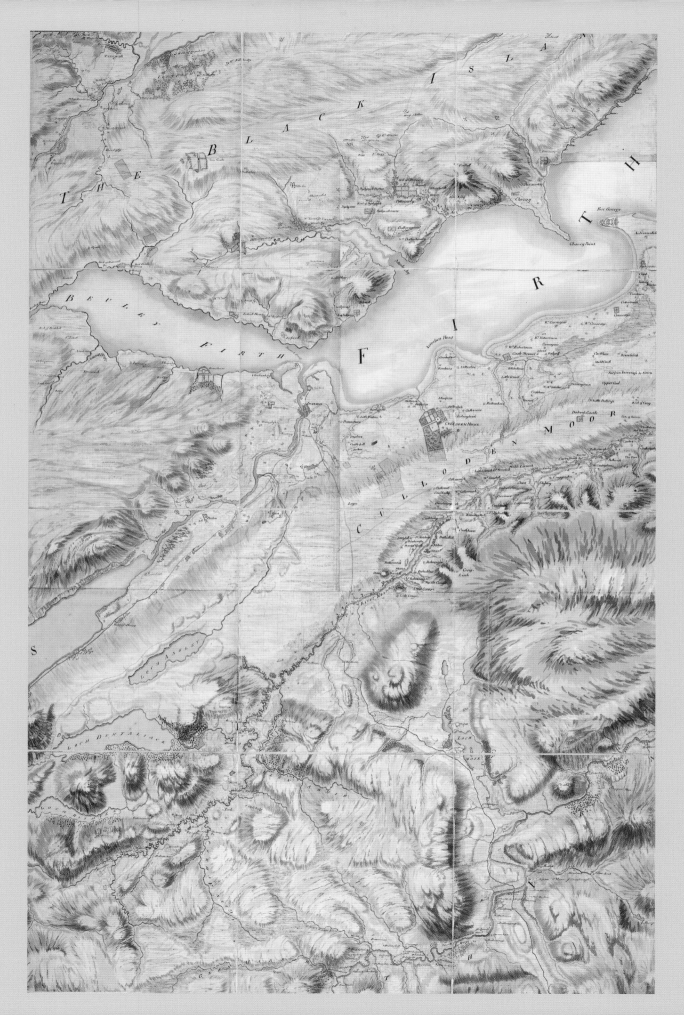

Chilhampton

River Wily

Fowlston

Wilton

Quidhampton

Conway's Howard's Albemarle's Rich's Cholmondley's Aucram's

LIEU.ᵗ GEN.ᴸ HAWLEY

Avon

Road from Salisbury to Devizes

100 200 300 400 500 600 700 800 900 1000   2000 Yards

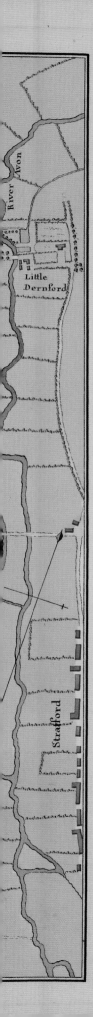

PREPARING FOR INVASION

George Morrison, 'Plan of the Encampment near Salisbury', 1757.

Showing an area about eight miles northwest of Salisbury, the map is at the scale of about five inches to the mile, and was probably made by Major General George Morrison (1703–99) in whose library it was unearthed. Joining the British Army in 1722, Morrison became a Practitioner Engineer in 1748, and was prominent in road construction in Scotland in 1749–50 in the aftermath of the Jacobite uprising, and he served on coastal operations against France in 1759, becoming a full general in 1796, based on longevity of service, according to the pattern of the period.

Military encampments were established near Amersham, Doncaster and Salisbury in 1757. The maps kept by Morrison covered such encampment plans for 1756 and 1762, and there are later maps for the encampments near Salisbury in 1778 and 1779 when a French invasion was feared during the War of American Independence, the latter group by Daniel Paterson (1739–1825), a major cartographer who also was part of the Quartermaster-General's Department. Joining the British Army in 1765, Paterson became a Lieutenant in 1772 and a Lieutenant Colonel in 1798. In 1771 he published the first edition of his book about roads, which was dedicated to Morrison. The first edition was entitled *A New and Accurate Description of all the Direct and Principal Cross Roads in Great Britain*. Paterson also produced *A Travelling Dictionary, or Alphabetical Tables of the Distances of all the Cities, Boroughs, Market Towns, and Seaports in Great Britain from each other* (1772). By 1829 the 18th and final edition of his first book was being published as *Paterson's Roads*.

Maps and encampments were, in their military origins and purpose, a prelude to the Ordnance Survey, although without such a systematic coverage. They also reflected the needs of a particular juncture, in this case raising troops in order to cope with the threat of invasion, which was to recur in 1778–79 and from 1793.

The location of encampments reflected a lack of certainty over areas of vulnerability, combined with the need to provide opportunities for militiamen from across the country. Road links were important, with Salisbury providing access to much of the south coast. As a result, maps of a particular locality have to be set in a wider spatial sense of the country.

In 1756 the French successfully invaded the British-ruled Mediterranean island of Minorca, and in 1757 there was the rapid development of a militia because during the Seven Years' War (1756–63) there were no defeats of the French fleet until 1759, when indeed the French tried to invade.

In 1757, William, Duke of Cumberland, mocked William Pitt the Elder's support for the militia:

'I have wrote my humble opinion for the raising more [regular] troops, but I do not know whether the dauntless Man Mountain [Pitt] will think it proper, or perhaps intend to meet the enemy at their landing in person at the head of his new valiant militia. If so, what has Old England to fear.'

In practice, the militia helped give the government confidence.

There were to be fresh encampments from 1792 in response to the crisis stemming from the French Revolution. For example, in 1792 there was a large militia encampment on Bagshot Heath that was inspected by George III and much reported in the press, including in the *Reading Mercury*, which was read in Steventon Rectory, where the young Jane Austen lived. In *Pride and Prejudice* she drew on the nearby quartering of the South Devon Militia to protect Portsmouth in 1793–95 as well as on the militia camps at Brighton in 1793–94. In the novel the attraction of the military, not least their uniforms, has implications for the frustrations of rural dullness and female sexuality.

THE RISE OF A GREAT PORT

John Eyes, 'Plan of Liverpool', 1765.

John Eyes's 1765 map was very much that of a port, with the docks along the Mersey made more prominent by the ships drawn in. The city had also grown since James Chadwick's 1725 map, a map commissioned by the Corporation of Liverpool, which similarly showed many ships on the river, but also a far less developed harbour. Daniel Defoe had been particularly impressed by Liverpool, which was praised in his *A Tour Thro' the Whole Island of Great Britain* (1724–26). Eyes's map depicted the south elevation of the new Exchange (1749–54), which confirmed the city's devotion to commerce and also the interest in urban improvement seen with the town commission to that end established in 1748 under the Liverpool Improvement Act. Much of the identifiable industry related to shipping is in the form of roperies and shipyards. A charitable infirmary opened in 1749 on Shaw's Brow to the north was testament to the civic benefits of trade.

The maritime trade of the city was varied. The emphasis today is on the slave trade. Indeed, by 1752 Liverpool had 88 slavers with a combined capacity of over 25,000 slaves and in 1750–79 there were about 1,909 slave trade sailings from the city compared to 869 from London and 624 from Bristol, which declined in relation to Liverpool and its better port facilities, not least the sole wet dock outside London (the Old Dock, shown in the inset, was the world's first enclosed dock when built in 1709–15 and could accommodate up to 100 ships). This dock was followed by the Salthouse Dock (1753), St George's Dock (1771) and Duke's Dock (1773). Money from the slave trade enabled investment in nearby transport links and manufacturing, and these further increased the port's importance.

Liverpool was also a key port in North American and Caribbean trade as a whole, as well as that of the Irish Sea, which was an important economic zone. Thus, much Lancastrian coal was exported through Liverpool to Dublin: Ireland was a coal-shortage area. In 1791, William, Marquess of Lansdowne, formerly Prime Minister as 2nd Earl of Shelburne, wrote to a traveller: 'If you think of Wales, you should see Liverpool. It is an amazing phenomenon.' In place of Bristol, Glasgow was now the principal competitor to Liverpool. The city's extensive commercial hinterland ensured widespread interest. Thus, the first number of

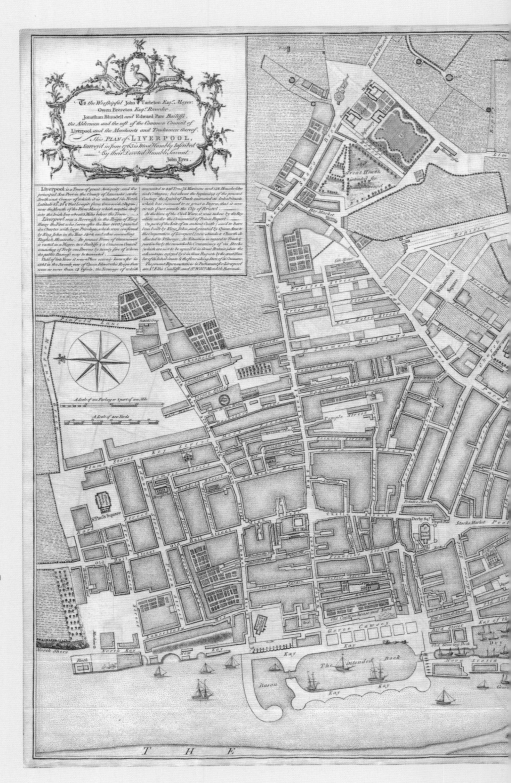

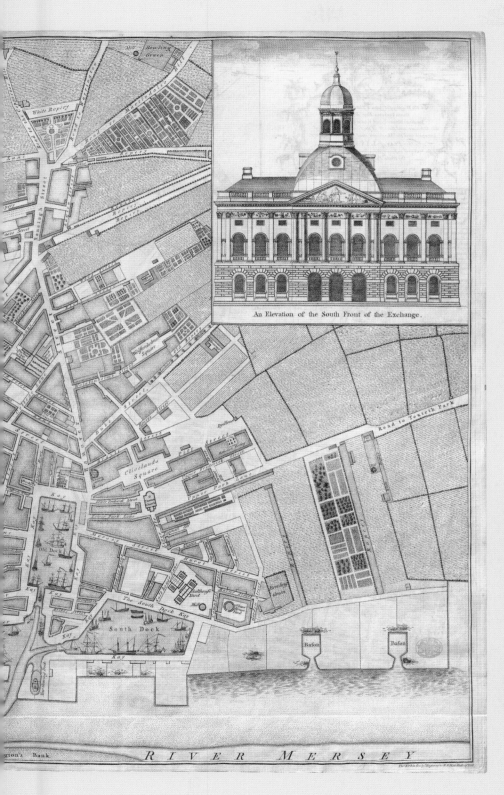

An Elevation of the South Front of the Exchange.

RIVER MERSEY

The Union Journal: or, Halifax Advertiser, that of 6 February 1759, announced:

> '...as the printer is a great well-wisher to trade, and would do everything to promote that most valuable blessing to the nation, he will oblige his subscribers with the exports, etc. at Liverpool.'

Having viewed the Bridgewater Canal in 1767, Joseph Banks reflected: 'Trade is opened between two very large towns [Liverpool and Manchester] before labouring under great inconveniences.' A sense of the past overcome was important to the significance of Liverpool. Another Liverpool map, that of 1785, was surveyed and published by Charles Eyes, who succeeded his uncle John as Town Surveyor in 1777. In 1803 Richard Horwood's survey took the story forward. Liverpool's population had risen to 83,250 in 1801, making it third largest in England after London and Manchester. Bristol had been long passed. The Old Dock was filled in during the 1820s as the city's docks expanded ninefold from 1756 to 1836 to cope with a 30-fold rise in tonnage. The rural areas in the map to the north (around Shaw's Brow) and to the east (Toxteth Park) became densely populated.

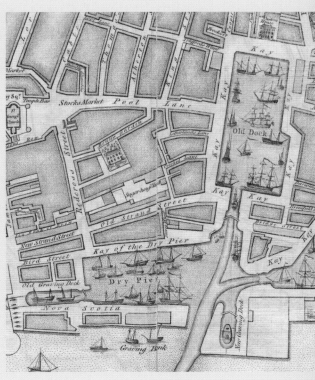

SURVEYING THE COUNTIES

John Chapman and Peter André, *A Map of the County of Essex...*, 1777.

On a longstanding pattern, Essex was surveyed by John Chapman and Peter André in 1772–74, and the resulting map was published in 1777. Produced at a scale of two inches to the mile, the map contained a range of detail lacking in earlier maps, including watermills and windmills, as well as the double gallows on Barking Level. As was often the case, the names of the owners of county seats appeared where appropriate. The county is divided on the traditional administrative boundaries, those of the hundreds, which had very little significance in this period. More important were the links provided by the road system and the resulting axes of activity and nodal points. As the map makes clear, the axes are out from London, which thus becomes the biggest node for Essex, with the key secondary nodes being Chelmsford and Colchester. As with all maps, what does not appear is as significant as what does. The map shows roads, and these were more significant in Essex because it was not a canal county nor one of improving rivers. Ironically, the principal river for Essex was the Thames. None of Essex's ports had a significant role in international trade.

The map was published in 25 sheets, each measuring 23 by 19 inches. A set of sheets could be bought for £1 15s od (£1.75 currently) if hand-coloured, £1 5d od (£1.25) if plain, or £2 12s 6d (£2.62½p) if bound into a leather-backed book. A countywide index map was included that helped the purchaser to identify the particular sheet of interest. The map, which included a list of the 224 subscribers who had supported the project (a key source of financing in much of the surveying and publishing of the period), was reprinted in 1785 and 1833.

Essex was greatly affected by the nearby London market, which was the destination of its production – a situation also seen elsewhere, notably in Middlesex and eastern Berkshire. Less positively, this proximity meant that many activities were dominated by London. The 'Market Herald' carried in the *Chelmsford Chronicle* in 1792 gave the London prices of grain, flour, seed, leather, raw hide, meat, tallow, coal, hay, straw and hops.

The role of accumulated experience was shown with Chapman, who had worked with Rocque's widow in London and been involved in the publication of county maps of Durham, Nottinghamshire and Staffordshire, while André, who was of Huguenot descent, had been involved in that of Surrey.

Until the mid-eighteenth century, the Elizabethan county maps had been reprinted with scant alteration, due to the absence of new fieldwork. After that period new surveys of entire counties were undertaken and maps produced on detailed scales: one or more inches to the mile. The first, that of Cornwall by Joel Gascoyne, appeared in 1699, but, by 1750, only eight counties had been mapped anew at that scale. However, the work from 1759 was in part encouraged by prizes awarded by the Royal Society of Arts, one of the major 'improving' bodies of the period. By 1775 nearly half of the English counties had been thus surveyed. Thomas Jefferys, 'Geographer to King George III', commissioned surveys and published maps of Bedfordshire, Huntingdonshire, Oxfordshire, County Durham, Buckinghamshire, Westmoreland, Yorkshire, Cumberland and Northamptonshire. His apprentice, John Ainslie, was a key figure, not least surveying Bedfordshire, Buckinghamshire and Yorkshire, and after the death of Jefferys in 1771 he returned to Scotland to do comparable work there. So also with the collection of such maps, as by Emanuel Bowen and Thomas Kitchin in *The Large English Atlas* (1749-60), which was a sequel to *The Small English Atlas* (1749) by Kitchin and Jefferys. Bowen was notable for filling the corners and spaces of the map with additional informative material, rather than the decorative ships and sea monsters of earlier maps. His map of Devon (which was somewhat out of proportion) included much text in this format but also a plan of Plymouth.

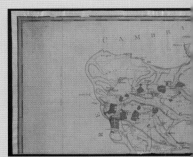

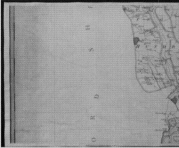

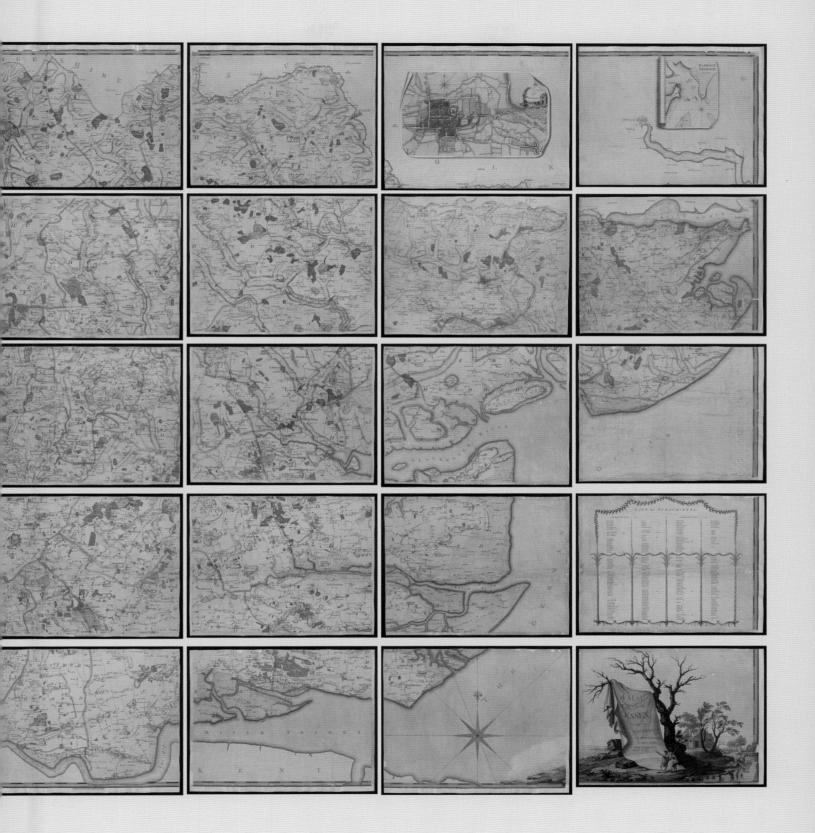

A PLAN of COLCHESTER

Colchester with the Liberty's contains Sixteen Parishes viz.
eight within the Walls four without & Lexden, Mile-end,
Greenstead, Bere Church alias West Doniland Parishes
within the Liberty's. Here are three Market days every Week
viz. Wednesdays, Fridays & Saturdays; but Saturday
is the most considerable, being for Corn & Provsions of
all kinds. Five Fairs are kept the 1st for Cattle & Wares of all
kinds, on the second Tuesday in April, and the three
following days. the 2d is held July the 5th on
St. Johns Green the 3d call'd the New Fair on
the 23 of July. the 4th on the 2d of August
kept on Magdalen
Green, the 5th call'd St.
Dennis Fair
on the 26
of
October.

RIVER COLNE

The Road to Ipswich

52 from London

Here the New
Fair &c is kept

St Anns
Chap.

Road to Ipswich

East Mill

East Street

East Hill

East Bridge

Mile from the Chelmer

The Road to Wivenhoe Brightlingsea

uld-well Lane

Water Lane

St Marys
Mag Chap

Magdalen Green
Here a Fair
is Kept

Magdalen   Street

Magdalen   Street

St Leonards
Ch.

The   Hythe

The Hythe

New Works

30   40 Chains or ½ a Mile.

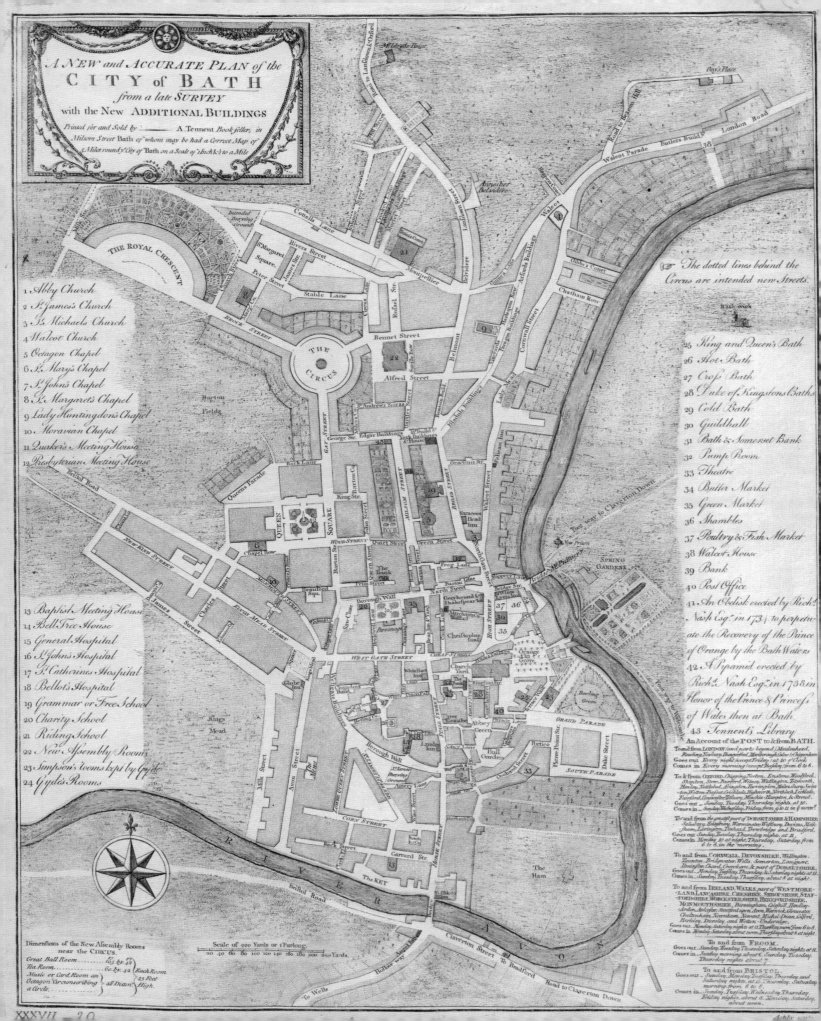

A NEW and ACCURATE PLAN of the CITY of BATH from a late SURVEY with the New ADDITIONAL BUILDINGS

Printed for and Sold by _____ A. Tennent Bookseller, in Milsom Street Bath of whom may be had a Correct Map of 5 Miles round y.e City of Bath on a Scale of 1 Inch & ¾ to a Mile

1 Abby Church
2 St James's Church
3 St Michaels Church
4 Walcot Church
5 Octagon Chapel
6 St Mary's Chapel
7 St John's Chapel
8 St Margaret's Chapel
9 Lady Huntingdon's Chapel
10 Moravian Chapel
11 Quaker's Meeting House
12 Presbyterian Meeting House
13 Baptist Meeting House
14 Bell Tree House
15 General Hospital
16 St John's Hospital
17 St Catherines Hospital
18 Bellot's Hospital
19 Grammar or Free School
20 Charity School
21 Riding School
22 New Assembly Rooms
23 Simpson's rooms kept by Gyde
24 Gyde's Rooms

25 King and Queen's Bath
26 Hot Bath
27 Cross Bath
28 Duke of Kingstons Baths
29 Cold Bath
30 Guildhall
31 Bath & Somerset Bank
32 Pump Room
33 Theatre
34 Butter Market
35 Green Market
36 Shambles
37 Poultry & Fish Market
38 Walcot House
39 Bank
40 Post Office
41 An Obelisk erected by Rich.d Nash Esq.r in 1734 to perpetuate the Recovery of the Prince of Orange by the Bath Waters
42 A Pyramid erected by Rich.d Nash Esq.r in 1738 in Honor of the Prince & Princess of Wales then at Bath
43 Tennent's Library

The dotted lines behind the Circus are intended new Streets.

An Account of the POST to & from BATH

To and from LONDON and parts beyond, Maidenhead, Reading, Newbury, Hungerford, Marlborough, Calne & Chippenham.
Goes out Every night except Friday, at 10 o'Clock
Comes in Every morning except Friday, from 6 to 8.

To & from OXFORD, Oxigving, Norton, Enstone, Woodstock, Shipton, Stow, Burford, Witney, Watlington, Elsworth, Henley, Nettlebed, Abingdon, Farringdon, Malmsbury, Swindon, Wotton Bassett & c.
Goes out Sunday, Tuesday, Thursday nights, at 10.
Comes in Sunday, Wednesday, Friday, from 9 to 11 in y.e morn.?

To and from the greatest part of DORSETSHIRE & HAMPSHIRE, Salisbury, Ringwood, Blandford & c.
Goes out Sunday, Tuesday, Thursday nights, at 11.
Comes in Monday, Wednesday, Saturday, from 6 to 8 in the morning

To and from CORNWALL, DEVONSHIRE, Wellington, Taunton, Bridgewater, Wells, Somerton & c.
Goes out Monday, Tuesday, Thursday & Saturday nights at 11.
Comes in Sunday, Tuesday, Thursday, about 8 at night.

To and from IRELAND, WALES, part of WESTMORELAND, LANCASHIRE, CHESHIRE, SHROPSHIRE, STAFFORDSHIRE, WORCESTERSHIRE, HEREFORDSHIRE, MONMOUTHSHIRE, Birmingham & c.
Goes out Monday, Saturday nights at 11 Tuesday morn from 6 to 8.
Comes in Monday, Saturday, about noon, Thursday & c.

To and from FROOM.
Goes out Sunday, Tuesday, Thursday, Saturday nights at 11.
Comes in Sunday, morning about 6, Sunday, Tuesday, Thursday nights about 7.

To and from BRISTOL.
Goes out Sunday, Monday, Tuesday, Thursday and Saturday nights at 11, Thursday, Saturday morning from 6 to 8
Comes in Sunday, Tuesday, Wednesday, Thursday, Friday nights about 6, Monday, Saturday about noon.

Dimensions of the New Assembly Rooms near the CIRCUS.
Great Ball Room 105 by 42
Tea Room 60 by 42
Music or Card Room an Octagon circumscribing a Circle 48 Diam.r Each Room 43 Feet High.

Scale of 220 Yards or 1 Furlong.

BUILDING FOR PLEASURE

Andrew Tennant, *A New and Accurate Plan of the City of Bath...*, 1779.

This map of Bath very much presented newness, emphasising the 'New Additional Buildings'. Moreover, as the map explained, the dotted lines behind the Circus were planned streets. As was the fashion of many maps of the period, additional information was offered, including transport routes to Bath, but there was no guide to heights or contours. While the map was new, Bath as a settlement dated back to pre-Roman days. But it was new as an eighteenth-century experience, both as a place of leisure – indeed, *the* place of leisure – and as a new townscape, one made dramatic by its rise up an impressive hill.

By 1800 Bath had a population of about 33,000 and was about the tenth-largest town in England and Wales, although the numbers there fluctuated with visitors and therefore the season. Popularised by the visits of Queen Anne in 1702–03, Bath became a city where it was fashionable to be seen. The social élite went, but so also did politicians and painters. Aside from Jane Austen, Bath was to attract a number of writers, including, among women, Fanny Burney, Catharine Macaulay and Hannah More. Although it was already successful, the development of Bath as a city of orderly leisure, and therefore a respectable and safe place to visit, owed much to Richard 'Beau' Nash (1674–1761), who, in 1705, succeeded Captain Webster as the city's second Master of Ceremonies. Nash's 'Rules' for the behaviour of visitors to Bath were first published in 1707. This was part of the process by which the codification of social propriety was expressed and debated, explicitly or implicitly, in print. Novels were another aspect of this process of codification, and the two combined in that, in fact and in fiction.

Health might be the basis of the resort, but Bath was often a destination for those seeking marriage, and this goal attracted visitors of all ages. Not only was this the case for men and women of all ages, but also for the parents acting as chaperones for the young women. The first Pump Room at Bath was built in 1706, followed in 1708 by Harrison's Assembly Rooms, and in 1730 by additional rooms in the Palladian style by John Wood the Elder. Both sets of rooms ran in parallel until the later eighteenth century.

The suburbs laid out to the north of the old core of Bath were to be influential for the establishment of urban forms. Circles, even if not the invention of John Wood the Elder, were first used on any scale by him in Bath. Wood began the King's Circus in 1754, the design and decoration reflecting his masonic and druidical beliefs. His son began the Royal Crescent in 1767. Palladianism greatly influenced the extension of Bath. This was most famously so with the Circus (1754–64) and the Royal Crescent (1767–74). It was also so with John Wood the Elder's Queen Square (1728–34) and Assembly Rooms (1730), his son's Assembly Rooms (1769–71), and the Palladian Bridge created in the nearby gardens of Prior Park. Other buildings included new churches, notably St Michael's (1734–42) and St James's (1768–69), as well as Robert Adam's Pulteney Bridge. 'The white glare of Bath' was a product of its being built largely of light yellow oolitic limestone.

By mid-century, a series of walks and gardens were major social attractions at Bath: the Gravel Walks and the Grove, Harrison's walks and gardens, the Terrace Walk, the Parades, and the Spring Gardens. The public spaces were lined by luxury shops, assembly rooms and socially acceptable accommodation.

Alongside its development as a fashionable resort, the effects of such construction and activity helped make Bath an attractive topic and space for the descriptive poetry, prose and painting of the period. Yet, Bath also attracted moral panic, as so much else of the different aspects and sites of urban life did in this far-from-secure age. The city indeed focused concerns about conduct and misrepresentation, both of which centered on the marriage market, and thus sex. Countering concerns, however, about the city's setting as a place for vice (notably gambling and sex) and the depiction of the worrying problems of luxury, the life of Bath was based on the fusion of gentility and equality. The assurance of the former made it possible in theory for the company to set aside status and act as equals, sidelining the concerns about social fluidity that played such a corrosive role in mixing, and was actively encouraged by Beau Nash. However threatening, social mixing, in practice, had its limits. Indeed, the organisation of space, both within towns and in individual sites such as buildings, excluded the bulk of the population in the cause of what in effect was an uneasy mix of hierarchy, status and profit. So also did the norms of behaviour that were encouraged. Like the West End of London, Bath became normative as a setting for the urban play of the social élite through their repetition in novels, plays and paintings. The town also had a rich cultural life, notably of music.

NORTH BRITAIN

John Ainslie, *Scotland Drawn and Engrav'd from a Series of Angles and Astronomical Observations*, 1789.

The map of Scotland by Jedburgh-born John Ainslie (1745–1828) represents a key stage in the mapping of the country, being the most accurate to date. After working in England, Ainslie returned to Scotland where he improved the accuracy of surveying and quality of mapping and was a prolific producer of surveys and maps. His work was particularly good for his coverage of the coasts, the islands being mapped in particular with greater accuracy (see detail, right), while he also (correctly) depicted the Great Glen as a straight line. Ainslie started in Scotland with county or town maps: Selkirkshire (1773), Fife (1775), Jedburgh (1780), Edinburgh (1780) and Wigtownshire (1782), but made his name with 'Ainslie's travelling map of Scotland showing the distances from one stage to another' (1783), a map that reflected the impact of turnpiking. This was followed by coastal charts published in 1785, and then by Ainslie's major nine-sheet map seen here, on which he had worked from 1787, a map that included insets of the Shetlands and Orkneys, and a table of distances.

Ainslie went on to produce more county maps (Angus 1794; Renfrew, 1796; Kirkcudbright, 1797), a map of southern Scotland (1821), and one of Edinburgh and Leith (1804), as well as estate maps. He worked as a surveyor on civil engineering projects, including the Forth and Clyde canal and the Glasgow, Paisley and Ardrossan canal, as well as an extension to Saltcoats harbour. The first was approved in 1768, left incomplete in 1775 due to a shortage of funds, and only completed in 1790. The second was proposed in 1791, begun in 1807 and opened, albeit not as far as Ardrossan, in 1811. Published in England in 1812, Ainslie's book, *Comprehensive treatise on Land Surveying comprising the Theory and Practice of all its Branches; in which the use of the various instruments employed in surveying, levelling, etc. is clearly elucidated by practical examples*, was long an important work in the field.

The great economic expansion of central Scotland, especially the area round Glasgow, that began in the mid-eighteenth century provided the setting for a major explosion of intellectual life known as the Scottish Enlightenment. Many new ideas about government, society and science were advanced, with the most famous individual work, Adam Smith's *The Wealth of Nations* (1776), providing the foundation of free-market economic analysis. The New Town of Edinburgh was built to make it a metropolis fit to be the chief city of

North Britain. The political élites of England and Scotland continued to combine, with the willing co-option through patronage and shared benefit in the expanding empire of Scots who had no alternative Jacobite or nationalist focus of loyalty. There was a diminishing emphasis on coercion in the control of Scotland and no comparison with the situation in Ireland, where a major rebellion was suppressed in 1798. Radical sentiment inspired by the French Revolution was limited, and paternalism – in the form of a more responsive Poor Law and subsidised grain prices – helped to lessen discontent. Aristocratic dominance of Scottish society remained strong, and was reflected in the Highland Clearances of people pressed into emigration in part to make way for sheep-rearing.

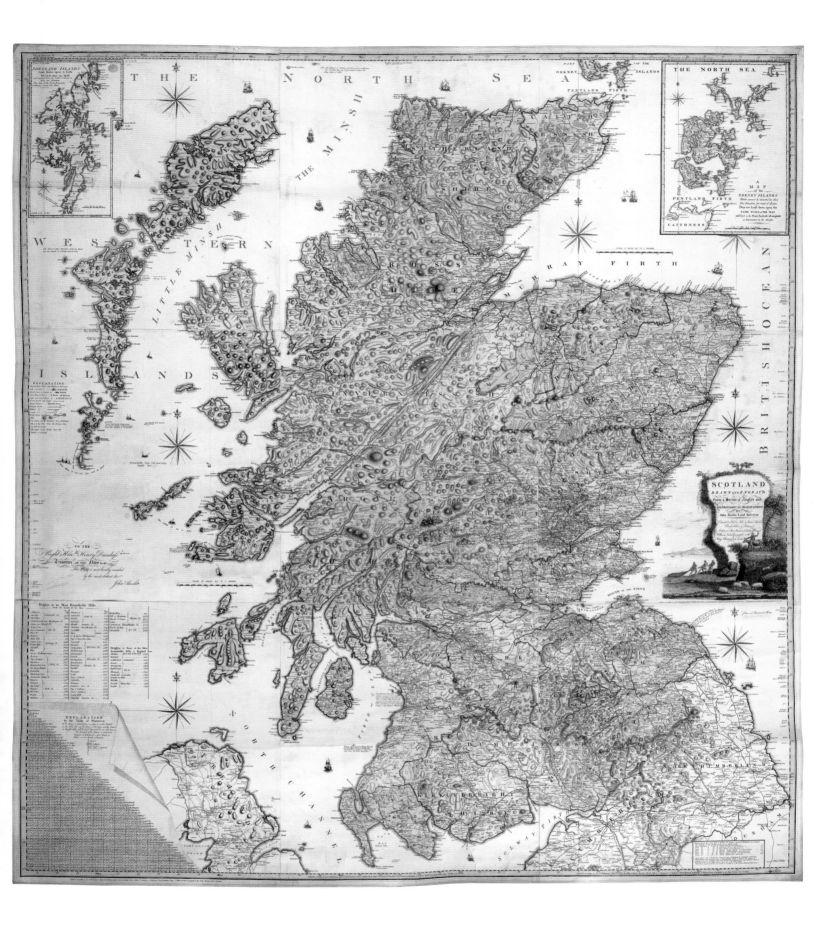

A Topographical Plan of MANCHESTER and SALFORD, with the ADJACENT PARTS, shewing also THE DIFFERENT ALLOTMENTS of LAND PROPOSED TO BE BUILT ON. As communicated to the Surveyor by the respective Proprietors.

By C. LAURENT, Engineer.

A Plan of MANCHESTER and SALFORD taken about 1650.

A Map of the Co

NORTHERN POWERHOUSE

Charles Laurent, A Topographical Plan of Manchester and Salford..., 1793.

The history of this work reflects the complex origins of many maps, not least as a result of entrepreneurship that was often ruthless. William Greene carried out the first large-scale surveying of Manchester between 1787 and 1794, but, using Greene's material, Charles Laurent produced a smaller-scale map first. Laurent's 1793 map includes the planned developments in the northeastern part of the area (labelled, in the box containing the extended title, 'with the adjacent parts shewing also the different allotments of land proposed to be built on as communicated to the Surveyor by the respective Proprietors') as well as three insets: one of Manchester and Salford in 'about 1650'; another mapping the strip road map from London to Manchester; and a survey of the environs round Manchester.

This map is a classic of a type of mapping becoming more significant in this period, and not only with cities but also in particular with mapping for agricultural and transport improvements, notably with enclosures, turnpikes and canals. As shown here, a key source of information was that of surveyors helping to turn agricultural land into the high income (rental)/capital (sales) of urban property. The value of the projected new property depicted in large part related to the existing configuration of Manchester and Salford, not least because there are no systems of rapid transit and or public transport. Instead, walking was the norm, with carriages for the more affluent. As a result, distance was a far greater issue than in cities a century later. For Manchester and Salford, the recent and projected developments were very much organised in a rectilinear street plan layout. This reflected plot size, landowner convenience and initiatives, survey norms and the largely flat topography that also emerges in the map, which helped greatly in the development of the area. In contrast, the older core of Manchester did not have this regular layout.

In industrial terms, cotton textiles were to see southern Lancashire become a major area of factory production, at first this was powered by water and later driven by coal, but as yet it was not the key aspect in land use or mapping.

The London map publisher John Stockdale bought Laurent's plates and used them to illustrate John Aikin's A Description of the Country from Thirty to Forty Miles Round Manchester (1795). The choice of Manchester for such a detailed map, already produced for London by Thomas Kitchin to accompany John Norrthouck's New History of London (1773), reflected the city's importance. Such maps became more significant as turnpike roads made it easier to travel. Helped by the dynamism of south Lancashire, the building of the Bridgewater Canal and the availability of coal, Manchester and Salford boomed.

Engineer James Brindley planned the canal by which Francis, 3rd Duke of Bridgewater, moved coal from his Worsley mines to nearby Manchester from 1761 onwards. By 1792 freight traffic on the canal was £80,000 a year. Bridgewater's role was an instance of the co-operation between the older landed order and the newly emerging powers of commerce. Joseph Banks wrote in 1767 of the canal: 'The benefits accruing to the country are almost invaluable. Trade is opened between two very large towns [Manchester and Liverpool] before labouring under great inconveniences … and a plan is struck out before deemed impracticable which has already been followed in several parts of the kingdom.'

Canal-building was especially active in the 1770s and 1790s. Demand for coal helped to drive the growth of the canal system. The Sankey Brook Navigation of 1755 carried coal from St Helens to Liverpool, and stimulated both the development of coal-consuming industries on Merseyside and the expansion of Cheshire's salt industry, which depended on coal-fired salt pans. In Warwickshire, Sir Roger Newdigate sought to link the coal mines developed by his father to Coventry by canal, and also actively promoted the Oxford canal and the Coventry to Leicester turnpike road. Similarly, Thomas Anson supported James Brindley, and one of his canals bordered his estate at Shugborough Park. The building of the Staffordshire and Worcestershire canal between 1766 and 1770 enabled the movement of Staffordshire coal and iron to the Severn, and thence to the sea, and the new town of Stourport was built at the junction of the canal and the Severn, while the first coal barge arrived in Birmingham on the new Birmingham canal in 1772. The Trent and Mersey canal, known as the Grand Trunk, and Brindley's most important canal, was completed three years later. The Coventry Canal brought coal to Coventry from the 1780s, and the opening of the Monkland Canal in 1793 stimulated the development of the Lanarkshire coalfield in order to serve the rapidly growing Glasgow market. Delayed, in part, by the need to build many locks, the Birmingham to Worcester canal was finished in 1815.

A GEOGRAPHY GAME

John Wallis, *Wallis's Tour Through England and Wales,*

a New Geographical Pastime, 1794.

A map board game with hand-coloured engraved paper on linen, with each player having a marker and four counters, and the game requiring an eight-sided teetotum spinner. The 117 playing spaces each designate a place, beginning with (1.) Rochester and ending with (117.) London. The places and their descriptions are listed at the sides of the playing surface with any rewards or penalties for landing on them. The descriptions of the towns emphasise manufacturing, as with Manchester and Leeds for cloth, and Worcester for china and gloves, 'manufactories' in Birmingham or other economic activities, as with Berwick and its salmon fishery. The tour through Scotland is a separate game.

The disaster is landing on the Isle of Man where the traveller is shipwrecked and has to leave the game. That island had recently been mapped by Peter Fannin, who had been master of the *Adventurer*, one of the ships on James Cook's first expedition, and had then set up a school on the Isle of Man where he taught navigation. In 1789 Fannin published his *A Correct Plan of the Isle of Man* (following pages), which offered a better account of the topography of the island than earlier maps, as well as the first indication of the island's roads and the first town plan of Douglas, the major town. However, the coastline was less accurate than Mackenzie's maritime survey of 1775, a contrast that underlined the significant difficulties of reconciling mapping on land and at sea.

Maps as puzzles were developed by John Spilsbury (1739–69), an apprentice to Thomas Jefferys, Royal Geographer to George III, and the producer himself of geographical board games, where 'dissected puzzles' or jigsaws, carved out of wood, included, as separate subjects, England and Wales, Ireland and Scotland. Wallis's game became very popular and was produced for many years. Based from 1775–76 in Ludgate Street, London, under the name Map Warehouse, and from 1805 at Warwick Square under the name Instructive Toy Warehouse. John Wallis died in 1818, but his sons, John and Edward, continued the trade until mid-century (see also pages 166–167). As an indicator of the scale of the market, Laurie and Whittle produced another such map in 1794.

The value of these games was highlighted by the ridicule attached to an ignorance of geography, as with Jane Austen's *Love and Friendship*, a juvenile work in which Edward sets off from Bedfordshire for Middlesex, '... and tho' I flatter myself with being a tolerable proficient

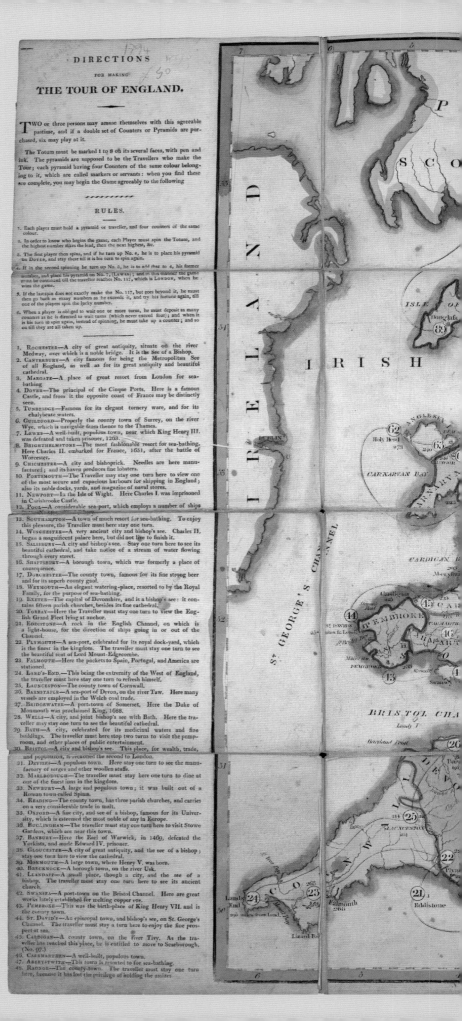

Walli's TOUR THROUGH ENGLAND and WALES, A NEW Geographical Pastime. London

Published 23d December, 1794, by John Wallis, at his Map Warehouse, No 16, Ludgate Street; Where may be had upon the same Plan, a Tour round the World, & another through Europe.

49. HEREFORD—Is an ancient, decayed place, with a large cathedral, in danger of speedy ruin. It is a city, and see of a bishop.
50. WORCESTER—A city, and capital of the county; also the see of a bishop. It has nine parish-churches, besides a cathedral. Here the traveller must stay two turns to see the several manufactories of china, gloves, &c.
51. WARWICK—An ancient and neat town, and the capital of the county. Here the Earl of Warwick has a noble castle.
52. NORTHAMPTON—A handsome county town, near which King Henry IV. was defeated and made prisoner, 1460.
53. OKEHAM—The capital of Rutlandshire.
54. LEICESTER—The county town, and a place of great antiquity. Stay one turn here to see the Abbey, where the great Cardinal Wolsey ended his life.
55. COVENTRY—A city, and joint bishop's see with Lichfield, celebrated for its ribbon manufactories.
56. BIRMINGHAM—A very large and populous town. Here the traveller must stay two turns, to inspect the amazing number of manufactories carrying on there.
57. LUDLOW—Celebrated for the remains of its magnificent Castle.
58. MONTGOMERY—The traveller must stay a turn here to admire the neatness of this town.
59. SHREWSBURY—A respectable ancient town, inhabited by a great number of genteel families, and famous for its excellent brawn.
60. BALA—A market town, where there is a considerable trade in knit worsted stockings.
61. HARLECH—A poor town, though the capital of the county.
62. HOLYHEAD—The most commodious place of passage to Dublin. The traveller must stay one turn here to see the passengers embark.
63. BEAUMARIS—A neat place, with a Castle, founded by Edward the First. As the traveller has neglected to secure a passage across the ferry to Bangor, he must be banished to the Isle of Wight, (No. 11,) and miss four turns.
64. BANGOR—A small city and bishop's see
65. ST. ASAPH—An episcopal city in Flintshire
66. DENBIGH—Is finely situated on a rocky declivity above the vale of Clwyd. Here the traveller must stay one turn to view its ruined Castle, which forms a noble object.
67. CHESTER—The capital of the county, is an ancient city, and the see of a bishop.
68. LIVERPOOL—Is reckoned the second port in the kingdom, with respect to extent of commerce.
69. STOCKPORT—A very flourishing town in the cotton manufacture.
70. NAMPTWICH—A market town, famous for its salt-works.
71. STAFFORD—The capital of that county.
72. LITCHFIELD—This city unites with Coventry in forming a bishop's see; it is a well-built place, and has a very elegant cathedral.
73. DERBY—The capital of the county; it is a handsome town, and well inhabited.
74. NOTTINGHAM—This town has of old been famous for its fine ale. Here the traveller must stay one turn to see the Castle.
75. NEWARK—A considerable and very neat town. Here died the inglorious king John; and it was here that Charles I. put himself into the hands of the Scotch army, who afterwards gave him up to his enemies.
76. SHEFFIELD—A large and populous town, celebrated for its various hardware manufactories.
77. BUXTON—Famous for its warm springs, which are extremely agreeable for bathing.
78. MANCHESTER—A very large and populous town on the river Mersey. Here the traveller must stay one turn to view their manufactories of linen, silk, and cotton, which are very extensive.
79. HALIFAX—A considerable town, and the great market for shalloons, calamancoes, everlastings, &c.
80. LANCASTER—A well-built county town, noted for the making of cabinet ware.
81. KENDAL—This town is situate near the lakes of Westmoreland; its trade is in woollen manufactures.
82. LEEDS—A large, well-built, populous town, and the great mart for coloured and white broad-cloth. Here the traveller must stay one turn to see the famous cloth-hall.
83. YORK—The capital of Yorkshire; it is the see of an archbishop, and its cathedral is a noble Gothic pile, equal, if not superior, to any in the kingdom.
84. NORTH-ALLERTON—Here was fought, in 1137, the battle of the standard, in which David, king of Scotland, was defeated.
85. RIPPON—A market town, celebrated for its fine minster.
86. RICHMOND—A handsome and pleasant town, with a stone bridge over the Swale. Here the traveller must pay one stake for his passage to the Isle of Man.
87. APPLEBY—The county town, but an inconsiderable place.
88. KESWICK—A market town, situate near the Lakes.
89. ISLE OF MAN—This island is situated in the Irish Sea, from some part of which the three kingdoms of England, Scotland, and Ireland, may be seen at once. The traveller will be shipwrecked on this Island, and thereby lose his chance of the game.
90. CARLISLE—This place surrendered to the rebels, 1745: it is an ancient city, walled round, and is the see of a bishop.
91. BERWICK—A borough town on the borders of Scotland. Here the traveller must stay one turn to see the salmon fishery in the river Tweed.
92. ALNWICK—The county town. Here the Duke of Northumberland has a princely castle.
93. NEWCASTLE—Upon the river Tyne; a very large and populous town, famous for its collieries.
94. DURHAM—Capital of the bishoprick and principality of Durham, beautifully situated on the River Ware.
95. STOCKTON—On the river Tees, an handsome, flourishing town, where there is a large manufactory of sail-cloth.
96. WHITBY—A port town, famous for being the birth-place of the celebrated Captain Cook.
97. SCARBOROUGH—A large sea-port, noted as a polite watering place.
98. HULL—A large sea-port town, which was the first that shut its gates against Charles I.
99. LINCOLN—Capital of the county, and a bishop's see; it was anciently one of the greatest cities in England. Here the traveller must stay one turn to see the fine cathedral.
100. BOSTON—A port on the river Witham. The elegant steeple of this town is a noted sea-mark.
101. LYNN REGIS—A port town, situate at the mouth of the Ouse.
102. NORWICH—One of the most populous cities in England, and the see of a bishop. It has 12 gates, 36 parish-churches, besides the cathedral and dissenting meeting-houses; here are great manufactories in crapes, stuffs, &c.
103. YARMOUTH—A sea-port, famous for its fisheries in herrings and mackarel.
104. LOWESTOFF—The most easterly point of Great Britain, and built on a cliff above the sea.
105. HARWICH—A borough and port town of Essex. It was here the Stadtholder of Holland and his family landed, January 22, 1795.
106. IPSWICH—A borough and port town on the river Orwell, and a place of great antiquity.
107. ST. EDMUND'S BURY—A handsome town, the trade of which is making of worsted yarn. Here the traveller must stay one turn to view the ruins of its once beautiful abbey.
108. ELY—A place of little consequence, though a city and bishop's see; and only remarkable for its fine cathedral.
109. PETERBOROUGH—A small city, and the see of a bishop, on the river Nen.
110. HUNTINGDON—The birth-place of Oliver Cromwell, and capital of the county.
111. BEDFORD—The county town, on the river Ouse.
112. CAMBRIDGE—The county town, and celebrated for its University. Here the traveller must stay two turns to visit its colleges, halls, &c.
113. ROYSTON—A market town, famous for its subterraneous Chapel of Rosia, a Saxon lady.
114. DUNMOW—Famous for giving a flitch of bacon to any married couple who will swear they never repented being married, in thought, word, or deed.
115. CHELMSFORD—The county town, on the river Chelmer.
116. HERTFORD—The county town, on the river Lea.
117. LONDON—The Game.

J. Pitman, Printer,
Warwick Square, London.

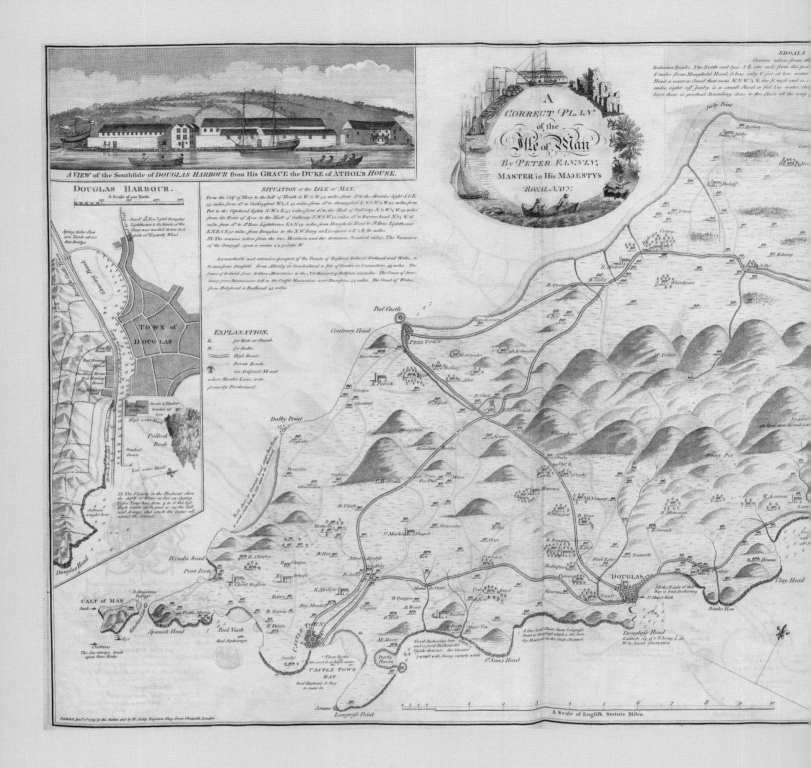

A VIEW of the Southside of DOUGLAS HARBOUR from His GRACE the DUKE of ATHOL's HOUSE.

A CORRECT PLAN of the Isle of Man By PETER FANNIN, MASTER in His MAJESTY'S ROYAL NAVY.

in geography, I know not how it happened, but I found myself entering this beautiful vale which I find is in South Wales, when I had expected to have reached my aunt's...'. So also for Fanny Price in *Mansfield Park* (1814): 'Do you know, we asked her last night which way she would go to get to Ireland; and she said, she should cross to the Isle of Wight.' In *Emma*, Harriet Smith asks, 'Will

Mr Frank Churchill pass through Bath as well as Oxford?', a question that shows she does not know the route from Yorkshire to Surrey.

This was a period of greater interest in Britain as a whole. In the dedication to his *Ode to the Sun* (1776), William Cumberland had called for an engagement with the English 'sublime', which he located in the landscape. This *Ode* and other early

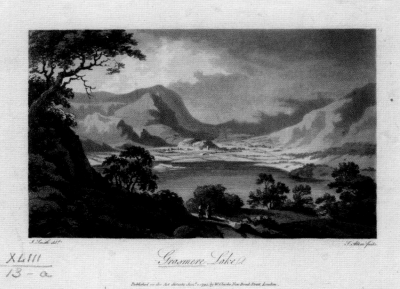

XLIII
13 - a

Grasmere Lake

Published as the Act directs Jan.^r 1 1793 by W.^r Clarke New Bond Street, London.

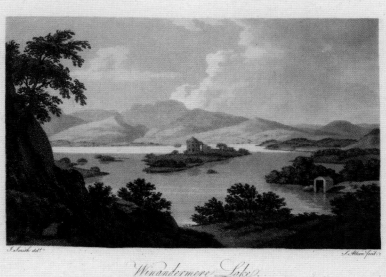

XLIII
16 - e

Winandermere Lake

Published as the Act directs June^t 1 1793, by W.^r Clarke, New Bond Street, London.

accounts of the Lakes, including John Dalton's *Descriptive Poem* of 1755, appeared in 1780 in the second edition of Thomas West's *A Guide to the Lakes: Dedicated to the Lovers of Landscape Studies, and to All who Have Visited, or Intended to Visit, the Lakes in Cumberland, Westmorland and Lancashire*, the first major guide to picturesque mountain scenery. The popularity of West's work ensured seven editions by 1799 and 11 by 1821. The collectable and display quality of these editions was enhanced, first, with maps and, subsequently, with aquatints. From the fifth edition (1793), the 16 aquatint *Views of the Lakes* by Samuel Alken (above, Grasmere and Windermere), after drawings by J. Smith and J. Emes, were advertised as of an appropriate size to bind with the *Guide*.

TRANSFORMATIVE TRANSPORT

John Philips, ...Lines of All the Navigable Canals; with those which have been proposed, 1795.

This map was engraved for *The General History of Inland Navigation* by Thomas Conder (1747–1831), a map engraver, publisher and bookseller based in the City of London, who produced maps of many areas, ranging from Asia, the United States and the West Indies to Wiltshire and Yorkshire, but the surveyor appear to have been John Philips.

Until the development of steam-powered railways, much was moved by sea or river because water was favourable for the movement of heavy or bulky goods, for which road transport was difficult, inadequate and expensive. It cost 33s 4d (£1.67 in modern currency) a ton to move goods by road from London to Reading in 1792, but only 10s (50 pence) by water. However, the river system was not always helpful. Many rivers were not navigable, transport was often only easy downstream, rivers did not always supply the necessary links and many were obstructed by mills and weirs.

The canalisation of rivers was the response to problems with the river system. The construction of canals represented a determined attempt to alter the environment and make it operate for the benefit of man. As with the turnpikes, and again unlike elsewhere in Europe, private enterprise and finance were crucial. The development of such a transport system was costly but it increased the comparative economic advantage of particular regions or interests within them and was therefore actively supported.

Landlocked countries found their relative position transformed. Canals were not separate to the process of industrial change, but integral to it. The location of new mine shafts, factories and wharves responded to the possibilities of canal transport. When the Britannia Foundry was established in Derby in 1818 to produce quality cast iron products, it was sited on the banks of the River Derwent and linked, via that and the Derby canal, to the Midlands' canal system and the sea. *Smart's Trade Directory* for 1827 noted that from Pickfords' canal wharf in Wolverhampton, a leading centre for the manufacture of iron products, goods could be sent direct to 73 towns, including Bristol, Liverpool, London and Manchester.

Although canals made it easier to transport bulk goods, it was only on a wharf-to-wharf basis. Unless the water froze, canals had a particular advantage over roads in the winter, when many of the latter became impassable. This was especially true of routes across the Midland clays. Canals were also more predictable than coastal shipping. Today, canals are noted for leisure activities, and it is difficult to visualise the major changes that they brought. There was a new geography, as landlocked counties, such as Derbyshire and Staffordshire, found their relative position transformed. Totally new links were created, and isolation lessened. This was not only true of industrial and mining areas. For example, the opening of the canal between Aberdeen and Inverurie in 1805 made it easier for the Leith Hall estate to sell and deliver goods.

It is appropriate that the eighteenth century is known for canals, just as the nineteenth is for railways, and the twentieth for roads. Each transport system was the product of the socio-political systems of the age and were central to economic transformation and to shifts in attitude. Each also led to geographical change, as new nodes emerged, although, unlike rail and road, canal was crucial only to freight and not to passenger traffic. Thus, London, the centre of passenger traffic, was not central to the canal system. Instead, thanks to the mutually stimulating interaction of canals and their industries, the West Midlands, South Lancashire and South Yorkshire became more important to communications within the country.

Canals, however, were expensive and faced problems, not least preventing leaks and securing an adequate water supply. Due to financial problems, the 38-mile Forth and Clyde canal, which had 39 locks, was begun in 1768 but not finished until 1790. Most goods and people in the British Isles continued to move by road. The canal network was sparse, somewhat fragmented and especially limited in Scotland, Wales and Ireland. Nevertheless, in the last, the Lagan Navigation, the Tyrone Navigation and the Strabane Canal were all completed in Ulster by 1796, while the Grand (1756–1805) – mapped by James Brownrigg in 1788 as work in progress (following pages) – and Royal (1789–1817) canals linked Dublin to the Irish midlands. The planning of canals required maps while, in turn, their construction ensured the need to insert new material on maps.

A Map of
ENGLAND;
Shewing the Lines of all the
NAVIGABLE CANALS;
with those which have been proposed.

Engraved for The General History of
Inland Navigation.
1795.

T. Conder Sculp.

Canals already executed
D.º proposed
Navigable Rivers

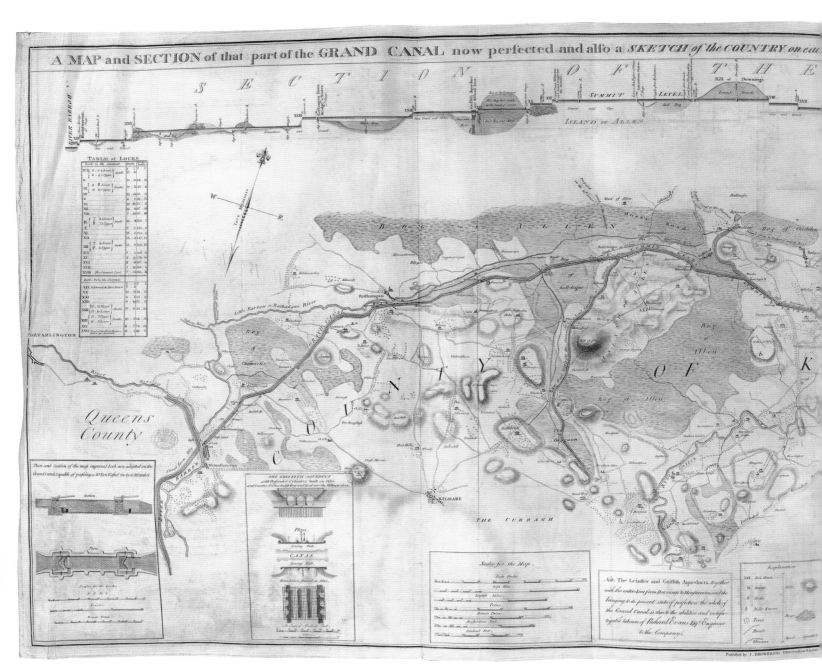

James Brownrigg, A Map and Section of that part of the Grand Canal now perfected..., c.1788.

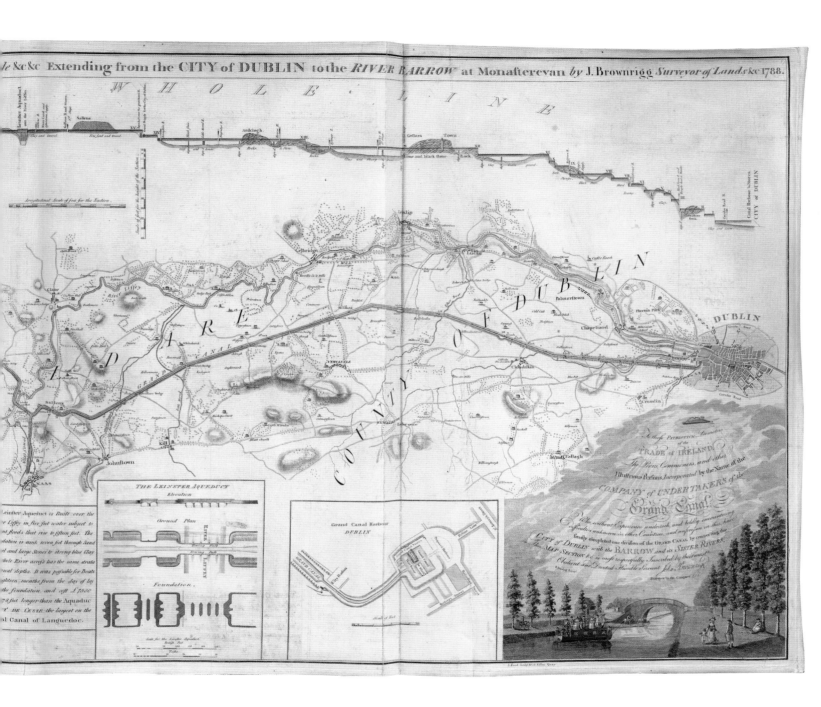

&c&c Extending from the CITY of DUBLIN to the RIVER BARROW at Monasterevan by J. Brownrigg Surveyor of Lands &c 1788.

A REBELLION CRUSHED

Richard Musgrave, 'View of Vinegar hill on the north east side', 1801.

This map, probably based on a topographical map created by Captain Alexander Taylor, an officer in the Royal Engineers, appeared in a book by Richard Musgrave published in 1801, but recording events in 1798. The map marks the positions of the 'Rebels' and those of the attacking government forces under the command of Lieutenant General Lake. Vinegar Hill, Wexford, was the key battle in the Irish rising of 1798, which was the most significant rebellion in Ireland between 1641 and the far smaller-scale Easter Rising of 1916.

British concern about possible internal discontent and French intervention helped to increase Protestant–Catholic tension, leading to rebellion. In 1798 the government thwarted action for an insurrection in Dublin; and throughout the rising, by controlling the major towns the authorities controlled the centres of communication, which helped them deploy forces and retain the initiative. The most serious military challenge was in County Wexford, where the local garrison was weak. Initially strong, the rebels overran most of the county but found it impossible to exploit this success. They then concentrated at Vinegar Hill, allowing the British to deploy reinforcements. On 21 June, Lieutenant General Gerard Lake, with 20,000 troops, attacked his 9,000 opponents, using his numerous cannon to devastate them. The rebels fought for two hours, sustained heavy casualties, and finally retreated when their ammunition ran out. Punitive operations in the following weeks harried survivors. More generally, the insurgents had limited experience and training and a shortage of firearms. In fact many used pikes, a weapon regular troops had not employed for nearly a century, and one with which readers would have been unfamiliar, therefore explaining the simple illustrations shown of several different types.

The insurgents were also weakened by the heavily divided nature of Irish political opinion. This was not the case of an imperial power suppressing a people, but of a more complex set of religious, social, political and economic relations that enabled the government to muster a significant amount of Irish support. In addition, French participation in 1798 was too late (an earlier attempt to land a sizeable force at Bantry Bay in December 1796 failed because of terrible midwinter weather). In 1798, the French, only 1,100 strong, did not land until 22 August, and did so in distant Connacht, not in Wexford. A force under Lake, largely of militia, was driven aside at Castlebar on 20 August, but there was no supporting insurrection, the British fleet blocked French reinforcements, and the French army was obliged to surrender at Ballinamuck to a far larger British one on 8 September. The British commander, Charles, Marquess Cornwallis, had himself been forced to surrender by the Americans and French at Yorktown in 1781.

Battle maps were frequently produced from the seventeenth century onwards. This map was somewhat crude and traditional in its pictorial quality, although that certainly brought out the terrain. At the time of the British Civil Wars from 1639 onwards, maps were generally accompanied by illustrations, but by the late eighteenth century that aspect had become far less significant and the focus instead was usually very much on a plan of the battle. That, however, could provide a false coherence and clarity that did not capture the extent to which battles were in reality far more confused, and not only at the level of individual experience. Waterloo (1815) was to be much represented in maps, but, even so, there were considerably different recollections of precisely where units were and when they were under fire.

View of Vinegar hill on the North east side

Pl. V

1 Light Infantry with Howitzer   4 & 5 Gen. Dundas's Brigade.   8 Rebels fort of Vinegar Hill
2 Gen. Lake where   his Horse was kill'd.   6 Gen. Loftus's Brigade   9 Rebel lines & forest of Pikes.
3 Gen. Wilford's Brigade.   7 Gen. Sr. J.n Duff's Brigade   10 Enniscorthy side of the Slaney.

IHS

A Scapular

1   Pike for cutting and stabbing.
2   Do. for stabbing only.
3   Do. for grappling and stabbing.

4

THE NINETEENTH CENTURY

The functional character of much mapping reflected an economy that was growing, a society that was changing and a state that was regulating. Thus, the dual impact on food supplies of war with France in 1793–1815 and population growth led to much enclosure of common land, which required mapping, while the 1836 Tithe Commutation Act led to the mapping and valuation of titheable land. Later in the century, the establishment of compulsory schooling increased the demand for maps in the classroom. With growing literacy and wealth, society was thirsting for knowledge, the book-reading public swelled and readers became more used to seeing maps – for example, in bibles, newspapers and magazines, and on stamps and consumer products, especially tins. There was also an interest in statistics, with increased mapping a part of the process. By 1851 thematic maps accompanied the decennial census.

Maps played an increasing role in scientific investigation and exposition, and an interest in maps more generally was encouraged by a conviction that the environment was influential. Thus, Charles Pearson, in his *Historical Maps of England* (1869), presented geography as playing a major role. Maps expressed confidence in human destiny, notably that of Britain.

As an aspect of a more general interest in statistical graphics and thematic mapping, maps recorded life's changing structures, not only railways and factories, but also the omnibus depots, board schools, police stations and mission halls all marked in Charles Booth's *Descriptive Map of London Poverty* (1889). Demand was in part a cause as well as consequence of increased supply,

the latter reflecting the application of mass-production techniques to what had hitherto been essentially a craft industry. The use of steam power made a key difference, replacing the manual operation of printing presses. The technology was developed in other contexts, notably for the newspaper and book trades, although, just as had happened earlier with printing itself, there were specific applications for maps. There was a move away from the original steam-powered cast-iron presses with rotary cylinders to rotary printing presses. In addition, paper was machine-made in rolls, and there were hot-metal typesetting machines.

A characteristic of the era was that technological innovation was generally important. Lithography provided greater flexibility in map-printing than copper engraving and was less expensive and made printing in colour possible. New forms of production included wood engraving, which was a type of woodcut that could be printed on smoother machine-made paper, and wax engraving, which used images incised in wax that were transferred by electrotyping onto metal printing plates. The application of colour was time-consuming: it was either manual or by means of engraving a different plate for each ink colour. The onset of commonplace printing in colour meant colours came to play a more prominent role in mapping, and colour was seen as both a commercial opportunity and a challenge. New, specialised map publishers came into being, including W. and A.K. Johnson in 1826 and John Bartholomew and Son in the 1820s, both in Edinburgh, and George Philip and Son in London in 1834.

A DOCK IN PROGRESS

John Fairburn, An Accurate Plan of the Docks for the West India Trade,

and the Canal, in the Isle of Dogs, 1800.

Published in May 1800, this impressive scale map captures key details of the West India docks begun earlier that year on the Isle of Dogs in London. As the map shows, there were two docks, the first for unloading (with planned warehouses in dark red), the other for loading for sailing to the Caribbean (with the extent of warehousing as yet undetermined). The map more generally carefully distinguished between before (the landholders in the area), definite change and possible change (the areas marked as 'not fully resolved on'), using a variety of devices to that end, as well as capturing the possibilities offered by building across the Isle of Dogs, thus providing two approaches to the Thames by means of a Limehouse Basin and a Blackwall Basin. Steam-powered vessels helped change the bulk and volume of shipping, but so also did the growth of the British economy and notably its booming trade. New docks both recorded and made possible this expansion. There was considerable specialisation of function, as with the building in South Wales of the Bute East, Roath Basin and Penarth docks, all linked to the Taff Vale Railway opened in 1841 that brought coal to Cardiff from the Glamorgan coalfield. But London's docks, shown here, were the most extensive. In Dickens's *Great Expectations*, Pip travels down the Thames and describes its: '...tiers of shipping. Here, were the Leith, Aberdeen and Glasgow steamers, loading and unloading goods ... colliers by the score and score.... to-morrow's steamer for Rotterdam ...; and ... tomorrow's for Hamburg...'

The Thames at London, indeed, was a phenomenally busy port by the early nineteenth century. The Pool of London had become outgrown and the longer the valuable cargoes waited to be unloaded the more vulnerable they were to well-organised gangs of thieves operating along the river. To speed up unloading times and improve security, Parliament passed the West India Dock Act in 1799 (so that West India produce 'might be effectually secure from loss by theft or other causes and the public revenue greatly benefited'), and in August 1802 the West India Dock Company opened the enclosed West India Docks on the Isle of Dogs, with an import dock and an export dock lined with five-storey warehouses, enclosed by walls and a ditch, overseen by an armed watch. The company had a 21-year monopoly on the trade with the West Indies, which centred around commodities produced on the slave plantations in the region,

including sugar, rum, coffee and timber. These cargoes provided a significant proportion of Britain's overall trade. Although docks at Wapping were under construction before the West India Docks, they did not open until 1805. (William Daniell produced a bird's-eye view of the proposed scheme in 1803, overleaf.) The East India Company then secured permission for a dock at Blackwall, which opened in 1806, requiring all ships going to and arriving from the East Indies and China to load and unload in the East India Docks.

In 1827 London received 1.9 million tons of coal, mostly from colliers (boats) sent from Newcastle and Sunderland; in 1855, 4.2 million tons (three million by sea); and in 1879, 6.6 million tons, although by then rail was more important as the means of supply. In Dickens's *The Old Curiosity Shop*, Daniel Quilp, the villainous moneylender, rentier, shipbreaker and smuggler, falls into the Thames near his wharf and drowns:

'Coming slowly on through the forests of masts was a great steamship, beating the water in short impatient strokes with her heavy paddles as though she wanted room to breathe, and advancing in her huge bulk like a sea monster among the minnows of the Thames. On either side were long black tiers of colliers; between them vessels slowly working out of harbour... The water and all upon it was in active motion, dancing and buoyant and bubbling up...'

Work on the river and in the London docks was generally poorly paid and casual, with most hiring done on a daily basis. Employments levels fluctuated greatly with trade. Many cargoes were moved by hand and injuries were frequent. The situation encouraged a hard-working environment in the docks and was to lead to bitter labour disputes. In an older world on the river, vessels would moor and their cargoes were transferred to small, unpowered barges known as lighters, which would take the goods to the wharves. Before steam tugs began to be used to tow the lighters, they were manoeuvred using long oars known as 'sweeps,' and by taking advantage of the tides and winds, making lighterman a skilled job that required good knowledge of the 'set' of the tides.

As the century progressed, and shipping increased in size and volume, new docks became ever larger and were built further downstream, in a process akin to industrialisation. Following on from earlier docks that were closer to the City –

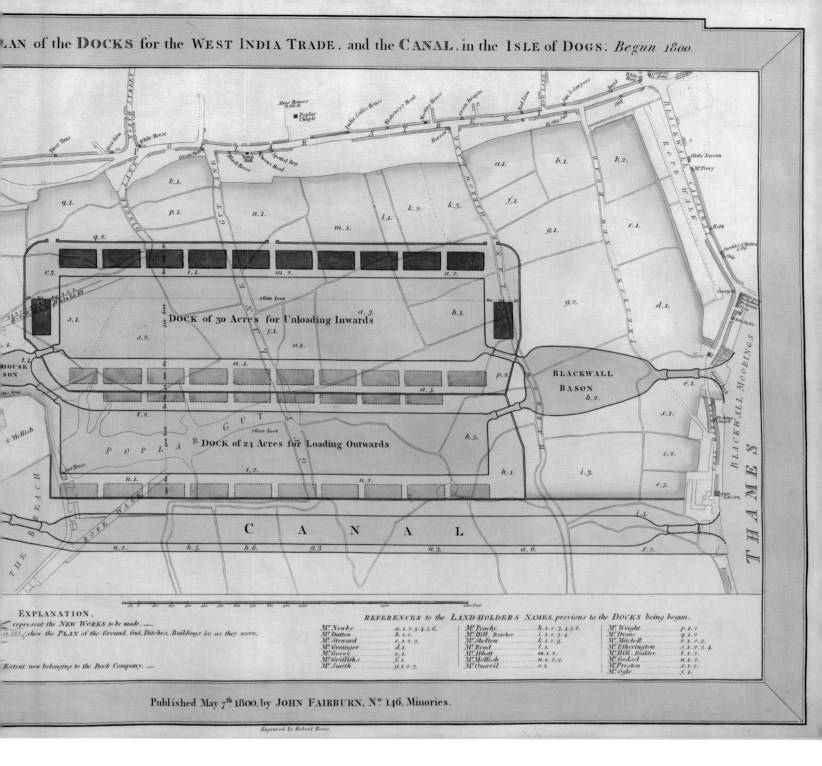

DOCK of 30 Acres for Unloading Inwards

2600 feet

BLACKWALL BASON

2600 feet

R. DOCK of 24 Acres for Loading Outwards

C A N A L

BLACKWALL MOORINGS

THAMES

EXPLANATION.

represent the NEW WORKS to be made.

shew the PLAN of the Ground, Gut, Ditches, Buildings &c. as they were.

Extent now belonging to the Dock Company.

REFERENCES to the LAND-HOLDERS NAMES, previous to the DOCKS being begun.

Mr Newby	a.1.2.3.4.5.6.	Mr Peachy	h.1.2.3.4.5.6.	Mr Wright	p.1.2
Mr Dutton	b.1.2.	Mr Hill, Butcher	i.1.2.3.4.	Mr Drane	q.1.2
Mr Steward	c.1.2.3.	Mr Shelton	k.1.2.3.	Mr Mitchell	r.1.2.3.
Mr Grainger	d.1.	Mr Read	l.1.	Mr Etherington	s.1.2.3.4.
Mr Govey	e.1.	Mr Abbott	m.1.2.	Mr Hill, Builder	t.1.2.
Mr Griffiths	f.1.	Mr Mellish	n.1.2.3.	Mr Gedsel	u.1.2.
Mr Smith	g.1.2.3.	Mr Quarril	o.1.	Mr Preston	x.1.2.
				Mr Ogle	y.1.

Published May 7th 1800, by JOHN FAIRBURN, No. 146, Minories.

Engraved by Robert Rowe.

notably London Dock (1801), the East India Docks (1805), Surrey Commercial Docks (1807) and St Katharine Docks (1828) – the Royal Victoria Dock of 1855, the first of the 'Royal' docks, was able to cater for the large steamships of the day, and could handle massive quantities of goods. The 'Royal' docks were commercial docks given the royal stamp of approval rather than being owned by the Crown. The expansion reduced congestion on the Thames, making it easier to control trade, and to cut the large-scale pilfering from open wharves (many of the new docks were surrounded by high walls for this very purpose), and this expansion also responded to the needs of the larger iron, and later steel, merchantmen. In turn, Millwall Dock (1868) was followed by Royal Albert Dock (1880) and Tilbury Docks (1886), the last downriver where it was easier for deeper-draught vessels. Built in 1912–21, the King George V Dock was the last of the upstream enclosed London docks. Together, at 245 acres, the three Royal docks constituted the world's largest area of enclosed docks.

An Elevated View of th

This view represents the first part of the Works, as they will appear when finished, which are now executing in Wapping near the Tower, by the patriotic exertions of the London Dock

accommodation of Vessels employed in every branch of Commerce, for which extensive ranges of appropriate Warehouses are preparing within the enclosure. This great public work is co

progress or contemplation, render this Metropolis ultimately the first Port, as it is already the first City in the World.

To the

Drawn & Engraved by Wm. Daniell, & Published by

Dock in Wapping.

...ny, for the improvement of the Port of London. The Bason which is here shewn is 1260 feet in length & 690 feet in breadth, containing an Area of 20 Acres, and its object is the ...n a scale calculated to support the dignity of the Nation, and the important interests of its Commerce: and will, when compleated, in conjunction with other magnificent works, either in ...n, Deputy Chairman, & other Directors of the London Dock Company, this Print is with their permifsion inscribed by their Obedient & obliged Servant *William Daniell*

Cleveland Street, Fitzroy Square, London, Jan.ᵗ 1 1803.

THE ORDNANCE SURVEY

William Mudge, An entirely new & accurate Survey of the County of Kent, With Part of the County of Essex, 1801.

In 1791 the Corps of Royal Military Surveyors and Draughtsmen was established. Because Britain was at war with France from 1793 to 1802 and 1803 to 1815, cartographic information was of great importance, and by 1795 the new corps had completed a double chain of triangles from London to Land's End. These trigonometrical maps were the first output of what was to become the national mapping agency, the Ordnance Survey (the term not coming into use until 1810, when first used for a map of the Isle of Wight).

A one-inch-to-the-mile map of Kent was published by William Faden in 1801. This different map, by William Mudge, was in accordance with surveying work carried out by the Board of Ordnance earlier, much of it in 1798. The map was printed at the Drawing Room in the Tower of London. Kent was seen as the likeliest county for a French invasion and the plan was to try to hold the French advance by taking advantage of the county's hilly topography. Faden had really produced another county map, and, thereafter, the Survey decided to publish its own maps, not stopping at county borders.

After the Southeast of England, the surveyors moved to the Southwest, another potential invasion area. There was considerable emphasis on depicting 'strong ground', terrain that could play a role in operations; relief and slopes were important, not only to help or impede advances but also for determining the sightlines of cannon. The 'Old Series' of published maps began with four covering Essex published in 1805, and Kent was reissued in the new format in 1819. From 1811 to 1816 the War Office had banned the sale of maps to the public, but thereafter it was allowed, in part to help cover the costs.

William Mudge (1762–1820) was trained at the Royal Military Academy in Woolwich and served in the American War of Independence. In 1791 he became Deputy Director of the Ordnance Survey, becoming Director in 1798 and a Lieutenant Colonel in 1804. In 1809 Mudge became Lieutenant-Governor at Woolwich.

By 1844 the first 90 sheets of England and Wales at one inch to the mile, covering up to a line from Preston to Hull, had been published, with all of England mapped, bar the Isle of Man, and published by 1869.

The Ordnance Survey mapping took longer than anticipated, because errors were discovered and most of the 1820s and early 1830s were spent resurveying. The issues came to light in 1820 when a naval survey ship discovered that the island of Lundy in the Bristol Channel had been inaccurately sited. This was serious because Lundy's reefs claimed many ships. Other errors had arisen in part from having paid surveyors by the square mile, leading to overly hasty work.

As well as the standard one-inch mapping, there was also mapping at six and 25 inches to the mile, with a six-inch-to-the-mile map of Ireland finished in 1846. The Ordnance Survey developed considerable skill in the depiction of terrain, by means of hachured drawings that were engraved for printing on copper plates. This was an aspect of the labour-intensive nature of mapmaking. Mapping the Ordnance Survey was far from easy because it entailed accurate measurement, transporting often heavy equipment, notably the 200-pound Great Theodolite delivered in 1787, and dealing with sometimes hostile locals as well as changes being made by humans to the landscape, not least by the growth of railways.

LAND EFFICIENCY

Thomas and William Denton, 'Plan of the Manor of East Bedfont with Hatton, in the Parish of East Bedfont in the County of Middlesex. Taken at the time of the Inclosure, 1816', 1816.

The surveyors, Thomas and William Denton of Staines, have copied on this map the numbers and acreage given to the holdings and fields in the Enclosure Award, with the names of all holders of land ('No 55 Freehold Govrs of Christs Hospital') and of purchasers ('No 115 Sold to Peter Henderson') under the Award. This map shows the regular, linear nature of most enclosure boundaries. The basic unit for surveying was the chain, of which there were 80 to a mile (one chain equals 66 feet or 20.17 metres).

As a result of this recording of valuable information, maps played a key role in the enclosure of agricultural land, which led to the local mapping of much of the country, and to the linked development and dissemination of surveying skills and methods. These practices were longstanding, as surveying had become more significant from the sixteenth century, which again had been a period of large-scale enclosure. There was relatively little opposition to the later enclosure, in large part because the landed élite were thoroughly behind the process, but also because, in contrast to the sixteenth, the opposition by the non-élite rural population was weaker: there was no equivalent to Kett's Rising in Norfolk in 1549 (see also page 56).

The process of obtaining enclosure Acts reflected the social politics of the period. Once the major landowners were convinced of the value of enclosure, they would petition Parliament for an Act. Between 1760 and 1797, 1,532 enclosure Acts were passed, with the Midlands particularly affected. Although about one-third of these Acts brought waste land into cultivation for the first time, the extent to which there was a peasantry with a proprietary interest in the soil was also reduced. Freehold tenure became more important, and other 'rights' over land were downgraded, notably common land. This loss of security of tenure increased uncertainty, not least by dislocating the senses of place and identity for many who worked on the land. The radical Newcastle bookseller Thomas Spence wrote in 1800: 'Are not our legislators all landlords? ... It is childish to expect ever to see small farms again, or ever to see anything else than the utmost screwing and grinding of the poor, till you quite overturn the present system of landed property.' However, this was a partisan comment – the view that enclosure drove the small farmer out of existence is a myth.

Alongside regional variety in the intensity of enclosure, the social context differed: in some areas, such as Northamptonshire, landlords secured parliamentary Acts to further their interests, but in others, for example Hampshire and Sussex, enclosure was by private agreement and caused less tension. Nevertheless, hostility to the enclosure of the former Malvern Chase in 1776 led local people to prevent the surveyor John Andrews from marking out the enclosure boundaries. As a reminder that cartographers acted to different purposes and at a variety of scales, he had already produced a topographical map of Kent in 1769.

If the general context was that of agricultural improvement, that was not easy. Thus, the *Gloucester Journal* of 10 April 1780 carried a report announcing the prizes being offered by the Glamorgan Society for the Encouragement of Agriculture, but adding:

> 'The form and situation of this country, as well as the illiterateness of the generality of small farmers make us near a century behind some parts of England in the art of agriculture.... The gentlemen of his county, from their observations in travelling, and from books and their own experience, discover many improvements as to mode of tillage, different kinds of manure, succession of crops, artificial grasses, implements, etc. which they cannot prevail upon the farmers to adopt so speedily, any other ways as by pecuniary rewards.'

At the local level, enclosure, a process that involved valuation and valuers as well as surveying, was frequently linked to changes in naming, not least of field names, local terrain features and roads. This naming reflected alterations in layout as well as in land use and agricultural practices. Enclosures required a detailed land survey. Indeed, information was crucial to the process, both to its economic value and as part of the legal procedure. To arrange their valuation and to replan the area, it was necessary to establish who owned lands. This involved determining what land would form the new plots, as well as the routes of roads and watercourses. The role of the surveyors could be seen in new, straight-edged fields and straight roads, reflecting the role of cartography as an aid to organisation and control. There was a linear aesthetic of form and function that corresponded with the usefulness of enclosure. Older enclosures were more responsive to the local topography.

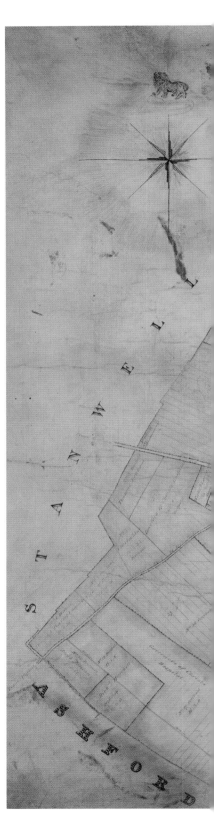

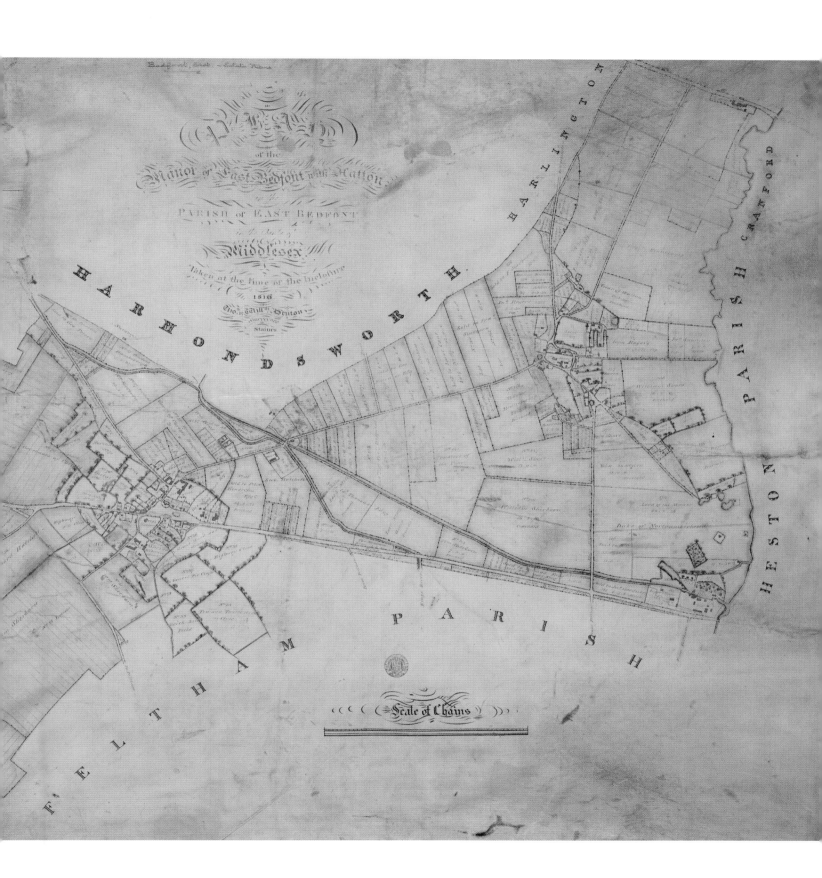

PLAN
of the
Manor of East Bedfont with Hatton
in the
PARISH of EAST BEDFONT
in the County of
Middlesex
Taken at the time of the Inclosure
1816
Thos. Tottill of Denton
Surveyor
Staines

HARMONDSWORTH

HARLINGTON

CRANFORD PARISH

HESTON

PARISH

FELTHAM

Scale of Chains

PETERLOO: A RIOT BY AUTHORITY

Pearson, Harmer and Denison, 'Map of St. Peter's Field,
Manchester, as it appeared on the 16th of August, last', 1819.

In August 1819 a panic charge by the Yeomanry
(militia), ordered by the Manchester magistrates,
on an enormous crowd of about 60,000 in St
Peter's Field gathered to support demands for
parliamentary reform by speakers such as Henry
'Orator' Hunt, led to 11 deaths and many injuries.
The over-excitable Manchester magistrates had
read the Riot Act and ordered the Manchester
and Salford Cavalry to seize the speakers (item
1 in the 21-item key identifies 'The HUSTINGS'
on Windmill Street), but the untrained, amateur
cavalry also attacked the crowd, eliciting
widespread revulsion. Newspaper reports were
given particular vividness by the presence of a
number of reporters on the platform, and one was
a target of the Yeomanry. *The Times* deplored:

> '...the dreadful fact that nearly a hundred of
> the King's unarmed subjects have been sabred
> by a body of cavalry in the streets of a town of
> which most of them were inhabitants, and in
> the presence of those magistrates whose sworn
> duty it is to protect and preserve the life of the
> meanest Englishman.'

The map reproduced here illustrated a
contemporary pamphlet that highlighted the
episode, printed by James Wroe, Observer-Office,
Manchester. The map was also sold separately.
The language used in the key is often emotive and
informative. For example, items 17 and 19: 'Foot
soldiers and Dragoons, striking and intercepting
Fugitives.' and 'Manchester Yeomanry cutting at
Men and Women, heaped on each other before the
houses. Some lives were saved here by Officers of
the 15th Hussars.' The map is also an insight into
the development of Manchester – an 'Intended
Street" is marked that runs right across the
site of 'St Peter's Ground'. George IV, as Prince
Regent, thanked the Manchester authorities, an
unsympathetic action that failed to condemn the
lack of judgement shown by the city's magistrates.

The use of the pun Peterloo was an ironic
counterpointing to Waterloo. The radical poet
Percy Bysshe Shelley referred in *The Mask of
Anarchy* to 'Trampling to a mire of blood/The
adoring multitude', and he called for a popular
rising: 'Ye are many – they are few.' In practice, the
radicals were divided and most, including Hunt,
rejected the use of force after Peterloo, which
received so much attention because it was an
untypical event.

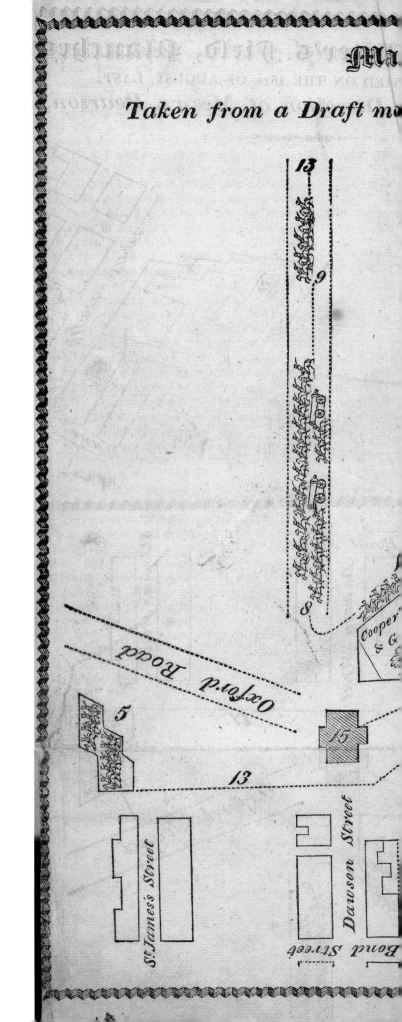

# of St. Peter's Field, Manchester,

A IT APPEARED ON THE 16TH OF AUGUST, LAST:

e u der the Direction of Messrs. Pearson, Harmer, and Denison.

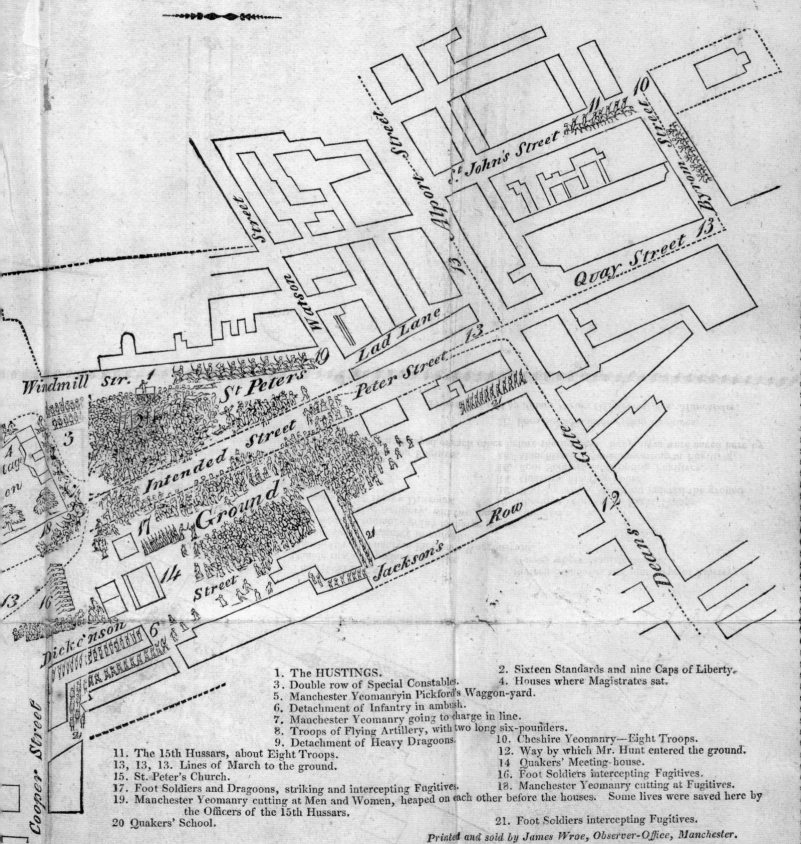

1. The HUSTINGS.
2. Sixteen Standards and nine Caps of Liberty.
3. Double row of Special Constables.
4. Houses where Magistrates sat.
5. Manchester Yeomanry in Pickford's Waggon-yard.
6. Detachment of Infantry in ambush.
7. Manchester Yeomanry going to charge in line.
8. Troops of Flying Artillery, with two long six-pounders.
9. Detachment of Heavy Dragoons.
10. Cheshire Yeomanry—Eight Troops.
11. The 15th Hussars, about Eight Troops.
12. Way by which Mr. Hunt entered the ground.
13, 13, 13. Lines of March to the ground.
14 Quakers' Meeting-house.
15. St. Peter's Church.
16. Foot Soldiers intercepting Fugitives.
17. Foot Soldiers and Dragoons, striking and intercepting Fugitives.
18. Manchester Yeomanry cutting at Fugitives.
19. Manchester Yeomanry cutting at Men and Women, heaped on each other before the houses. Some lives were saved here by the Officers of the 15th Hussars.
20 Quakers' School.
21. Foot Soldiers intercepting Fugitives.

Printed and sold by James Wroe, Observer-Office, Manchester.

MAPS OF A MURDER

George Henry Jones, 'Plan of the Country in the Neighbourhood of Gills-Hill' and 'Plan of Gill's-Hill Cottage, late in the Occupation of Mr William Probert', 1824.

In the eighteenth century the press had not printed many illustrations, still less maps, but the situation changed thereafter. Crime, a major draw in the newspapers, provided one source, with murders being of particular fascination. Four-and-a-half columns of the *Birmingham Chronicle* of 6 November 1823 were devoted to the murder of William Weare in Gills Hill Lane, Radlett, on 24 October, illustrated with two maps. The maps, which were were produced by lithography, a new method devised in 1796 that allowed drawing directly onto the plate and did not require the expense of engraving, show where the murder was committed, along Gills Hill Lane, and the separate place where the body was found, the pond at Hill Slough. In addition, the editorial, which noted that the reporting had driven out reports from abroad, commented on the wealth and respectability of the principal accused, adding a note of drama:

'Another trait in the evidence brings the affair into a resemblance with those banditti establishments, hitherto peculiar to the Continent, and which have been known to us only as the plots of our melodrames. Incredible as it may appear ... a fraternity existed for the express purpose of robbery and murder.'

The following issue (13 November) devoted two entire pages, including four sketches and a map, to the murder, as well as an editorial referring to 'the deep interest which the late horrid murder has excited, to the exclusion of all other subjects'. There was also extensive coverage in chapbooks and ballads, including the immortal lines that amused Sir Walter Scott: 'They cut his throat from ear to ear, His brains they battered in, His name was Mr William Weare, He dwelt in Lyon's Inn.'

A map of the surrounding area and a ground plan of the cottage, each with an explanatory key, were subsequently used to illustrate George Henry Jones' book about the case, published in 1824.

Weare was a London solicitor and gambler owed a debt by a man named John Thurtell, a dubious but powerful character who won much public sympathy as a sporting man defrauded by gamesters. Weare's corpse was put in a pond near the cottage where he had been going with Thurtell and his confederates to gamble, and then it was moved to another pond in Elstree further from the cottage. However, Thurtell foolishly left the weapons he used on the road, and was identified. Tried in Hertford, he was hanged, admitting the

crime on the gallows, the building of which was started before the trial had even started.

Much of the plot would have done credit to a Dickens novel, which reiterated the message across the country that London, where all the people involved were from, was violent and sinful. Thus, *Drewry's Staffordshire Gazette* of 2 August 1827 provided details of a London poisoning, while the *Sherborne Mercury* of 10 January 1837 devoted over a column to an item headlined 'Atrocious Murder in Ratcliff Highway. Examination of the Murderer.' This was followed by another item headlined 'The Edgeware Road Murder'. The impact of such reporting was seen in Dickens's novel *Martin Chuzzlewit* (1842), when Tom Pinch arrives in London from Salisbury:

'He was particularly anxious, among other notorious localities, to have those streets pointed out to him which were appropriated to the slaughter of countrymen; and was quite disappointed to find, after half-an-hour's

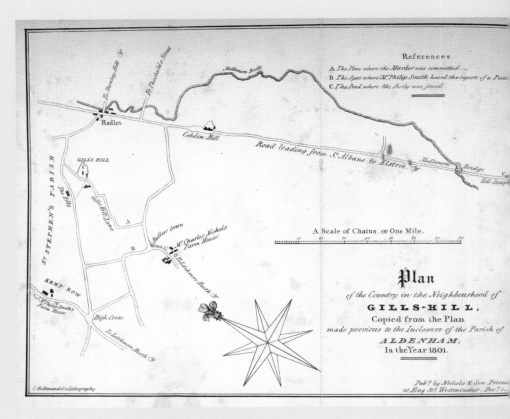

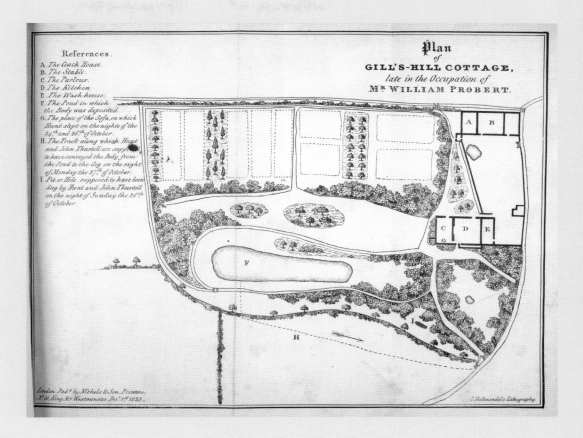

References.
A The Coach House.
B The Stable.
C The Parlour.
D The Kitchen.
E The Wash house.
F The Pond in which
  the Body was deposited.
G The place of the Sofa on which
  Hunt slept on the nights of the
  24.th and 26.th of October.
H The Track along which Hunt
  and John Thurtell are suppo[sed]
  to have conveyed the Body from
  the Pond to the Gig on the night
  of Monday the 27.th of October.
I Pit or Hole supposed to have been
  dug by Hunt and John Thurtell
  on the night of Sunday the 26.th
  of October.

Plan
of
GILL'S-HILL COTTAGE,
late in the Occupation of
Mr WILLIAM PROBERT.

London Pub.d by Nichols & Son, Printers,
N.º 18. King St. Westminster, Dec.r 1.st 1823.

C Hullmandel's Lithography.

walking, that he hadn't had his pocket picked. But on John Westlock's inventing a pickpocket for his gratification, and pointing out a highly respectable stranger as one of that fraternity, he was much delighted.'

Although Dickens noted the frequent display of murder in the press, in London Tom did not in the event fall into 'the dens of any of those preparers of cannibalistic pastry, who are represented in many standard country legends as doing a lively retail business in the Metropolis'.

Believing that society could survive in turbulent times only if authority was resolutely defended, Sir Robert Peel, the Tory Home Secretary and a Staffordshire gentleman from a paternal background in textile manufacturing, conflated threats he and others perceived from crime, radicalism and immorality, and had a hostile view of London as a centre for all three that required rigorous control.

Peel's Metropolitan Police Act, passed in 1829 (in part also to deal with systemic corruption in existing police provision), created a uniformed and paid police force that was under governmental direction. This professional service was designed to maintain the law and to keep order, not only against radicals, but also checking what was seen as working-class immorality. Despite being unpopular to those used to libertarian views about English freedoms, the police were a means to defend the existing system, as well as an alternative to the military, which otherwise was the major force at the disposal of the government, as was shown with the disastrous use of the Yeomanry in the Peterloo Massacre of 1819. A bill to create a national police failed in 1832, but under the County Police Act of 1839 Parliament enabled counties to raise uniformed police forces. These were designed to supersede parish policing, which was no longer regarded as adequate to the tasks of maintaining law and order in what was seen as a disorderly society. The move from the parish to the county level represented a major shift, not only in policing but also in the surveillance, control and governance of the countryside, and it contributed to the bureaucratisation, or at least systematisation, that replaced earlier more personal and diverse relationships. Attempts were also made to maintain and improve parochial policing, but these proved unsuccessful, and this led to the County and Borough Police Act of 1856, which consolidated the 1839 legislation and made the formation of paid police forces obligatory.

THE NINETEENTH CENTURY 157

CAPITAL GROWTH

Christopher and John Greenwood, *Map of London, from an Actual Survey...*, 1827.

The Greenwoods were brothers from Yorkshire who formed a partnership in 1821 and intended to map England at one inch to one mile, only to meet competition from the Ordnance Survey. Nevertheless, they produced large-scale folding maps of all bar seven of the counties, going on to produce an *Atlas of the Counties of England* (1834). In 1824–26 they surveyed London, which was expanding unconstrained by city walls and not yet disfigured by railways.

This map appeared after a large number of bridges had just been built across the Thames, including Vauxhall (1816), Waterloo (1817), and Southwark (1819), opening up South London, where the draining of marshland, for example in Waterloo, was also significant. There was extensive industrial activity on the South Bank, notably in Lambeth and Vauxhall, and this contributed to the pollution that brought the fishing industry on the Thames to an end by the 1820s. 'Hell is a city much like London – A populous and a smokey city,' the poet Shelley had stated in *Peter Bell the Third* (1819). Two years earlier, in his *A Morning's Walk from London to Kew*, Sir Richard Phillips commented: 'It must in a future age be ... difficult to believe that the Londoners could have resided in the dense atmosphere of coal-smoke.' Meanwhile, as London sprawled outwards, areas of countryside were swallowed up by new suburban developments, villages such as Dulwich, Haringey and Hampstead all at risk. The expansion led to fresh thinking, as in John Claudius Loudon's *Hints on Breathing Places for the Metropolis* (1829), in which he proposed:

> 'Surrounding London, as it already exists, with a zone of open country, at the distance of say one mile, or one mile and a half, from what may be considered the centre, say from St Paul's. This zone of country may be half a mile broad, and may contain ... part of Hyde Park, the Regent's Park, Islington, Bethnal Green, the Commercial Docks, Camberwell, Lambeth, and Pimlico; and it may be succeeded by a zone of town one mile broad, containing Kensington, Bayswater, Paddington, Kentish Town, Clapton, Limehouse, Deptford, Clapham, and Chelsea; and thus the metropolis may be extended in alternative mile zones of buildings, with half mile zones of country or gardens, till one of the zones touched the sea.'

Such ideas became influential in the late 1890s with Ebenezer Howard's garden-city movement.

THE AGE OF THE TRAIN

George Stephenson, *A Plan and Section of an intended Railway or Tram-Road from Liverpool to Manchester...*, 1829.

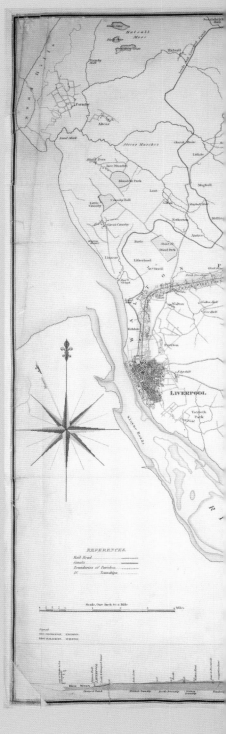

This map shows the precision possible in planning maps as well as the use of colour to convey more information. Like canals before them, railways required maps for planning and then use. Plans had to be drawn up for any proposed railway and deposited with both Parliament and the local Justice of the Peace. For example, more than 1,000 plans were submitted during the subsequent 'mania', or building-boom, of 1844–45.

As with the earlier canal, completed in 1767, the proposed railway shown in this plan was projected in a fashion separate to existing transport routes. That offered, as this plan showed, both possibilities and problems – the first in terms of a relative flexibility, but the latter that of constraints. This map provided no guidance in terms of the attitudes of landowners, favourable or not, but it does in terms of terrain, not least the waterlogged parts of South Lancashire. Engineer George Stephenson received approval in April 1826 to tackle what was to be a four-year challenge presented by rivers, valleys, hills and Chat Moss, a four-mile stretch of bog that swallowed the tracks. Stephenson overcame the bog by floating the track on tree trunks and shingle across its length. The other natural obstacles required 63 bridges to traverse the terrain.

The British led the way with the technology and practice of rail traffic. Wagonways had existed for many years, with horses drawing wagons along rails, especially from the collieries to the coal-loading staithes on the Tyne and Wear, and elsewhere. Other products, such as stone, were also carried. The Surrey Iron Railway Company, the world's first railway company and public railway, operated between Wandsworth and Croydon from 1803.

The situation was changed radically by self-propelled steam locomotives, not least by making long-distance movement possible. In 1804, Roger Hopkins built a tramroad between Pen-y-darren and Abercynon in South Wales upon which Richard Trevithick tried the first steam railway locomotive engine, essentially a mobile beam engine. In 1812–13, the first locomotives at work in the Greater Manchester region used a geared driving wheel engaging with racks cast on the iron rails to haul coal from a colliery to the Leeds and Liverpool Canal.

Locomotive technology achieved a breakthrough in the 1820s. The development of the locomotive from the stationary steam engine provided the technology for the rail revolution,

and industrialisation supplied the necessary demand, capital and skills. George Stephenson opened the Hetton Railway in 1822. The more famous Stockton and Darlington Railway followed in 1825, which opened with a ceremonial journey from Witton Park colliery to Stockton. Economic considerations were foremost. Thomas Meyneel, a wealthy merchant who was a leading promoter of the Stockton and Darlington Railway, had argued that a railway was preferable to a proposed canal, as it was likely to yield a better return. The 40-mile-long line was designed to transport coal from the coalfields near Bishop Auckland to the port of Stockton. The Stockton and Darlington was extended to Middlesborough in 1830 and a suspension bridge took the line across the Tees.

When Goldsworthy Gurney's steam-jet (or blast) was applied to Stephenson's *Rocket* locomotive in 1829 speeds rose from 16 to 29 miles an hour. *Rocket* won the Liverpool and Manchester Railway's locomotive trials at Rainhill. Direct drive from the cylinders and pistons to the wheels increased efficiency, as did an engine design that boiled water more rapidly. The Liverpool and Manchester Railway was the world's first steam-powered, inter-urban railway designed to transport both passengers and goods (notably raw cotton, shipped into Liverpool and turned into textiles in Manchester's mills). A global revolution in trade and travel had begun.

The development of wrought-iron rails in the 1820s and 1830s was also very important. Railways offered new links and cut journey times for both freight and passengers. Initially, the railways were mostly small-scale, independent concerns which provided local links. As demonstrated, the movement of coal was crucial. The first public railway in the Midlands, the Leicester and Swannington Railway of 1830, was designed to move coal to the expanding Leicester market and to undercut canal-borne supplies from Nottingham and Derby. In 1839 the company paid an 8 per cent dividend, which was a good return.

Other lines, such as the 1838 Carlisle–Newcastle line, were important for more than local reasons as they became part of regional and then national networks. With time, bolder trunk schemes were advanced and financed, and, in addition, the already existing lines were linked to create long-distance networks. Glasgow and Edinburgh were linked by rail in 1841.

Services from London reached Birmingham in 1838, Southampton in 1840, Bristol and Brighton in

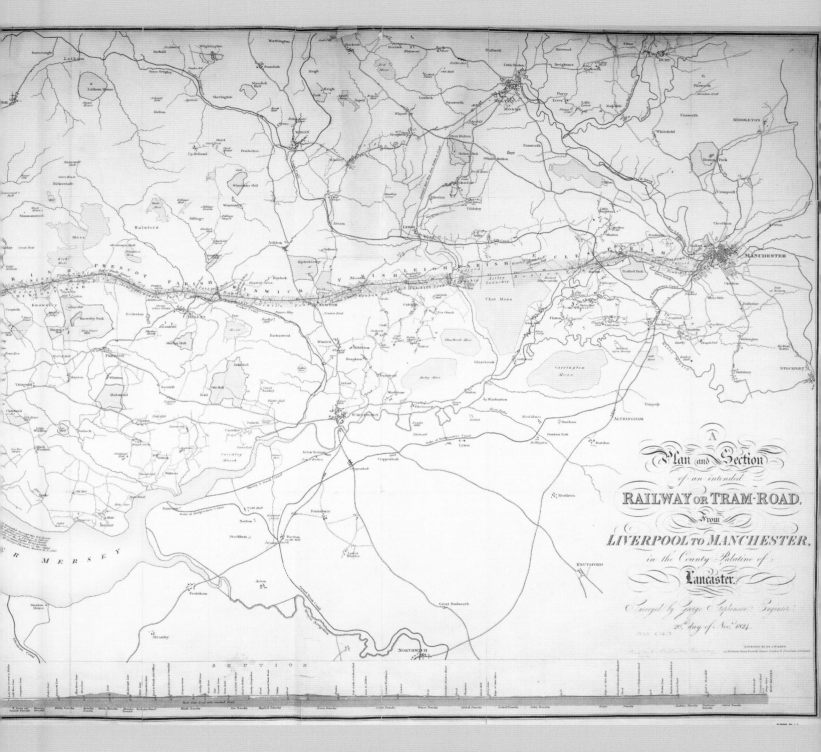

A Plan and Section of an intended RAILWAY OR TRAM-ROAD from LIVERPOOL TO MANCHESTER, in the County Palatine of Lancaster.

Surveyed by George Stephenson, Engineer. 20th day of Nov.r 1824.

1841, Oxford in 1844, Norwich in 1845, Portsmouth and Plymouth in 1847. By 1850 services from London could reach Holyhead, the Menai Straits having been bridged in 1849.

A formidable amount was invested in building the rail system. The London to Brighton line, including the spur to Shoreham, alone cost £2,569,359. Rivers were crossed and tunnels were blasted through hills: the Kilsby tunnel (1834–38) between London and Birmingham, and the Woodhead tunnel (1839–52) between Manchester and Sheffield.

Meanwhile, travellers on the railways were provided with maps, including in timetables. In 1842 the Railway Clearing House was created to apportion through revenues and it was responsible for plans, which were published in book form from 1867. The railways also led to the rebuilding of central urban areas, thus making earlier street maps redundant.

PUBLIC HEALTH

Robert Perry, 'Glasgow and Suburbs', 1844.

Robert Perry (1783–1848), Senior Physician to Glasgow Royal Infirmary, had graduated from the University of Glasgow in 1808 and was a prominent member of the city's medical world, being President of the Faculty of Physicians and Surgeons of Glasgow from 1843 to 1845. He was also interested in research, distinguishing typhus from typhoid fever in 1836. This was an era of many debates about how disease spread, which had encouraged thematic mapping. In 1844 Perry was studying the relationship between disease and poverty, using reports collected from the local medics. In *Facts and Observations of the Sanitary State of Glasgow during the last year; with statistical tables of the late epidemic, shewing the connection existing between poverty, disease, and crime*, he demonstrated that the districts where the fever epidemic was most prevalent were the most densely inhabited and poorest, which he highlighted in the map by using numbers (1–17) and coloured shading. Three areas were especially problematic with over 1,000 cases in each district. Located near the Hutchison Bridge crossing of the Clyde (see detail, numbered 2, 3 and 4), the cluster was in the area bordered by Bridgegate Street, Stockwell Street, Trongate Street and Saltmarket.

The report and map were published by the Glasgow Royal Asylum for Lunatics at Gartnaval 'in order to aid the laudable design of Dr Hutchison in exercising the mental and bodily faculties of the inmates of the Lunatic Asylum, the Printing of this Paper, the Colouring the Maps, etc, is wholly the work of the inmates'. Opened in 1814, the asylum (visible in the map in Cowcaddens, just above district 16) had been relocated to Gartnaval in Glasgow in 1843 and had a liberal policy, which resulted in the publishing in 1845 of the *Gartnaval Minstrel*, written and edited by the patients.

The process by which Perry assessed the situation was typical of the research-based nature of public policy that proved so important to Victorian governance, as also for John Snow with the analysis and mapping in his *On the Mode of Communication of Cholera* (1849), a work supplemented in a second edition published in 1855 by an analysis of the 1853–54 epidemic. Cholera was linked to poverty by William Alison, Professor of Physiology in Edinburgh, in his *Observations on the Epidemic Fever in Scotland, and its Connection with the Destitute Condition of the Poor* (1846). In 1848 the Public Health Act created a General Board of Health and an administrative structure to improve sanitation, especially water supply. The new Act provided for the creation of local Boards of Health, and they took action.

Glasgow's population had risen from 77,000 in 1801 to 275,000 by 1841, and was to reach 762,000 by 1901. As a commercial port, Glasgow, like Liverpool, had expanded rapidly in the eighteenth century, with textiles, engineering and shipbuilding all becoming increasingly important in the second half of the century. It was the hub for a cluster of growing Clydeside towns, while the Clyde's dock frontage also provided many jobs that were organised into small units, for the Industrial Revolution was not all about factories. By the mid-nineteenth century, 10 per cent of the Irish-born population in Britain were in Glasgow. There was also more disease in the densely packed city; cholera (a bacterial infection transmitted largely by water infected by excrement from victims) hit hard in 1847, as it had in 1832, and typhus in 1817–18 and 1837. Glasgow had annual average death rates of 33 per 1,000 in 1835–39.

Crowded big cities where people lived cheek-by-jowl, such as Dundee, the leading juteworking city in the world, posed particular issues, while the Bradford Sanitary Committee visited over 300 houses in 1845 and found an average of three people sleeping per bed, and mortality under five was about 50 per cent in Manchester from 1789 to 1869. Population density rose as the urban population grew: the number of people in Sunderland nearly trebled between 1825 and 1865, the built-up area did not keep pace and the overcrowded east end was the centre of the 1831 cholera epidemic in the town. In 1843 Pipewellgate in Gateshead had 2,040 people crammed into a street 300 yards long and mostly only eight feet in breadth; there were only three privies in the street. That year, fewer than 10 per cent of the homes in Newcastle had water directly supplied, and a reliance on Tyne water was linked to major cholera outbreaks in 1832, 1850 and 1853.

Yet, there were also serious problems outside the major cities. A 1850 report on the Sussex town of Battle recorded:

'There is no provision for the removal of any offensive or noxious refuse from the houses and gardens of the poorer classes; all the decomposing and putrescent animal and vegetable matter which is brought out of the house is thrown into a pool, around which is engendered an atmosphere favourable to the production of febrile epidemics.'

GLASGOW and SUBURBS

REFERENCES to PARISHES.
No I. Inner High Church Parish
II. Blackfriars Parish
III. Outer High Church Parish
IV. St Davids Parish
V. St Georges Parish
VI. St Enochs Parish
VII. St Mary's Parish
VIII. St Andrew's Parish
IX. St James Parish
X. St Johns Parish
XI. Barony Parish which also comprehends
Bridgeton & the Burghs of Calton & Anderston

MAP GAMES

Edward Wallis, *Wallis's Picturesque Round Game of the Produce & Manufactures, of the Counties of England & Wales*, 1844.

Produced by the London games-maker Edward Wallis (c.1787–1868), and accompanied by counters, this hand-coloured map provided, as earlier games-maps had done, an image of a changing country, its economy growing through the Industrial Revolution. This was notably so in the use of steam alongside sail by some of the ships. Moreover, steam was shown powering the Cornish tin mines, and there were also scenes of mining and railways. There are 151 playing spaces, starting at the Thames estuary, proceeding anti-clockwise up the east coast and ending in London. Each county has an accurate boundary and a landmark scene that tries to convey what is iconic about the area's local industry, commerce and craft. The area might also be famous for something topographical, such as Stonehenge in Wiltshire (see 105 in detail, right).

In 1835 Wallis had produced a *New Railway Game, or Tour through England and Wales*. Other maps included *Wallis's New Game including a Voyage Around the World* (1823), *Game of Star-Spangled Banner, or emigrants to the United States* (c.1842) and his *Wallis's New Game of Wanderers in The Wilderness* (c.1844).

Taking forward the work of his father John, responsible for *Wallis's Tour Through England and Wales, a New Geographical Pastime* (see pages 134–135), Edward was based for a long time at Skinner Street in London. In about 1847, Wallis sold his business to John Passmore.

Education itself changed greatly during the century, which enabled more of the population to follow maps. The 1870 Education Act divided the country into school districts and specified a certain level of educational provision, introducing the school district where the existing parish provision was inadequate.

Map games of Britain for children continue to be produced in the modern era, as with the *Race Around Britain* board game that was released in 1992, following the 1988 *Journey Through Britain* game. The *Great Game of Britain* was a version focused on the historic rail network.

PORT OF EMPIRE

John Tallis, 'Liverpool', 1845.

John Tallis (1817–76) was a cartographer with a London-based company for most of the period from 1842 to 1854 who covered a range of topics. These included the Great Exhibition of 1851 (with its setting, the Crystal Palace, an engraved frontispiece), *The Illustrated Atlas, and Modern History of the World; Geographical, Political, Commercial, Statistical*, a work edited by R. Montgomery Martin. The map of Liverpool was 20 by 16 inches, and came with handsome illustrations of principal buildings: St George's Hall, the Sailor's Home, the Custom House and the Mersey view from Birkenhead. Liverpool, the port of empire, was also the main departure point for travellers to America, as with Dickens's two voyages there. Following the famine of the late 1840s, Irish migration into Britain peaked in about 1861, when nearly 25 per cent of the population in Liverpool was Irish. Liverpool also drew heavily on migrants from North Wales.

Decades of commercial activity and growth, including the leading role in the Atlantic slave trade, had resulted in the creation, under dock surveyor Jesse Hartley, of the world's first fully enclosed wet dock system that added 10 miles of quay space and 140 acres of docks to the system, including the Albert Dock (1843–47). By the 1840s, Samuel Cunard was operating his transatlantic service. The wealth from this trade resulted in the development of new residential park suburbs, such as Princes Park (1842), visible on the right side of the map, above the older district of Toxteth Park. For the Victorians, parks were very much a characteristic of attractive residential areas.

The confidence, in the sense of potent commercial activity, shown by the map was an aspect of a more general sense of a less fractured and more prosperous society after the often divisive and difficult experiences of the 1830s and 1840s, notably the contentious repeal of the Corn Laws and the pressure from the Chartist movement for political reform. This was seen with the Great Exhibition, which was intended to speak for Britain past, present and future, and to proclaim the nation's mission, duty and interest to put itself at the head of the diffusion of civilisation. To some extent, the Great Exhibition was also a political stunt of the Free Traders.

Liverpool contained some of the country's worst housing and suffered from a high death rate. In 1846 the city contained 538 brothels and in 1857 there were at least 200 regular prostitutes under the age of 12. Alongside the extensive and

FROM BIRKENHEAD

ST GEORGE'S HALL.

LIVERPOOL

[1848]

The Plan Drawn & Engraved by J. Rapkin.

impressive world-leading docks prominent in the foreground, waterfront area, of the map, these sombre statistics hinted at the human suffering that accompanied the growth in trade. Dickens left a somewhat grim account of the treatment of the unfortunate of Liverpool.

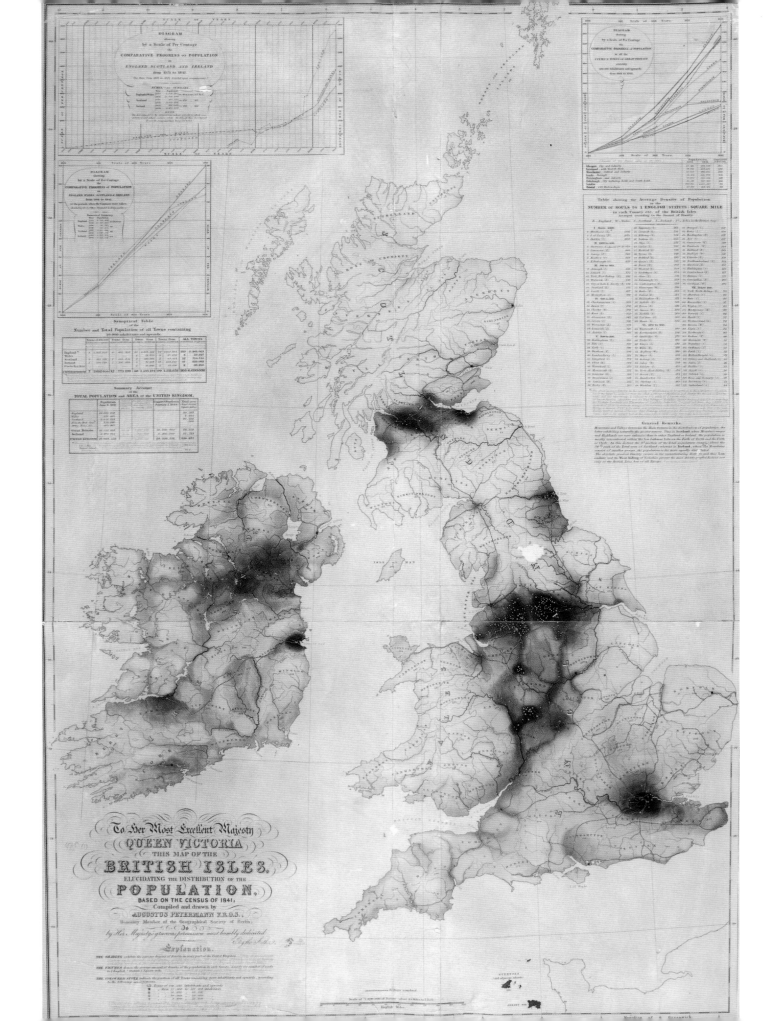

To Her Most Excellent Majesty
QUEEN VICTORIA
THIS MAP OF THE
BRITISH ISLES,
ELUCIDATING THE DISTRIBUTION OF THE
POPULATION,
BASED ON THE CENSUS OF 1841;
Compiled and drawn by
AUGUSTUS PETERMANN F.R.G.S.
Honorary Member of the Geographical Society of Berlin;
by Her Majesty's gracious permission most humbly dedicated

WHERE THE PEOPLE BE

August Petermann, *Map of the British Isles, Elucidating the Distribution of the Population Based on the Census of 1841*, 1849.

Dedicated to Queen Victoria, and based on the census of 1841, the map was compiled and drawn by August Petermann (1822–78), engraved by John Dower, and published in London by W.S. Orr. Innovative in its techniques, the map employed shading to indicate differences in population density, and graduated 'coloured spots' in order to show the relative sizes of towns. Railways were marked. The graphs on the map indicated population growth, including in the major cities.

This distribution was of greater significance because of the reorganisation of parliamentary representation in 1832 under the Great Reform Act in order to reward growing towns – such as Birmingham, Bradford and Manchester – and counties at the expense of 'rotten boroughs', seats with a small population. So also with the Reform Act (Scotland) of 1832, under which representation was extended to industrial centres such as Paisley. Representation remained a contested issue, with the working-class Chartist mass movement that developed in the late 1830s calling for universal adult male suffrage and equal constituencies, although neither was then achieved.

Educated in cartography in Germany, Petermann worked in Britain from 1845 to 1854, first in Edinburgh for the major mapmaker Alexander Keith Johnston, and from 1847 in London, where in 1850, the year he became Under-Secretary of the Royal Geographical Society, he also founded 'The Geographical Establishment, Engraving, Lithographic and Printing Office'. Petermann published a number of works, including *Physical Statistical Maps of the British Isles*, and, in 1852 and 1853, maps on cholera in Britain.

The distribution of population very much reflected the growth of industrial regions and the cities, which owed much to the relative stagnation of rural and small town Britain and Ireland, especially those areas lacking coal and suffering deindustrialisation, such as East Anglia and Devon, in each of which the textile industries were hit hard by the rise of Lancashire and Yorkshire production. Other areas that became relatively less significant in population and economic terms included the Welsh Marches, Sussex, Kent and Lincolnshire. At the same time, there was growth within particular counties not otherwise expanding significantly. Thus, in Devon, Plymouth, with its naval base, grew at the expense of Exeter, while in Lincolnshire there was to be growth linked to iron ore extraction. The growth rate in County Durham was 34.7 per cent in 1861–71, with the population of Tudhoe, where an ironworks was opened in 1853 and pits sunk in 1866–69, rising from 400 in 1851 to 5,007 in 1871.

In Scotland, the Central Belt grew at the expense of the Southern Uplands, the Highlands and the Islands. Its percentage of the population rose from nearly 40 per cent in 1755 to nearly 50 per cent in 1821 (and 80 per cent today). By 1861 the majority of the Scottish population lived in towns. Much of the population of the Highlands and Islands was affected by landowners determined to encourage them to emigrate.

North Wales suffered at the expense of South Wales, which also drew in migrants from the Southwest of England. The population of Cardiff rose from fewer than 2,000 in 1801 and 10,000 in 1841 to 200,000 in 1921. Glamorgan and Monmouthshire had about 20 per cent of the Welsh population in 1801, but 57.5 per cent by 1901.

The dislocation caused by extensive movement of people was part of the pattern of economic growth, essential to the provision of labour and yet disruptive for individuals and communities. Of the 225 iron workers at the Britannia Foundry in Derby in 1871, over half were born outside the town, although most came from the county. Most of the new inhabitants of Tudhoe came from exhausted mining areas in the west of the county and from the Midlands, while London drew heavily on East Anglia and the West Country.

The mass Irish migration following the famine transformed the situation in some of the big cities. The 1851 census revealed that 18.9 per cent of Liverpool's population was Irish-born, compared to 4.6 per cent of London's, where the Irish communities first developed in poor central areas such as St Giles, and then in the East End.

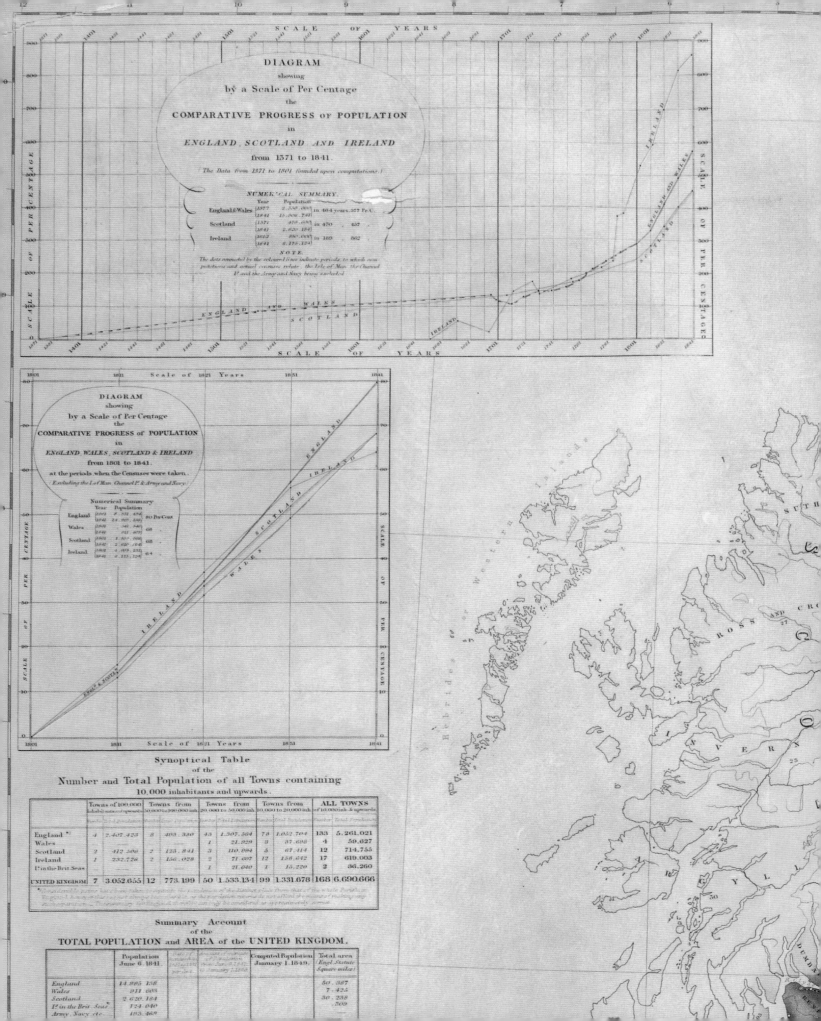

DIAGRAM
showing
by a Scale of Per Centage
the
COMPARATIVE PROGRESS of POPULATION
in
ENGLAND, SCOTLAND AND IRELAND
from 1571 to 1841.
(The Data from 1571 to 1801 founded upon computations.)

NUMERICAL SUMMARY.

	Year	Population		
England & Wales	1377	2.350.000	in 464 years.	577 Pr Ct.
	1841	15.906.741		
Scotland	1371	470.000	in 470	457
	1841	2.620.184		
Ireland	1652	850.000	in 189	862
	1841	8.175.124		

NOTE

The dots connected by the coloured lines indicate periods to which computations and actual censuses relate : the Isle of Man, the Channel I.ˢ and the Army and Navy being excluded.

SCALE OF YEARS
SCALE OF PER CENTAGE

ENGLAND AND WALES
SCOTLAND
IRELAND

DIAGRAM
showing
by a Scale of Per Centage
the
COMPARATIVE PROGRESS of POPULATION
in
ENGLAND, WALES, SCOTLAND & IRELAND
from 1801 to 1841.
at the periods when the Censuses were taken.
(Excluding the I. of Man, Channel I.ˢ & Army and Navy.)

Numerical Summary

	Year	Population	
England	1801	8.331.434	80 Per Cent
	1841	14.995.138	
Wales	1801	541.546	68
	1841	911.603	
Scotland	1801	1.559.068	68
	1841	2.620.184	
Ireland	1801	4.499.252	64
	1841	8.175.124	

Scale of Years
SCALE OF PER CENTAGE

ENGLAND
IRELAND
SCOTLAND
WALES
ENG.ᴰ & SCOT.ᴺ

Synoptical Table
of the
Number and Total Population of all Towns containing
10.000 inhabitants and upwards.

	Towns of 100,000 inhabitants and upwards		Towns from 50,000 to 100,000 inh.		Towns from 20,000 to 50,000 inh.		Towns from 10,000 to 20,000 inh.		ALL TOWNS of 10,000 inh. & upwards	
	Number	Total Population	Number	Total Population	Number	Total Population	Number	Total Population	Number	Total Population
England	4	2.407.423	8	493.330	43	1.307.564	78	1.052.704	133	5.261.021
Wales					1	21.929	3	37.698	4	59.627
Scotland	2	412.506	2	123.841	3	110.994	5	67.414	12	714.755
Ireland	1	232.726	2	156.028	2	71.607	12	158.642	17	619.003
I.ˢ in the Brit. Seas							1	21.040	1	15.220	2	36.260
UNITED KINGDOM	7	3.052.655	12	773.199	50	1.533.134	99	1.331.678	168	6.690.666

Summary Account
of the
TOTAL POPULATION and AREA of the UNITED KINGDOM.

	Population June 6. 1841	State of increase &c	Amount of increase of population from June 6. 1841 to January 1.1849	Computed Population January 1.1849	Total area Engl. Statute Square miles
England	14.995.138				50.387
Wales	911.603				7.425
Scotland	2.620.184				30.238
I.ˢ in the Brit. Seas	124.040				.309
Army, Navy etc.	185.469				

SUTHERLAND
ROSS AND CROMARTY
INVERNESS
ARGYLL
Western Islands
Hebrides
DUNBARTON

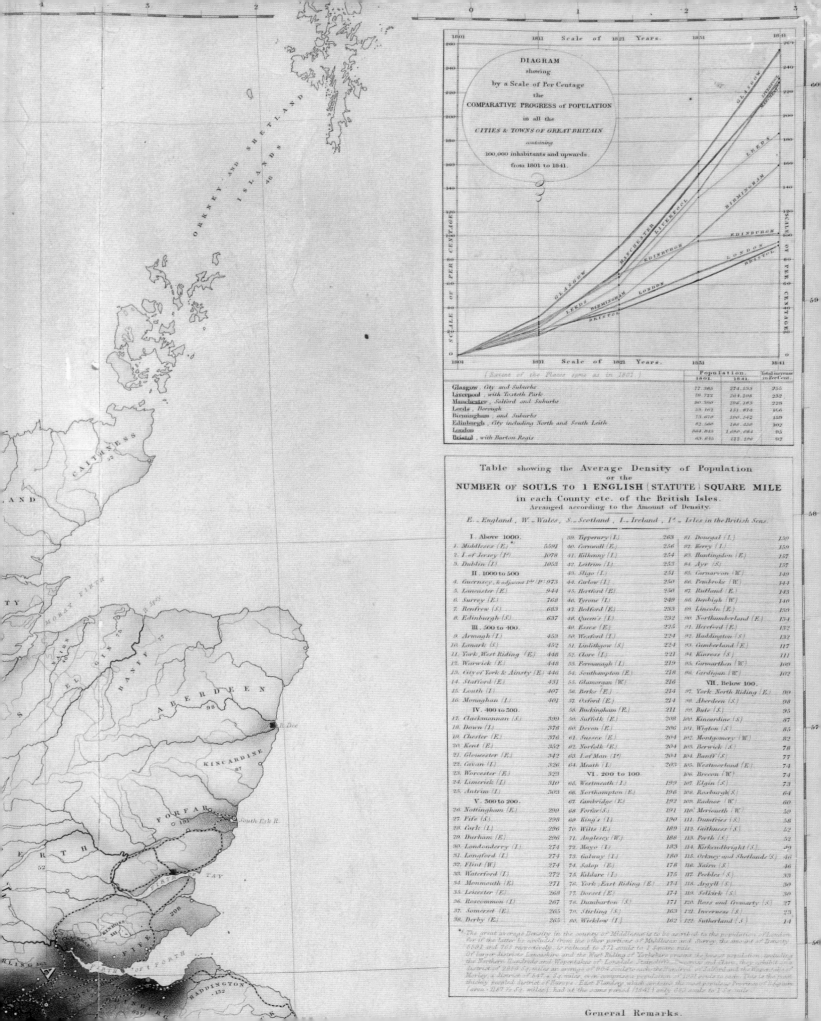

DIAGRAM
showing
by a Scale of Per Centage
the
COMPARATIVE PROGRESS of POPULATION
in all the
CITIES & TOWNS OF GREAT BRITAIN
containing
100,000 inhabitants and upwards.
from 1801 to 1841.

1801   1811   Scale of 1821 Years.   1831   1841

SCALE OF PER CENTAGE

SCALE OF PER CENTAGE

1801   1811   Scale of 1821 Years.   1831   1841

(Extent of the Places same as in 1801)

	Population 1801	Population 1841	Total increase in Per Cent
Glasgow, City and Suburbs	77,385	274,533	255
Liverpool, with Toxteth Park	79,722	264,298	232
Manchester, Salford and Suburbs	90,399	296,183	228
Leeds, Borough	53,162	151,874	166
Birmingham, and Suburbs	73,670	190,542	159
Edinburgh, City including North and South Leith	82,560	166,430	102
London	864,845	1,690,084	95
Bristol, with Barton Regis	63,645	122,296	92

Table showing the Average Density of Population
or the
NUMBER OF SOULS TO 1 ENGLISH (STATUTE) SQUARE MILE
in each County etc. of the British Isles.
Arranged according to the Amount of Density.

E. = England, W. = Wales, S. = Scotland, I. = Ireland, I⁵. = Isles in the British Seas.

I. Above 1000.
1. Middlesex (E.) — 5591
2. I. of Jersey (I⁵.) — 1078
3. Dublin (I.) — 1053

II. 1000 to 500.
4. Guernsey, & adjacent I⁵. (I⁵.) — 973
5. Lancaster (E.) — 944
6. Surrey (E.) — 768
7. Renfrew (S.) — 683
8. Edinburgh (S.) — 637

III. 500 to 400.
9. Armagh (I.) — 453
10. Lanark (S.) — 452
11. York, West Riding (E.) — 448
12. Warwick (E.) — 448
13. City of York & Ainsty (E.) — 446
14. Stafford (E.) — 431
15. Louth (I.) — 407
16. Monaghan (I.) — 401

IV. 400 to 300.
17. Clackmannan (S.) — 399
18. Down (I.) — 378
19. Chester (E.) — 376
20. Kent (E.) — 352
21. Gloucester (E.) — 342
22. Cavan (I.) — 326
23. Worcester (E.) — 323
24. Limerick (I.) — 310
25. Antrim (I.) — 303

V. 300 to 200.
26. Nottingham (E.) — 299
27. Fife (S.) — 298
28. Cork (I.) — 296
29. Durham (E.) — 296
30. Londonderry (I.) — 274
31. Longford (I.) — 274
32. Flint (W.) — 274
33. Waterford (I.) — 272
34. Monmouth (E.) — 271
35. Leicester (E.) — 268
36. Roscommon (I.) — 267
37. Somerset (E.) — 265
38. Derby (E.) — 265

39. Tipperary (I.) — 263
40. Cornwall (E.) — 256
41. Kilkenny (I.) — 254
42. Leitrim (I.) — 253
43. Sligo (I.) — 251
44. Carlow (I.) — 250
45. Hertford (E.) — 250
46. Tyrone (I.) — 249
47. Bedford (E.) — 233
48. Queen's (I.) — 232
49. Essex (E.) — 225
50. Wexford (I.) — 224
51. Linlithgow (S.) — 224
52. Clare (I.) — 221
53. Fermanagh (I.) — 219
54. Southampton (E.) — 218
55. Glamorgan (W.) — 216
56. Berks (E.) — 214
57. Oxford (E.) — 214
58. Buckingham (E.) — 211

VI. 200 to 100.
65. Westmeath (I.) — 199
66. Northampton (E.) — 196
67. Cambridge (E.) — 192
68. Forfar (S.) — 191
69. King's (I.) — 190
70. Wilts (E.) — 189
71. Anglesey (W.) — 188
72. Mayo (I.) — 183
73. Galway (I.) — 180
74. Salop (E.) — 178
75. Kildare (I.) — 175
76. York, East Riding (E.) — 174
77. Dorset (E.) — 174
78. Dumbarton (S.) — 171
79. Stirling (S.) — 163
80. Wicklow (I.) — 162

59. Suffolk (E.) — 208
60. Devon (E.) — 206
61. Sussex (E.) — 204
62. Norfolk (E.) — 204
63. I. of Man (I⁵.) — 204
64. Meath (I.) — 203

81. Donegal (I.) — 159
82. Kerry (I.) — 159
83. Huntingdon (E.) — 157
84. Ayr (S.) — 137
85. Carnarvon (W.) — 149
86. Pembroke (W.) — 144
87. Rutland (E.) — 143
88. Denbigh (W.) — 140
89. Lincoln (E.) — 130
90. Northumberland (E.) — 134
91. Hereford (E.) — 134
92. Haddington (S.) — 132
93. Cumberland (E.) — 117
94. Kinross (S.) — 111
95. Carmarthen (W.) — 109
96. Cardigan (W.) — 102

VII. Below 100.
97. York, North Riding (E.) — 99
98. Aberdeen (S.) — 98
99. Bute (S.) — 95
100. Kincardine (S.) — 87
101. Wigton (S.) — 85
102. Montgomery (W.) — 82
103. Berwick (S.) — 78
104. Banff (S.) — 77
105. Westmorland (E.) — 74
106. Brecon (W.) — 74
107. Elgin (S.) — 64
108. Roxburgh (S.) — 64
109. Radnor (W.) — 60
110. Merioneth (W.) — 59
111. Dumfries (S.) — 58
112. Lanark (S.) — 52
113. Perth (S.) — 52
114. Kirkcudbright (S.) — 50
115. Orkney and Shetlands (S.) — 46
116. Nairn (S.) — 46
117. Peebles (S.) — 33
118. Argyll (S.) — 30
119. Selkirk (S.) — 30
120. Ross and Cromarty (S.) — 27
121. Inverness (S.) — 23
122. Sutherland (S.) — 14

*. The great average Density in the county of Middlesex is to be ascribed to the population of London; for if the latter be excluded from the other portions of Middlesex and Surrey, the amount of Density 5591 and 768 respectively is reduced to 371 souls to 1 Square mile.
Of larger districts Lancashire and the West Riding of Yorkshire present the largest population including the Northern Hundreds and Wapentakes of Lonsdale Staincliffe, Ewcross and Claro, they exhibit in a district of 2954 Sq. miles an average of 964 souls to each ... in Salford and the Wapentakes of Morley, a district of 647 ... Sq. miles ... a comparative population of 1031 souls to each. This is the most thickly peopled district of Europe. East Flanders which contains the most populous Province of Belgium (area 1267½ Sq. miles) had at the same period (1841) only 582 souls to 1 Sq. mile.

General Remarks.

DATA JOURNALISM

John Snow, 'Showing the deaths from cholera in Broad Street, Golden Square,

and the neighbourhood, from 19th August to 30th September 1854', 1855.

Dr John Snow's book *On the Mode of Communication of Cholera* was published originally in 1849, and its second, much expanded edition in 1855 contained two maps, statistical tables and an appendix detailing the key local rates of cholera infection and deaths. Snow was also a prominent contributor to the *Report on the Cholera Outbreak in the Parish of St. James, Westminster, During the Autumn of 1854*, published by the Cholera Inquiry Committee in July 1855. The report also contained a map of the same Broad Street area founded on one produced in 1854 by Edmund Cooper for the Commissioners of Sewers (see detail, below), but with St. Anne's Court and neighbourhood added, tracing 351 deaths by house number. Cooper uses thick black lines to indicate homes in which cholera deaths occurred and shorter black bars stacked under the black lines to signify multiple deaths at a single location. Cooper's map contains an erroneous location for a 1665 plague burial site.

The boundaries are not easy to see in Snow's map of the Soho district, but within the outer boundary showing the area within which all the deaths are indicated there is a faint dotted line that shows the boundary of equal distance between the Broad Street Pump and other pumps. Within this, most of the deaths are located. As Snow summarised his presentation of the data: 'A black mark or bar for each death is placed in the situation of the house in which the fatal attack took place. The situation of the Broad Street Pump is also indicated, as well as that of all the surrounding Pumps to which the public had access.' Snow had identified the potentially fatal consequences of using contaminated public water supplies. His data-driven insight into cholera transmission was later reflected in a caricature called 'Death's Dispensary. Open to the Poor, Gratis, by Permission of the Parish', which showed Death pumping water for the poor, a bitter commentary on poverty, poor law, health and mortality – not as a consequence of individual moral failure but inadequate public sanitation and appalling urban living conditions.

Snow also mapped the boundaries of the Registrar-General's districts on the south side of the Thames and also the water supply of those districts. He used blue to indicate the Southwark and Vauxhall Company, red for the Lambeth Water Company and purple for the area in which the pipes of both companies intermingled.

In 1852, the Lambeth Water Company had changed its source of supply to Thames Ditton,

which was free from pollution by London sewage. In the red-shaded areas served exclusively by this company, there were only five deaths per 1,000 households. In contrast, the blue-shaded Southwark and Vauxhall Company's areas, served by water from the Thames at London Bridge, had a mortality rate of 71 per 1,000.

In the *Punch* cartoon 'Father Thames Introducing His Offspring To The Fair City of London' of 3 July 1858, a facetious design for a fresco for the new Houses of Parliament, a filthy Thames, polluted by factories, sewage and steamships, presented diphtheria, scrofula and cholera. This episode of foul-smelling atmosphere, known as the Great Stink, was an ironic counterpart to the triumphalist character of the rebuilding of Parliament after it was largely destroyed by fire in 1834.

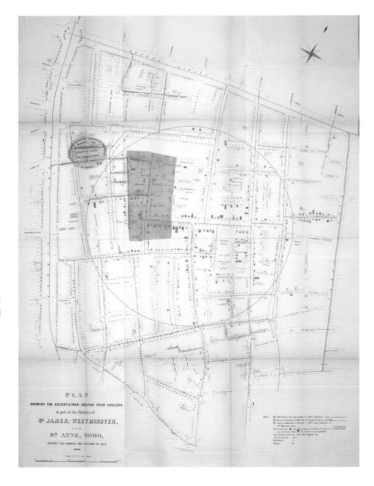

NOTE. Boundary within which all the Deaths are indicated, is shewn thus, ... Divisions between Sub-Districts, thus, ... Boundary of equal distance between Broad Street Pump and other Pumps, thus, ...

SCALE 30 INCHES TO A MILE.

AS DIVIDED INTO UNIONS BY THE POOR LAW COMMISSIONERS.

The Name of the Union is underlined in Red.

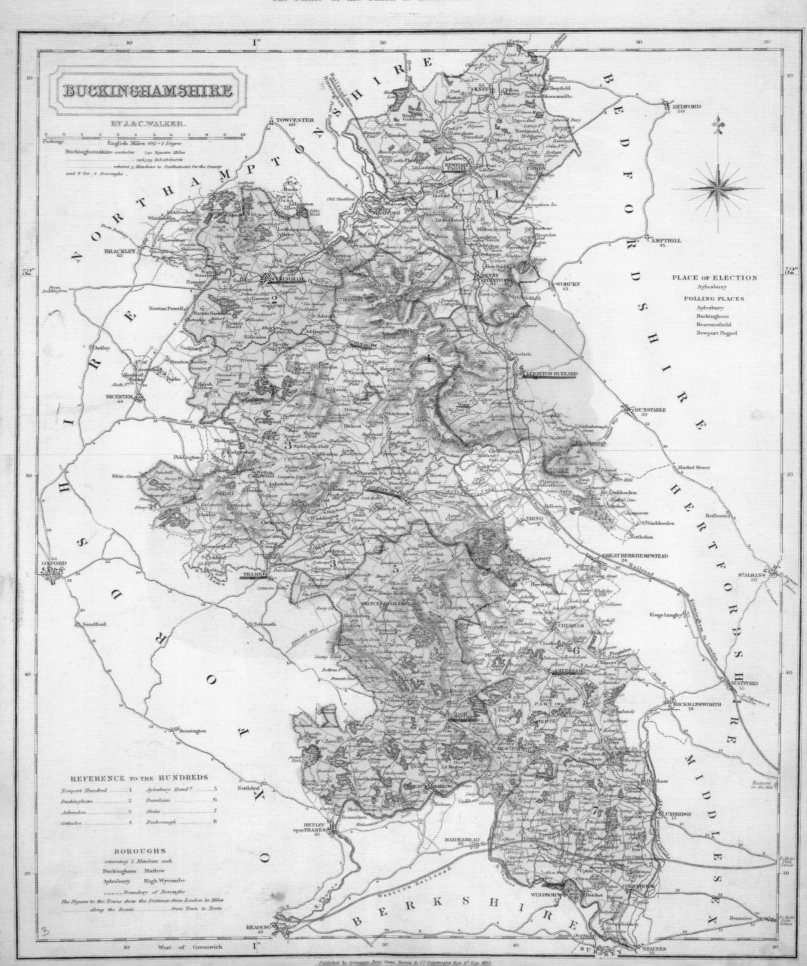

BUCKINGHAMSHIRE

BY J. & C. WALKER.

English Miles 69½ = 1 Degree

Buckinghamshire contains 740 Square Miles
146,529 Inhabitants
returns 3 Members to Parliament for the County
and 8 for 4 Boroughs.

PLACE OF ELECTION
Aylesbury

POLLING PLACES
Aylesbury
Buckingham
Beaconsfield
Newport Pagnel

REFERENCE TO THE HUNDREDS

Newport Hundred	1	Aylesbury Hund.d	5
Buckingham	2	Burnham	6
Ashendon	3	Stoke	7
Cottesloe	4	Desborough	8

BOROUGHS

returning 2 Members each

Buckingham   Marlow
Aylesbury   High Wycombe

———— Boundary of Boroughs

The Figures to the Towns show the Distance from London in Miles
along the Roads   from Town to Town

Published by Longman, Rees, Orme, Brown & C.º Paternoster Row 1st Nov.r 1835.

POOR LAW

J & C. Walker, 'Buckinghamshire as Divided into Unions by the Poor Law Commissioners', 1870.

The attempt to replace the parish-based system of localised relief of poverty that had existed in England since the sixteenth century by creating a comprehensive national system of social welfare under the 1834 Poor Law Amendment Act created much need for mapping. Indeed, this mapping was a feature of the reform legislation of the period – as with electoral reform and that of the administration of tithes. The Poor Law Commission oversaw the division of the country into Poor Law Unions. Alongside reports seeking to guide this process came maps that recorded its stages, for both national and local attention, with the inclusion and exclusion of particular parishes reflecting lobbying by the local magistrates. For example, a report in 1835 by William Gilbert, an Assistant Poor Law Commissioner, was accompanied by a map describing the envisaged Newport Pagnell Poor Law Union, duly formed that September. By the time the county maps were being compiled some years later, Newport Pagnell was one of seven unions, each underlined in red in the map, within Buckinghamshire, alongside Amersham, Aylesbury, Buckingham, Eton (Windsor), Winslow and Wycombe.

The plan (below) for Thurgarton workhouse in Southwell, Nottinghamshire, was particularly important because it was regarded by the Poor Law Commission as a model for the Union Workhouses. It was designed by William Nicholson to plans by the Reverend J.T. Becher and built in 1824 at the cost of £6,596 to house 158 paupers. In 1836 it became the Southwell Union Workhouse. Most of the inmates were younger women or older men. Initially, there was a punishment regime for reprobates, of breaking stones and being locked in solitude, but this was dropped. The main block of the workhouse provided an architecture of control. Aside from the central hub for the Master's accommodation, there were wings for

the three segregated groups: men, women and children, while, in accordance with Becher's views, the stairs were intended to divide the idle and profligate poor from the blameless and infirm, a spatial segregation that extended to the exercise and work yards.

Overseen by the Poor Law Commissioners in London, the uniform workhouse system that the legislation sought to create was deliberately not generous to its inmates for fear that this would both discourage people from working and impose too high a burden on ratepayers. Outdoor relief was abolished for the able-bodied. Instead, they were obliged to enter the workhouse, where they were to be treated no better than the conditions that could be expected outside, in order to deter all bar the very destitute from being 'a charge' on that community. Bastardy, and indigent marriage and parenthood, were to be discouraged. In general, expenditure on the workhouses was severely controlled, discipline was harsh and the stigma attached to dependent poverty grew.

As a result, in Wimborne in Dorset, for example, workhouse beds had to be shared, meat was only provided once a week, there were no vegetables other than potatoes until 1849, men and women were segregated, and unmarried mothers had to wear distinctive clothes. Revealed in 1845, the Andover workhouse scandal indicated an abusive and corrupt master of the workhouse and totally inadequate rations. In response, the House of Commons set up a committee in 1846 that revealed serious mismanagement in the oversight of the Act.

There was some active popular opposition to the workhouses. That at Gainsborough in Lincolnshire was destroyed while it was being built in 1837, and there were also disturbances elsewhere. Todmorden in Yorkshire was for many years the sole English Poor Law Union area without a workhouse. Opposition there owed much to John Fielden, a wealthy cotton manufacturer and radical MP. More generally, far from there being a total shift to the workhouses, a degree of outdoor relief continued in many places.

Dickens was opposed more to the nature of the administration of the Poor Law, as in *Oliver Twist*, than to the particular regulations themselves, but the latter are also castigated in the shape of their impact. In *Our Mutual Friend*, Betty Higden is terrified of the workhouse: 'Kill me sooner than take me there.' Dickens used this to criticise the 'Lords and gentlemen and Honourable Boards'.

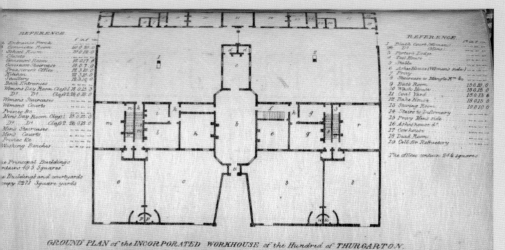

GROUND PLAN of the INCORPORATED WORKHOUSE of the Hundred of THURGARTON.

GEOGRAPHY OF RELIGION

Edwin H. Tindall, 'Wesleyan Methodist Map of the Macclesfield, Sheffield, and Nottingham & Derby Districts', *c.*1873.

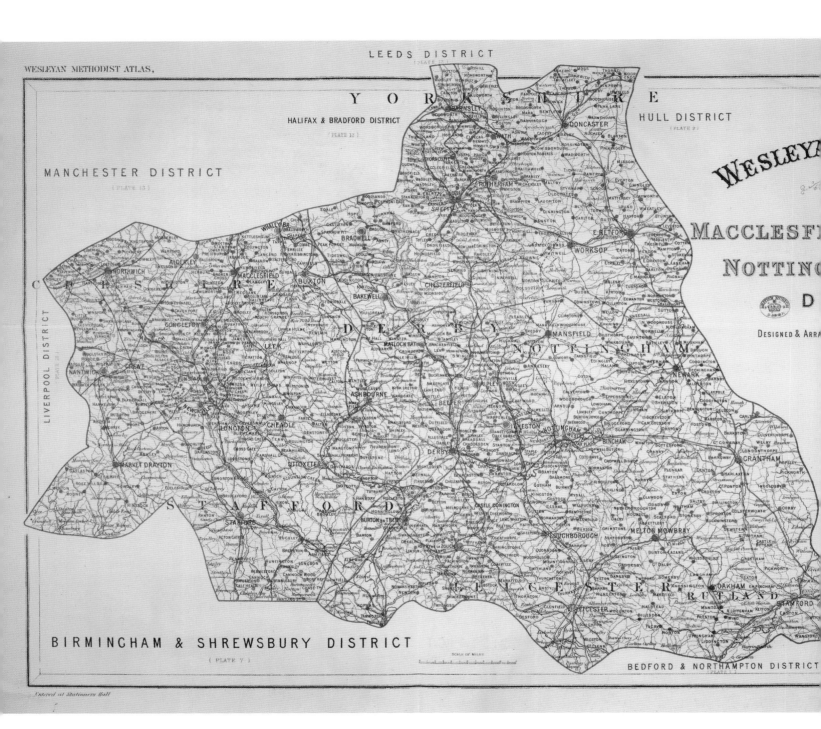

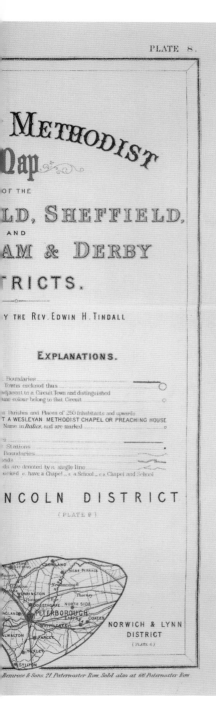

PLATE 8.

METHODIST
Oap
OF THE
LD, SHEFFIELD,
AND
AM & DERBY
RICTS.

Y THE REV. EDWIN H. TINDALL

EXPLANATIONS.

Boundaries
Towns enclosed thus
adjacent to a Circuit Town and distinguished
ame colour belong to that Circuit

s Parishes and Places of 250 inhabitants and upwards
T A WESLEYAN METHODIST CHAPEL OR PREACHING HOUSE
Name in *Italics*, and are marked

Stations
Boundaries
vais
ds are denoted by a single line
arked c. have a Chapel ... s. a School ... cs. Chapel and School

NCOLN DISTRICT
[PLATE 9]

NORWICH & LYNN
DISTRICT
[PLATE 6]

Bemrose & Sons 21 Paternoster Row Sold also at 66 Paternoster Row

Reverend Edwin H. Tindall's *The Wesleyan Methodist Atlas of England and Wales* (c.1873) is an enormous volume that includes 15 two-page maps of Methodist districts showing circuits, chapels, towns and railway lines. Tables cover the 1871 census population of parishes, the provision of chapels (and whether owned or rented), with their sitting accommodation (on the basis of a need of 20 inches per person), and the fluctuation in Wesleyan Society members every census year from 1801. The use of colour serves well to capture the circuit areas without having to use linear boundaries that would clash with the use of lines for communication routes. This particular map also provides a clear visual guide to the density of Methodist facilities, with clear concentrations in areas of industrial activity, notably the Potteries, as well as round Derby, Macclesfield, Northwich and Sheffield. This linkage of industry and Low Church activity went back to the sixteenth century, being seen for example in those parts of Derbyshire that supported the Parliamentary cause in the 1640s. In part, the Established Church (the Church of England) proved poor in serving such areas of expanding population.

Tindall's effort followed William Buckley Haigh's synopsis of *Wesleyan Methodism in Yorkshire and Companion to the County Plan of Circuits* (1830) and the *Agency and Progress of Wesleyan-Methodism as Exemplified by Statistical Details, and Considered with Reference to its Facilities for Promoting and Sustaining a General Revival of Religion throughout the Country* (1845).

Circuit plans were a major form of Methodist mapping that the organisation felt to be important, but the energy for new activity came from the 1851 religious census of England and Wales, which reported more irreligion than had been anticipated (only 60.8 per cent of the population were in church that 30 March), and led to subsequent Nonconformist attempts to establish the nature of public devotion. On Census Sunday, 48.6 per cent of those in church were in Anglican churches, especially in the rural south and in small towns, and 51.4 per cent in others, notably in the cities.

The expansion of the industrial cities, such as Sheffield, stretched existing church provision. In many cases, despite the goals of the Nonconformist denominations insufficient places of worship were built. Also, as suggested by Dickens, the mission of the churches did not necessarily elicit a response. Nevertheless, industrialisation was also linked to religious revival in some areas. There was a powerful movement of reform, with committed clerics seeking to make Christian teaching more accessible.

The number of religious newspapers rose markedly from the late 1820s, and their confessions, often lurid tales of sin, redemption and retribution, provided readily grasped content, notably an exciting series of individual morality tales that paralleled crime literature and secular newspaper reporting. The religious press overlapped with other religious publications, including sermons, poetry and novels. Indeed, sermons probably sold more than novels and poetry until the 1850s, and Charles Spurgeon, the magnetic Baptist preacher (1834–92), possibly sold more sermons than the works of any individual novelist.

The churches were also in competition, with local circumstances playing a major role. The Church of England faced particular difficulties in Wales and northern England, while the re-emergence of 'public' Catholicism, with the re-establishment of the Catholic hierarchy in England in 1850 and in Scotland in 1878, caused tension, accentuated by massive Irish immigration that had greater impact due to its concentration in particular centres, notably London, Liverpool and Glasgow. While anti-Catholicism was strengthened by anxiety about the Irish, there was also a fear of growing 'unbelief', gaining respectability through the development of Darwinism, which encouraged a relativism about religion. In addition, drink kept devotion at bay, and concern about alcohol encouraged a growing temperance movement. John Davis, the Anglican Rector of St Clement's Worcester, reported in 1851 that his working-class parishioners: '...seldom ever attend Sunday Morning Service. The Saturday Market and the late payment of wages on the evening of that day contribute probably in no small degree to produce this.'

THE NATIONAL RAIL NETWORK

John Airey, *Airey's Railway Map of England & Wales*, 1877.

John Airey was an employee of the Railway Clearing House, which existed from 1842 to 1963, and a prolific producer of railway maps. From 1859 onwards the Clearing House issued these maps, which initially had been restricted to diagrams showing the junctions where two or more railway companies met. This map provides an overview of the extensive railway network in England and Wales, including the companies running the principal lines, whereas Airey's series of district maps provided more detail, from stations, junctions and sidings to private lines, canals and docks. Airey's *Railway Map of London and the Suburbs* (1875) was particularly skilful in depicting the complex system with clarity by using the possibilities offered by chromolithographic printing to employ many different colours in order to identify the different lines. Both overground and underground lines were shown, and thus their integration was made clear, notably the role of the Metropolitan Underground Railway in linking mainline London termini.

The integration of railway lines meant infrastructure that wrought massive change upon the existing urban landscape – or 'improvements', in the language of the day: replacing ancient streets and neighbourhoods with the creations of a new civilisation. For example, in London Camden Town and nearby areas were transformed by the building of Euston, King's Cross and St Pancras stations, and their extensive supporting marshalling yards and lines, the biggest concentration of major stations and railway facilities in the country. As Dickens captured it:

'The first shock of a great earthquake had … rent the whole neighbourhood to its centre… Houses were knocked down; streets broken through and stopped… Everywhere were bridges that led nowhere… mounds of ashes blocked up rights of way, and wholly changed the law and custom of the neighbourhood… the yet unfinished and unopened Railroad was in progress, and, from the very core of all this dire disorder, trailed smoothly away, upon its mighty course of civilisation and improvement.'

Airey published a railway map of Scotland in 1875, and others of Yorkshire in 1883, the West of England in 1886 and of Lancashire in 1887. Railway Clearing House maps went on being produced until the mid-twentieth century. Maps for internal company purposes, such as junction diagrams and signalling, had a need for exactness that was less of a priority for those maps for public consumption, where clarity was more important and mapping therefore more schematic. The latter could exaggerate ease of use and directness, and also downplay the role of competitors. Advertising provided an important part of the economics.

There is no perfect way to map a rail system because a number of factors play a role, including the purpose, audience and type of system. As far as the last is concerned, there are major contrasts between freight and passenger, and between intercity and intracity. There is also the contrast between the individual route and the system as a whole. In each case, there is a tendency to ignore many geographical features because what may bulk large in the construction, notably the topography and hydrology, can be superseded, notably by tunnels, cuttings and bridges.

Thanks to the train, the meaning of place in Victorian Britain changed both locally and nationally. Edinburgh and Glasgow were now closer to London as an aspect of a national network for which York and Manchester were merely important stages. Dublin was brought closer, with expresses from London to Holyhead (crossing the Menai Strait on a dramatic bridge in 1850), followed by steamships thence to Ireland. The journey time from London to Holyhead was cut to nine hours 35 minutes compared to 40 hours by mail coach.

The number of letters delivered in the British Isles rose from 82.5 million in 1839 to 411 million in 1853, with a relatively inexpensive uniform charging system introduced in 1840 and the Penny Black, the world's first postage stamp, released. Pride in the system even led to the production of ceramic tiled maps – for example in York and Manchester Victoria stations.

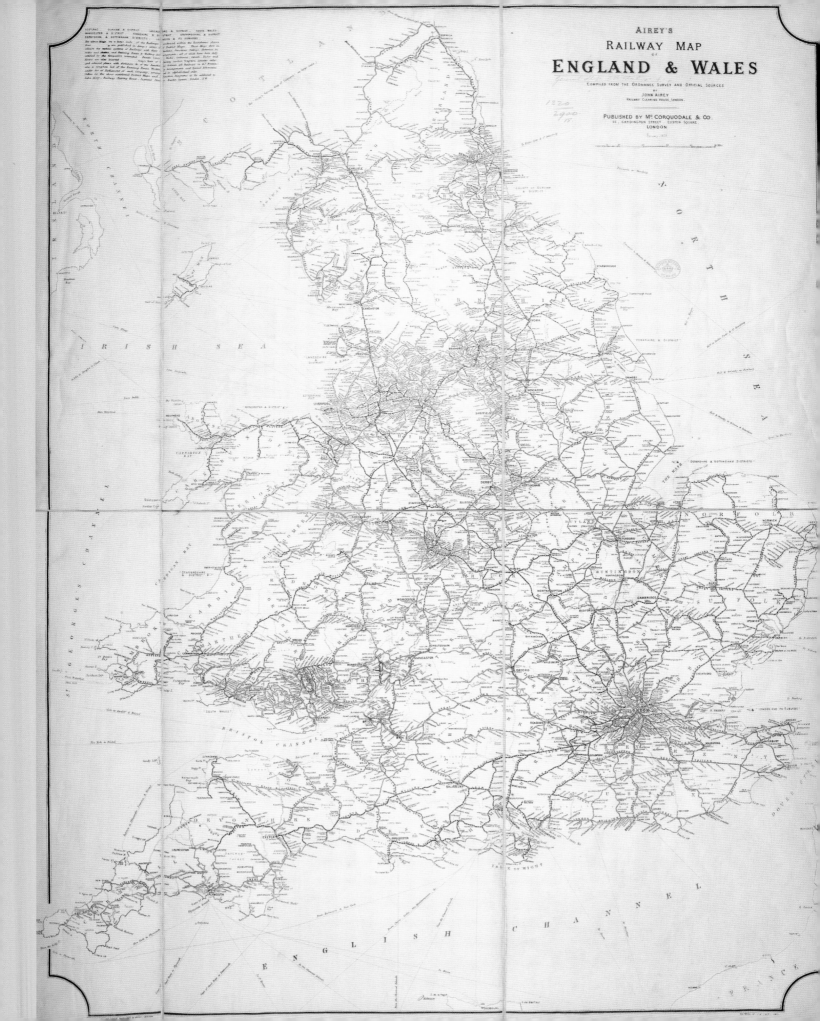

AIREY'S
RAILWAY MAP
OF
ENGLAND & WALES

COMPILED FROM THE ORDNANCE SURVEY AND OFFICIAL SOURCES
BY
JOHN AIREY
RAILWAY CLEARING HOUSE, LONDON.

PUBLISHED BY McCORQUODALE & CO.
31, CARDINGTON STREET, EUSTON SQUARE,
LONDON

Charles Booth, 'North-Eastern sheet, comprising parts of Hackney, Islington, and Holborn; the whole of the City, Shoreditch, Bethnal Green, Whitechapel, St. George's-in-the-East, Stepney, Mile End, and Part of Poplar', 1889.

Charles Booth's 12 maps of London poverty took several years work and cover London from Hammersmith in the west to Greenwich in the east, and from Hampstead in the north to Clapham in the south. The City of London is not covered and therefore unclassified. The maps were published in the book *Descriptive Map of London Poverty* (1889), with the East London part of his survey originally prepared in 1887. There was a subjective dimension to Booth's classification, but the context was a scientific one of the gathering, depiction and analysis of information. He classified and coloured streets in terms of the general condition of the inhabitants, who were categorised in seven bands from the lowest to the highest classes. The lowest was denoted by black and presented as 'vicious, semi-criminal'; the highest was indicated by yellow, consisting of the upper classes and wealthy. Yellow is not the dominant colour of East London, but along the main roads, where the houses were more substantial, there was much red and that indicated the second-highest tranche: 'Middle class. Well-to-do.' In between these ranged four other categories: 'Fairly comfortable. Good ordinary earnings.' in pink; 'Mixed. Some comfortable, others poor.' in purple; 'Poor. 18s. to 21s. a week for a moderate family.' in light blue; and 'Very poor, casual. Chronic want.' in dark blue.

Poverty, both moral and material, were associated in the Victorian mind with idleness, drunkenness and depravity. Booth's mapping accentuated the idea of location and social degredation. The East End of London, overwhelming populated by British and Irish migrants and foreign immigrants, such as Eastern European Jews and Chinese, was both alien and intimidating for many. Charles Booth recorded that by 1888 the Jews of Whitechapel had begun to expand beyond Commercial Street and into 'Hanbury Street, Fashion Street, Pelham Street, Booth Street, Old Montague Street, and many streets and lanes and alleys...'. At more or less the same time as Booth was surveying these areas, from 1888 to 1891 a series of 11 murders took place in Whitechapel, five of which have become world famous. Like other *causes célèbres*, the case of Jack the Ripper brought out Victorian phobias – sex and the city, as well as immigration. Interest in crime was a preoccupation of newspapers. London's East End was created as an area of crime in part by such depictions in both newspapers and

New York World, 9 November 1888.

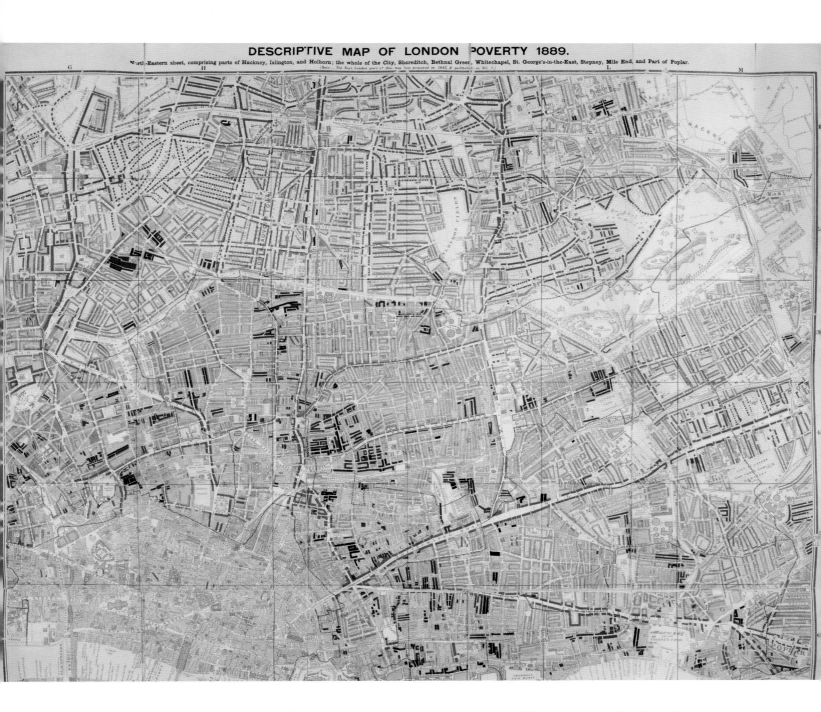

DESCRIPTIVE MAP OF LONDON POVERTY 1889.

North-Eastern sheet, comprising parts of Hackney, Islington, and Holborn; the whole of the City, Shoreditch, Bethnal Green, Whitechapel, St. George's-in-the-East, Stepney, Mile End, and Part of Poplar.

[Note.—The East London part of this map was prepared in 1887, & published in Vol. 1.]

fiction, as in Dickens's *The Mystery of Edwin Drood* (1870), Thomas Burke's *Limehouse Nights* (1917) and the *Fu Manchu* stories of Arthur Sarsfield, a one-time crime reporter in Limehouse, who wrote under the pseudonym Sax Rohmer. East London was soon to provide the setting for stories of innocents seduced in Chinese opium dens. Arthur Conan Doyle made use of their sinister reputation, while Agatha Christie in *The Lost Mine* (1923) presented an opium den in Limehouse, its trapdoor and Limehouse's evil-smelling streets. In *The People of the Abyss* (1903), the popular American writer Jack London described the East End as somewhere 'the obscenities and brute vulgarities

of life are rampant'. He added: 'There is no privacy. The bad corrupts the good, and all fester together. Innocent childhood is sweet and beautiful; but in East London innocence is a fleeting thing, and you must catch them before they crawl out of the cradle, or you will find the very babes as unholily wise as you.'

Dorset Street in Spitalfields, where the infamous Jack the Ripper claimed his final victim, Mary Jane Kelly (see detail, opposite, reported as 'Lawrence') in 1888, was said to be the worst street in London: 'There were pubs every few yards. Bawdy houses [brothels] every few feet. It was peopled by roaring drunken fighting – mad killers.'

PLACE IMAGINED

Thomas Hardy, 'The Wessex of The Novels', 1895.

Maps of Britain included those of places realised by novelists writing 'Condition of England' novels. To readers, these were part of a real world, and they deserve attention accordingly. The frontispiece of Thomas Hardy's *The Return of the Native* (1878) contains a topographical map of Egdon Heath with place names marked. The map is not particularly attractive, but it helped the reader to locate the action.

The map of Wessex specifically endorsed by Hardy first appeared in the 1895–97 edition published by Osgood, McIlvaine, and Co., and has continued to appear thereafter, as with the endpapers in the 1920 edition in which the real place names appear in a regular font while Hardy's fictional names appear in italics. In his preface to the 1895 edition, Hardy emphasised the reality of the Wessex background:

'In the present edition it may be well to state, in response to inquiries from readers interested in landscape, pre-historic antiquities, and especially old English architecture, that the description of these backgrounds in this and its companion novels has been done from the real. Many features of the first two kinds have been given under their existing names... In respect of places described under fictitious or ancient name – for reasons that seemed good at the time of writing – discerning persons have affirmed in point that they clearly recognise the originals, such as Shaftesbury in 'Shaston' ... I shall not be the first to contradict them.'

Dorchester is Casterbridge, Exonbury is Exeter, Christminster is Oxford, Melchester is Salisbury and Toneborough is Taunton. Wessex was a movable feast for Hardy. It could be his native county of Dorset, which, as this map shows, has the densest set of references, but it came to encompass much of Southwest and even South England. Yet, for Hardy, Wessex came to represent an identity, that of a rural world with a strong link to nature and an often harsh environment. As a result, Wessex was differentiated from the urban, industrial world that was becoming so dominant in Britain.

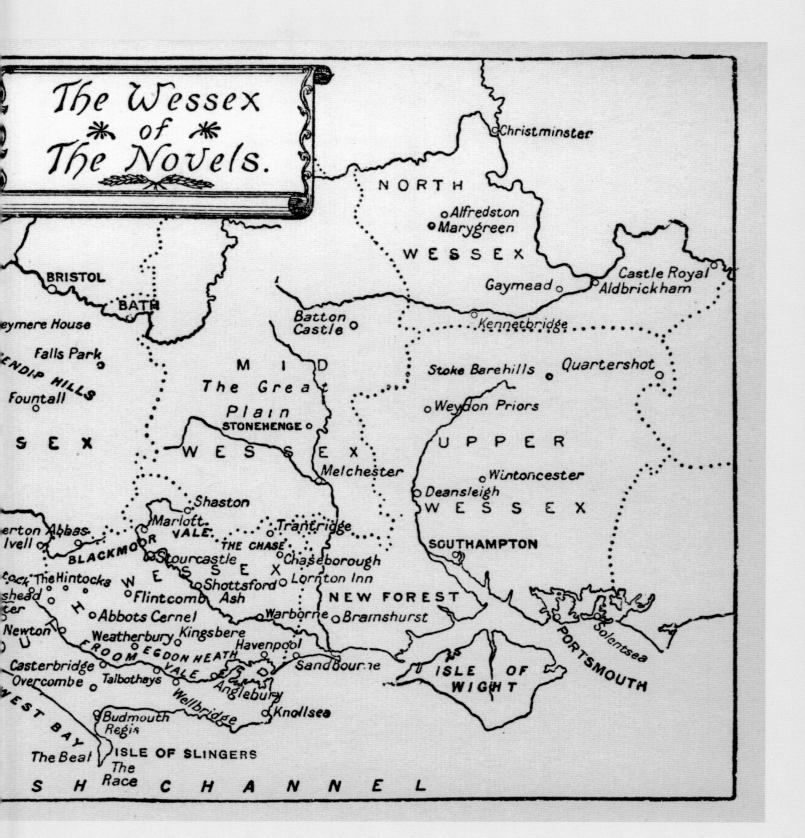

The Wessex
* of *
The Novels.

Christminster

NORTH

Alfredston
Marygreen

WESSEX

BRISTOL

BATH

Castle Royal
Gaymead
Aldbrickham

eymere House

Batton
Castle

Kennetbridge

Falls Park

MID

Stoke Barehills
Quartershot

ENDIP HILLS

Fountall

The Grea

Plain

Weydon Priors

UPPER

STONEHENGE

SEX

WESSEX

Melchester

Wintoncester
Deansleigh
WESSEX

Shaston

erton Abbas
Ivell

Marlott
VALE

Trantridge

SOUTHAMPTON

BLACKMOR

THE CHASE

tock The Hintocks
shead
ter

Stourcastle
W E S S E X
Shottsford

Chaseborough
Lornton Inn

Flintcomb Ash

NEW FOREST

Newton

Abbots Cernel

Warborne
Bramshurst

Weatherbury
Kingsbere

FROOM

EGDON HEATH

Havenpool

Casterbridge

VALE

Sandbourne

ISLE OF
WIGHT

Overcombe

Talbothays

Anglebury

Wellbridge

Knollsea

WEST BAY

Budmouth
Regis

The Beal

ISLE OF SLINGERS

The
Race

CHANNEL

Solentsea

PORTSMOUTH

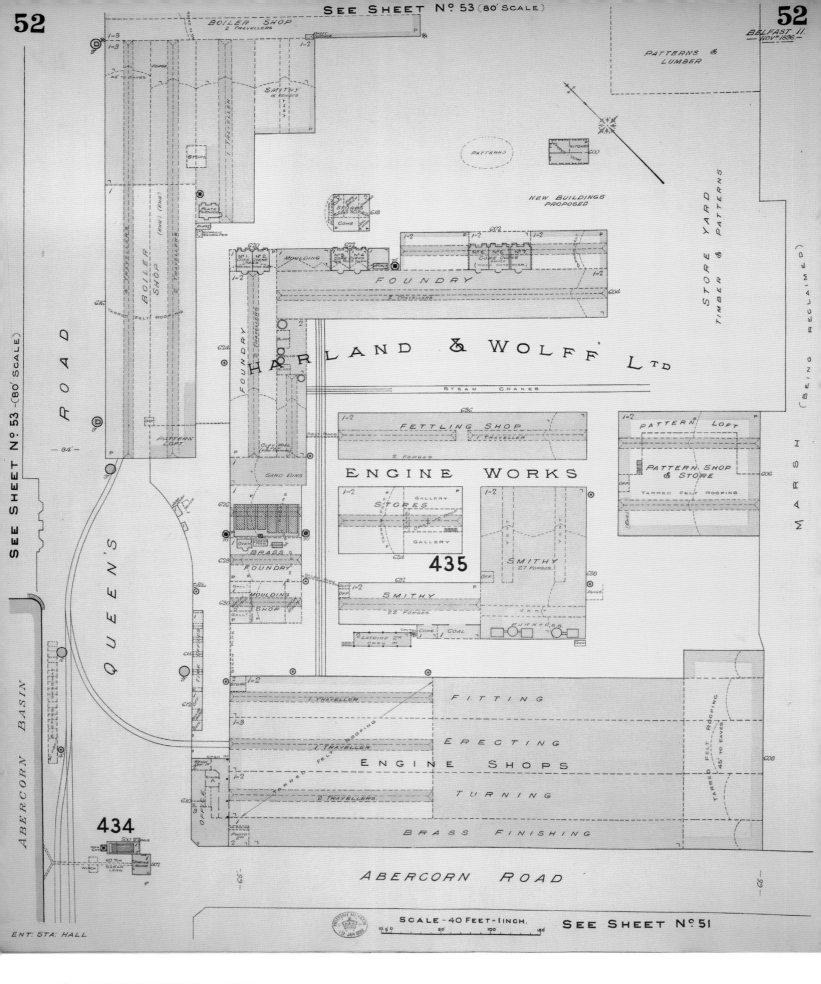

TITANIC TOWN

Charles E. Goad Ltd., 'Insurance Plan of Belfast', 1898.

Urban and industrial growth in late Victorian Britain created a new demand for mapping that detailed urban structures and land use. Whereas in the past the destructiveness of fires had resulted in a need for new maps of new areas, in the nineteenth century the high-density centres of trade and industry fire represented a quantifiable risk to commercial interests, which gave rise to mapping that could help insurance companies to assess the fire risks they were underwriting. Numerous mapping companies specialised in this activity, but the largest in Britain was the civil engineering firm Charles E. Goad Ltd., established in 1885. Its large-scale plans of urban areas include footprints and addresses for each building, its height, use (commercial, residential, educational) and construction materials (and thus its risk of burning), as well as information about special fire hazards (chemicals, kilns). The mapped information might also indicate whether there was a likelihood of a large group of people in a building, such as in a school or a place of worship. This plan is sheet 52 of the company's map of Belfast from its 1887–1898 series of fire insurance maps of cities in Britain and Ireland. The plan of the Harland and Wolff shipyard is clearly scaled and makes readily apparent the complexity of a major shipbuilder and the probity of a range of activities and stores, including the boiler shop, smithy, foundry, plate furnace, brass foundry and various ovens. The plan was accompanied by a detailed explanatory key for the various signs used (see detail, left).

The economy of Ireland grew as part of the expanding imperial economy, although the canal network was less extensive than in Britain and the railway system was established more slowly. Belfast developed as a great port and with manufacturing industry based on linen, shipyards and tobacco. Its expansion, however, saw the growth of patterns of urban segregation rooted in religion.

Britain was then the leading shipbuilder in the world, albeit with changing patterns in the location of activity. London had been a key centre. Peter the Great of Russia had visited the dockyard of Deptford in 1698 to learn shipbuilding techniques, but, despite its use by Brunel, London declined in the nineteenth century to the benefit of Glasgow, Sunderland and Newcastle.

Cork had been the main place for Irish shipbuilding, but by the 1900s both Harland and Wolff (founded in 1861) and the lesser-known Workman Clark (founded in 1880) were launching 150,000 tons annually despite a lack of local coal, timber and steel, as well as being distant from the sea on the narrow River Lagan. The launching of the Titanic in 1912 and the Britannic in 1914 reflected a specialty in building liners and more specifically the building of a massive twin slipway and associated gantry structure.

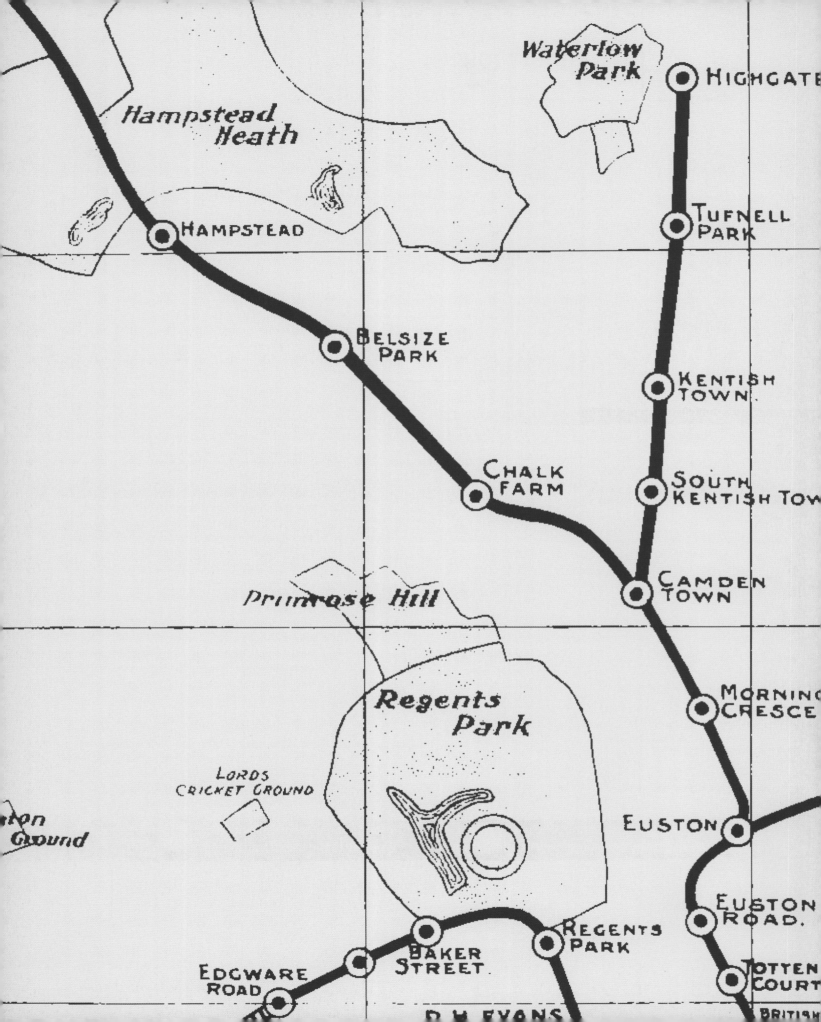

5
1900–60:
WAR AND TRANSFORMATION

Although cartography in some respects remained traditional in its contents and forms, notions of environmental influence became more pronounced, with atlases devoting more attention to physical details, especially terrain. Moreover, such influence could apparently be mapped, and could demonstrate the value of mapping, maps and map-reading, with the maps both descriptive and explanatory.

Demand for maps grew in both scale and range. The increase in the scope of government played a role. So also did the rising disposable income of a growing population. Many households acquired an atlas.

Production methods continued to develop, offering greater scale and ease. Lithographical printing dominated map reproduction, with chromolithography employed to produce multi-colour printed maps. In addition, pre-printing enhancements made it easier to use printable images for the purpose of creating a map. Photomechanical processes saved on labour and also produced multiple exact copies. All the while, photographic equipment and materials improved.

Moreover, advances in colour printing made it easier both to include more physical detail, most obviously by colour-coding elements (to indicate contour or rainfall or poverty zones), and to juxtapose such details with others to suggest causation. The use of colour increased the density and complexity of information that could be conveyed, as well as the aesthetic appeal. Aside from the degree to which the 'lesson' of the map had to be presented and grasped, there was now more information to assimilate, not least through a process of separating out the components and then integrating them in a comprehensible form. With maps being used as a tool for analysis rather than merely as illustration, distribution maps were particularly important in investigation and exposition. Moreover, they brought the authority of scholarship to the evaluation of the present, and vice versa. Difference helped to define regions, and in *The Geography behind History* (1938), Gordon East claimed that 'the efforts of geographers ... converge above all on one common goal – the discovery, description and demarcation of regions – broadly uniform areas of country which can be distinguished on a scientific basis'. Allowing for variations in scale, that was indeed the case.

In the interwar period, there was a shift that stressed mass production rather than craftsmanship. The changes threatened traditional standards of quality. It is not surprising that map-readers prefer nineteenth-century maps, with their copper engraving or lithographic drawing, to the atlases of the first half of the twentieth century.

Yet, if graphic quality and appeal were compromised, most atlases were still well up to their task technically, and a decline in precision of line was not too serious given the scale used in most maps. Moreover, the greater availability of maps ensured that more information was spatially depicted. After the Second World War, the use of transparent overlaps of plastic material for drawing and scribing spread rapidly, with photography taking a key role in map production: maps were compiled as a multi-layered system of overlays, with information registered on a base map on which typographers had placed type.

PROVINCIAL POVERTY

Benjamin Seebohm Rowntree, 'Plan of the City of York', 1901.

In 1901, inspired by Charles Booth's work in London, the book *Poverty: A Study of Town Life* by Benjamin Seebohm Rowntree (1871–1954) was published, which included two colour-coded maps of York. Rowntree's stated aim was to investigate the social and economic conditions of 'the wage-earning classes' in his native, provincial city. In particular, he was keen to discover whether poverty was the result of 'insufficiency of income' or 'improvidence'.

The demographic map of York is shaded in four colours, indicating areas ranging from poor to affluent. Grey represented: 'The poorest districts of the city, comprising the slum areas. Some of the main streets in these districts are, however, of a better class.' Yellow represented: 'Districts inhabited by the working classes, but comprising a few houses where servants are kept.' Pink represented: 'The main business streets, consisting of shops and offices. Between these principal streets are many old and narrow lanes and courts.' Green represented: 'Districts inhabited by the servant-keeping class.'

Although subjective views played a role, the context was the scientific one of a gathering, depiction and analysis of information. Based on Booth's study of London, a study presented with the support of maps, but adopting a different approach, Rowntree also found that poverty and ill-health were linked, and he argued that poverty was largely due to low wages. He determined that 27.8 per cent of the people in York, a key railway town, were living below the poverty line.

At the same time, Rowntree was critical of expenditure on drink, which was a standard theme of Nonconformist and Liberal politicians. So also with Booth, who had very harshly argued that the life of the lowest social class '... is the life of savages, with vicissitudes of extreme hardship and their only luxury is drink,' and thus presented poverty as a threat to civil society. Rowntree's second map showed, atop the base of the first map, the location of the city's licensed premises, including clubs, off-licences and public houses. The lower frequency of pubs outside the city's centre owed much to the hostility of Justices of the Peace to the granting of licences. Pubs were the centre of sociability, particularly for singing, gaming and prostitution for the poor, who had few alternative places, as well as offering well-lit, warm and dry premises and a group privacy protected by frosted glass. In Dickens's *Martin Chuzzlewit*, Mark Tapley found the Dragon Inn a centre of activity:

'...skittles, cricket, quoits, nine-pins, comic songs, choruses, company round the chimney corner every winter's evening.' The snobbish Pecksniff, in contrast, typically finds 'the very sight of skittles ... far from being congenial to a delicate mind,' and an amusement of the 'very vulgar'.

Rowntree wrote of York: 'Many of the songs are characterised by maudlin sentimentality; others again are unreservedly vulgar. Throughout the whole assembly there is an air of jollity and an absence of irksome restraint which must prove very attractive after a day's confinement in factory or shop.' In contrast, York's central streets where the wealthy lived, notably Bootham, Clifton and Monkgate, had very few pubs, because they were not part of the society of that social group.

A member of a Quaker chocolate manufacturing family, Rowntree focused on the structural causes of poverty rather than presenting it as a product of moral failure. He proved that poverty was not focused on London but rather widespread. Rowntree also developed the idea of the poverty cycle, with childhood and old age being particular periods of absolute poverty where basic needs could not be covered.

Poor urban housing, sanitation and nutrition were widely blamed for the physical condition of much of the population. The British Army found this a serious problem at the time of the Boer War (1899–1902), while the Metropolitan Police thought their London recruits were physically weak, and defeats at the hands of the visiting New Zealand All Blacks rugby team in 1905 led to discussion about a supposed physical and moral decline arising from the country's urban and industrial nature.

Rowntree's ideas were to influence the Liberal social reforms of the late 1900s, which included temperance. In 1908, the Liberal Prime Minister, Herbert Asquith, suggested closing a third of the pubs, but this was defeated in the House of Lords, although taxation on pubs increased. In 1918, in *The Human Needs of Labour*, Rowntree pressed for a national minimum wage and for family allowances.

In 1936, Rowntree published *Poverty and Progress*, another survey of York poverty in which he demonstrated a fall in the rate of absolute poverty since the previous survey, but a switch in cause from low wages to high unemployment. His third study of York, *Poverty and the Welfare State* (1951), found an expanding economy and social welfare greatly improving the situation.

PLAN
OF THE
CITY OF YORK

Scale

FEET 1000   500   0   1000   2000   3000 FEET.

The poorest districts of the city, comprising the slum areas. Some of the main streets in these districts are, however, of a better class.

Districts inhabited by the working classes, but comprising a few houses where servants are kept.

The main business streets, consisting of shops and offices. Between these principal streets are many old and narrow lanes and courts.

Districts inhabited by the servant-keeping class.

Note.—The circle is drawn to represent a radius of a quarter of a mile from the centre of the old town.

BRAINS OF BRITAIN

Emil Reich, 'Map showing geographical distribution of British genius...', 1903.

One of the more innovative maps of the era was based on the *Dictionary of National Biography* (DNB, published 1885–1900), in which Emil Reich (1854–1910) traced the birthplaces of about 21,000 people from 'over 28,000 prominent men and women of thought or action', belonging to one of 12 categories: authors, artists, divines, engravers, inventors, judges/lawyers, physicians, miscellaneous, poets, scientific men, soldiers (army and navy) and statesmen. He mapped them, in three parts, in order to establish 'many a striking correlation between locality and genius'. Reich saw his approach as a means to indicate environmental influence. He acknowledged that place of birth might be less important than that of education, but argued nevertheless that the mapping indicated what he termed 'the prevalent tendencies' in counties. He considered it important that Glamorganshire had produced 11 poets of note and Monmouthshire only two, or that London and Middlesex were particularly deficient in inventors and soldiers, 'both classes forming the smallest portion of persons of genius born in the capital', whereas 'Devonshire, Kent, and Yorkshire are particularly rich in eminent soldiers'. He observed: 'Warwickshire, the county of Shakespeare, produced more poets than either of its four neighbours to the east, north, and west; while Denbighshire exceeds, considering its size and population, all the other English counties in point of poets.'

Reich argued: 'The influence of the locality, which is both spiritual, through its historical traditions, and physiological, through its climatic and other physical factors, has as yet been so little examined, and the whole question is so much obscured and marred by vague considerations of "race"...'. Although Reich felt that his maps would be seen as interesting, rather than significant, he asserted their importance and compared them to maps employed in 'botanical, zoological, or pathological geography'. This was a scientific comparison that the method employed in the DNB map might not seem to justify, but it was a comparison that reflected the intellectual values of the period, the scientific aspirations of history, the degree to which scientific mapping – for example of the distribution of species – also faced important problems, and, more generally, the sense of expanding knowledge and, with it, issues of methodology.

Reich was a Hungarian-born historian who had worked in the United States and France before moving to England, where he lectured and also taught candidates for the Civil Service. He wrote widely, being preoccupied, as many others at the time were, by the ideas of national character and power politics. His historical works included *Foundations of Modern Europe* (1904), *General History of Western Nations from 5000 B.C. to 1900 A.D.* (1908) and *Handbook of Geography* (1908).

In his *A New Student's Atlas of English History* (1903), Reich emphasised the role of pedagogic purpose and environmental concerns:

'Historical maps giving nothing but the locality and names of the places where events happened can, however, not be held to project these events plastically. Considering that of all the powers of recalling things or ideas, the memory for movements and their incident places is by far the commonest and strongest; considering, further, that the events of History are mostly not static but of a decidedly dynamic nature, it is evident that any means of representing the movements of historical events by graphic methods suggesting movements will necessarily give a truer and more impressive mental picture of the events than mere words can ever do. ... The paramount importance of geography as the basis of a study of history has been brought home to Englishmen by the late war in South Africa... The present atlas endeavours to initiate the student into the knowledge of the strategy of events, and to accustom him to look at history from that most fertile point of view, the geographical correlation of events... .'

The relationship between the physical environment and human geography was a given of the period, linking politicians, researchers and novelists, notably those who focused on the 'condition of England'. Indeed, proposals for social amelioration drew on these assumptions, and were reflected in the activist tendencies of Victorian and Edwardian government, particularly the mid-nineteenth century public health policies of Gladstonian Liberalism, the New Liberalism that succeeded it, and the extent to which the Conservatives also, from the late 1870s, supported a reform drive that led to mapping by Booth, Rowntree and others.

By 1900, widespread urbanisation and industrialisation had brought massive social change. Deference and traditional social patterns, never as fixed as some thought, had ebbed, and the new and newly expanded cities and towns created living environments in which the role and rule of the old world was far less influential. Only 10.4 per cent of the United Kingdom's workforce was employed in agriculture in the 1890s (compared to 40.3 per cent in France), and this had implications for the nature of rural society and its gentry leadership. Growing pressure for more radical policies increasingly led political opinion to coalesce and polarise along social and class lines, with the more radical Liberals increasingly politically linked to Labour. Education itself was brought under greater regulation: the 1870 Education Act required all areas to provide schools for those aged five to 12, although as yet attendance was not mandatory, while not all schools were free. The Elementary Education Act of 1880 dealt with the former and the Free Education Act of 1891 with the latter. Education for all was now intended as the means to national renewal and excellence.

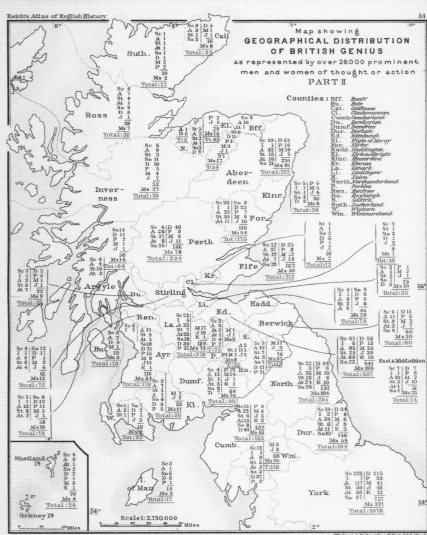

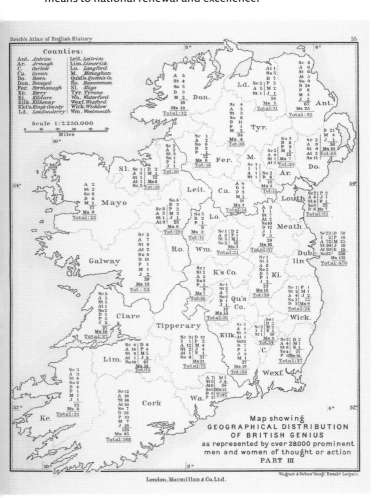

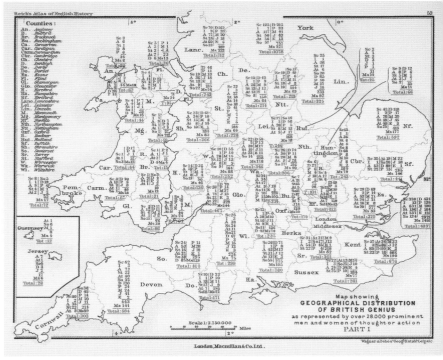

MAPS FOR MOTORISTS

Pratt's Road Atlas, 'Manchester', 1905.

The cycle and the car brought greater individual flexibility, speed and range for travellers, but also increased their need for information because of requirements for gradients, fuel, accommodation and refreshment. Map producers responded to such possibilities and helped shape them. The first national road atlas for cars was *Pratt's Road Atlas of England and Wales for Motorists* (1905). Published by the Anglo-American Oil Company, the brand name used until the mid-1930s was Pratt's Perfection Motor Spirit (Charles Pratt was an oil company director). The brand competed with Shell and Royal Dutch by commissioning from George Philip and Son, in 1904–05, the small-format *Pratt's* road atlases with sectional maps at a scale of six miles to the inch, profiles at eight miles to the inch and town plans at one mile to the inch. The *Oxford English Dictionary* cites this as being the first recorded instance of the phrase 'road atlas'.

The scale of six miles to an inch was well designed for route planning. To aid in the general understanding of routes and locations, railway lines and stations were marked. The role of leisure in encouraging journeys into the countryside was shown by the marking of golf courses. There was no numbering system for the roads; instead they were distinguished between main and cross roads, and the figures attached gave the mileage between the towns. The emphasis on terrain, presented in a standard colour-coded fashion, reflected the then norms of mapping, but it also had specific relevance for drivers in the crucial form of height, where engine performance on steep slopes presented difficulties for many cars. Access to much of the terrain to the north and west of Manchester involved ascending several hundred feet above sea level, which the colour scheme helped to make clear (see key detail, right.)

Maps for motorists, mostly produced by the Edinburgh cartographers John Bartholomew, were offered by the Automobile Association, including, from 1925, set itineraries along the major roads in the editions of the *AA Road Book of England and Wales*.

Autocar, the world's oldest car magazine, was soon offering *Everybody's 'Avoid-the-Traffic' Road Maps of Britain*. The maps were at the scale of six miles to the inch, and were commissioned by the company from George Philip and Son.

By 1939 there were nearly two million cars and half a million goods vehicles on British roads, and maps and guides for them came to be a major staple for cartographers, not least due to the major programme of road-building that, under the Trunk Roads Programme devised in 1929, began in the 1930s and resumed in the 1950s. The trunk roads of the 1930s were impressive and represented major changes to traditional local road patterns.

'The sound of horns and motors' of T.S. Eliot's poem *The Waste Land* (1922) became more insistent as part of a changed culture of sounds, smells and sights. Roads led not only to new demand for maps but also for signs, lampposts, manhole covers and traffic lights. As with the earlier games illustrated in this book, the new technology resulted in motorcar-based board games – in about 1910 *A Motor Tour* was produced.

Maps reflected the extent to which travel with road generally led to the need for individual decisions which were not required when making journeys by rail. Road transport by car, most of which were individually owned, offered access at every point along the road.

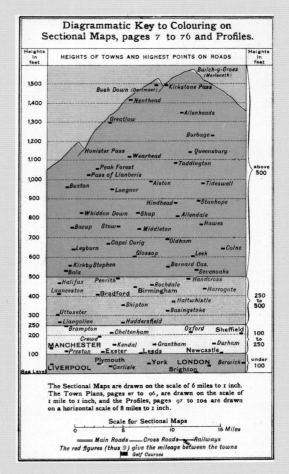

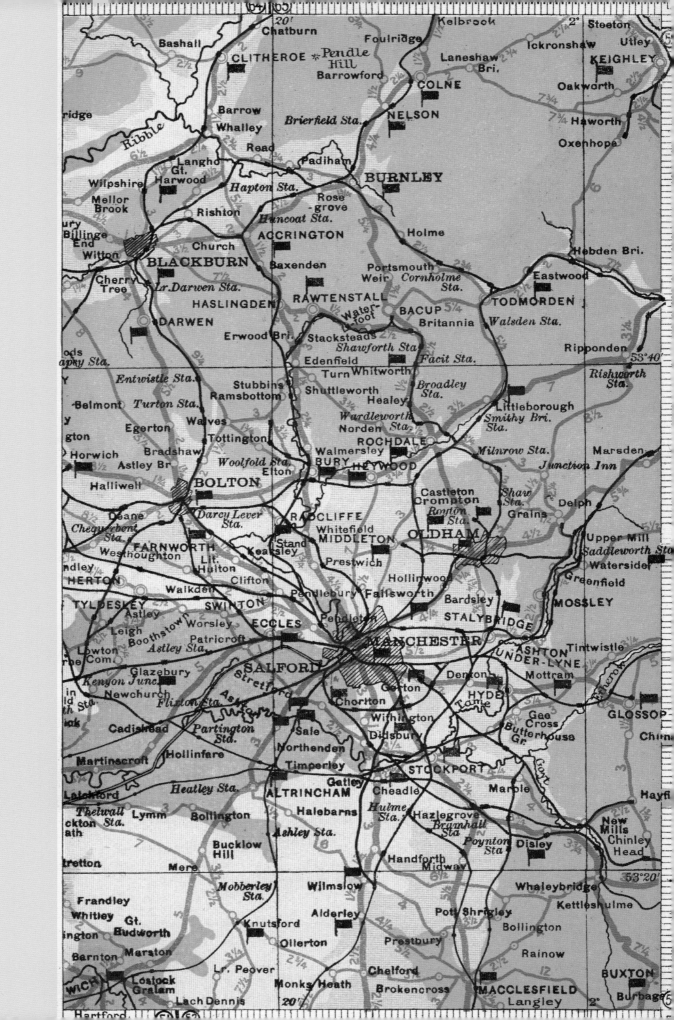

SUBURBIA

Hampstead Garden Suburb Trust, 'Proposed Garden Suburb at Hampstead North London', 1905.

The growth of suburbia reflected the desire for a life away from factory chimneys and inner-city crowding, a desire catered to in the publicity advocating life in the new suburbs. In 1905 architects and planners Barry Parker and Raymond Unwin created this map, drawing upon William Morris-inspired Arts and Crafts values and the ideas of the Garden City Movement founded by Ebenezer Howard, which reflected a desire to unify town and country to create a new form of civilisation. Rather than the monotonous urban expansion previously considered suitable for the working classes, Parker and Unwin balanced building density with the preservation of open spaces and the natural environment, first for Letchworth Garden Suburb in 1903 and then with this suburb in North London, begun in 1906 and expanded north of the A1 in the 1930s.

Place and movement were particularly susceptible to change in the early twentieth century as the cities altered and the motor car spread in a symbiotic development: cars encouraged housing of a lower density, while the new suburbs were shaped by the road systems constructed for these cars. The tightly packed terraces characteristic of Victorian England, for the middle as well as the working class, were supplemented by miles of 'semis': semi-detached houses with some mock-Tudor elevations, red-tiled roofs and walls of red brick or pebbledash, with a small front and a larger back garden. Each house had a small drive and a separate garage, which was often structurally linked to the house. This was a suburbia, later eulogised by the poet John Betjeman, representing the application of pre-First World War ideas of garden suburbs, notably with an emphasis on space, calm and the separateness expressed in individual gardens. Betjeman observed in 1939: 'Londoners, like all English people, prefer to live in a house.'

Suburbia had spread earlier, in the late nineteenth century, with the railways, but development then had generally not moved far from the stations. In contrast, car transport permitted less-intensive development, although in practice this often meant more extensive estates that were otherwise as densely packed by the developers as the basic housing model permitted. As with the car, the 'semi' expressed the desire for freedom: a freedom to escape the constraints of living in close proximity to others, as most people did, and, instead, to enjoy space. Semis were not the most individual of residences, like

larger suburban villas for the wealthier members of the middle class built round Victorian cities in upmarket suburbs such as London's St John's Wood, which continued to exist in what were now enclaves, but they reflected a similar aspiration for space and privacy. Moreover, semis captured the aspirations of millions, and offered them a decent living environment, including a garden. Stanley Baldwin's speeches in the 1920s helped to capture suburbia for the Conservatives by emphasising that its inhabitants were country-dwellers, and hence custodians of the core English values.

Semis were certainly more of a realisation of the suburban ideal than terraced housing. In *English Journey* (1934), J.B. Priestley, a sensible observer, could see that the country was changing, and wrote that alongside the old industrial and rural Englands was a new England of suburbs and road houses: pubs built along trunk roads. In Scotland, in contrast, the cities remained more like Continental ones, as to an extent they still do, with the well-to-do living quite close to the centre and the poorest in peripheral housing schemes.

In part, suburbia was a response to the cult of the outdoors, one mediated through, and in, the suburban garden (which greatly attracted the middle class) and the parks of new suburbs. I grew up in a 'Parkside Drive', built in the 1930s alongside a new suburban park taken from farmland. Suburbia, moreover, was linked to a ruralist image that was found across the arts: in music, in the positive response to Edward Elgar and Ralph Vaughan Williams, notably pieces that became iconic such as the *Enigma Variations*, *Pomp and Circumstance* and *The Lark Ascending*; and, in painting, in the popularity of 'authentic' rather than modernist works.

Suburbia, which came into use as a pejorative noun in the 1890s, certainly reflected sameness and national standardisation. Indeed, a predictability of product helped to make the new housing sell: these were mass-produced houses, with standardised parts and they looked similar, as did their garages. A degree of individuality was provided by the gardens, but they generally had similar plantings. The garden cities also allowed only a very narrow diversity.

In part, the similarity of the new housing was because of the role of brick as the standard building material and the dominance of much brick-making by the Fletton process using the Jurassic clays of the East Midlands, whose high carbon content cut the cost of firing. Feeding

PROPOSED GARDEN SU

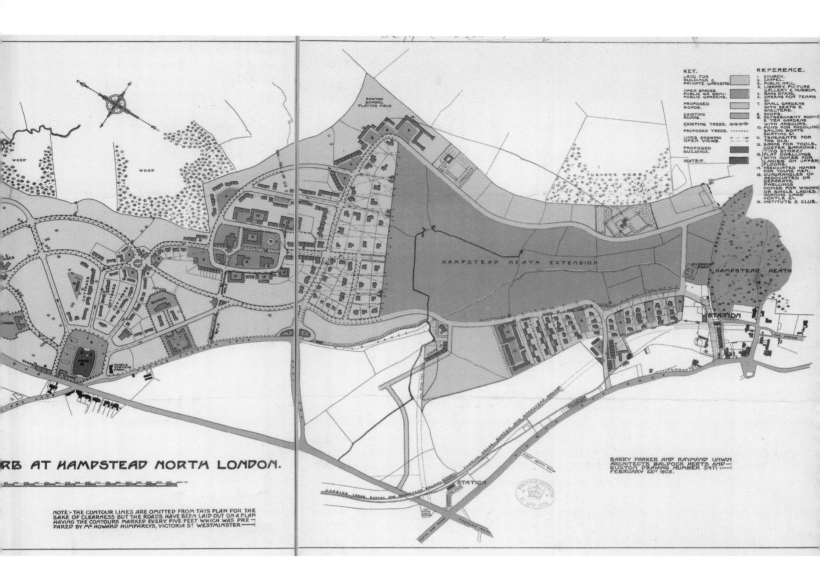

RB AT HAMPSTEAD NORTH LONDON.

NOTE:- THE CONTOUR LINES ARE OMITTED FROM THIS PLAN FOR THE
SAKE OF CLEARNESS BUT THE ROADS HAVE BEEN LAID OUT ON A PLAN
HAVING THE CONTOURS MARKED EVERY FIVE FEET WHICH WAS PRE—
PARED BY M.r HOWARD HUMPHREYS, VICTORIA ST WESTMINSTER—

BARRY PARKER AND RAYMOND UNWIN
ARCHITECTS BALDOCK HERTS AND—:
BUXTON DRAWING NUMBER 3471 :—
FEBRUARY 22nd 1905.

KEY.
LAID FOR
BUILDINGS &
PRIVATE GARDENS.
OPEN SPACES
PUBLIC OR SEMI-
PUBLIC GARDENS.
PROPOSED
ROADS.
EXISTING
ROADS.
EXISTING TREES.
PROPOSED TREES.
EXISTING
BUILDINGS.
LINES SHOWING
OPEN VIEWS.
PROPOSED
BUILDINGS.
WATER.

REFERENCE.
1. CHURCH.
2. CHAPEL.
3. PUBLIC HALL.
4. LIBRARY PICTURE
   GALLERY & MUSEUM.
5. BAND STAND.
6. GREENS FOR TENNIS
   &c.
7. SMALL GARDENS
   WITH SEATS &
   SHELTERS.
8. SHOPS.
9. REFRESHMENT ROOMS
   & TEA GARDENS
   WITH ARBOURS.
10. POND FOR PADDLING
    SAILING BOATS
    SKATING &c.
11. TENEMENTS FOR
    THE OLD.
12. BARNS FOR TOOLS,
    COSTER BARROWS,
    &c.
13. FLAT DWELLINGS
    WITH ROOMS FOR
    LADIES ON UPPER
    FLOORS.
14. ASSOCIATED HOMES
    FOR YOUNG MEN.
15. QUADRANGLES OF
    ASSOCIATED
    SEPARATE
    DWELLINGS.
16. HOMES FOR WIDOWS
    OR SINGLE LADIES.
    WORKING LADIES
    HOSTLE &c.
17. INSTITUTE & CLUB.

the new suburbia, brick-making developed as a massive industry between Bedford and Bletchley and also near Whittlesey on the Cambridgeshire–Huntingdonshire border. Bricks, and other products for the housing market such as prefabricated doors and windows, could be moved not only by rail, but also by the new expanding road system; and there was more profit in mass producing and absorbing the costs of long-range distribution, which impacted on production that was more locally sourced.

Much new building was by private enterprise, and often by speculative builders, such as John Laing and Richard Costain. They were largely responsible for the plentiful supply of inexpensive houses by the mid-1920s. The ability of purchasers to borrow at low rates of interest from building societies was also important. In the mid-1920s, houses cost between £400 and £1,000. This new housing was crucial to the process by which suburban culture became increasingly defined and important within Britain; and this importance was true for both politics and social assumptions. The suburbs had fairly standard mock-Tudor parades of shops (with accommodation above) on their high streets and also enormous and lavishly decorated cinemas ('picture palaces'), which represented the move to the suburbs of leisure.

"Cycling" MAP
OF
ENGLAND & WALES
SHOWING THE BEST TOURING ROADS
REDUCED BY PERMISSION FROM THE ORDNANCE SURVEY

Scale 12 English Miles to an Inch

Main Roads coloured brown

N O R T H

S E A

I R I S H   S E A

ISLE OF MAN

ST GEORGE'S CHANNEL

CARDIGAN BAY

CARNARVON BAY

B R I S T O L   C H A N N E L

ISLE OF WIGHT

E N G L I S H   C H A N N E L

Longitude West 2 from Greenwich

EXERCISING LEISURE

John Bartholomew & Co., "Cycling" Map of England & Wales Showing the Best Touring Roads, 1908.

Leisure, because of its particular requirements was important to the growth of the maps trade. The press runs of Bartholomew's cycling maps rose from 2,000 in the early 1890s to 60,000 in 1908, with demand for bikes having grown greatly as a result of the introduction of safety bikes in the 1880s and the comfort and ease of maintenance resulting from the invention of pneumatic tyres. Indeed, the boom in cycling during the 1890s, which provided individuals with the private means to wander freely and flexibly, transformed the way that tourist maps were produced.

By the early 1900s the mechanisation of folding ensured that these maps were more user-friendly, being able to fit into a pocket. *Philips' Clear Print Half-Inch Cycling Map of England and Wales*, consisting of 31 sheets, first appeared in 1903, improving a genre of maps first produced in 1876.

Safety bicycles encouraged young women to cycle, an activity that could not be chaperoned, and this both reflected and encouraged a major shift in gender relations, with young women gaining an important degree of personal freedom, as well as being able to dress in a way that enabled them to cycle. Arthur Conan Doyle and other writers put women cyclists into their stories.

Cycling contributed to a cult of the countryside in Britain that became increasingly significant, as with the foundation of the National Trust in 1895 and with books such as Henry Williamson's *Tarka the Otter* (1927).

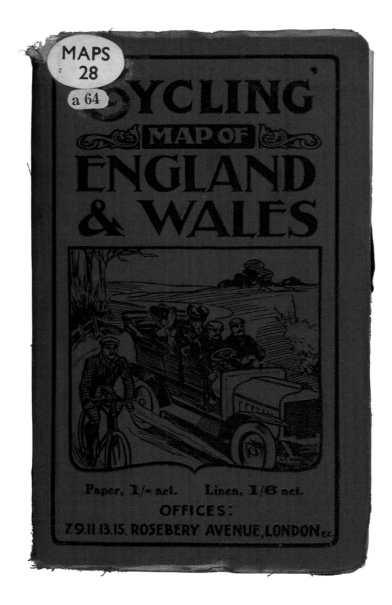

"Cycling" MAP

OF

ENGLAND & WALES

SHOWING THE BEST TOURING ROADS

REDUCED BY PERMISSION FROM THE ORDNANCE SURVEY

Scale 13 English Miles to an Inch

0 5 10 15 20 25 30 35 40

Main Roads coloured brown

N O R T H

S E A

UNDER THE GROUND

D.H. Evans and Co. Ltd., 'Map of the "Tubes" of London in One Mile Squares', 1908.

The enlargement of London and its facilities posed issues for cartographers, but also opportunities in terms of a massive and growing market. The spreading extent of the city was indicated by the contrast between Washington Bacon's 1886 edition of *New Large-Scale Ordnance Atlas of London and Suburbs*, which offered 25 four-inch maps, and the 1912 edition, which both covered new streets and houses in these areas and an extension of London that necessitated 34 maps.

The expansion of the subterranean rail system or 'Tube', a nickname adopted widely from around 1900, was designed to help serve this urban growth, but it also required dedicated maps. In *Anticipations* (1901), H.G. Wells wrote about transport networks making possible the expansion of cities into large metropolitan spaces. This map was produced by D.H. Evans & Co. Ltd., 'silk mercers' with a department store on Oxford Street (depicted in red in the map), and was distributed for free within the retailer's *Brief Guide to London* (1908). Founded in 1879, the store moved into larger premises on Oxford Street in 1893, being expanded in 1895 and 1898, and rebuilt from 1906. This was a key example of a wider change in which shopping became a leisure activity.

D.H. Evans's map provided a scale by means of the one-mile squares, as well as pictures of the leading sites, including the Earl's Court Exhibition Centre opened in 1887. The treatment of the 'Tube' was different to the usual basis and purpose of maps of the underground railway, which were system-orientated and produced either by the individual companies responsible for particular lines, or those of the network as a whole (as with that in 1908 produced by the Underground Electric Railways Company of London and four other underground railway companies – a map designed to be accurate in terms of distance and direction, and that showed other railways, roads and major features as a background).

The street-map background was dropped by Fred Stingemore in his 1927 map, by when the Northern Line had reached Edgware (1924) and Morden (1926). In turn, the first diagrammatic map

of the system, the basis of the modern tube map, was designed by Harry Beck and published from 1933. That year, the system spread further when the Piccadilly Line reached Cockfosters. The Beck map shrank the apparent distance between suburbia and the inner city (where a relatively large scale meant that station names did not overlap), and ensured that movement to places such as Morden did not appear to be a case of leaving London. Instead, the ease of travel into the centre was emphasised, a visual effect encouraged by the use of straight lines for individual underground routes. Beck, however, sought to minimise typology only as necessary to lessen crowding. He also retained the River Thames, the colour-coding of routes, and the northward orientation of the map.

In 1862 the Metropolitan Railway had made a first run over the full length of its new underground railway in London, initially powered by steam engines. That line, from Bishop's Road Paddington to Farringdon, is unmarked in the map because, as cut-and-cover work, it was regarded as a surface line rather than a truly underground line. The early steam-operated routes needed open-air sections at regular intervals to reduce smoke build-up in the tunnels. After a tunnelling shield and cylindrical cutter was developed the deep-bore 'Tube' tunnels could be created, the first of which opened under the Thames between Tower Hill and Bermondsey in 1870. The City and South London Railway opened in 1890, which is now the City branch of the Northern Line, and was the first underground electric railway in the world. This line was followed in 1898 by the Waterloo and City Line, and in 1900 by the Central Line between Shepherd's Bush and Bank.

The success of the Central Line encouraged the building of other lines, notably the Bakerloo, the Piccadilly, and the Hampstead to Charing Cross lines. A key figure was Charles Tyson Yerkes, an American financier of dubious practices but boundless energy. The Piccadilly, opened in 1906, initially ran from Hammersmith to Finsbury Park, making it the longest line that fed commuters and shoppers from West London into the West End.

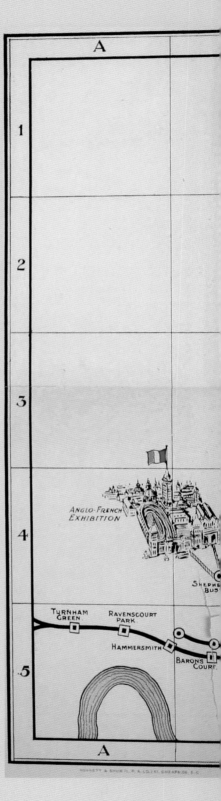

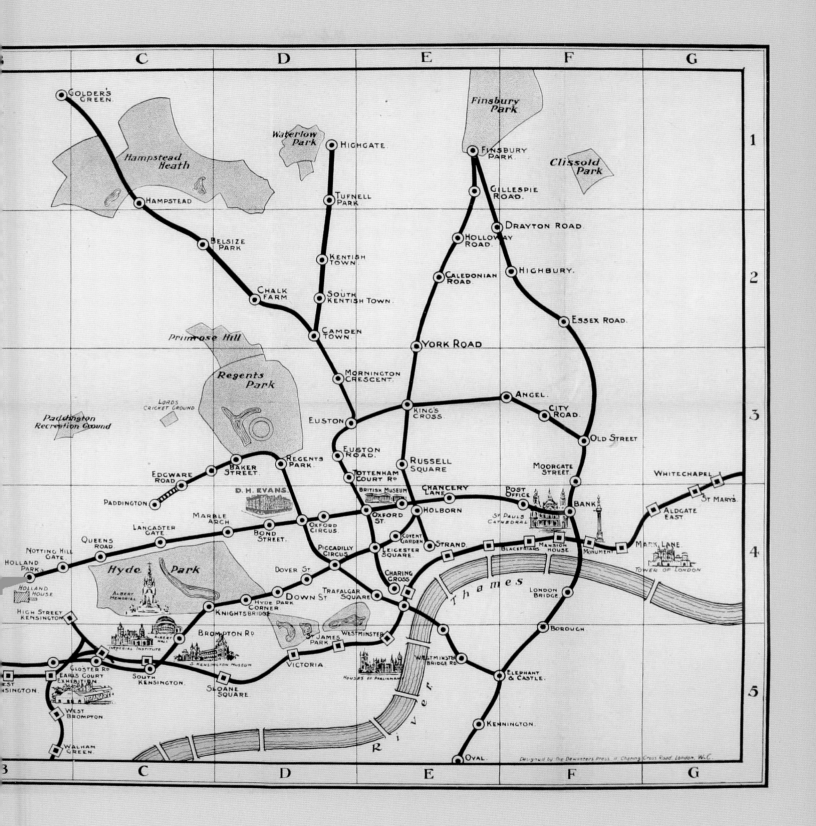

TERROR FROM THE AIR

Western Daily Press, 'How the Zeppelins Came to England', 1915.

As had been feared prior to the war, air attacks brought the damage and uncertainty of war to the home front. On 19 January 1915 three Zeppelin airships were sent against England. One turned back with engine trouble but the others dropped bombs on targets in Norfolk, which was exposed to attack from across the North Sea. In total, there were 51 Zeppelin attacks involving 208 sorties, during which 196 tons of bombs were dropped, causing 557 fatalities, 1,358 injuries and £1.5 million worth of property damage.

This map from the *Western Daily Press* newspaper on 23 January 1915 demonstrated how standard maps could be readily used to provide war news, and the British public expected such explanatory maps in order to follow reports. The standard base used is one of the many maps produced by the London Geographical Institute and published by George Philip and Son, and superimposed on that are the details of bases and of the zeppelin route. Looking back to earlier mapmaking practices, the latter was supported by a picture.

The Zeppelins set out from a base near Hamburg at around 11.30 a.m. and arrived over the coast of East Anglia at about 8.30 p.m. They then separated in the dark, with one going north to Cromer and another south to Yarmouth. Not long after that the Zeppelin passed over the town and the crew dropped bombs for ten minutes. Two people were killed and a soldier was injured. Meanwhile, following the coast and along the Wash, although Cromer was missed, bombs were dropped over Sheringham, without results, and then around 11 p.m. King's Lynn was bombed, killing a soldier's widow and a boy of 14 in his bed.

In response to the deadly raids civilians took refuge in basements, the London Underground stations and in the countryside. The attacks also affected troops at the front, collapsing the distance between it and the homeland. Lieutenant Colonel Alan Thomson, a gunner, worried about his wife in London, referred to the Zeppelins as 'those infernal devils'. However, tactics for the effective use of intercepting aircraft were rapidly developed and spelled doom for the latter. Much effort was spent in developing anti-Zeppelin rounds, although a problem with incendiary rounds was that the pilot had to get very close because otherwise the phosphorus, which ignited when the round was fired, burned up too early. The vulnerability of Zeppelins became apparent, but they tended to attack at night, could fly at a great height, and could climb rapidly, all challenging requirements for intercepting fighters.

Blackouts to make targeting harder showed the consequences of the war for civilian life. In July 1916 John Monash, an Australian divisional commander, wrote to his wife from London: 'You can hardly imagine what the place is like. The Zeppelin scare is just like as if the whole place was in imminent fear of an earthquake. At night, the whole of London is in absolute darkness.'

Heavy Zeppelin losses led the Germans to switch in 1917 to aircraft attacks, made by twin-engined Gothas that caused significant casualties. The Gotha Mk IV could fly for six hours, had an effective range of 520 miles, could carry 1,100 pounds (500kg) of bombs, and could fly at 21,000 feet, which made interception difficult. The crew members were supplied with oxygen and with electric power to heat their flying suits.

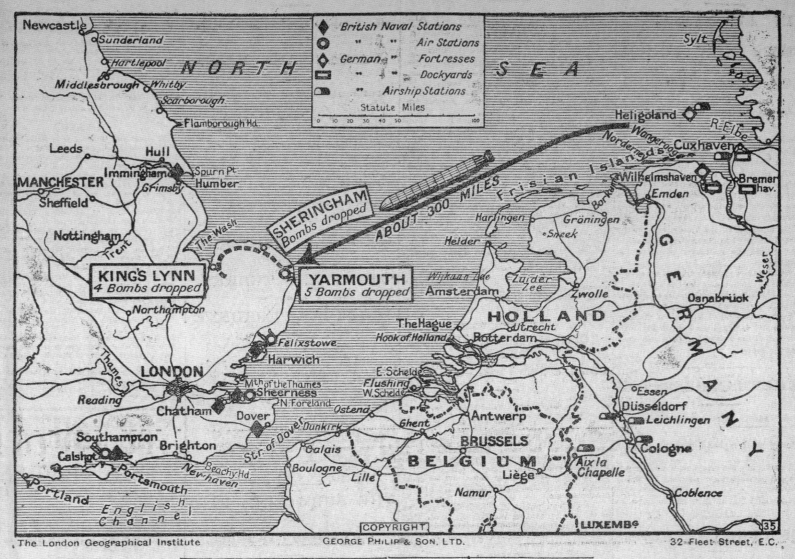

HOW THE ZEPPELINS CAME TO ENGLAND.

The Map shows the approximate route followed by the Airships which effected the raid on certain unfortified East Coast Towns. On their return, in all probability, they followed much the same course, being sighted off the Dutch Frisian Islands, bound East, some hours later.

ELECTORAL GEOGRAPHY

Edward Krehbiel, 'The Parliamentary Constituencies of the British Isles and the Results of the General Elections since 1885', 1916.

This four-ink map, covering the eight general elections from 1885 until the two in 1910, appeared in Edward Krehbiel's article 'Geographic Influences in British Elections' published in *The Geographical Review* (issue 2, 1916). The then recently launched journal was published by the American Geographical Society and it indicated interest in cartographic techniques and their application to new topics. British elections provided an obvious instance of something that was significant and had available data.

The map showed differences in the scale of volatility of particular seats. The significance of Wales and Scotland to the Liberals, and of Southeast and southern England to the Conservatives, emerged clearly. The map can be compared with later ones of British electoral geography, but it also looks to Charles Pearson's discussion of the physical geography affecting Britain (see pages 20–21). The method employed in this map was a good way to demonstrate electoral consistency.

Thanks to the divisive effect that Irish Home Rule had on the Liberals from 1886, the Conservatives – under Robert, 3rd Marquess of Salisbury, and, from 1902, his nephew Arthur Balfour, with the support of Liberal Unionists – were in office in 1886–92 and 1895–1905. The

Conservatives also benefitted from their growing urban strength following the 1885 constituency redistribution, the long-term expansion of the middle classes, and from the popularity of their imperialist policies. The Conservative Party gained an effective popular organisation with the Primrose League, which stood for Church, Crown, Empire, property and order. Although headed by the establishment, the Conservatives were keen to reach out and win the active backing of what they saw as the inherent conservatism of the populace.

Lancashire (see detail, below) and London were the areas of most contention in English campaigning because each had large numbers of parliamentary seats and also switched between the Conservatives and the Liberals. In the 1906 election, when the Conservatives did badly and lost some of their urban working-class support, the Liberals took the former Conservative strongholds of London and Lancashire, and also made important gains in rural and suburban areas of southern England, the Conservative heartland. Many of the latter gains were lost in the two general elections of 1910, but the Liberals then retained Lancashire and London, ensuring that they were the major party in all the leading industrial areas.

EASTER RISING

Irish Life, 'The Cordon System', 1916.

On 24 April, about 1,200 men and women seized a number of sites, then proclaimed an independent Irish republic. But the Easter Rising enjoyed scant support and was rapidly crushed. The rebels suffered from bad planning, poor tactics and a lack of German help, as well as a strong British reaction, which included an uncompromising use of artillery to shell targets. Under heavy pressure, the insurgents surrendered unconditionally on 29 April. This map is from a 64-page booklet *The Record of the Irish Rebellion of 1916*, published by *Irish LIfe* magazine and printed in 1916 to serve as a contemporary record. It shows the cordon system the British Army established, with the thin red line surrounding the city, while the thick red represents the wedge of troops that divided the rebels in two and split their communications. The rebel strongholds are circled: in the north, the North Union Workhouse, Four Courts and General Post Office (GPO); in the south, the South Union Workhouse, Marrowbone Lane Distillery, Jacob's Factory, Stephen's Green and Boland's Mill.

Outside Dublin, the planned nationalist uprising failed to materialise, while in Dublin the numerous soldiers' wives, when informed by the rebels that the establishment of a republic meant that the payment of separation allowances had now ended, responded with anger rather than nationalist enthusiasm. The firm British response was to play a major role in Irish public memory, notably in encouraging opposition to Britain. However, given that the United Kingdom of Great Britain and Ireland was at war in 1916, and indeed not doing well, the declaration of martial law, the series of trials, the execution of 15 rebels for treason and the internment of many were scarcely surprising responses.

In the 1918 general election, 73 out of the 105 parliamentary seats were won by the Sinn Féin party, republican nationalists led by Eamonn de Valera, who refused to attend Westminster and demanded independence. They rejected the earlier policy of Home Rule and Sinn Féin replaced the Irish Parliamentary Party as the focus of Irish nationalism. An independence war was then launched that led to the Anglo-Irish Treaty of December 1921, partition and effective independence for the new Irish Free State, which governed most of the island while retaining Dominion status at this stage and was therefore still part of the British Empire, albeit in effect independent. The Protestant Unionists of the north refused to accept being part of this state, and six out of the nine counties of Ulster opted out and became Northern Ireland, which, while self-governed, remained part of the United Kingdom and retained representation at Westminster.

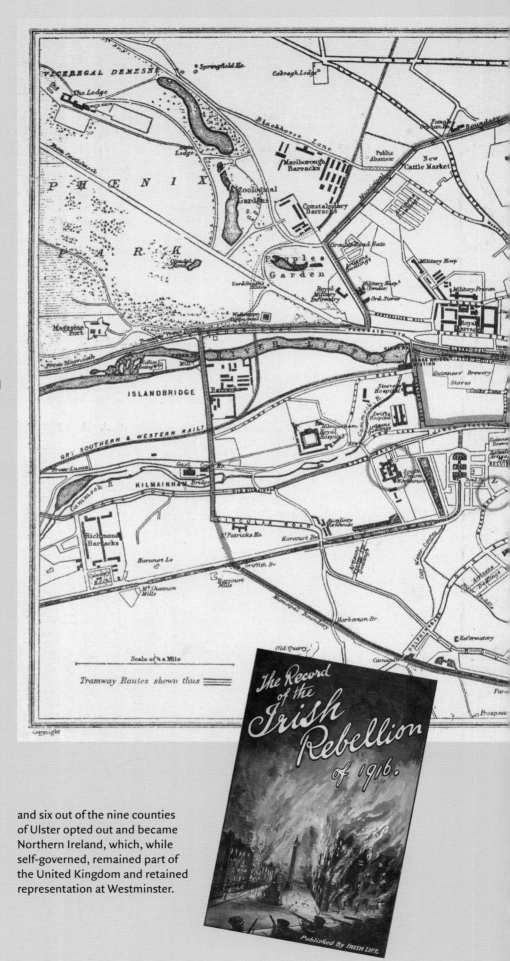

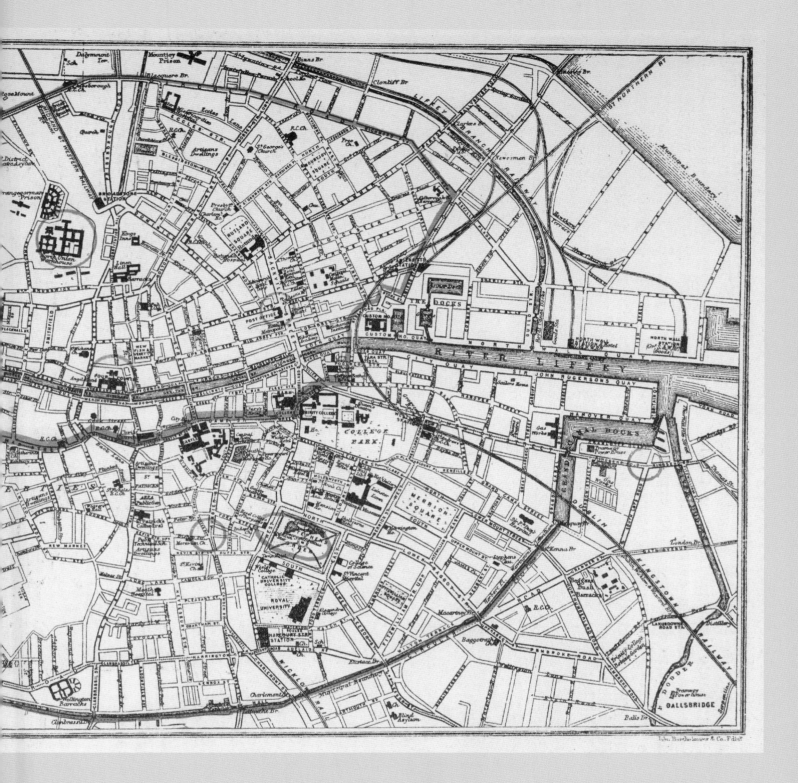

HEART OF EMPIRE

Stanley Kennedy North, *British Empire Exhibition 1924*, 1924.

This skilful map is part of an illustrated folding guide to the British Empire Exhibition (1924), providing both the layout of the exhibition and also locating it with reference to the London underground system.

Stanley Kennedy North (1887–1942) was an artist and stained glass designer. He was devoted to medieval art and illustrated in a medievalist mode, as shown by the plants in the garden (top) in this map and in the place name calligraphy. His technique of pictorial cartography looked also to that of Leslie MacDonald Gill (1884–1947), whose maps reflected skills as an artist and graphic designer. Gill created the 'Wonderground Map of London Town' to promote the London Underground and his map of the South Pole at the Scott Polar Research Institute in Cambridge.

A tremendous success, the British Empire Exhibition showed the vitality of the imperial theme in the aftermath of the war, as well as London's role as 'the heart of the empire'. The exhibition, for which Wembley Stadium was built in 1923, was a major public occasion, celebrated in the press and the newsreels and commemorated by a set of stamps. The Empire Marketing Board, created in 1926, sought to encourage trade within the Empire. Another British Empire Exhibition followed in Glasgow in 1938.

Empire was presented at the time as a progressive force and differentiated from the empires of Continental Europe. Thus, in 1904, Winston Churchill asked the voters of North West Manchester:

> 'Whether we are to model ourselves upon the clanking military empires of the Continent of Europe, with their gorgeous imperial hierarchy fed by enormous tariffs, defended by mighty armies, and propped up by every influence of caste privilege and commercial monopoly, or whether our development is to proceed by well-tried English methods towards the ancient and lofty ideals of English citizenship.'

In 1905, he referred in a speech to the 'regular, settled lines of English democratic development' underpinning the 'free British empire', again without any sense of contradiction.

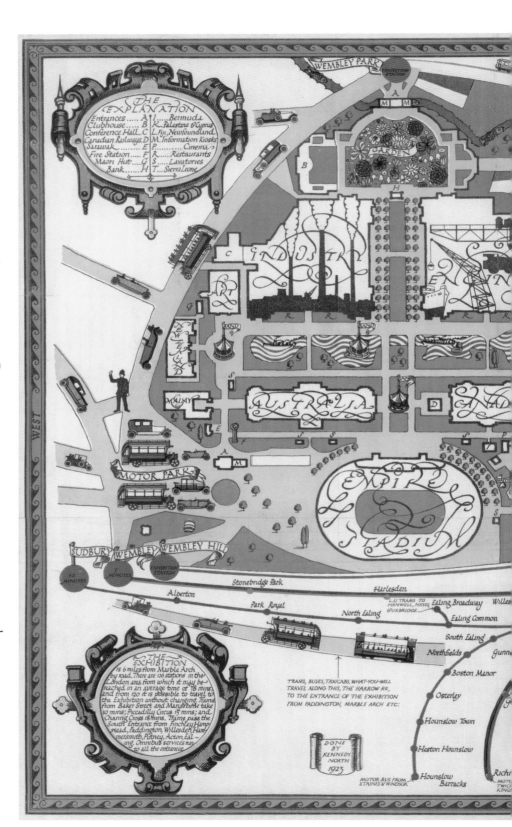

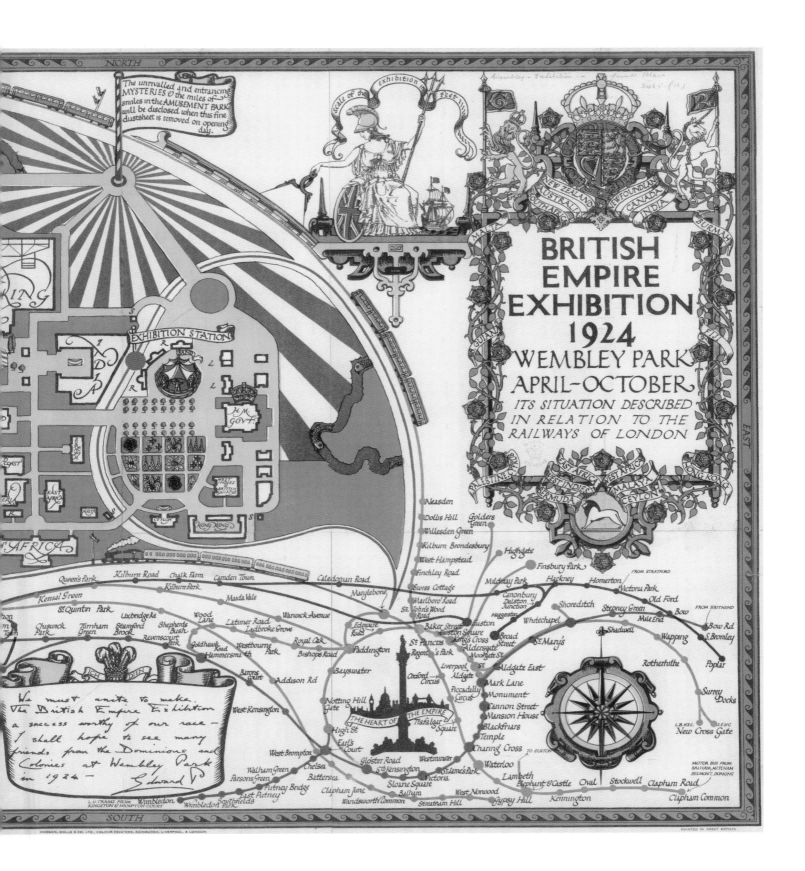

CRIME IN THE SHIRES

Agatha Christie and Edmund Crispin, *Murder at the Vicarage* and *The Moving Toyshop*, 1930 and 1946.

Originating with Wilkie Collins' *The Moonstone* (1868), in which the protagonist is a detective, detective fiction is a major British contribution to literature. The Golden Age of the genre was the 1920s and 1930s. Maps were a key feature in much of this fiction – the value of them demonstrated, for example, in Agatha Christie's *Murder at the Vicarage* (1930), which included no fewer than three. The first, illustrated here (below), showed both the vicarage, where the murder occurred, and the house and garden of Jane Marple, and helps to explain why she is a key witness of the action. The narrator, the vicar, refers directly in the text to the map: 'I append a rough sketch here which will be useful in the light of after happenings, only sketching in such details as are necessary.' The second map provided the plan of the room where the murder occurred ('For the convenience of my readers I append a sketch plan of the room'), and the third covered the surrounding buildings and lanes, being particularly helpful for following the relevant clues.

Edmund Crispin's *The Moving Toyshop* (1946) was far more whimsical, not least because it engages with a shop that has two separate locations, both of which are shown on the map (opposite), as are a number of real places in

Oxford including St John's, Balliol and Trinity colleges, the Sheldonian Theatre, the market and the police station, as well as fictional locations, notably Rosseter's office and St Christopher's College. The early morning walk through Oxford by Richard Cadogan is as if through 'an underwater city', which leads him to the shop and into the mystery.

Detective novels like these showed the prominence of maps in British culture, a culture in which maps were reproduced in a variety of printed media, while the popularity of these novels reflected rising prosperity and leisure. Maps of the neighbourhood featured in Margery Allingham's *The Mystery Mile*, Mavis Doriel Hay's *Death on the Cherwell* and Ellis Peters's *The Rose Rent*, while maps or plans of a building appeared in Anna Green's *The Leavenworth Case*, Agatha Christie's *The Mysterious Affair at Styles*, Michael Gilbert's *Smallbone Deceased* and *Death Has Deep Roots*, and Dorothy L. Sayers's *Clouds of Witness* and *The Nine Tailors*, which were used to help the reader understand the precision of the plot. A London street that cannot be found is important in John Dickson Carr's *The Lost Gallows*, which, significantly, does not have a map. Maps clarify issues of access, sightlines and possibilities for

KEY

A. Toyshop (second position).
B. St. Christopher's.
C. St. John's.
D. Balliol.
E. Trinity.
F. Lennox's.
G. The "Mace and Sceptre."
H. Sheldonian.
I. Rosseter's office.
J. Market.
K. Police Station.
L. Toyshop (first position).

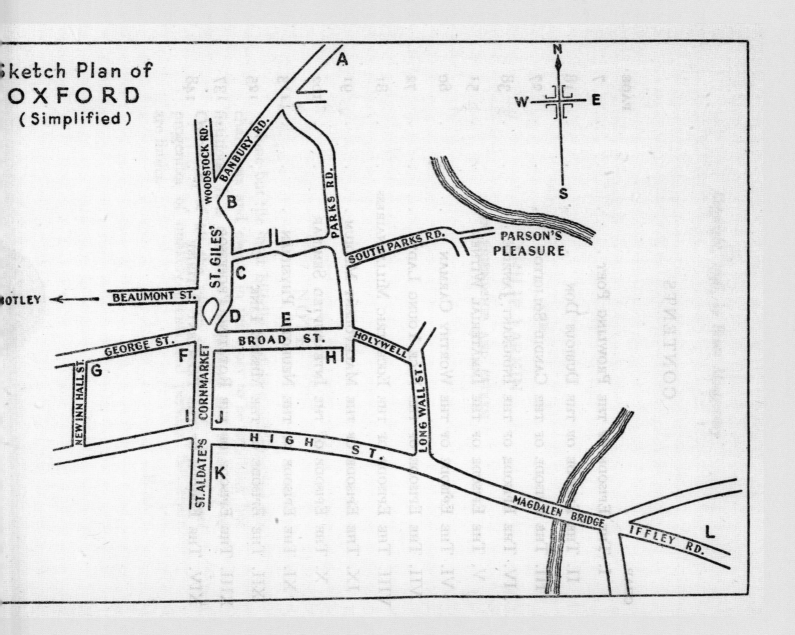

Sketch Plan of
OXFORD
(Simplified)

PARSON'S PLEASURE

WOODSTOCK RD.
BANBURY RD.
PARKS RD.
ST. GILES'
SOUTH PARKS RD.
BEAUMONT ST.
←BOTLEY
GEORGE ST.
BROAD ST.
HOLYWELL
CORNMARKET
NEW INN HALL ST.
LONG WALL ST.
ST. ALDATE'S
HIGH ST.
MAGDALEN BRIDGE
IFFLEY RD.

overhearing. The detective-themed board game *Cluedo* is a variant on this linkage of crime and mapping. It was invented by Anthony Pratt, originally as *Murder*, released in 1949 and is known in the United States under the name *Clue*. Recent novels make less use of the technique of the map, in part due to a focus on psychological factors rather than plot possibilities.

Detective fiction reflected social mores. In *After the Funeral* (1953), Agatha Christie commented on 'vast houses nowadays. No one would buy them to live in. It would be pulled down, perhaps, and the whole estate built over ... Would it be turned into an hotel, or an institute?' In Patricia Wentworth's

The Listening Eye (1957), Ethel Burkett writes to her aunt about her sister: '...who had taken the unjustifiable step of leaving an excellent husband whom she complained of finding dull. "As if anyone in their senses expects their husband to be exciting", wrote Mrs Burkett. "And she doesn't say where she is, or what she is doing, so all we can hope and trust is that she is *alone*, and that she hasn't done anything which Andrew would find impossible to forgive. Because what is she going to live on?"' Thus, Ethel's sister is demanding change and willing to seek it herself, notably by breaking family constraints, while Ethel still offers a traditional view of husbands sitting in judgement.

YESTERDAY'S FUEL

Geological Survey of Great Britain, *Map of the Coalfields of England and Wales...*, 1935.

Britain was the leading European coal producer of the eighteenth century, with an annual average output in 1870–74 of 121 million tons, compared to 40.4 million tons for Germany; and for 1910–14, 270 million tons and 243 million tons respectively. The areas of prime production changed, notably with the development of the Yorkshire–Derbyshire–Nottinghamshire coalfield (detail, below), and with previous areas of production becoming less important or ceasing production, as in Kent and Somerset.

Mapping coal resources was seen by government as an urgent task that the Geological Survey of Great Britain had hitherto underrated, and the economic crisis after the First World War – more particularly, anxiety about the coal industry – led to pressure for action. In addition to surveys of particular areas – some, such as Kent, so far largely neglected – there was mapping at the national scale under Sir John Smith Flett, Director of the Survey from 1920 to 1935 and a sometime President of the Mineralogical Society. This 1935 map crucially distinguished (using colour coding) between exposed and concealed coal deposits, while separating the latter that were proved from those that were only partly proved or probable.

The map was a gauge of potential, but it did not provide any indication of key variables.

In particular, there was a failure to match the rate of technological and organisational improvement shown by foreign coal mining competitors. Productivity gains were too low, in part due to a managerial failure to adopt and invest in technological innovation, but also to unwillingness on the part of miners to respond to change. Necessary restructuring through amalgamation of the large number of mines was not pressed ahead with. Exports were also hit by the development of competing power sources, as well as by an overvalued currency. Labour disputes were serious.

The map offered no hint about the industrial difficulties. The miners rejected the recommendation of a Royal Commission for the rationalisation of numerous pits and a cut in wages, and the crisis led to a national miners' strike in 1926, which in turn produced a short-lived General Strike. That failed, and in late 1926 the miners returned on the employers' terms. The map provides no information on qualitative material of which commentators were well aware, such as the greater militancy of the South Wales miners. Nor does it record the underlying crisis of rising unemployment. Thus, in 1934 there were only 126,000 Welsh miners whereas there had been 272,000 at the start of 1920.

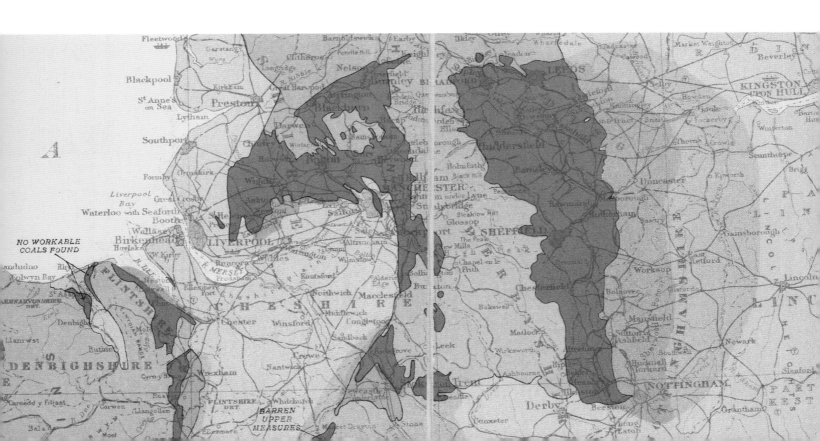

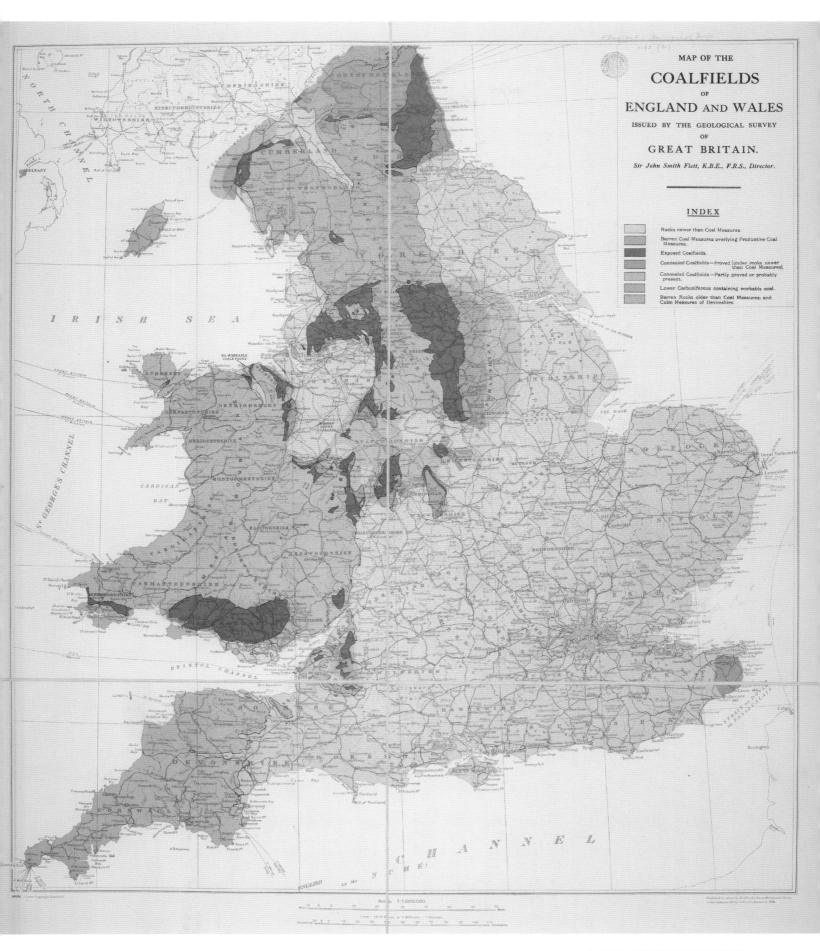

MAP OF THE

COALFIELDS

OF

ENGLAND AND WALES

ISSUED BY THE GEOLOGICAL SURVEY

OF

GREAT BRITAIN.

Sir John Smith Flett, K.B.E., F.R.S., Director.

INDEX

Rocks newer than Coal Measures.

Barren Coal Measures overlying Productive Coal Measures.

Exposed Coalfields.

Concealed Coalfields—Proved (under rocks newer than Coal Measures).

Concealed Coalfields—Partly proved or probably present.

Lower Carboniferous containing workable coal.

Barren Rocks older than Coal Measures; and Culm Measures of Devonshire.

Scale 1:1,000,000

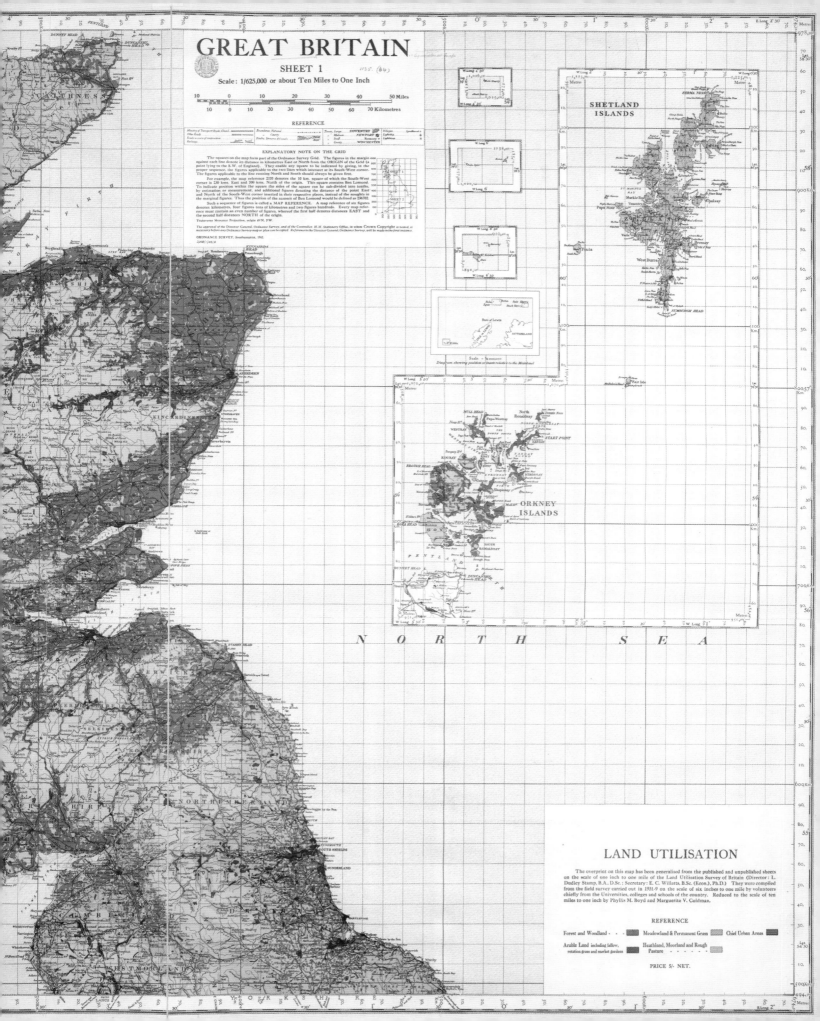

GREAT BRITAIN

SHEET 1

Scale: 1/625,000 or about Ten Miles to One Inch

SHETLAND ISLANDS

ORKNEY ISLANDS

N O R T H   S E A

LAND UTILISATION

The overprint on this map has been generalised from the published and unpublished sheets on the scale of one inch to one mile of the Land Utilisation Survey of Britain (Director: L. Dudley Stamp, B.A., D.Sc.; Secretary: E. C. Willatts, B.Sc. (Econ.), Ph.D.) They were compiled from the field survey carried out in 1931-9 on the scale of six inches to one mile by volunteers chiefly from the Universities, colleges and schools of the country. Reduced to the scale of ten miles to one inch by Phyllis M. Boyd and Marguerite V. Guldman.

REFERENCE

Forest and Woodland

Meadowland & Permanent Grass

Chief Urban Areas

Arable Land including fallow, rotation grass and market gardens

Heathland, Moorland and Rough Pasture

PRICE 5/- NET.

CHANGE AND CONTINUITY

Land Utilisation Survey of Britain, 'Land Utilisation', 1942.

The Land Utilisation Survey of Britain, conducted by L. Dudley Stamp, was carried out during the 1930s. It was the first time that anyone in Britain had tried to determine how all the land in Britain was being used, field by field. The work was carried out largely by volunteers, including 250,000 schoolchildren, who helped categorise Britain between 1931 and 1933, shading maps of the fields in their surrounding area, and people at universities who were responsible for collating these into a series of national land use maps. Land use was depicted as a colour overlay on top of Ordnance Survey topographic mapping. The relationship between arable land (brown), particularly in East Anglia, and pasture (yellow) further west emerged very clearly, as did the extent of heathland and moorland, notably in Wales, the Pennines and southwestern England.

Agriculture changed radically from the late twentieth century, being hit hard by the development of trans-oceanic food imports, notably of meat from Australasia, Argentina and North America, and of grain from the last. Refrigerated holds in large steamships aided meat imports, as did developing techniques in meatpacking and the extension of railway systems overseas, which enabled food to be transported for export to ports such as Buenos Aires.

Once transported to Britain, it was then unloaded in the expanding harbour facilities in Britain, notably in Liverpool, Britain's main North Atlantic port, London and Southampton. All this competition produced a sustained agricultural depression in Britain. This was not true of all products, for milk, fruit and vegetables required a freshness that aided domestic production, for example milk in the West Country, and market gardening near cities.

Competition was accentuated by the development of Danish bacon, German sugar beet and Eastern European grain. The resulting squeeze on food prices benefitted urban workers but hit their agricultural counterparts. Employment, rents and profits were all hit. So also with the local towns that had existed primarily to process products and service communities. They declined or became stagnant.

Additional disruption to earlier agricultural methods came with the spread of technology, in which machinery replaced workers and, notably, manual farm work, as in the threshing scene in Thomas Hardy's *Tess of the d'Urbervilles* (1891). So also with the railway, which changed the methods and geography of distribution and processing. The pressure on the rural economy lessened the value of land, and certainly so relative to capital. The economics of rural estates were far worse than is suggested by visiting many of the surviving stately homes of the period.

In 1897 Herbrand Russell, 11th Duke of Bedford wrote about his 'ruined' estate. Rent rebates were common: 10 per cent on the Blanchland estate of Lord Crewe's Charity in County Durham from 1887 until 1893, and on most of the estate's holdings the 1895 rent was equal to or less than that from 1870. Rents there did not improve until the 1900s. The agricultural depression hit arable farming particularly hard on the heavier soils such as Essex where 30 per cent of the arable area was officially 'derelict'. More generally, routine tasks such as hedge-laying were badly neglected, and many fields were left to be occupied by thistles and dandelions.

The total area devoted to agriculture in Britain fell by half a million acres between the 1870s and 1914 as more marginal farmland was abandoned while the leisure use of land grew. With German submarines (U-boats) hitting food imports, the First World War saw a marked revival in agriculture. However, after the war the depression returned. In 1921–39, the number of agricultural labourers fell by one-quarter.

Although woodland had been destroyed over much of the country, notably East Anglia, its continuing presence was captured by Arthur Conan Doyle in *The Adventure of Black Peter* (1904), which is set in Sussex and provides more than one sense of change:

'Alighting at the small wayside station, we drove for some miles through the remains of widespread woods, which were once part of that great forest which for so long held the Saxon invaders at bay – the impenetrable "weald", for sixty years the bulwark of Britain. Vast sections of it have been cleared, for this is the seat of the first ironworks of the country, and the trees have been felled to smelt the ore. Now the richer fields of the North have absorbed the trade, and nothing save these ravaged groves and great scars in the earth show the work of the past.'

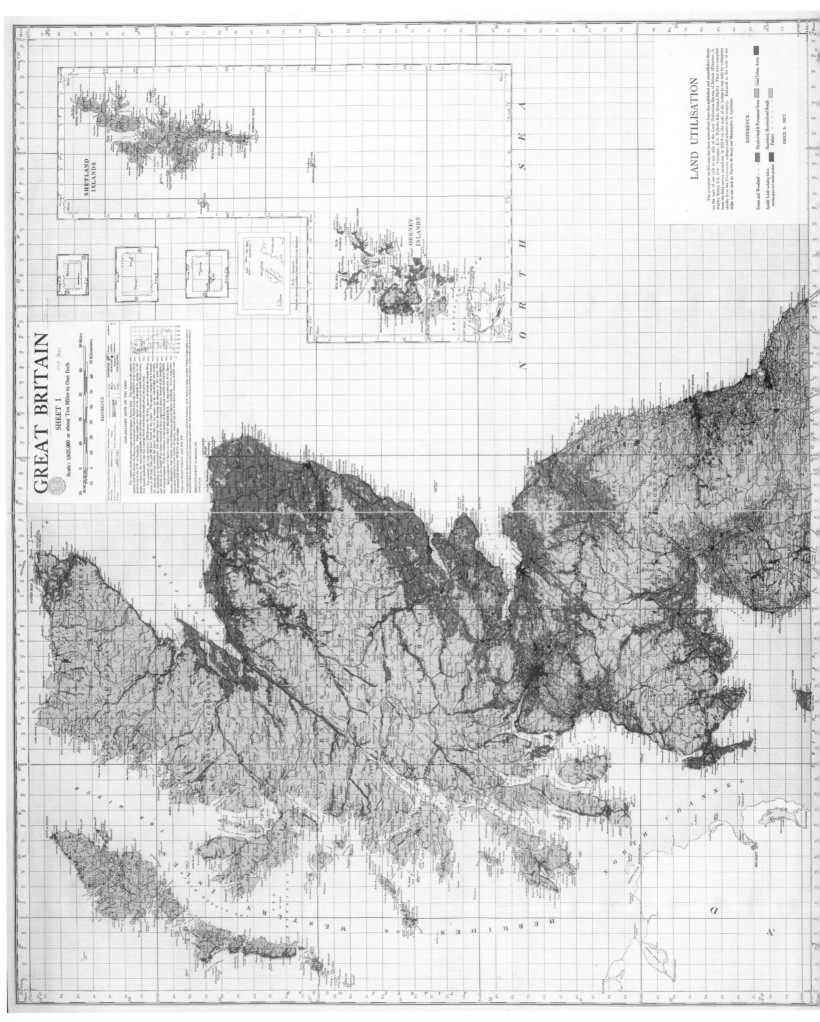

GREAT BRITAIN

SHEET 1

Scale: 1/625,000 or about Ten Miles to One Inch

SHETLAND ISLANDS

ORKNEY ISLANDS

N O R T H   S E A

A T L A N T I C   O C E A N

O U T E R   H E B R I D E S or W E S T E R N   I S L E S

NORTH CHANNEL

LAND UTILISATION

The overprint on this map has been compiled from the published and unpublished sheets on the scale of one inch to one mile of the Land Utilisation Survey of Britain (Director: L. Dudley Stamp, B.A., D.Sc.; Secretary: E. C. Willatts, B.Sc.(Econ.), Ph.D.) They were compiled from the field surveys carried out in 1931-9 on the scale of six inches to one mile by volunteers, chiefly drawn from the Universities, schools and colleges of the country. Reduced to the scale of ten miles to one inch by Phyllis M. Boyd and Marguerite V. Coldman.

REFERENCE

Forest and Woodland

Meadowland & Permanent Grass

Arable Land including fallow, rotation grass and market gardens

Chief Urban Areas

Heathland, Moorland and Rough Pasture

PRICE 3/- NET.

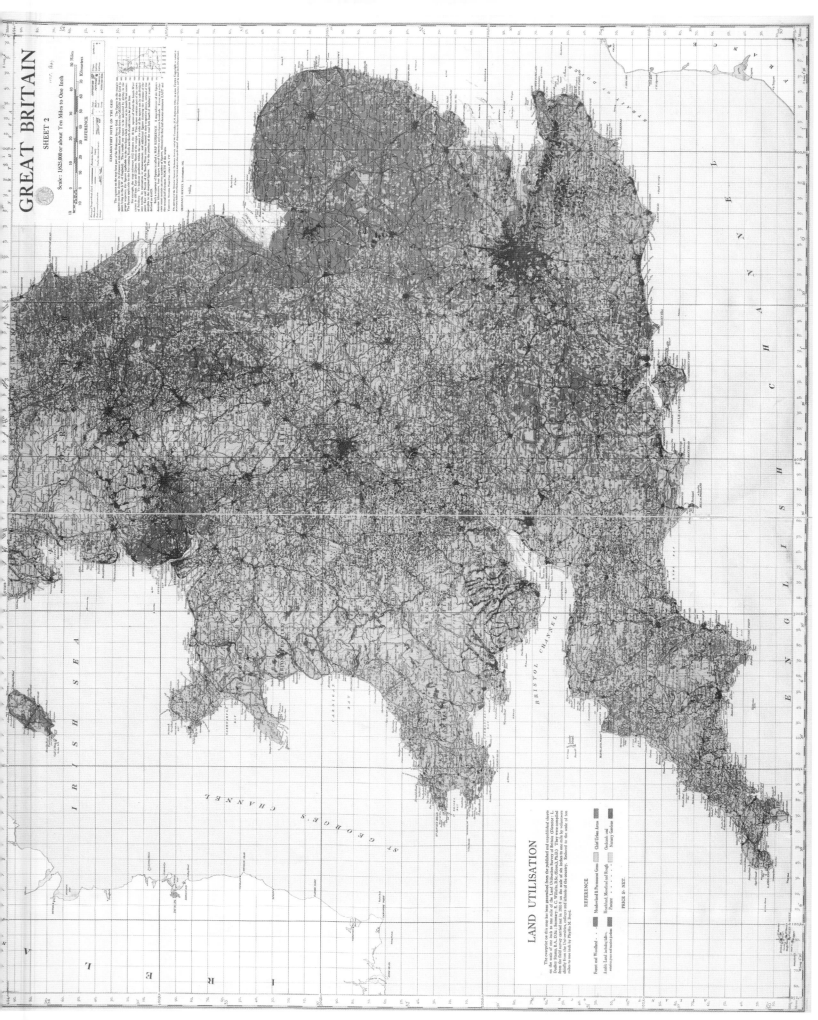

GREAT BRITAIN

SHEET 2

Scale: 1/625,000 or about Ten Miles to One Inch

LAND UTILISATION

The viewprint on this map has been generalised from the published and unpublished sheets on the scale of one inch to one mile of the Land Utilisation Survey of Britain (Director: L. Dudley Stamp, B.A., D.Sc.; Secretary: E. C. Willatts, B.Sc. (Econ.), Ph.D.) They were compiled from the field survey carried out in 1931-34 on the scale of six inches to one mile by reductions chiefly from the Universities, colleges and schools of the country. Reduced to the scale of ten miles to one inch by Phyllis M. Boyd.

PRICE 2/- NET.

REFERENCE

Forest and Woodland	Meadowland & Permanent Grass
Arable Land including fallow, rotation grass and market gardens	Heathland, Moorland and Rough Pasture
	Chief Urban Areas
	Orchards and Nursery Gardens

BRAVE NEW WORLDS

Patrick Abercrombie and James Paton Watson, 'City of Plymouth: New City Centre', 1943.

The Second World War transformed Britain, not least its cityscapes, with enormous damage done by bombing and rocket attack, principally to London and the other major ports. Much of the housing stock was destroyed or damaged, but there were marked variations between and within cities, reflecting both German planning and operational vagaries, not least because bombs were 'dumb' munitions rather than the 'smart' guided ones that came several decades after the war. The Germans devoted much effort to hitting London, dropping by mid-November 1940 over 13,000 tons of high explosive bombs on the city as well as nearly one million incendiaries. This was part of an attempt to destroy civilian morale by terror bombing, yet there were also other strategies at play. In particular, there was an attempt to starve Britain into surrender by destroying the docks through which food was imported. London, Liverpool, Plymouth and Southampton were heavily attacked for that reason, as well as to deny the navy bases. Opportunity also encouraged attack on settlements on or close to the South coast, such as Plymouth, Exeter, Weymouth and Southampton. The range of cities that received heavy attacks included Coventry (which received 818 tons of bombs), Manchester (578 tons), Belfast and Hull.

Bomb damage was mapped to provide a key tool for post-war planners, who often carried out their rebuilding with a determination to break from the patterns of the past in land use and housing, building instead what they viewed as a new future for a new society. Their achievement often failed to match up to the hopes they had raised. Men like Patrick Abercrombie for London and Plymouth and Thomas Sharp for Exeter felt they had been presented with a blank slate on which to build, an opportunity to realise their pre-war inclinations for slum removal and 'improvement' through modern, progressive urban architecture.

The post-war planners faced a difficult task because, in their view (rather than that of the public), it was not an option to rebuild cities devastated by bombing in a re-creation of history; meanwhile, the context echoed the situation after the Great Fire of London in 1666, with a shortage of resources and funds, and a pressure for speed. Although Abercrombie's work appreciated the nature of community, there was an excessive willingness to remould the street pattern for the sake of motorists. His map reflected the major rethinking possible when presented with the opportunity provided by the devastation of Plymouth and its flatness – again similar in many respects to the planned rebuilding of London after the Great Fire. However, there was a deceptive character to the mapping because it was two-dimensional with no indications of the height of the likely buildings and the impact on sight lines. As with the earlier Wren maps, the emphasis on street planning was placed on circulation. But in Plymouth there was a failure to assess the consequences of opening up the city for exposure to wind and wind-driven rain, and notably so in the shape of the prevailing Atlantic westerlies.

Abercrombie's colour-coded plans reflected his strong commitment and that of other planners to separate residential, commercial and industrial areas into precincts (see detail, below). These measures were seen as likely to enhance efficiency and the quality of life but they were ones that hit communities as well as damaging workshop-based employment. However, the boldness of his plans, including their visual strength as maps, encouraged many. In practice, the city centres, while easier of access for cars and lorries, and praised in some guidebooks of the 1950s, proved unattractive, and by the 1970s somewhat tired.

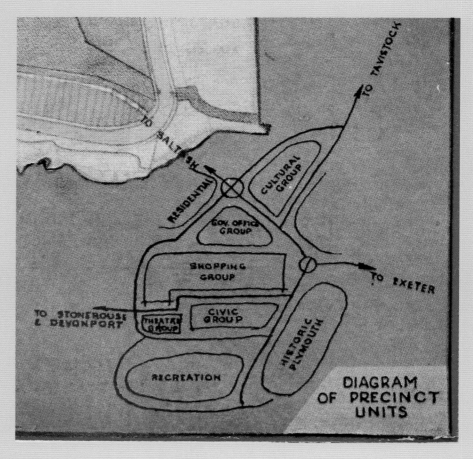

CITY OF PLYMOUTH

NORTH ROAD STATION

ST MATTHIAS CHURCH

CHRIST CHURCH

SHERWELL CHURCH

ALL SAINTS CHURCH

PUBLIC LIBRARY

GREAT WESTERN RAILWAY

UNION STREET

ST ANDREW'S CHURCH

ROYAL CINEMA

THE CRESCENT

SUTTON HARBOUR

MAYFLOWER STONE

THE PROMENADE

THE HOE

THE SOUND

KEY TO COLOURS

CIVIC & THEATRE GROUP
SHOPPING GROUP
GOVERNMENT OFFICE GROUP
STATION HOTEL & TERMINUS
OTHER BUILDING AREAS

Scale of feet
100 0 100 200 300 400 500

RAILWAY COMMUNICATIONS
THROUGH TRAFFIC ARTERIES
PRECINCT ROADS
PEDESTRIAN WAYS
OPEN SPACES ETC

DIAGRAM OF PRECINCT UNITS

PROTECTING THE REALM

Ministry of Home Security, 'Defence of Britain:
Defences as at "D" Day 6 June 1944', 1945.

Prepared in May 1945 to accompany a memorandum issued by the Ministry of Home Security's Key Points Intelligence Directorate's Cartography Section, this map covers events from the year before, more specifically the situation on the day of the invasion of France. The purpose of the compilation is unknown. Although the scale of the original map was one inch to one mile, this is drawn at a scale of four miles to an inch. The map shows the country's defences against air attack, in the shape of guns and balloons. The grouping of defences in belts indicated the need to protect both ports and coastal areas, the point of access, and also London, which remained a prime target with vulnerabilities that were to be exploited by German V-rockets, a form of drone. The map indicated the need to prepare against dive-bombers ('Anti "Diver" Defences'). 'HAA' signifies high-altitude artillery.

The small blue boxes with an R and a date (for example, 'R 11.6.44' off Hastings) report German aerial reconnaissance, and give an indication of how infrequent it was. Hitler never put sufficient emphasis on reconnaissance, but most of the Luftwaffe was anyway fully occupied at home to defend against the Anglo-American Combined Bomber Offensive. Moreover, British air defences were excellent. The contrast between the Luftwaffe's ability to threaten the British retreat from Dunkirk in 1940 and its failure to disrupt the Normandy landings was striking. Only two Luftwaffe pilots fired shots in anger on 6 June.

The lines on the map for marshalling and embarkation areas indicated key locations to keep from German air attack and reconnaissance. The defences indicated included decoys and smoke screens. The red lines represent belts of high- and low-altitude artillery to defend against potential dive-bomber attacks.

The Germans continued to mount bomber attacks, and Hitler remained committed to them. Indeed, in June 1944 he ordered the title of the Me-262, the first jet aircraft to enter service, changed to Blitzbomber because he wanted it used as a high-speed bomber rather than as an interceptor of Allied bombers. There were also plans for the Ju-287, a jet bomber with four engines. However, it was to be rockets that were used: V-1s, launched at Britain from 13 June, were followed from 8 September by V-2s, which were too fast to be destroyed by anti-aircraft fire, as the V-1s could be.

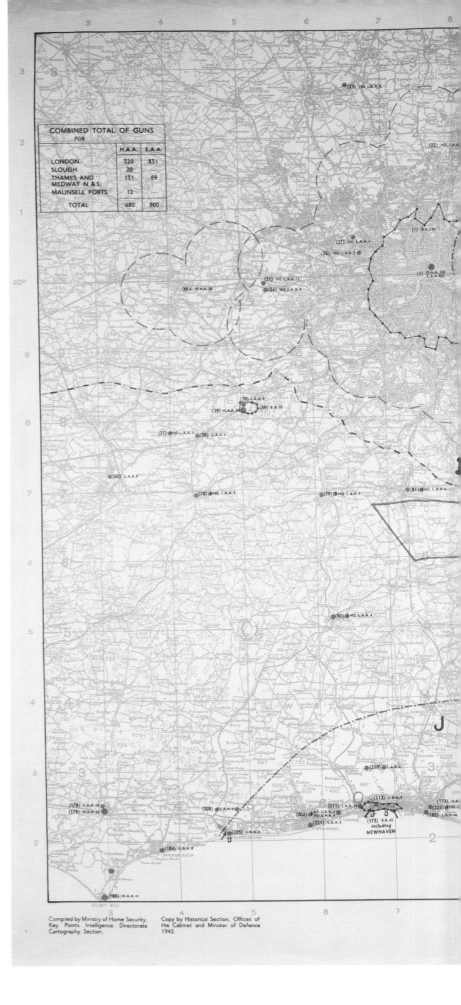

COMBINED TOTAL OF GUNS FOR		
	H.A.A.	Z.A.A.
LONDON	320	831
SLOUGH	20	
THAMES AND MEDWAY N. & S.	131	69
MAUNSELL FORTS	12	
TOTAL	480	900

Compiled by Ministry of Home Security, Key Points Intelligence Directorate Cartography Section.

Copy by Historical Section, Offices of the Cabinet and Minister of Defence 1945.

ANTI-DIVER
BALLOON BARRAGE

ANTI-DIVER
S. COASTAL BELT AND BOX   PEAK TOTALS — H.A.A. = 703
L.A.A. = 1312 $^{40}_{MM}$
= 790 $^{20}_{MM}$

Maunsell Forts

MAUNSELL FORTS

ANTI-DIVER
BALLOON BARRAGE
FROM 479 TO PEAK
TOTAL OF 2003

BELT

GUN

ANTI-DIVER   INLAND
PEAK TOTALS — H.A.A. = 375
L.A.A. = 1198

ANTI-DIVER
S.COASTAL BELT
AND BOX
PEAK TOTALS — H.A.A. = 703
L.A.A. = 1312 $^{40}_{MM}$
= 790 $^{20}_{MM}$

TO BOULOGNE

Scale: Quarter-Inch to One Statute Mile · 1/253440

25 Miles

8000   16,000   24,000   32,000   40,000   44,000 Yards

HS/8/1

DEFENCE OF BRITAIN
DEFENCES AS AT "D" DAY 6 JUNE 1944
and
ANTI "DIVER" DEFENCES

MAPS X.293

THE NEW FUEL

Electrical Press, '*Electrical Industries* Graded Supply Map of England & Wales...', 1947.

The Electricity Supply Act of 1926 established a National Grid for electricity, under the control of the Central Electricity Board. Schemes for supply areas were prepared by the Electricity Commission and adopted by the Central Electricity Board (see boards' boundaries map, right). Household electricity supplies expanded greatly, replacing human effort and other sources of energy and lighting, including gas and candles. Electricity was seen as clean and convenient, and as a way to improve the environment; power, heat and light were increasingly dependent on electricity.

This map (opposite) integrated the use of colour in order to provide a considerable amount of information. In particular, it displays the geographical structure of organisation combined with more specific data on demand – aggregate consumption is supplemented by per capita usage. Published by Electrical Press Ltd, the map had been compiled by the editor of *Electrical Industries* and it represented original research in the shape of working out the per capita usage by dividing output by population. Clear colour contrasts differentiate the output of companies.

The percentage of homes wired for electricity rose from 31.8 per cent in 1932 to 65.4 per cent in 1938 by when the grid was operating as an effective national system. In his novel *Invisible Weapons* (1938), John Rhode captured change in a British cottage: 'Everything here's absolutely up to date ... all the latest gadgets – tiled bathroom, latest type of gas cooker, electric refrigerator, coke boiler for constant hot water ... a labour-saving house.'

Refrigeration had a major impact on food storage and thus on the range of food available in households with fridges. Sales of electrical goods became economically important. Advertisements from the County of London Electric Supply Company for electric irons and kettles referred to 'The extra comforts which electrical services provide' and 'You must move with the times'. Such expenditure reflected, and helped to define, class differences. Whereas radios, vacuum cleaners and electric irons were widely owned, in part thanks to the spread of hire purchase, electric fridges, cookers and washing machines were largely restricted to the middle class. New owner-occupied suburban houses tended to have electricity supply and appliances; working-class terraces less so. Social differences had a regional component, with ownership of such goods, and access to electricity consumption, higher in the Southeast than in areas such as South Wales.

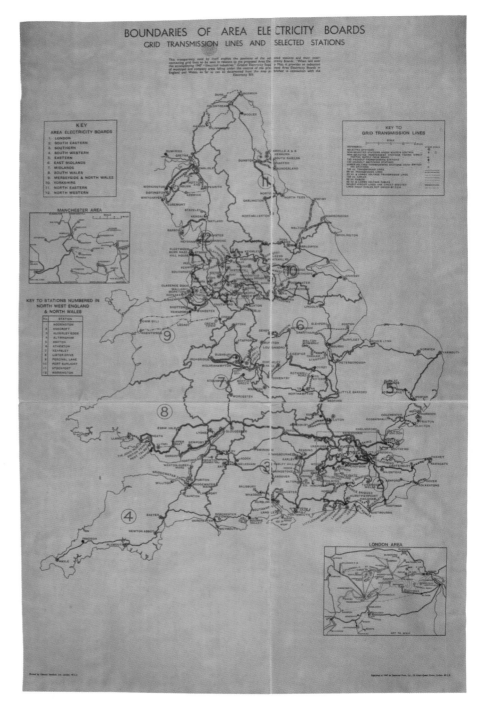

"ELECTRICAL INDUSTRIES" GRADED SUPPLY MAP of ENGLAND & WALES

Showing Areas of Authorised Distributors, Output of
Undertakings (excluding traction and bulk supplies),
and Consumption per head of population per annum

*(The grading is based upon the latest official statistics
available at the time the map was prepared.)*

THE MARK OF 'THE WORLD'S STANDARD IN CABLES & WIRES'

CERTIFICATION MARK

STREET ATLAS

Geographers' Map Co., Ltd., 'Saltley', 1956.

This is mapping organised around thousands of streets, with the index crucial. The 1956 *Geographers' A to Z Street Atlas of Birmingham and the West Midlands* in fact covered the contiguous built up area, notably including Walsall and Wolverhampton. The 76 sectional maps included public transport in the shape of railways, bus, trolleybus and tram routes, as well as public buildings in the form of post offices, fire stations, police stations and hospitals. House numbers on the main thoroughfares were also provided. Separately, there was a map for main roads and a complete index of the 11,000 plus streets depicted.

This map of the inner-city district of Saltley shows the prominence of railway lines and facilities, notably goods stations, as well as the gas works and gas holders that were conspicuous prior to the landing of natural gas from the North Sea. Adderley Park, marked here south of the landmark Saltley Viaduct, which crosses the Grand Union Canal, was the first public park in Birmingham, with its own free public library and museum at the entrance. Saltley in part reflects the subsuming of the granulated variety of past life by the uniformity of change. In the late nineteenth century a philanthropic Lord of the Manor built attractive streets for ordinary people and endowed public buildings and parkland, but this heritage has largely been lost. In part, there was a failure to compensate for the inroads and disrepair of time; however, the lack of commitment, as in so many municipal areas, reflected the agglomeration of local government areas and the resulting lack of interest by distant local government officials.

In the 'A-Z'ing of life, habitations emerge as the spaces between streets. Differences within the city or town, for example of wealth, or environmental or housing quality, are ignored. Political canvassers, estate agents, police officers and residents are aware of detailed variations among streets, of a geography of zones and boundaries, of ownership and residence patterns that do not appear on any street plan. Instead, the perceptions that create and reflect senses of urban space – often rival, contested and atavistic – are neglected in favour of a bland uniform background that is described, and thus experienced, insofar as there is any explanation, in terms of routes (although the latter are not depicted with sufficient attention to

their problems as routes, notably traffic density). This is not so much a world of neighbourhoods as it is a road system.

Moreover, these maps of cities are very much ground level, with little, if any, suggestion of the vertical, and thus of the many who live and work in skyscrapers or more modest multi-storey buildings, and indeed of the transport problems these buildings pose and the links they offer. There are hints about urban environmental quality, as with the presence of parkland and the distance between streets: the wider the gap the more likely that there are gardens of some size.

The focus in discussion of England on London ensured that the significance of Birmingham, the country's second-biggest city, was often underplayed. In part this was because it was not widely perceived as a social or political problem. In reality, an area that had been an industrial powerhouse faced growing problems and by the 2010s had relatively low rates of business start-ups and economic output per head.

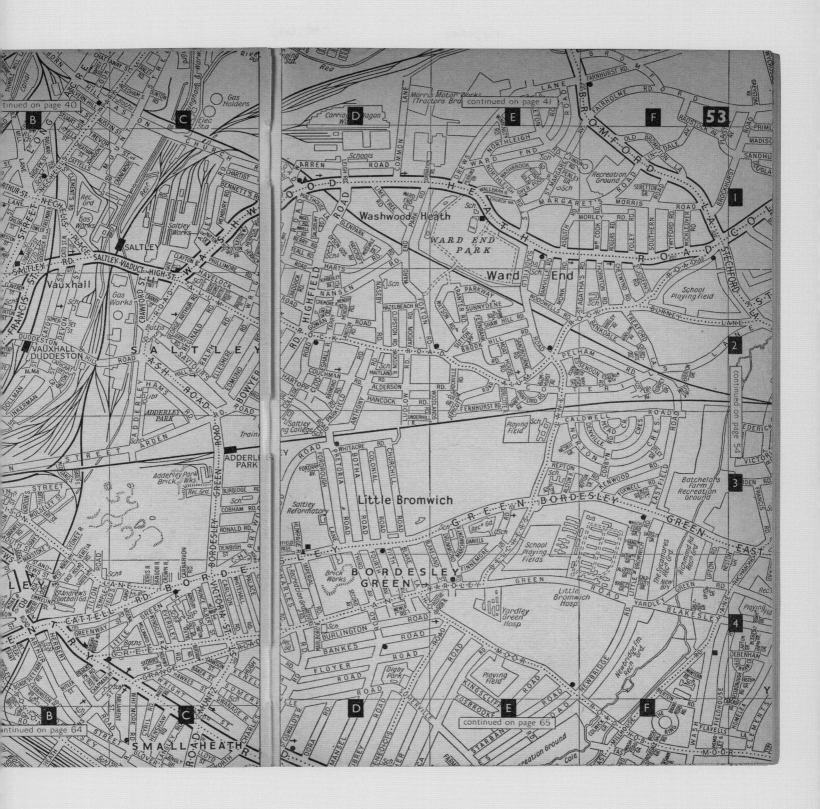

tinued on page 40
continued on page 41
continued on page 54
continued on page 64
continued on page 65

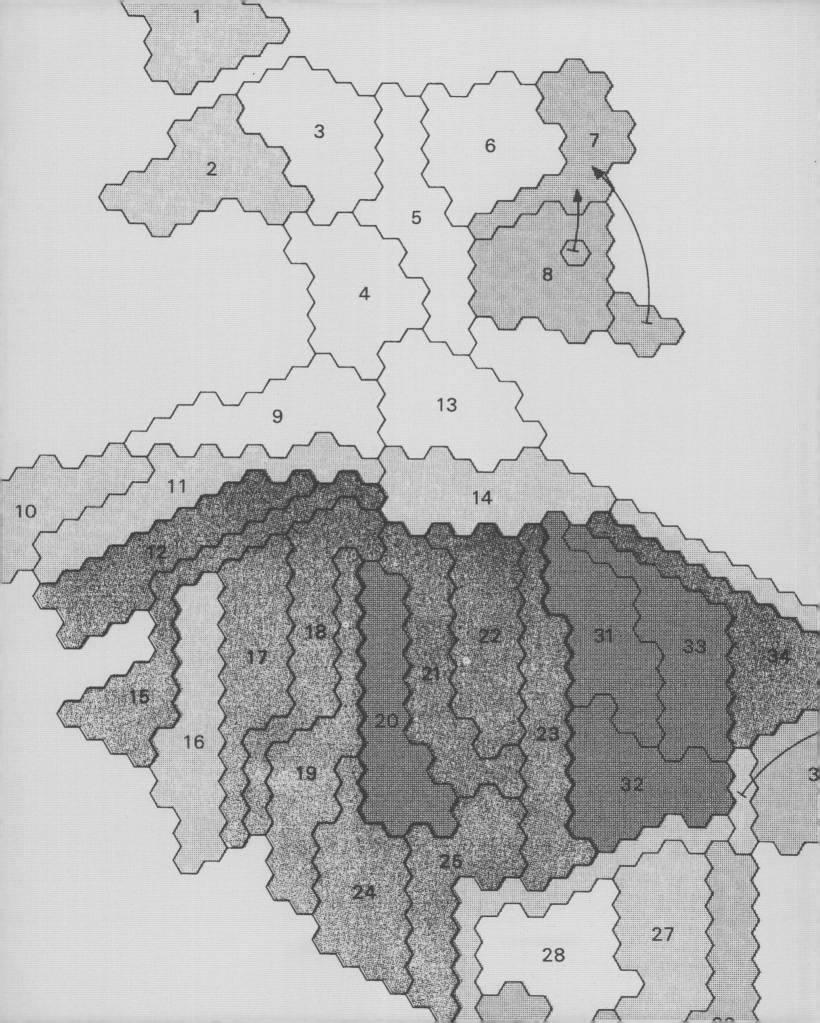

6

1960–TODAY:
NEW SUBJECTS, NEW TECHNIQUES

As part of a greater interest in locational analysis, spatial processes and proactive governance, new subjects included environmental issues and a greater engagement with social inequality. New techniques included a major use of computers in analysis, presentation and production, and, more specifically, navigation systems for travellers using Global Positioning System (GPS), which were operational for civilian use from the 1980s. Computer-based mapping drew on Geographic Information Systems (GIS), which ensured that the printed map, the only section of earlier cartographies seen by consumers, whether public or private, was but one outcome from a spatial database, with the relevant software allowing a variety of approaches to, and presentations of, the data.

Because computer graphics software was adopted for map production, for example for weather maps, most maps were computer generated by the late 1990s, and existing information was digitised. The use of dot matrix printers and then inkjet printers helped in the reproduction of colour. Laser printers followed, and in 1993 colour laser printers. As a result, photomechanical film work was no longer necessary and the flexibility of map design, already increased by photomechanical techniques, was greatly enhanced, although this democratisation was not always accompanied by an understanding of the limitations of maps.

The flexibility of use with digital data was seen with 'zoomable maps', which offered particular magnification of selected portions, and with the ready printing of maps from websites such as Google and MapQuest. The recent and current situation is dynamic, and with a multitude of stakeholders

in cartography, because the production of maps has become much easier and the interface of maps and diagrams more widespread. Readily available data-processing and printing software ensures that mapmaking is now within the scope of anyone with a computer, and the results contrast less with those produced by specialists than was the case in the age of engraving and hot-metal typesetting and printing. This, however, does not mean that data analysis and presentation are free of problems. Indeed, to a degree, the opposite is the case because it is easier now to produce maps that, deliberately or not, are seriously flawed, if not actively misleading. The contentiousness of some of the issues involved may well encourage this process. For example, a central subject is that of communications, with directions of flow a key topic for depiction in maps, in terms of goods, people, ideas and more.

Many older map formats have been revived, for example maps for cyclists and walkers such as those in Alfred Wainwright's *Pennine Way Companion* (1968). However, in-vehicle navigation systems are new, not least because they can now communicate with the driver. There is also the use of mapping as an aspect of lobbying and public advocacy, not least in order to highlight apparent problems. Britain itself has changed greatly over the last 60 years. It is more urbanised, more built up, more diverse ethnically and culturally, less industrial and with a larger service sector. Growth, both demographic and economic, has been particularly pronounced in southern England, with maps increasingly covered by symbols relating to built-up space.

A REDUCED RAIL SYSTEM

British Railways, 'Proposed Withdrawal of Passenger Train Services, Map No. 9', 1963.

The rail system in Britain was hit hard by the rise of road transport, while limited investment in the 1940s had also left much of the system obsolescent, and the inflexibility of the rail unions to adapt and accept change posed major problems. In terms of thousand million passenger miles, private road transport shot up from 47 thousand million passenger miles in 1954 to 217 thousand million passenger miles in 1974, an increase from 39 per cent to 79 per cent of the total and again made at the expense of bus, coach and rail transport. The proportion of goods traffic moved by road rose from 37 per cent in 1952 to 58.3 per cent in 1964, exacerbating the already poor finances of British Rail. Warehousing and distribution increasingly responded to supplies being carried by road-based transport.

The geography of Britain's rail system was transformed in 1963 with the publication of *The Reshaping of British Railways*, which was better known after Dr Richard Beeching, the chairman of the British Railways Board, as the Beeching Report. The operating deficit had increased from £16.5 million in 1956 to nearly £50 million in 1958 and £104 million in 1962, despite measures introduced as part of the major railway modernisation programme begun in 1955, such as diesel railbuses, much of it due to wage increases.

The report used maps extensively in order to present data and also to justify its conclusions. The maps differentiated between freight and passenger services and thus offered different ways to consider usage and revenues. Maps 1 and 9 covered the key passenger points. Map No. 1, on density of usage ('Density of Passenger Traffic', right), showed that most of the network was little used, although the data was not offered proportionate to the local population. Map No. 9 covered the withdrawal of services, which was closely related to Map No. 1. In the event, some lines such as Exeter to Exmouth were saved.

The report proposed the closure of 2,500 stations and one-third of the passenger rail network. The conclusion that half the network carried only one-twentieth of its traffic hit hard, and the policy was to be continued by the Labour government when it was elected in 1964.

There were dramatic cuts in the national network, with freight and services greatly curtailed, the workforce cut, lines taken up, and many stations converted to other uses. Rural and small-town Britain changed as railways that had integrated it into an urban-centred network

were dramatically and finally removed. The focus was on a core network, one made possible and necessary by the move from steam to diesel, and one designed to provide speed, efficiency and profit. In practice, largely rural areas, such as East Anglia, Lincolnshire, Mid-Wales, the Welsh borders and north Cornwall, tended to have inadequate services, while the emphasis on routes into London was not matched by necessary attention to cross-Pennine routes.

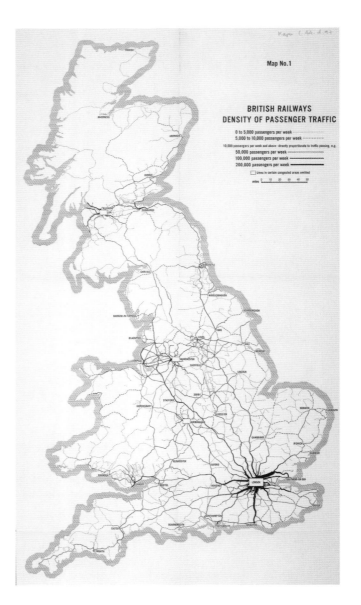

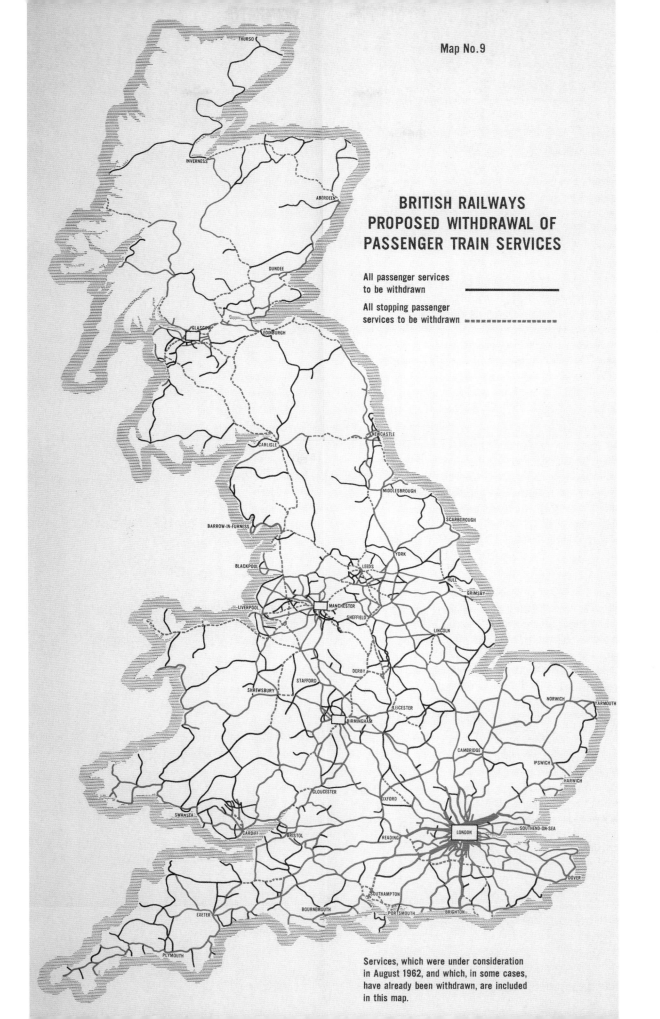

**BRITISH RAILWAYS
PROPOSED WITHDRAWAL OF
PASSENGER TRAIN SERVICES**

All passenger services
to be withdrawn ————————————

All stopping passenger
services to be withdrawn ------------------

Services, which were under consideration
in August 1962, and which, in some cases,
have already been withdrawn, are included
in this map.

THURSO

INVERNESS

ABERDEEN

DUNDEE

GLASGOW EDINBURGH

CARLISLE NEWCASTLE

MIDDLESBROUGH

SCARBOROUGH

BARROW-IN-FURNESS

BLACKPOOL YORK

LEEDS HULL

GRIMSBY

LIVERPOOL MANCHESTER

SHEFFIELD

LINCOLN

DERBY

STAFFORD

SHREWSBURY

LEICESTER

NORWICH

YARMOUTH

BIRMINGHAM

CAMBRIDGE

IPSWICH

HARWICH

GLOUCESTER

OXFORD

SWANSEA

CARDIFF BRISTOL

READING LONDON SOUTHEND-ON-SEA

DOVER

SOUTHAMPTON

EXETER

BOURNEMOUTH

PORTSMOUTH BRIGHTON

PLYMOUTH

FATAL VARIATIONS

Royal Geographical Society, 'Arteriosclerotic Heart Disease, including Coronary Disease (Males)', 1963.

This map is from the *National Atlas of Disease Mortality in the United Kingdom* by Professor George Melvyn Howe, an innovative medical demographer who skilfully assembled and deployed, notably through mapping, medical statistics in order to test and clarify subjective and impressionistic assumptions. He thereby helped to provide a basis for public policy at a time when the National Health Service was starting to address major differences in the public provision of healthcare – differences which he showed interacted with variations in health outcomes. The varied public health of a country with state provision of care for health and social welfare was a problematic issue.

The relationship between higher-than-average mortality and industrial areas, and notably the strong local and regional character of disease rates and health indicators, was readily apparent for both men and women. These maps were snapshots of a dynamic pattern, but the data presented in 1963 has been confirmed by subsequent trends. Alongside increased longevity, not all illnesses retreated, which was unsurprising because people do not live forever.

The assault on health came from a variety of directions. Although other factors also played a significant role, high and rising rates of obesity helped to explain high and rising rates of heart disease and Type 2 diabetes, the former especially acute in Scotland and notably in Clydeside. In England, blood pressure rates are especially high in the North and West Midlands. The poor tend to have less variety and fewer fresh ingredients in their diet, and less opportunity to take exercise.

The Standardised Mortality Ratio used in the atlas was a highly effective way of establishing and then depicting a range within the data, although it required an input from other data sources to provide the social dimension of the causation of these variations.

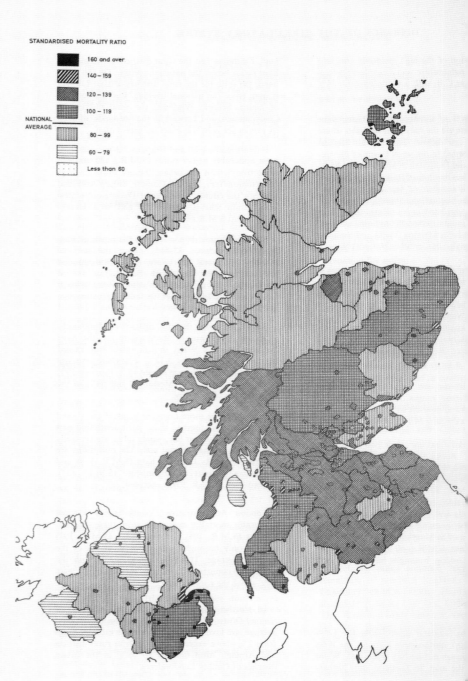

ARTERIOSCLEROTIC HEART DISEASE, INCLUDING CORONARY DISEASE
(MALES)

46

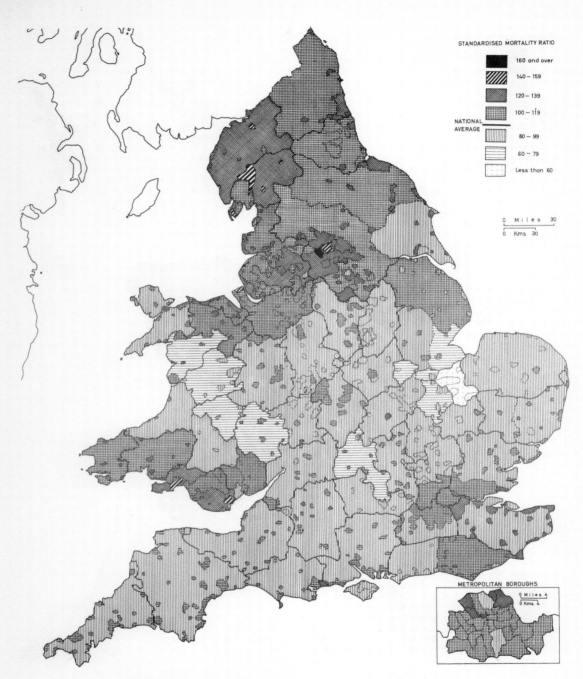

STANDARDISED MORTALITY RATIO

160 and over

140 — 159

120 — 139

100 — 119

NATIONAL
AVERAGE

80 — 99

60 — 79

Less than 60

0 Miles 30

0 Kms 30

METROPOLITAN BOROUGHS

0 Miles 4

0 Kms. 4

ARTERIOSCLEROTIC HEART DISEASE, INCLUDING CORONARY DISEASE
(MALES)

47

GREEN BELT

Catherine Lawrence, 'Map of Cherished Land', 1973.

This map, from the October 1973 edition of *Geographical Magazine*, revealed the range of designations of protected land and also its location with reference to major urban areas and motorways. As an exercise in mapmaking, it made good use of colour, employing it to discriminate between types of protected land (including National Parks existing and proposed, Areas of Outstanding natural beauty existing and proposed, approved Green Belt and Green Belt under consideration, and local authority-controlled country parks and picnic sites), while the urban areas and motorways are reduced to a monotone. The use of numbers and boxes enables the listing of a mass of information. The use of brown, a standard terrain colour on maps, to capture a physical rather than a legal or institutional designation of the landscape provides a way to contextualise, locate and look at the latter. The limited provision of protected land in the Midlands and East Anglia emerges clearly.

Pressure from the public for national parks had led the Labour government to establish an inquiry, which in 1931 recommended a National Parks Authority, but with the Conservatives reluctant, due to landowner interests, such a body had to wait until the Labour Party regained power after the Second World War.

In 1949 the government created a National Parks Commission (NPC) and gave it power to designate national parks in England and Wales. The first, established in 1951, were the Lake District (see detail, right), the Peak District, Snowdonia and Dartmoor. They were followed by the North York Moors (1952), the Pembrokeshire Coast (1952), Exmoor (1954), the Yorkshire Dales (1954), Northumberland (1956) and the Brecon Beacons (1957). The NPC did not own the parks, but instead had to operate through the county councils. The Broads in East Anglia gained status equivalent to that of a national park in 1988, while since then the New Forest (2005) and South Downs (2010) also became national parks. Of the original 12 national parks proposed for England and Wales, two remained undesignated: the Cambrian Mountains and Cornish Coast. In Scotland, the Loch Lomond and the Trossachs National Park was established in 2002, followed by the Cairngorms National Park in 2003.

Areas of Outstanding Natural Beauty (AONB) were established for England and Wales in 1949. They lack the legislative powers of national parks, but also receive protection. The Green

Belt areas depicted had, however, undesirable consequences, including higher house prices, and longer commuting distances from new housing having to be built beyond them.

The National Trust-owned land highlighted was important because it was the largest private landowner in England and Wales, owning for example over 250,000 hectares by 2022. By that year, its Enterprise Neptune covered 780 miles of coast.

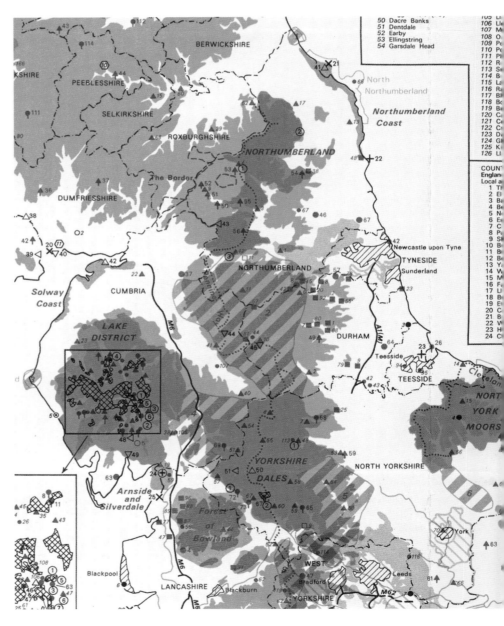

MAP OF CHERISHED LAND

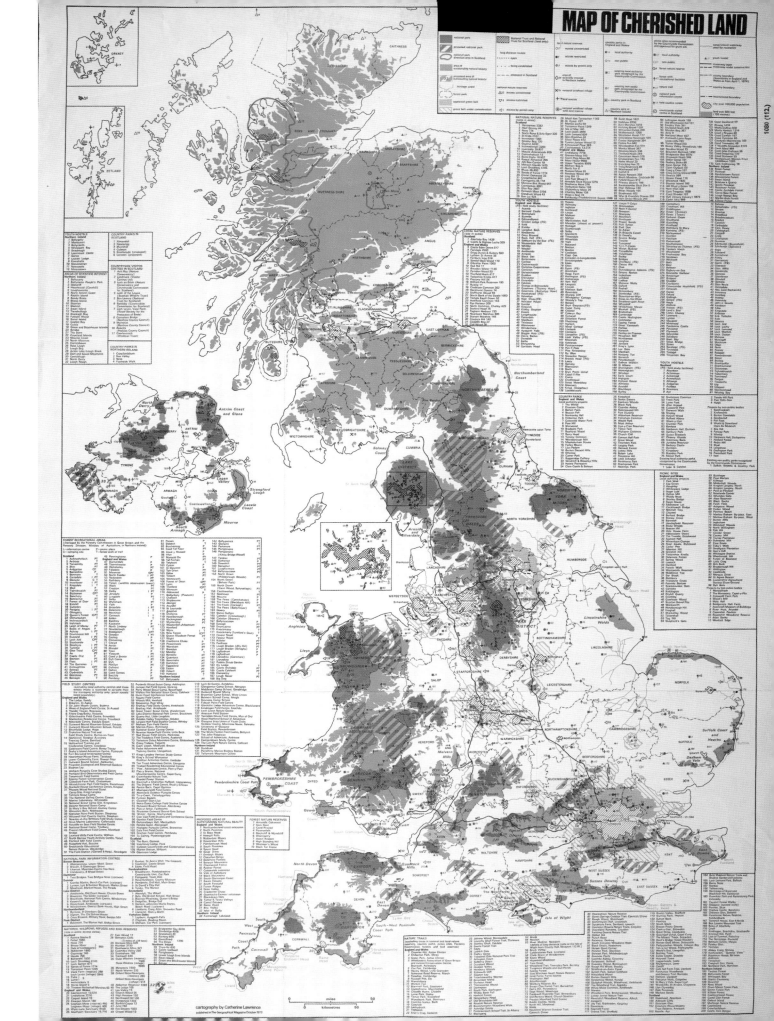

cartography by Catherine Lawrence
published in The Geographical Magazine October 1973

SOILSCAPES

D. Mackney and A.J. Thomasson, 'Winter Rain Acceptance Potential', 1977.

This map was created by the cartography department at the Soil Survey of England and Wales, from work undertaken between 1939 and 1976, mostly as a result of the systematic surveys that followed the establishment of the Soil Survey of England and Wales at Rothamsted Experimental Station in Hertfordshire in 1954. In addition to the individual sheets of maps produced after the survey, the data assembled provided an opportunity for mapping at the national level, as with this map of rainfall acceptance, which provided guidance to likely soil saturation. The contrast (opposite) between Midland clays and the light soils of East Anglia emerge clearly, as do those between the Wealden Greensand and the surrounding Downland.

The map is an important indicator of an area's agricultural capability, and therefore parallels William Smith's 1815 geological map (see pages 12–13). Organised soil classification moves beyond the knowledge of individual farmers. The detailed understanding of soil is important for the often competing interests of farmers and planners, interests that played a clashing role in development until the fertility of agricultural land was subordinated to planning requirements from the 2000s. Soil maps were a variant on the underlying geological ones, but more complex due to the factors affecting soil types, including recent surface erosion.

The local Bangor sheet (right) showed not only much of Snowdonia, but also the lowlands to the east as well as the Menai Strait to the northwest and Anglesey beyond. The use of colour served well to distinguish between soil types and notably the soils to the east from Snowdon's rocks. The use of symbols and colours, with a considerable range offered for the latter, ensured that a considerable amount of information could be conveyed by these maps, which here includes the Soil Group, Drainage Class and Parent Material. Unlike most of the survey sheets, the Bangor area map was supported by a prominent perspective block, which employed a vertical perspective to underline terrain differences.

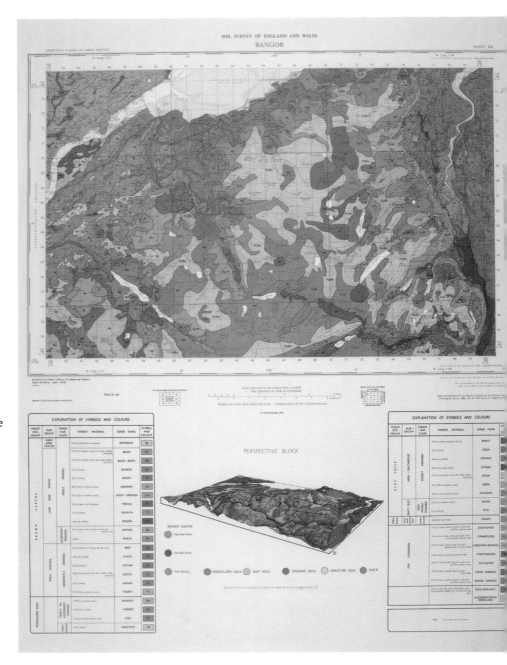

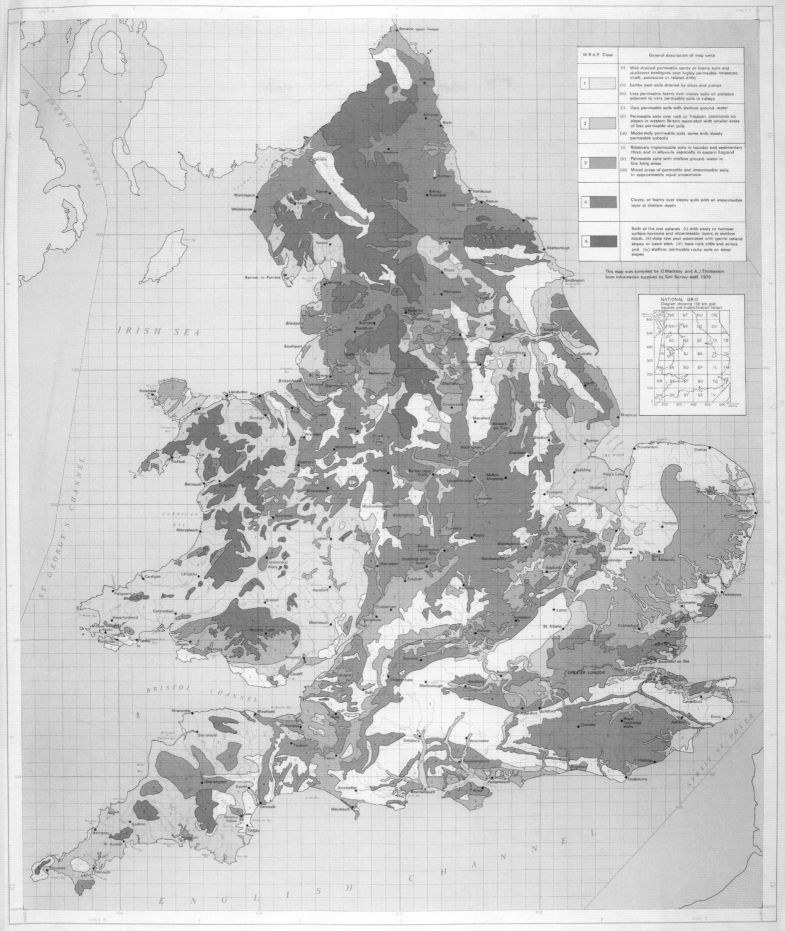

Soil Survey of England and Wales
Winter Rain Acceptance Potential

W.R.A.P. Class		General description of map units
1	(i)	Well drained permeable sandy or loamy soils and shallower analogues over highly permeable limestone, chalk, sandstone or related drifts
	(ii)	Earthy peat soils drained by dikes and pumps
	(iii)	Less permeable loamy over clayey soils on plateaux adjacent to very permeable soils in valleys
2	(i)	Very permeable soils with shallow ground-water
	(ii)	Permeable soils over rock or fragipan, commonly on slopes in western Britain associated with smaller areas of less permeable wet soils
	(iii)	Moderately permeable soils, some with slowly permeable subsoils
3	(i)	Relatively impermeable soils in boulder and sedimentary clays, and in alluvium, especially in eastern England
	(ii)	Permeable soils with shallow ground-water in low lying areas
	(iii)	Mixed areas of permeable and impermeable soils, in approximately equal proportions
4		Clayey, or loamy over clayey soils with an impermeable layer at shallow depth
5		Soils of the wet uplands (i) with peaty or humose surface horizons and impermeable layers at shallow depths, (ii) deep raw peat associated with gentle upland slopes or basin sites, (iii) bare rock cliffs and screes and, (iv) shallow, permeable rocky soils on steep slopes

This map was compiled by D. Mackney and A.J. Thomasson from information supplied by Soil Survey staff, 1976

NATIONAL GRID
Diagram showing 100 km grid squares and identification letters

Head of Soil Survey K.E. Clare

Map drawn by the Cartography Dept.
Soil Survey of England and Wales 1977

Based on the International Map of the World 1:1 000 000 Sheet NN-30 1966

Made and published by the Director General of the Ordnance Survey
Southampton, for the Soil Survey of England & Wales

SCALE 1:1 000 000

BARTHOLOMEW

WEATHER MAP
OF THE BRITISH ISLES

Compiled and written by D. M. Houghton, Meteorological Office

INFLUENCE OF WEATHER ON MAN

Every day we have to make decisions based upon what the weather is likely to do. We want to know whether to take an umbrella, whether we should wear our plkinis in the garden, whether the wind will be suitable for sailing, whether we should water our plants in case of frost. If we are travelling we need to know whether there is a likelihood of fog, frost or snow. In many areas of commerce and industry the weather is important economically. The ice cream manufacturer and soft drinks supplier want to know the temperature so that they can predict consumption. Building contractors and fruit growers need warnings of frost, tower crane operators need warnings of high winds, railway operators and local authorities warnings of snow and ice. The gas and electricity industries need detailed forecasts of temperature, wind and sunshine, and the offshore industry forecasts of wind and waves. The farmer is particularly interested in rain and sunshine in summer and frost and snow in winter.

CIRRUS ABOVE CUMULUS
ALTO-STRATUS
STRATUS
COLD FRONT APPROACHING

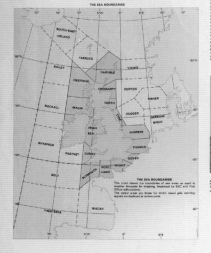

THE SEA BOUNDARIES

This chart shows the boundaries of sea areas as used in weather forecasts for shipping, broadcast by BBC and Post Office radio stations.

THE SEA BOUNDARIES

WEATHER FORECASTS

OLD SAYINGS

STRATO-CUMULUS
ALTO-CUMULUS CASTELLANUS
SEA BREEZE CUMULUS

SYMBOLS USED ON BBC TV WEATHER FORECASTS

PRESSURE DEFINITIONS

AIR MASSES

WEATHER OBSERVATION

WEATHER INFORMATION BY SATELLITE

WEATHER-RECORDING INSTRUMENTS

PRECIPITATION

TEMPERATURE

ANNUAL RANGE OF TEMPERATURE AND TOTAL PRECIPITATION

AIR FLOW MAP

TYPICAL WEATHER SEQUENCE

WEATHER EXTREMES BRITISH ISLES

ACKNOWLEDGEMENTS

All photographs are copyright R K Pilsbury except:

BEAUFORT SCALE SPECIFICATIONS

BEAUFORT SCALE

CUMULUS OVER BURNING STUBBLE
LIGHTNING

RAINBOW
HEAVY RAIN

FOGGY AFTERNOON

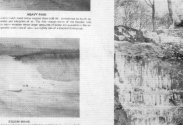

FROZEN WATERFALL

THAMES FROZEN

SNOW
HAIL
STORM WAVE

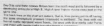

FORECASTING

D.M. Houghton, 'Weather Map of the British Isles', 1978.

Mapping the weather requires the presentation of masses of data in four dimensions, with all the complexity that entails. A specialist mapping language has developed in order to present such data, although it faces the additional challenges posed by contrasting requirements and understanding on the part of particular user groups. This weather map, compiled and written by D.M. Houghton, a member of the Meteorological Office, provided help on a key area of notation – that for a typical weather sequence. The passage of two depressions, Low A and Low B, is shown (opposite left, bottom), followed by the development of an anticyclone, High B. There is then an explanation of isobars and cyclonic fronts. This period of mapping was one requiring more knowledge and work on the part of the reader than that which simply used symbols.

Weather maps had appeared in *The Times* from 1875 onwards. For a long time, weather maps were black and white, and in newspapers were produced with limited detail and in a highly conventional style. The information offered remained limited; indeed, it remained of limited interest. Isobars were smoothly curved, and fronts were absent in the maps printed daily in *The Times* in the 1930s.

After the Second World War had brought greater knowledge about weather, fronts were presented. This was an important aspect of change, which then accelerated, with television providing the public with weather maps that were explained, while radar and then weather satellites provided meteorologists with more information. The public came to expect accurate prediction. Early television weather maps were frequently manually drawn onto a background of the country.

Eventually a version of radar displays was adopted, and with particular colour notations, notably for temperature and rainfall. Colour helped lead to a further development, and newspapers had to respond to the increased visual interest provided by the treatment of weather on television. In both cases, there was a move away from the depiction of air pressure and instead a focus on the end results in the shape of vivid graphics. Time-lapse weather animation shows the movement of clouds or high- and low-pressure systems. Weather maps on television were transformed by the use of computer graphics. In particular, the weather presenter, using a computer-control device, brings up background images from a computer onto a screen, producing a composite image of person and map, each providing a narrative. The BBC uses highly detailed Meteorological Office (Met Office) data, with the density of isobars an easy indicator of the severity of storms (for example, this mean sea level pressure analysis, left). On 16 October 1987 many trees were felled and travel chaos brought to southern England, although further north there was far less disruption and damage. The previous day, giving the BBC television weather forecast, Michael Fish had said 'batten down the hatches, there's some really stormy weather on the way', but he was remembered for saying there was no hurricane on the way, although he was in fact referring to Florida at that point.

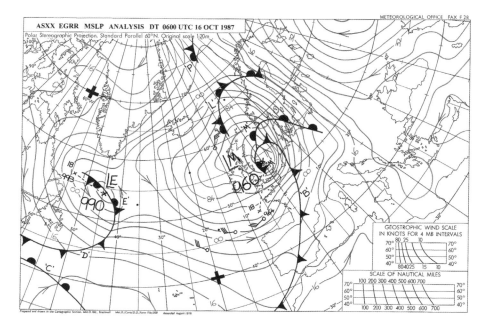

CAPTURING THE INVISIBLE

Cornwall County Council, 'Cornwall County Structure Plan', 1981.

Maps are used in local government to highlight development issues, notably the impact on a partly controlled landscape of regulated land use. In Cornwall, the economy acts to link both, not least due to the economic value of leisure. However, local and regional planners have found it difficult to implement such models. There were no specific plans for new settlements in the plan, but there were housing allocations for each area. The stress was on the provision of housing in existing urban areas, and only in villages with high levels of service provision; a measure intended to reduce driving.

The notion of Tourism Restraint Areas, of which 11 were designated, was a reaction to development pressures. The reference in the key items to 'structure plan area policy numbers' captured the top-down nature of the plan. Moreover, it was not designed as a commercial product and the list of agencies involved reflects the degree of wide consultation underlying such projects. In such cases, maps were very much a group activity

involving clear protocols. More generally, this was a characteristic of the institutional mapping that came to be the norm from the time of the foundation of the Ordnance Survey onwards.

The designation of an area for St Austell China Clay reflected a determination to keep an important extractive industry. There were no comparable hopes for tin. The map gave no attention to fishing, a far more significant Cornish industry. Due to the county basis, the role of Plymouth in Cornish life was underrated

Produced in May 1986 by the Directorate of Development Services, Planning Section, the Upper Airedale Local Plan (below) reflected the significance of current land use policies, regulations and requirements for development, notably for housing, industry and roads. This land use proposals map provided a powerful visual support for what otherwise was sometimes difficult for people to visualise.

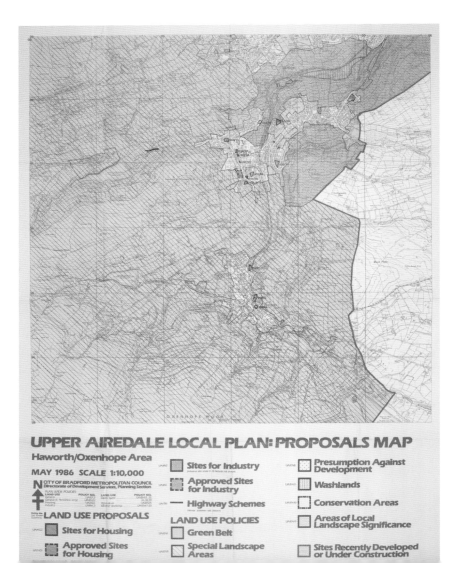

COUNTY WIDE POL■
EMPLOYMENT, IND■
HOUSING
TRANSPORTATION
TOWNS, VILLAGES
EDUCATION, HEAL■
COAST AND COUN■
HOLIDAY INDUSTR■
RECREATION
MINING AND QUAR■
REFUSE DISPOSAL

UPPER AIREDALE LOCAL PLAN: PROPOSALS MAP

Haworth/Oxenhope Area

MAY 1986 SCALE 1:10,000

N CITY OF BRADFORD METROPOLITAN COUNCIL
Directorate of Development Services, Planning Section

LAND USE PROPOSALS

Sites for Housing

Approved Sites for Housing

Sites for Industry

Approved Sites for Industry

Highway Schemes

LAND USE POLICIES

Green Belt

Special Landscape Areas

Presumption Against Development

Washlands

Conservation Areas

Areas of Local Landscape Significance

Sites Recently Developed or Under Construction

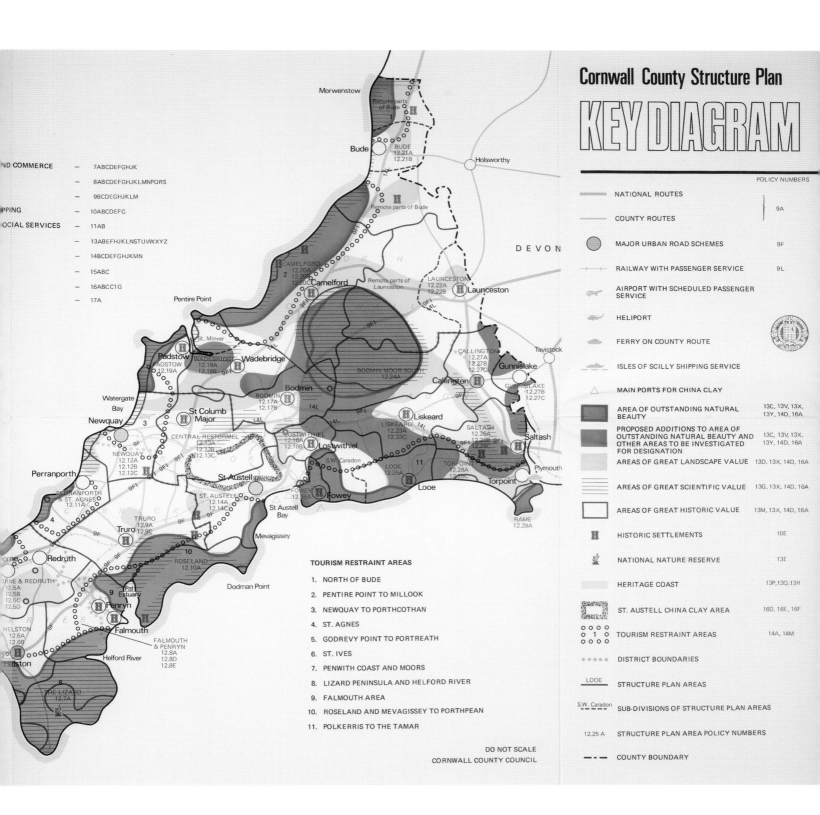

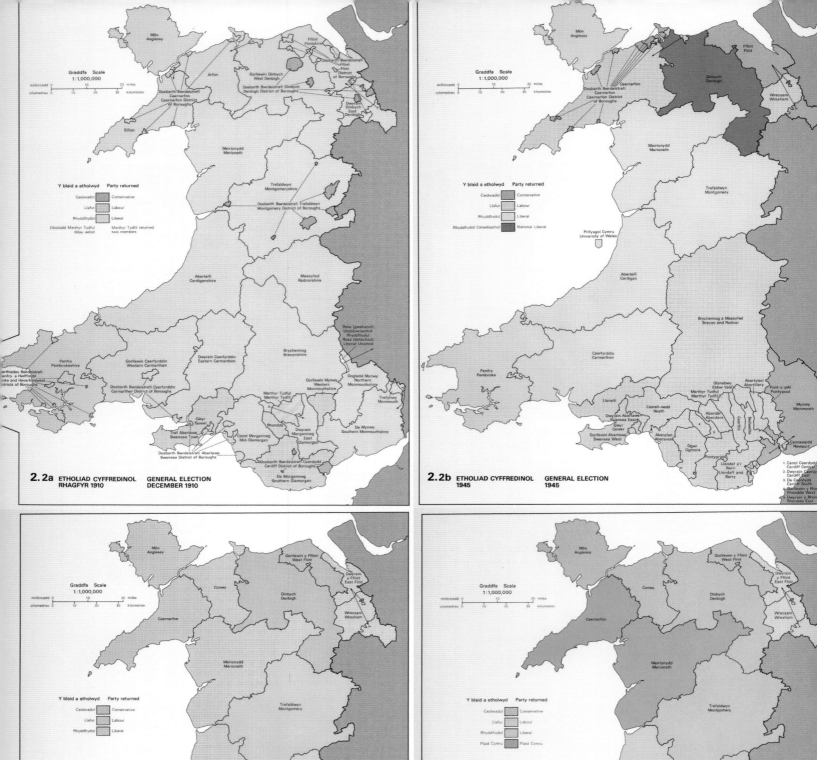

2.2a
ETHOLIAD CYFFREDINOL
RHAGFYR 1910

GENERAL ELECTION
DECEMBER 1910

Graddfa Scale
1:1,000,000

Y blaid a etholwyd — Party returned

Ceidwadol	Conservative
Llafur	Labour
Rhyddfrydol	Liberal

Etholodd Merthyr Tudful — Merthyr Tydfil returned
ddau aelod — two members

2.2b
ETHOLIAD CYFFREDINOL
1945

GENERAL ELECTION
1945

Graddfa Scale
1:1,000,000

Y blaid a etholwyd — Party returned

Ceidwadol	Conservative
Llafur	Labour
Rhyddfrydol	Liberal
Rhyddfrydol Cenedlaethol	National Liberal

2.2c
ETHOLIAD CYFFREDINOL
1966

GENERAL ELECTION
1966

Graddfa Scale
1:1,000,000

Y blaid a etholwyd — Party returned

Ceidwadol	Conservative
Llafur	Labour
Rhyddfrydol	Liberal

2.2d
ETHOLIAD CYFFREDINOL
1979

GENERAL ELECTION
1979

Graddfa Scale
1:1,000,000

Y blaid a etholwyd — Party returned

Ceidwadol	Conservative
Llafur	Labour
Rhyddfrydol	Liberal
Plaid Cymru	Plaid Cymru

RURAL-URBAN DIVIDE

Harold Carter, 'Relative Strength of the Principal Parties 1950–79', 1989.

Maps both clarify and yet also confuse. As observed in the notes to this map in the *National Atlas of Wales* (*Atlas Cenedlaethol Cymru*), the use of area-based constituencies leads to an overemphasis on the role of rural constituencies. In practice, applied to political support, this approach underrated the Labour position because Labour support was concentrated in densely populated areas (see detail, below).

The hardships of the interwar years helped cement an identity of Wales and Labour that persisted in the post-war decades of economic growth. Whereas David Lloyd George of the Liberal Party was the dominant Welsh figure in British politics in the opening decades of the century, in the 1940s and 1950s this role was assumed by Aneurin Bevan, MP for Ebbw Vale, a radical socialist who played the key role in the foundation of the National Health Service and Bevan was no Welsh separatist.

Indeed, Plaid Cymru did badly in elections, winning fewer than 70,000 votes in the 1964 and 1966 general elections. However, in 1966–68, there was an upsurge in support, with the first parliamentary seat won by Gwynfor Evans in a by-election at Carmarthen in July 1966. Plaid provided an attractive alternative for those angered by national and local Labour policies, specifically the unpopularity of national economic policies and a reaction against the dominance of local government, which seemed somehow stale. The party also benefitted from an upsurge of nationalist feeling.

In the 1970 election Plaid contested all the Welsh seats for the first time and won 175,000 votes (11.5 per cent of those cast), but the first-past-the-post electoral system ensured that Labour won 27 parliamentary seats, the Conservatives seven, the Liberals one and Plaid none. In February 1974 Labour's share of the Welsh vote fell to less than half for the first time since the Second World War, but they still won 24 seats, the others gaining eight, two and two respectively. Plaid's support then dipped to only 7.6 per cent in 1979.

Devolution was heavily defeated in the 1979 referendum but narrowly supported in another in 1997, after which a Welsh Assembly was established in Cardiff. The first elections for the new body, held in 1999, left Labour as the largest party with Plaid as the official opposition. Labour proved able to maintain this dominance. The situation was helped by Plaid's problems, seen in this map, in winning support across Wales and particularly in the populous southeast, although Plaid was able to win occasional victories there.

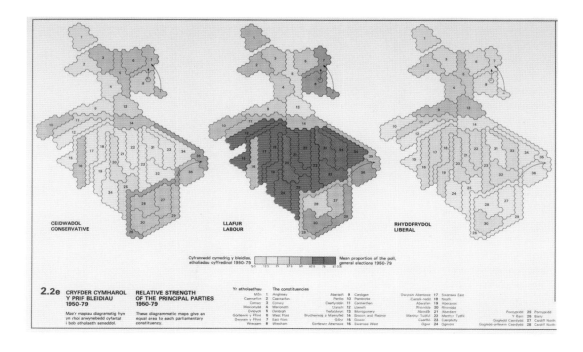

800th BIRTHDAY

Stephen Walter, 'Liverpool', 2008–09.

The disorganised energy of Liverpool and the panopticon cacophony of the artist combine in this highly personal response of filled-in tiny details in words and symbols, created by Stephen Walter to celebrate the city's 800th anniversary. These include footballs (right) to mark the Goodison Park stadium of the city's oldest professional club Everton, in the Walton district, and the nearby stadium of its rival Liverpool, in the Anfield district. Words fill the map, notably the River Mersey.

The comments are sometimes sarcastic. The map is diachronic, including events across time. Although the use of symbols and words may strike some as unusual, there is no reason why a map should not depart from standard procedures as long as it can provide clarity. Indeed, doing so may provide this very clarity.

Liverpool has been hit hard in recent decades, while also displaying impressive signs of resilience. The October 2016 Office of National Statistics figures suggested that of the 11 largest city regions, Liverpool had 1.2 per cent growth in 2011–15, with only Glasgow, at 1 per cent, being lower. Both were former ports of empire, and were hit in part by the decline of the economic links of the imperial period and the corresponding shift of trade towards a focus on the European mainland, as well as by containerisation and the problems in addition to opportunities it posed, not least to areas with a relatively inflexible labour force. Liverpool had a particularly poor reputation for labour relations. In contrast, Felixstowe – which adapted well to containerisation, had good labour relations and was well placed for Europe – boomed as a port.

Liverpool has also done poorly on the Barclays Prosperity Map, which calculates scores based on median household wealth, gross domestic product per capita, the unemployment rate, average household expenditure and house prices, working hours and charitable giving. Serious urban rioting in 'inner-city' Toxteth in 1981 affected the image of Liverpool as a whole, as did the political militancy of its council in the 1980s.

Very different images emerge from the worlds of music and sport. The Beatles, with their debut single 'Love Me Do' released in 1962, set the 'Mersey beat' and offered global prominence to and a sound that invigorated working-class experiences of life. Many other groups and performers also came from Liverpool, including Cilla Black. Interest in the city was also shown by

the popularity of *The Liver Birds*, a television sitcom set there that began in 1969.

However, this impression could not be sustained, and both London and Manchester provided more potent images, with Liverpool's relative decline also seen in football. Urban regeneration from the 2010s, nevertheless, has offered hope and a variety of new possibilities.

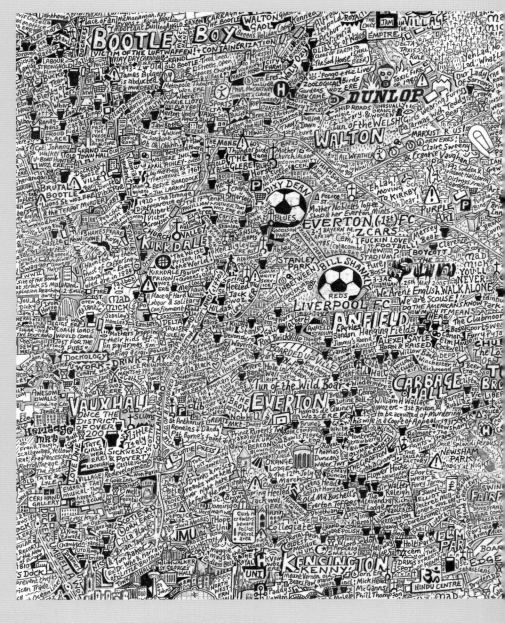

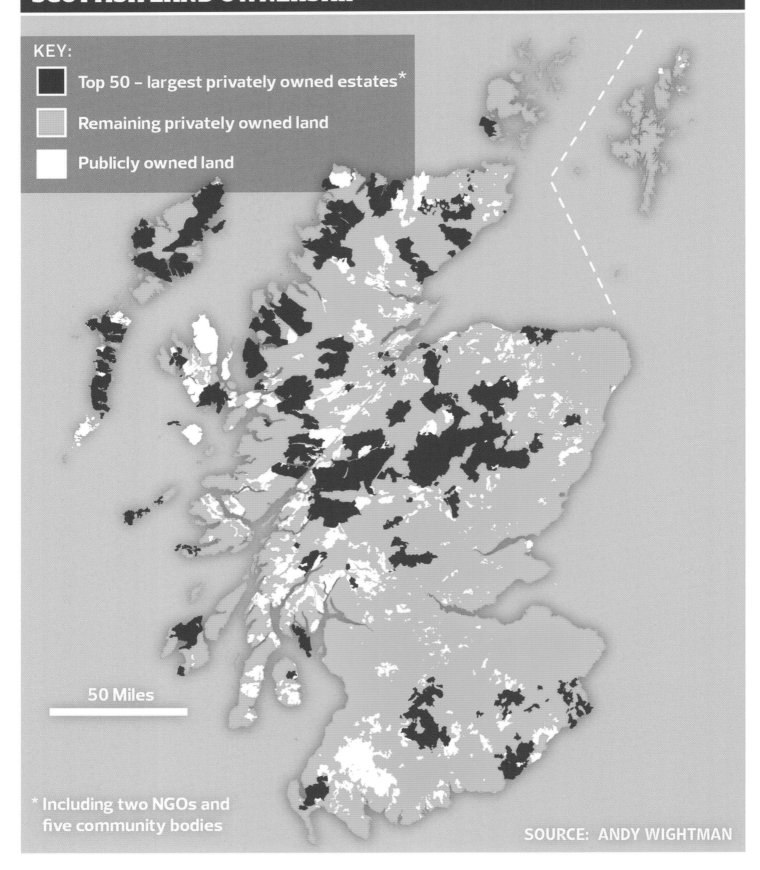

SCOTTISH LAND OWNERSHIP

KEY:

■ Top 50 – largest privately owned estates*

▪ Remaining privately owned land

□ Publicly owned land

50 Miles

* Including two NGOs and
five community bodies

SOURCE: ANDY WIGHTMAN

A LAND OF ESTATE LAIRDS

Andy Wightman and *The Observer*, 'Scottish Land Ownership', 2013.

Maps have always served to demonstrate landownership, both recording its detailed bounds and showing the general extent of individual estates and of landownership as a whole. Thus, the Lanhydrock map (see pages 104–105) reflected the pride of ownership of a wide-ranging estate.

This map, from the 10 August 2013 edition of *The Observer*, a politically left of centre newspaper, was produced by Andy Wightman and is intended to demonstrate the inequitable nature of Scottish land ownership. The map very much conveys that impression, not least by using the boldest colour for the largest privately owned estates, and a muted colour, white, for its counter, publicly owned land.

Andy Wightman, an activist in the field of land ownership, became a Scottish Green Party MSP in 2016 before resigning in 2020 over the party's stance on trans rights, thereafter serving as an independent until 2021. Prior to that he was best known for his book *Who Owns Scotland* (1996), and had continued his concern with the issue in *Land Reform The Way Ahead* (2011) and *Forest Ownership in Scotland* (2012). In 2022 he began writing on that topic for *The National*. The arresting map does not capture any other data including land value or terrain. It is both descriptive and campaigning.

Scotland has seen a greater percentage of the great estates maintained than in England, in part because of the buoyant economy in the Highland region built on shooting, stalking and fishing, an economy that draws heavily on international wealth. Moreover, the costs of sustaining these estates, while considerable, were often less than those of comparable English estates. At the close of the nineteenth century the Duke of Buccleuch, Duke of Sutherland and Cameron of Lochiel each owned major estates, but although large-scale traditional landholding continued, the number, extent and role of such estates were less than in the past. However, there was no equivalent in Scotland or England to the collapse in Ireland in the first quarter of the twentieth century of Anglo-Irish landowners due to land reform and civil violence. Nor was there an equivalent to the growth of owner-occupation of farmland in England after 1918 as aristocratic land-sales gathered pace. In England, in so far as new country houses were built, they were not for landed families but for rich businessmen or foreigners who did not wish to build up extensive landholdings.

In 2019 the second largest of Scotland's individual big landowners was a traditional one, the Duke of Buccleuch, who owned about 200,000 acres. The largest was Anders Holch Povlsen, a Danish clothing tycoon and advocate of re-wilding, who had about 220,000 acres in 12 estates in Sutherland and the Grampian area. The Rausing sisters, of Tetra Pak fame, have 100,000 acres, while the ruler of Dubai has about 63,000 acres. In comparison, Forestry and Land Scotland, the government agency responsible for managing the country's forest and land, looks after over a million acres of public forest, the National Trust for Scotland owns about 180,000 acres, and the Church of England has about 32,000. There is a significant Crown holding centred on the Balmoral Estate. Although the largest British Army training area is on Salisbury Plain in England, there are important Ministry of Defence holdings in Scotland, including the Faslane naval base and the Lossiemouth air base.

EXPLORER

OS Explorer, *Torquay & Dawlish*, 2015.

Founded in 1791, the Ordnance Survey had long focused on its established methods and markets, yet it also offered new maps. In 1897, following permission from the Treasury for the necessary funds to enable the publication of an experimental colour map, the monochrome and hachured Old Series of one-inch maps was replaced by a Popular Series that used colour and thus developed standard symbols accordingly, as with different road types, which was of particular interest to purchasers. The introduction of more precise and measured contours rather than hachures meant more opportunities for symbols.

In 1920, selling for four shillings (25p), then a high price, the Ordnance Survey produced its first tourist map, a one-inch-to-the-mile map of Snowdonia with a vivid cover (see illustration, right). For walkers, folding systems were important to the usefulness of such maps, and a number were devised, including the Ansell, Bridges and Bender systems. The contents of such maps changed over the years, reflecting what were seen as customer requirements, not least those of drivers.

Revised in 1996 and 2013, and published in 1997 and 2015 respectively, largely showing urban expansion, this map of Torquay and Dawlish was similar in its use of colour to sheet 202 of the one-and-a-quarter-inch-to-the-mile, 1:50,000 Landranger series published in 1992. However, the 'customer information' was more focused on tourism, with the depiction of sites by symbols, such as viewpoint and golf course, and also words printed onto the map, such as Model Village (referring to Babbacombe). The use of blue for tourist information helped to focus the user's attention, although there was no indication of the difference between types of resort, notably Torquay and Paignton.

The Ordnance Survey also had to respond to new expectations in production and presentation from the 1970s, notably digitisation and metrication. Each was a formidable operation, but by ending expensive manual redrawing the Ordnance Survey was able to continue to provide high-quality printed maps with lower production costs, and because of commercial considerations the metric system had to be adopted.

In 1935 the Ordnance Survey had already begun a process of retriangulation to replace the primary network established over a century before. The process was completed in 1962. In so doing thousands of concrete 'trig pillars' were built on hilltops and high points across the country to serve as solid triangulation points for theodolites and the metric national grid reference system was launched.

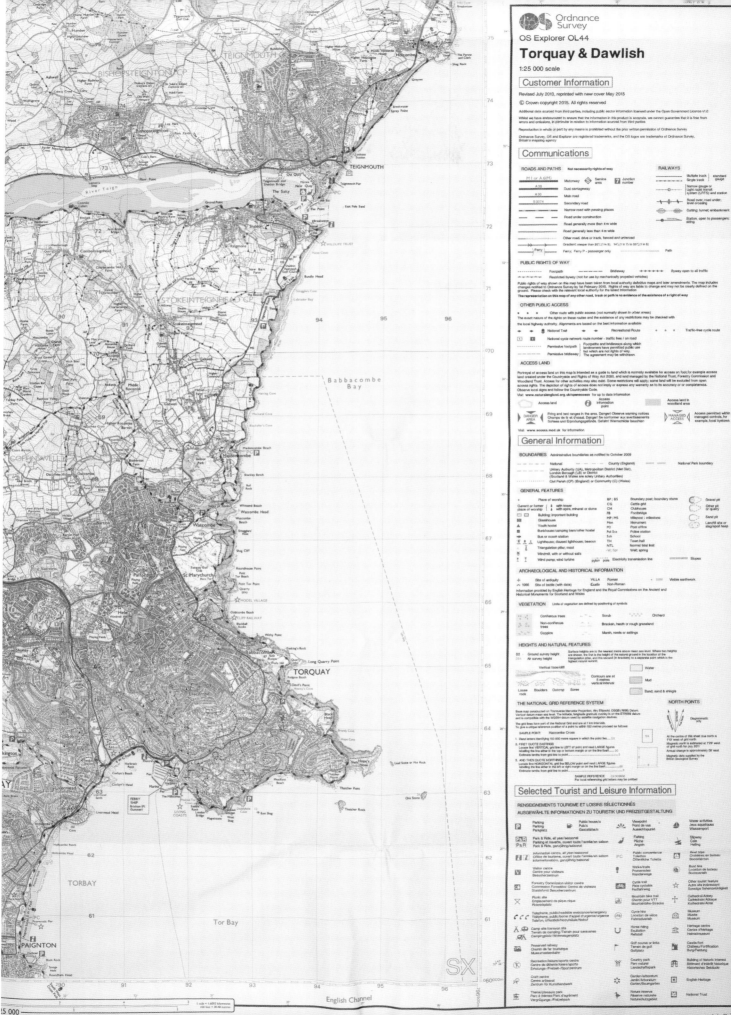

Torquay & Dawlish

OS Explorer OL44

1:25 000 scale

Customer Information

Revised July 2013, reprinted with new cover May 2015

© Crown copyright 2015. All rights reserved

Communications

ROADS AND PATHS Not necessarily rights of way

RAILWAYS

PUBLIC RIGHTS OF WAY

Public rights of way shown on this map have been taken from local authority definitive maps and later amendments. The map includes changes notified to Ordnance Survey by 1st February 2013. Rights of way are liable to change and may not be clearly defined on the ground. Please check with the relevant local authority for the latest information.

The representation on this map of any other road, track or path is no evidence of the existence of a right of way

OTHER PUBLIC ACCESS

The exact nature of the rights on these routes and the existence of any restrictions may be checked with the local Highway authority. Alignments are based on the best information available

ACCESS LAND

Portrayal of access land on this map is intended as a guide to land which is normally available for access on foot, for example access land created under the Countryside and Rights of Way Act 2000, and land managed by the National Trust, Forestry Commission and Woodland Trust. Access for other activities may also exist. Some restrictions will apply; some land will be excluded from open access rights. The depiction of rights of access does not imply or express any warranty as to its accuracy or or completeness. Observe local signs and follow the Countryside Code.

Visit www.naturalengland.org.uk/openaccess for up to date information

Visit www.access.mod.uk for information

General Information

BOUNDARIES Administrative boundaries as notified to October 2009

GENERAL FEATURES

ARCHAEOLOGICAL AND HISTORICAL INFORMATION

Information provided by English Heritage for England and the Royal Commissions on the Ancient and Historical Monuments for Scotland and Wales.

VEGETATION Limits of vegetation are defined by positioning of symbols

HEIGHTS AND NATURAL FEATURES

THE NATIONAL GRID REFERENCE SYSTEM

NORTH POINTS

Selected Tourist and Leisure Information

RENSEIGNEMENTS TOURISME ET LOISIRS SÉLECTIONNÉS

AUSGEWÄHLTE INFORMATIONEN ZU TOURISTIK UND FREIZEITGESTALTUNG

A WESTWARD MIGRATION

The Migration Observatory, 'Distribution of EU migrants in Great Britain', 2015.

The political contentiousness of the extent of immigration into Britain changed from the mid-2000s. Prior to then, it had very much been an issue focused on newcomers from Commonwealth countries, but in 2004 the Labour government, alone among the major Western European states, permitted unrestricted entry for work to the new EU accession countries. In part, this was because of a failure to anticipate the extent of immigration. By 2013 there were 1.24 million people born in Eastern Europe, principally Poland, living in the UK, compared with 170,000 in 2004. The numbers subsequently continued to grow, so that by the end of March 2016 there were believed to be 3.2 million EU nationals in the UK. In 2011, of the 13.4 million non-natives living in the UK, the largest group were the 729,000 Indian-born, followed by the 646,000 Poles. In the year ending March 2016, the Poles, at 831,000, exceeded the Indian-born for the first-time. There were also large numbers from Slovakia, Romania and Bulgaria. London, the focus of immigration both EU and non-EU, saw its population rise from 6.7 million in 1988 to 8.7 million by mid-2015.

The map produced here captured a reality that was not that of popular concerns, which tended to be strongest not where immigrants were most numerous (such as London, where EU citizens represented an estimated 18 per cent of the population in 2020, which voted Remain in the 2016 EU referendum), but rather where the percentage was rising rapidly, for example in parts of East Anglia, with accompanying claims of communities being 'overwhelmed'. Brexit campaigners predicted that continued membership would lead to an annual immigration of 300,000 people, and would rapidly result in a UK population of 80 million, and they drew attention to what they claimed was the risk that Turkey would join the EU. In response, David Cameron correctly argued that there was no current prospect of longstanding accession negotiations leading to such an outcome. Less contentiously, given high unemployment rates in much of the EU, and attractive minimum-wage provisions in the UK, continued inward movement at a high rate appeared likely.

The immigration issue contributed to the referendum vote of 2016 to leave the EU. Although many immigrants came from non-EU countries, a sense among the British public that the jurisdiction of European courts and institutions had eroded the country's ability to control all

16,000 ▭ 984,000

Ireland

Denmark

Netherlands

Belgium

Germany

Poland

Czechia

Li

immigration played a role, as did the concern that German pressure for a distribution across the EU of Syrian refugees proportional to the size of the existing population would lead to a substantial additional increase.

Immigration from the EU fell after the referendum but net migration of EU citizens remained positive until the Covid-19 pandemic began in early 2020. Free movement ended on 31 December 2020, and by the end of September 2021 an estimated 5.2 million EU citizens had applied to the British government's EU Settlement Scheme. This represented a major increase in population.

RUPTURE

Iwan Bala, *The Dis-united Kingdom (Eton Mess)*, 2016.

The idea of personalising Britain and parts thereof for maps is long established. William Harvey, a London doctor and journalist, as part of his atlas *Geographical Fun* (London, 1868), published anthropomorphic maps by Lilian Lancaster (although she was not identified by name), including England in the form of Queen Victoria, Scotland as a piper struggling through the bogs, Ireland as a woman 'peasant, happy in her baby's smile' and Wales as 'Owen Glendowr. In Bardic grandeur'.

Iwan Bala, a Welsh artist, has used imaginary maps in order to comment on Welsh culture, as with 'Cymru Ewropa' (2016), which presents Wales as linked to Europe rather than as part of the British Isles. In his November 2016 exhibition in Penarth he offered a critique of Brexit, not least with a map of Britain running away from Europe toward President Trump's America.

In *The Dis-united Kingdom* (2016), Bala gave a fresh critique of the Brexit referendum. The subtitle, *Eton Mess*, refers to David Cameron and Boris Johnson, both Prime Ministerial old boys of Eton College, and is a pun on a popular dessert of that name. England is seen in terms of xenophobia, and the waters to the south, west and east are titled to make political points while a republican future is predicted for Scotland and an imaginary Channel of Sanity separates it from xenophobic England.

Although Welsh nationalists were very interested in the idea of a Wales of the regions, promised by the EU's Committee of the Regions, created by the Maastricht Treaty in 1993, in the 2016 European referendum a majority of Welsh voters opted for Brexit: 17 out of the 22 Welsh council areas voted for Brexit, not least the industrial areas of South Wales where 56.4 per cent voted thus in Merthyr Tydfil and 62 per cent in Blaenau Gwent.

Plaid Cymru, the Welsh Nationalist Party, was formed at a meeting held at a temperance hotel during the Pwllheli *eisteddfod* in 1925 to campaign for self-government. But by 1930 it had only 500 members, and its concern with the Welsh language and agrarianism were not shared by the bulk of the population. In the 1966 general election only 4.3 per cent of the voters backed the party, but there was a revival thereafter, in part due to dissatisfaction with the Labour government, and the percentage rose to 11.5 in 1970, only to fall thereafter.

Wales gained an assembly after the narrow 1997 referendum result, but Labour proved able to maintain its dominance, helped by Plaid's problems in winning support across Wales and notably in its populous southeast, although Plaid won occasional victories there.

A geographical image was particularly to the fore in the case of the Conservative general election victory of 2019, in the shape of the 'Red Wall' of traditional Labour seats in northern England, many of which went Conservative in a major electoral surprise. The previous spatial pattern of elections was transformed.

The analysis was even more apparent if, instead of the geographic view showing land area, the constituency view showing seats in Parliament or maps based on population distribution were used. These indicated Labour's still-strong presence in the North, and notably the Northeast and Merseyside, as well as South Wales, but also the very strong significance of London and of university cities such as Cambridge, Canterbury, Exeter, Oxford and Plymouth, with Labour support in all of them.

Mapping elections provides a key instance of the need to represent the consequences of a highly varied population density. Cartograms, with the scale proportional to the population, did so although they could lead to a situation in which areas not joined in the cartography were in fact joined in practice. In the cartogram mapping of elections, the cartogram base changes over time. Constituencies appear and disappear and alter shape as the size of their electorates change. For example, as the percentage of the population in southern England has risen, so its area in the map has grown.

These points are exemplified in the maps made by Benjamin Henning, an Icelandic geographer who is an expert in the depiction of gridded cartography. Alongside the contrasts, there are common features such as the weakness of the Liberal Democrats whichever system is used.

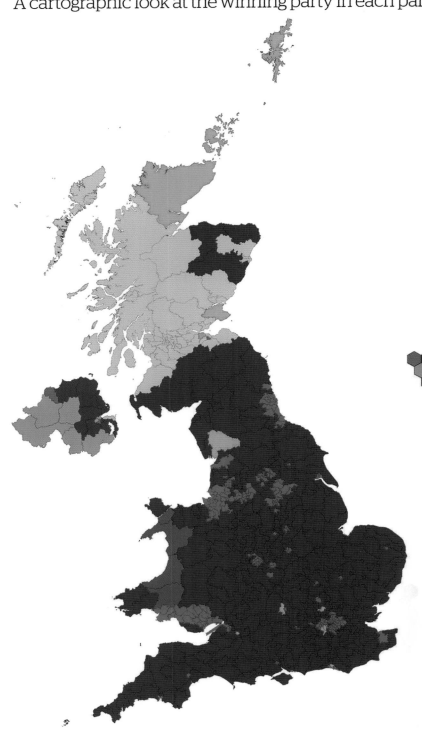

Mapping the 2019 General Election
A cartographic look at the winning party in each parl

Geographic view
Map showing land area

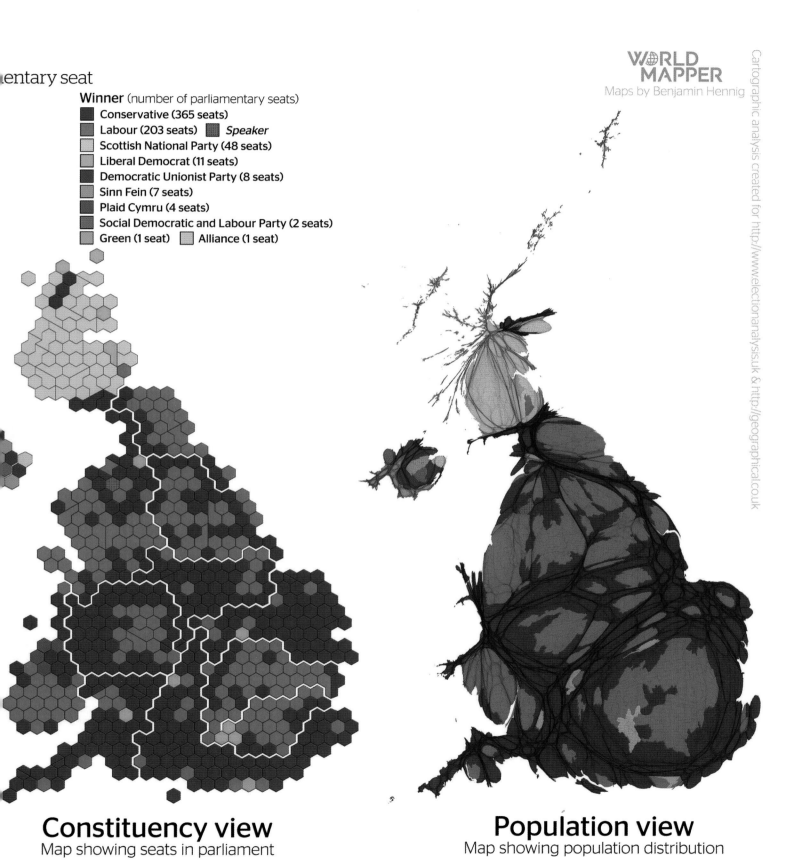

entary seat

Winner (number of parliamentary seats)

- Conservative (365 seats)
- Labour (203 seats) *Speaker*
- Scottish National Party (48 seats)
- Liberal Democrat (11 seats)
- Democratic Unionist Party (8 seats)
- Sinn Fein (7 seats)
- Plaid Cymru (4 seats)
- Social Democratic and Labour Party (2 seats)
- Green (1 seat) Alliance (1 seat)

Cartographic analysis created for http://www.electionanalysis.uk & http://geographical.co.uk

Constituency view
Map showing seats in parliament

Population view
Map showing population distribution

The Daily Telegraph, 'Covid Tiers in the UK', 27 November 2020.

The public use of maps became more prominent during the Covid-19 pandemic of 2020–22 for two reasons. First, to show where the disease was particularly virulent; this was done both within government and publicly, although for different purposes. Government was concerned about the means and rate of transmission of a new disease. As with other new phenomena, mapping distribution proved to be a key element in the relevant research. At the public level, there was linked concern. Second, maps became more prominent because of the means developed in an attempt to control the spread of the disease by regulating human contact.

The significance of the issue was shown by the prominence given to the maps in the media, both on television and in newspapers. It became commonplace to see maps on the front page of the latter, and notably in the prime position under the masthead, a spot previously taken by photographs.

The maps published in *The Daily Telegraph* on 27 November 2020 also related to a third, more marginal, use: to support political dissension. The paper was in the position of being a Conservative one attacking a Conservative government, and both the headline and the captions attached to the maps indicated this disapproving stance. Tier 3 was the most restrictive and was coloured in red, the colour of alarm, while Tier 1, in green, was the least restrictive. With the standard mapping by omission, Wales and Scotland were not included in the map because those countries were regulated by their devolved assemblies.

The text brought out a number of points about the maps, namely the area that moved from Tier 3 to Tier 2 in Merseyside, although there was a contrast between the map showing a change for Merseyside, and the text referring to Liverpool, Warrington and Cheshire.

The text also brought out the political dimension not shown in the maps, notably that Conservative strongholds such as Essex, Hertfordshire, Surrey and Dorset, had all moved up a tier, while London had not moved into Tier 3 due to the intervention of the Prime Minister.

34 million worse off than before lockdown

PM facing Tory rebellion over 'unfair' tiers, and may be left relying on Labour's support

By **Camilla Tominey** *and* **Harry Yorke**

BORIS JOHNSON is facing a Tory rebellion after the Government's "authoritarian" and "unfair" new tier system left 34 million people facing tougher restrictions than before lockdown.

MPs were described as being "in open revolt" after 98 per cent of England's population were placed in Tiers 2 and 3, with only Cornwall, the Isle of Wight and the Scilly Isles put in the lowest level.

Mr Johnson defended the measures saying they were necessary to prevent a "New Year national lockdown".

More than 23 million people, including in large swathes of the Midlands, the North East and North West, were placed in the most restrictive Tier 3, with almost all household mixing banned and bars and restaurants limited to takeaways and deliveries. A further 32 million were placed in Tier 2, which bans household mixing indoors and only allows pubs and restaurants to sell alcohol with a "substantial" meal.

In total, 34.1 million people (61 per cent of the population) were moved into a higher tier than that which they were in before the second national lockdown began on Nov 5. More than 55 million people in England are in Tiers 2 and 3, which have even tougher rules this time around. Mr Johnson faces a revolt when the measures are put to a vote on Tuesday, the day before they come into force.

Depending on the scale of the Tory opposition, the Prime Minister may rely on Labour votes to get the measures through. Labour last night refused to confirm how its MPs would vote.

Speaking in Downing Street after emerging from 14 days in self-isolation, Mr Johnson said: "I know this will bring a great deal of heartache and frustration, especially for our vital hospitality sector – our pubs, our restaurants, our hotels, in so many ways the soul of our communities – which continue to bear a disproportionate share of the burden.

"I really wish it were otherwise, but if we are to keep schools open – as we must – then our options in bearing down on the disease are necessarily limited."

The new system came after the Government announced the rules would be relaxed from Dec 23 to 27 to allow up to three households to meet for Christmas.

But despite guidance suggesting there would be no need to maintain social distancing within a Christmas bubble, Prof Chris Whitty, the Chief Medical Officer, warned: "Would I encourage someone to hug and kiss their elderly relatives? No I would not…

BRITAIN'S BEST QUALITY NEWSPAPER

aily Telegraph

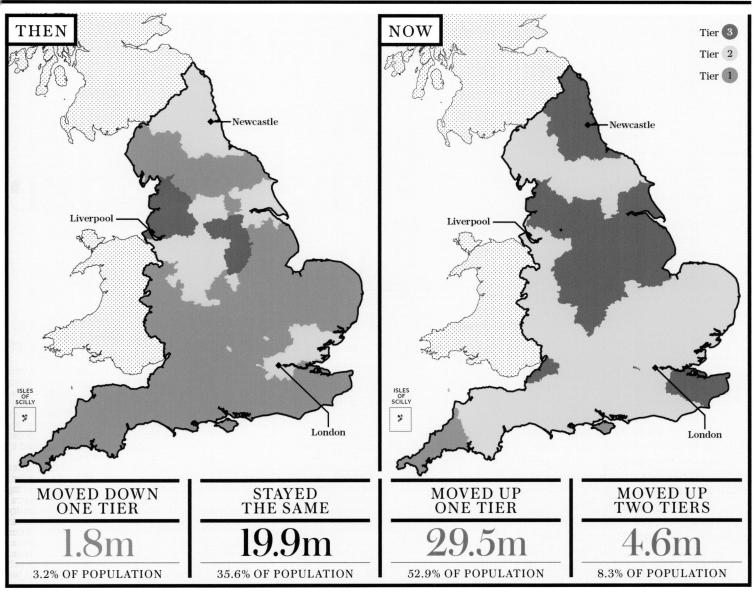

THEN

Newcastle
Liverpool
ISLES OF SCILLY
London

NOW

Tier 3
Tier 2
Tier 1

Newcastle
Liverpool
ISLES OF SCILLY
London

MOVED DOWN ONE TIER	STAYED THE SAME	MOVED UP ONE TIER	MOVED UP TWO TIERS
1.8m	19.9m	29.5m	4.6m
3.2% OF POPULATION	35.6% OF POPULATION	52.9% OF POPULATION	8.3% OF POPULATION

if you want them to survive to be hugged again."

Liverpool, Warrington and Cheshire were the only areas to move from Tier 3 to Tier 2 thanks largely to mass testing.

London was placed in Tier 2 after the Prime Minister, a former mayor of the capital, overruled Michael Gove, the Cabinet Office minister, who had insisted the city should be in Tier 3 at a meeting of the Cabinet's Covid Opera-

tions subcommittee on Wednesday. Shires in Conservative strongholds such as Essex, Hertfordshire, Surrey and Dorset, all previously in Tier 1, will move up a level, prompting anger. Some southern areas, including Kent, Slough, Bristol, North Somerset and South Gloucestershire, went from Tier 1 to 3, the toughest measures, along with War-wickshire and Leicestershire. Most of the North East joined Greater Manches-

ter, Lancashire, the Humber and most of Yorkshire in Tier 3.

Northern mayors reacted angrily, with Sheffield's Dan Jarvis warning "lockdown must not become limbo" and Manchester's Andy Burnham call-ing for "a strong cross-party appeal" against the "devastating" measures he said would "cause real hardship". Mark Harper, leader of the 70-strong Covid Research Group of lockdown sceptic

backbenchers, called for the Govern-ment to publish the impact assessments and modelling that supported their decision-making.

"There are colleagues who've already publicly said they will be voting against these regulations next week. A lot of MPs are unhappy," he said. "There's a
Continued on Page 6

Editorial Comment: Page 21

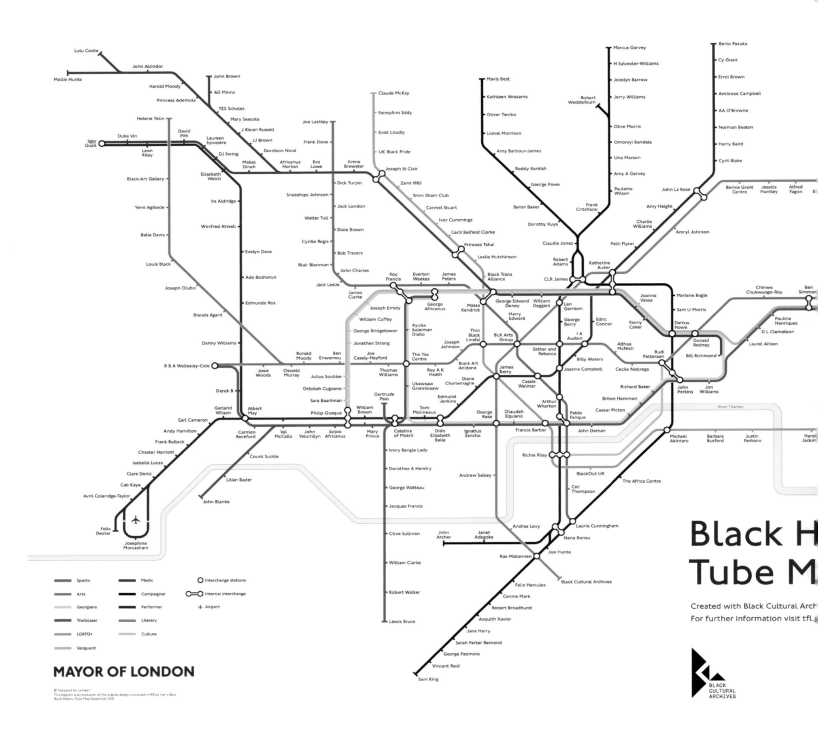

Black H
Tube M

Created with Black Cultural Arch
For further information visit tfl.

AFRICAN AND CARIBBEAN LONDON

TfL and the Black Cultural Archives, *Black History Tube Map*, 2021.

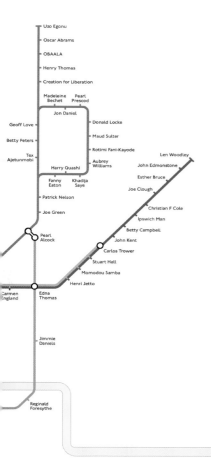

tory

home of Black British history
ack-history-map

The iconic London Underground map was updated in 2021 to launch the first *Black History Tube Map*, a joint project of Transport for London (TfL) and the Black Cultural Archives. Designed to celebrate the rich and varied historical contribution made by Black people in Britain, the map transposes modern-day station names for those of individuals and institutions.

The range of both encourages readers to find out more. For example, Embankment Station is renamed after Pablo Fanque (1810–71), an equestrian performer, tightrope walker, acrobat and the first Black British equestrian producer, who had already been celebrated in The Beatles' song 'Being for the Benefit of Mr Kite!'

St Paul's Station has become Cécile Nobrega (1919–2013), a Guyanese-born British teacher, poet, playwright, composer and community activist who led an eventually successful campaign to establish *The Bronze Woman*, the first public monument to Black women in the United Kingdom. The monument is in Stockwell Memorial Gardens, which makes it somewhat surprising that Stockwell was not the chosen station for her.

Sudbury Town Station was awarded to Evelyn Dove (1902–87), the first Black singer to feature on BBC Radio (in 1939); John Edmonstone (1820–90), representing Upminster, began life as a slave in Guyana but became a taxidermist who taught at the University of Edinburgh; Cesar Picton (1755–1836, corresponding to Blackfriars) was slave-born but became a successful coal merchant in Kingston upon Thames; Barbara Burford CBE (1944–2010, standing for Bermondsey) was a distinguished medical researcher and writer; and Justin Fashanu (1961–98, Canada Water) was a high-profile footballer who had a £1 million transfer fee in 1981 and in 1990 became the first footballer to reveal he was gay.

The British Nationality Act of 1948 reflected the wartime experience of strong imperial links and confirmed the existing position in guaranteeing freedom of entry from the Commonwealth and colonies. From the late 1950s, immigration became a major feature of British life. Large-scale immigration was the case initially with West Indians from British colonies, especially Jamaica. This immigration was a result of colonial links and, in part, of labour shortages in Britain where post-war unemployment was low. Thus, many West Indians found work in London as bus conductors. Many others, however, had no job to go to and were seeking whatever work they could get. There was social tension in response to immigration, and many West Indians felt unwelcome – often rejected as tenants by racist landlords.

In 1962 the first Commonwealth Immigrants Act was passed. These restrictions were accompanied by a transformation in citizenship, so as to draw a strong distinction between citizens of the United Kingdom and those living in the Commonwealth or in former imperial possessions. Previously, all had shared a common citizenship.

In 1981 poor relations between the police and Black youth were a key element in the urban disturbances that erupted that year. The Scarman Inquiry that was set up after the riots focused on racial disadvantage. However, inner-city discontent was arguably not simply a matter of racial issues, but in part a consequence of an economic transformation caused by the decline of manufacturing. The loss of unskilled and semi-skilled work, and the development of an economy of shifts and expedients, led some into criminal behaviour that increased tension with the police. In London in October 1985 a policeman was murdered during riots at Broadwater Farm Estate, a supposedly model estate that had rapidly become a classic instance of the social failure of some of these urban environments. Inner-city rioting on this scale was certainly a new phenomenon for the twentieth century, and the 'inner cities' have remained a topic of analysis and concern ever since.

WIND ON THE WAVES

The Crown Estate, 'Offshore Activity', 2022.

The Crown Estate was established by an Act of Parliament and is tasked with benefiting the nation's finances by generating a profit for the Treasury, which in the past decade or so has totalled £3 billion. As well as some of London's best-known retail and leisure destinations, the Crown Estate manages the seabed and half the foreshore around England, Wales and Northern Ireland, and it plays a crucial role in the sustainable development of this national asset, including the UK's world-leading offshore wind sector. Crown Estate Scotland runs ScotWind, which leases areas of the seabed around Scotland for wind farm developments. ScotWind hopes that farms built in the next decade will have as much as 25GW of new generating capacity. The map, dated 25 May 2022, shows wind energy evolution in UK territorial waters. The key uses colours and symbols to denote offshore wind activity at various stages, from pre-planning application areas to operative wind farms already contributing to the national grid.

Wind power attracted more governmental and public attention from the 2000s. It was seen in terms of an overall contribution to renewable energy, the natural potential of the British Isles, both onshore and offshore, and international standing in terms of renewable energy. These led to government targets, further encouraged by the obsolescence of existing power plants and the fall in the production of natural gas and oil from the North Sea – 2000 having been the year of peak production there. 'Green' policies were also a factor, in particular in the move away from coal-fired power stations, encouraged by carbon taxes, and that despite a rapidly rising population that had high expectations of energy provision.

By 2015 renewables accounted for 24.7 per cent of UK electricity production, notably from wind turbines and solar panels, with Scotland producing about half the UK output. Of the 337.7 terawatt hours of electricity generated in 2015, gas-fired power stations supplied 99.8 and renewables 83.3.

Wind turbines were controversial. It was claimed that they were dangerous to birds, although the Royal Society for the Protection of Birds supports the turbines provided they are located correctly. It was claimed that they were eyesores, especially apparent in upland areas; although that response is a matter of emphasis. The difficulties and costs of eventually dismantling them attracted attention, although many of the claims were exaggerated.

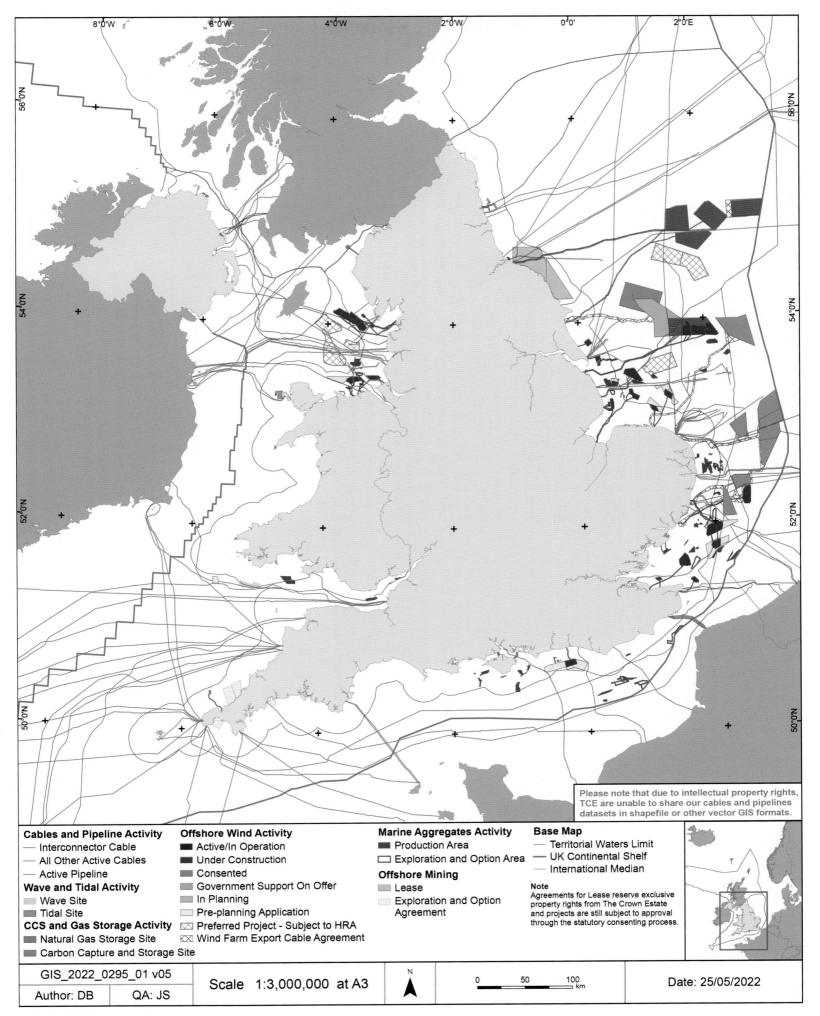

Cables and Pipeline Activity
— Interconnector Cable
— All Other Active Cables
— Active Pipeline

Wave and Tidal Activity
Wave Site
Tidal Site

CCS and Gas Storage Activity
Natural Gas Storage Site
Carbon Capture and Storage Site

Offshore Wind Activity
Active/In Operation
Under Construction
Consented
Government Support On Offer
In Planning
Pre-planning Application
Preferred Project - Subject to HRA
Wind Farm Export Cable Agreement

Marine Aggregates Activity
Production Area
Exploration and Option Area

Offshore Mining
Lease
Exploration and Option Agreement

Base Map
— Territorial Waters Limit
— UK Continental Shelf
— International Median

Note
Agreements for Lease reserve exclusive
property rights from The Crown Estate
and projects are still subject to approval
through the statutory consenting process.

Please note that due to intellectual property rights,
TCE are unable to share our cables and pipelines
datasets in shapefile or other vector GIS formats.

| GIS_2022_0295_01 v05 | | Scale 1:3,000,000 at A3 | N | 0   50   100 km | Date: 25/05/2022 |
| Author: DB | QA: JS | | | | |

FURTHER READING

Anderson, Carolyn and Christopher Fleet, *Scotland: Defending the Nation: Mapping the Military Landscape*, Edinburgh: Birlinn Ltd, 1999.

Andrews, J.H., *A Paper Landscape: The Ordnance Survey in Nineteenth-Century Ireland*, Dublin: Four Courts Press Ltd, 1975.

Andrews, J.H., *Shapes of Ireland: Maps and their Makers, 1564–1839*, Dublin: Geography Publications, 1997.

Chapman, J., Oliver, R.R. and Kain, R.J.P., *The Enclosure Maps of England and Wales 1595–1918*, Cambridge: Cambridge University Press, 2004.

Cunningham, I.C. (ed.), *The Nation Survey'd: Timothy Pont's Maps of Scotland*, Edinburgh: John Donald Publishers, 2001.

Delano-Smith, C. and Kain, R.J.P., *English Maps: A History*, Toronto: University of Toronto Press, 1999.

Dorling, Danny, *A New Social Atlas of Britain*, London: John Wiley and Sons, 1995.

Foxell, Simon, *Mapping England*, London: Black Dog Publishing, 2008.

Gardiner, Leslie, *Bartholomew, 150 Years*, Edinburgh: J. Bartholomew, 1976).

Garland, K., *Mr Beck's Underground Map*, London: Capital Transport Publishing, 1994.

Harvey, P.D.A., *The History of Topographical Maps: Symbols, Pictures and Surveys*, London: Thames & Hudson, 1980.

Harvey, P.D.A., *Medieval Maps*, London: British Library Publishing, 1991.

Harvey, P.D.A., *Maps in Tudor England*, London: British Library Publishing, 1993.

Harvey, P.D.A., *Mappa Mundi: The Hereford World Map*, Toronto: University of Toronto Press, 1996.

Hellyer, R., *The 'Ten-Mile' Maps of the Ordnance Surveys*, London: The Charles Close Society, 1991.

Hewitt, Rachel, *Map of a Nation: A Biography of the Ordnance Survey*, London: Granta Publications, 2011.

Hodgkiss, A.G., *Understanding Maps: A systematic history of their use and development*, Folkstone, Kent: Dawson & Sons, 1981.

Hodgson, Y., *Popular Maps: The Ordnance Survey Popular Edition One-Inch Map of England and Wales, 1919–1926*, London: The Charles Close Society, 1999.

Hoskins, W.G., *The Making of the English Landscape*, London: Hodder & Stoughton, 1955.

Nicholson, T.R., *Wheels on the Road: Maps of Britain for the Cyclist and Motorist 1870–1940*, Norwich: Geo Books, 1983.

Oliver, R.R., *Ordnance Survey Maps: A Concise Guide for Historians*, London: The Charles Close Society, 1992.

Oliver, R.R., and Kain, R.J.P., *The Tithe Maps of England and Wales: A Cartographic Analysis and County-by-County Catalogue*, Cambridge: Cambridge University Press, 1995.

Oliver, R.R., and Kain, R.J.P., *British Town Maps: A History*, London: British Library Publishing, 2015.

Smith, David, *Victorian Maps of the British Isles*, London: Batsford Ltd, 1985.

Snow, John, *On the Mode of Communication of Cholera*, London: John Churchill, (2nd edn) 1855.

Tyacke, S. (ed.), *English Map-Making, 1500–1650*, London: British Library Publishing, 1983.

Whyte, I.D., *Landscape and History since 1500*, London: Reaktion Books, 2002.

Withers, Charles W.J., *Geography, Science and National Identity: Scotland since 1520*, Cambridge: Cambridge University Press, 2001.

LIST OF MAPS

Note: All maps and illustrations are from the collections of the British Library unless otherwise specified. Printed titles are in *italics* whereas manuscript/handwritten and plate titles are in 'inverted commas'.

Introduction: The Geological Past to Medieval Britain

A delineation of the Strata of England and Wales, with part of Scotland; exhibiting the Collieries and Mines, the Marshes and Fen Lands originally overflowed by the sea, and the varieties of Soil … By W. Smith. London: J. Cary, 1815. Maps *1180.(20.).

Sheet for Exeter, 1995, *Geological Survey of England and Wales 1:63,360/1:50,000 geological map series, New Series.* Southampton: Ordnance Survey, 1972–. © British Geological Survey.

The Invasions of England and Ireland, with all their civill wars since the conquest by John Speed, London, 1601. Maps CC.5.a.178.

'Saxon England'. Charles Henry Pearson, *Historical Maps of England, during the first thirteen centuries.* London, 1870. Cup.1247.h.27.

'Map of Britain', *Claudii Ptholemaei Alexandrini liber geographiae cum tabulis et universali figura et cum additione locorum quae a recentioribus reperta sunt, diligenti cura emendatus et impressus.* Venetiis: Per Iacobum Pentium de leucho, 1511. Maps C.1.d.7.

'World Map', S. England, second quarter of eleventh century. Cotton MS Tiberius B.V/1, f.56v.

'Hereford *Mappa Mundi*', c.1300. Hereford Cathedral.

Matthew Paris, 'Map of Great Britain', c.1255. Cotton MS Claudius D VI/1.

'London to Dover, Itinerary from London to the Holy Land with images of towns, their names, and descriptions of places', Matthew Paris, *Historia Anglorum, Chronica majora*, Part III, 1250–1259. Royal Ms 14 C VII, f.2.

'The Gough Map', England, c.1360. Bodleian Libraries, University of Oxford, MS Gough Gen. Top. 16.

'Map of Scotland depicting the main fortifications and towns with an array of castles, walled towns, gatehouses, churches and bridges', John Hardyng, *Chronicle* (first version), 1440–1450. Lansdowne MS 204, ff.226v-227r.

Chapter 1 The Sixteenth Century

'Map of the coast of Cornwall and Devon from the Scilly Isles and Land's End to Exeter', 1539–1540. Cotton MS Augustus I i 35. tributaries

'Map of the River Trent and its tributaries between Nottingham and Newark', c.1540. Cotton MS Augustus I i 65.

'Proposals for Dover Harbour', 1552. Add MS 69824 A.

The Moorfields section of the Copperplate Map. Etched copper base-plate for map of the City of London, c.1559. Museum of London, 62.75.

'Cambriae Typus auctore Humfredo Lhuydo Denbigiense Cambrobritanno', the Burghley Atlas, 1574–1592. Royal MS 18 D III, f.99

'The Counties of England', 1579, the Burghley Atlas, 1574–1592. Royal MS 18 D III, f.6.

'Edenburgum, Scotiae Metropolis'. Georg Braun, *Civitates Orbis Terrarium.* Cologne: P. von Brachel, c.1600–1623. Maps C.29.e.1.

'Map of the Parish of Smallburgh, Norfolk'. John Darby, 1582. Maps Roll 527.

Isca Damnoniorum … Latine Exonia, Anglice Exeancestre vel Exestre at nunc vulgo Exeter … Opera et impensis J. Hokeri … hanc tabella[m] sculpsit R. Hogenbergius. London?, 1587. Maps C.5.a.3.

Sheldon Tapestry Map of Warwickshire, 1580s. Warwickshire Museum Service.

'The River Thames from Westminster to Tilbury Hope, and showing the progress of Queen Elizabeth to the camp at Tilbury 1588 and the scheme for the defence of the Thames against the Spanish Armada', 1588. Add MS 44839.

Map of Chelmsford. Part of a survey of the manor of Bishop's Hall by John Walker, 1591. Essex Record Office, D/DM P1.

A New Description of Kent. Divided into the fyue Lathes thereof: and subdivided into Baylywiekes; and Hundredes: with the parishe Churches conteyned within euery of the same Hundredes by Philip Symonson, 1596. Maps M.T.6.f.1.(4.).

Chapter 2 The Stuart Age

'A Plott of the Six Escheated Counties of Ulster', drawn by John Norden, c.1610. Cotton MS Augustus I ii 44.

The assault upon Enniskillen Castle, 17 February 1593/4, drawn by John Thomas, 1594. Cotton MS Augustus I ii 39.

Map of Bassingham. 'Reasons for the petition to the Lady Francis, Countess Dowager of Warwick, from her tenants in Bassingham in favour of improvement of Bassingham by farming in severalty, inclosure and drainage', 1629. Image courtesy of Lincolnshire Archives, Misc DEP 264/2.

'The Mannar of Brainston and part of Nutford, late the land of Richard Rogers Esqr deceased, in the Countie of Dorset' by Margaret and William Bowles, 1659. Maps CC.6.a.85.

A True Mapp and Description of the Towne of Plymouth and the Fortifications thereof, with the workes and approaches of the Enemy at the last Siege A°. 1643. W. Hollar fecit, 1643. Maps 2140.(5.).

'Scotia Regnvm cum insulis adjacentibus. Robertus Gordonius a Straloch descripsit'. Joannis Blaeu, *Theatrum Orbis Terrarum, sive Atlas Novus. Pars Quinta.* Amsterdam: Apud Ioanneum Blaeu, 1654. Maps 1.tab.28.

'The London Plan' by Christopher Wren, 1666. © The Warden and Fellows of All Souls College, Oxford, Drawing 396 (l.7) recto.

A Plan for Rebuilding the City of London After the Great Fire in 1666: Design'd by that great architect S.r Christopher Wren and Approv'd of by King and Parliament, but unhappily defeated by faction. John Gwynn. London: Edward Rooker, 1749. Maps K.Top.20.20.

A description of al[l] the postroads in England, from London to Edenborough in Scotland … drawn and perfected by R. Carr. Amsterdam?, 1668. Maps CC.5.a.43.

An Exact Delineation of the Famous Citty of Bristoll and Suburbs. Bristol: James Millerd, 1673. Maps K.Top.37.32.2.

The Roads of England According to Mr. Ogilby's Survey. London: George Willdey, 1712. Maps K.Top.5.84.

'The Road from London to King's Lynn'. *Britannia, volume the first: or, an illustration of the Kingdom of England and Dominion of Wales; by a geographical and historical description of the principal Roads thereof. Actually admeasured and delineated in a century of whole-sheet copper-sculps … By John Ogilby, Esqr; his Majesty's Cosmographer, etc.* London: John Ogilby, 1675. Maps C.6.d.8.

'Edinburgh Firth'. *Great Britain's Coasting Pilot by Capt. Greenvile Collins.* London: Freeman Collins, 1693. Maps C.8.d.7.

'The Lanhydrock Estate'. Page of the Lanhydrock Atlas, surveyed by Joel Gascoyne in the 1690s. Lanhydrock, Cornwall. © National Trust Images/ John Hammond.

A mapp of the kingdom of Ireland, newly corrected & improvd by actuall observations : divided into its provinces, counties & baronies and supply'd with many market towns & other places of note omitted in former mapps with all the principall roades & the distances from place to place in com[m]on reputed miles by inspection by Henry Pratt, engraved by John Harris, London, 1708. Maps K.Top.51.18.11.

Chapter 3 The Hanoverians

'Newcastle Upon Tyne' by James Corbridge, London, 1723. Maps K.Top.32.51.

An Exact Survey of the City's of London, Westminster ye Borough of Southwark and the country near Ten miles round begun in 1741 & ended in 1745 by John Rocque, engraved by Richard Parr. London: John Rocque, 1746. Maps Crace Port.19.18.

Detail, 'Map of the City of London, Westminster and Southwark'. London: John Rocque, 1751–1754. Maps K.Top.20.37.

'The Military Survey of Scotland' by William Roy, 1747–1755. Maps CC.5.a.441.

Salisbury, Wiltshire: Plan of encampment there. Drawn by Captain, afterwards Major-General, George Morrison, 1756–1771. Add MS 15532, f.12r.

'Plan of Liverpool', surveyed by John Eyes, 1765. Liverpool?: John Eyes, 1765. Maps K.Top.18.71

A Map of the County of Essex from an actual survey taken in MDCCLXXI, LXXIII & MDCCLXXIV. London: J. Chapman & P. André, 1777. Maps K.Top.13.6.

A New and Accurate Plan of the City of Bath from a late Survey with the New Additional Buildings. Bath: A. Tennent, 1779. Maps K.Top.37.20.

Scotland Drawn and Engrav'd from a Series of Angles and Astronomical Observations by John Ainslie. Edinburgh: John & James Ainslies; London: William Faden, 1789. Maps K.Top.48.31.8.

A Topographical Plan of Manchester and Salford with the Adjacent Parts; Shewing also the Different Allotments of Land proposed to be built on, As communicated to the Surveyor by the respective Proprietors by Charles Laurent, 1793. London: C. Laurent, 1793. Maps K.Top.18.79.2.

Wallis's Tour Through England and Wales, a New Geographical Pastime. London: John Wallis, 1794. Maps C.44.b.79.

A Correct Plan of the Isle of Man by Peter Fannin, Master in His Majesty's Royal Navy. London: P. Fannin & H. Ashby, 1789.

A Map of England, showing the Lines of all the Navigable Canals; with those which have been proposed. London: I. & J. Taylor, 1795. Maps *1190.(7.).

A Map and Section of that part of the Grand Canal now perfected, and also a Sketch of the Country on each Side &c &c, Extending from the City of Dublin to the River Barrow at Monasterevan. Dublin: J. Brownrigg, 1788. Maps K.Top.51.33.2.

'View of Vinegar hill on the north east side'. *Memoirs of the different rebellions in Ireland, from the arrival of the English: with a particular detail of that which broke out the XXIII D of May, MDCCXCVIII; the history of the conspiracy which preceded it; and the characters of the principal actors in it. Compiled from original affidavits and other authentic documents; and illustrated with maps and plates, by Sir Richard Musgrave.* Dublin: Printed by Robert Marchbank for John Milliken and John Stockdale, 1801. Maps C.44.e.13.

Chapter 4 The Nineteenth Century

An Accurate Plan of the Docks for the West India Trade, and the Canal, in the Isle of Dogs engraved by Robert Rowe. London: John Fairburn, 1800. Maps Crace Port.18.39.

An Elevated View of the New Dock in Wapping. Drawn & Engraved by Wm Daniell. London: William Daniell, 1803.

Maps K.Top.21.31.a.Port.11.Tab.
*General Survey of England and Wales.
An entirely new & accurate Survey of
the County of Kent, with Part of the
County of Essex, Done by the Surveying
Draftsmen of His Majesty's Honourable
Board of Ordnance, on the basis of the
Trigonometrical Survey carried on by
their Orders under the direction of Capt.n
W. Mudge of the Royal Artillery, F.R.S.*
London: W. Faden, 1801. Maps 148.e.27.
'Plan of the Manor of East Bedfont with
Hatton, in the Parish of East Bedfont
in the County of Middlesex. Taken at
the time of the Inclosure, 1816', Thos.
& Willm. Denton, Surveyors, Staines,
1816. Maps M.T.6.b.1.(21.)
'Map of St. Peter's Field, Manchester'.
*Peterloo Massacre, containing a faithful
narrative ... Edited by an Observer.*
Manchester: J. Wroe, 1819. 601.
aa.9.(1.).
'Plan of the Country in the
Neighbourhood of Gills-Hill', George
Henry Jones, *Account of the Murder of
the Late Mr. William Weare, of Lyon's
Inn, ... and the execution of J. Thurtell,
etc.* London: J. Nichols and Son, 1824.
6495.cc.13.
'Plan of Gill's-Hill Cottage, late in the
Occupation of Mr William Probert',
George Henry Jones, *Account of the Late
Mr. William Weare, of Lyon's Inn, ... and
the execution of J. Thurtell, etc.* London: J.
Nichols and Son, 1824. 6495.cc.13.
*Map of London, from an Actual Survey
made in the years 1824, 1825 & 1826 by C.
and I. Greenwood.* London: Greenwood,
Pringle & Co., 1827. Maps 15.b.17.
*A Plan and Section of an intended Railway
or Tram-Road from Liverpool to
Manchester, in the County Palatine of
Lancaster. Surveyed by George Stephenson
... 20th day of Nour. 1824.* London,
Liverpool, 1824. Maps 1223.(14.).
'Glasgow and Suburbs', Robert Perry,
*Facts and Observations on the Sanitory
State of Glasgow during the last year.*
Glasgow: Glasgow Royal Asylum for
Lunatics, 1844. C.T.249.(18.)
*Wallis's Picturesque Round Game of the
Produce & Manufactures, of the Counties
of England & Wales.* London: Edward
Wallis, 1844? Maps C.29.b.16.
'Liverpool', London: John Tallis & Co.,
1845. Maps 25.a.2.
*Map of the British Isles Elucidating the
Distribution of the Population Based on
the Census of 1841,* Compiled and drawn
by A. Petermann, London, 1849. Maps
*1125.(1.).
'Plan showing the Ascertained Deaths
from Cholera in part of the Parishes
of St James, Westminster and St.
Anne, Soho, during the summer and
autumn of 1854' in *Report on the Cholera
Outbreak in the Parish of St. James,
Westminster, During the Autumn of 1854.*
Presented to the Vestry by the Cholera
inquiry Committee, July 1855. London,
1855. 7560.c.58.

Map of the Soho District (reproduced
originally in *On the Mode of
Communication of Cholera,* 2nd edition,
1855, as 'Showing the deaths from
cholera in Broad Street, Golden
Square, and the neighbourhood, from
19th August to 30th September 1854')
accompanying 'Dr. Snow's Report' in
*Report on the Cholera Outbreak in the
Parish of St. James, Westminster, During
the Autumn of 1854. Presented to the
Vestry by the Cholera inquiry Committee,
July 1855.* London, 1855. 7560.c.58.
'Buckinghamshire as Divided
into Unions by the Poor Law
Commissioners', London: J. & C.
Walker, 187-? Maps 195.d.16.
'Plate 8: Map of the Macclesfield,
Sheffield and Nottingham & Derby
Districts', *The Wesleyan Methodist Atlas
of England and Wales, Containing Fifteen
Plates Carefully Designed and Arranged
by the Rev. Edwin.H. Tindall.* London:
Bemrose & Sons, 1871 [c.1873?]. Maps
1174.(1.).
Airey's Railway Map of England & Wales.
London: McCorquodale & Co, 1877.
Maps 1220.(18.).
Descriptive Map of London Poverty 1889,
'North-Eastern sheet, comprising parts
of Hackney, Islington and Holborn; the
whole of the City, Shoreditch, Bethnal
Green, Whitechapel, St. George's-in-
the-East, Stepney, Mile End, and part
of Poplar', as reproduced in Charles
Booth, *Labour and Life of the People,*
London, 1891. Maps C.21.a.18.
Hardy's 'The Wessex of the Novels'
(1895–97), reproduced here from
Thomas Hardy, *Under the Greenwood
Tree,* London: Macmillan & Co., 1925.
W9/8284.
'Insurance Plan of Belfast' by C.E. Goad.
London, 1887–1898. Maps 145.b.5.

**Chapter 5 1900–60: War and
Transformation**
'Plan of the City of York', B. Seebohm
Rowntree, *Poverty: A Study of Town Life.*
London: Macmillan & Co., 1901. 8285.
eee.4.
'Map showing geographical distribution
of British genius as represented by over
28000 prominent men and women
of thought or action', E. Reich, *A
New Student's Atlas of English History.*
London: Macmillan & Co., 1903). Maps
29.b.40.
'Manchester', *Pratt's Road Atlas of England
and Wales for Motorists.* London: Anglo-
American Oil Co. Ltd, 1905. Maps
14.a.72.
'Proposed Garden Suburb at Hampstead
North London', Barry Parker and
Raymond Unwin Architects, February
1905. London: Hampstead Tenants Ltd
& The Garden Suburb Trust, c.1935.
Maps 3479.(35.).
"Cycling" Map of England & Wales
Showing the Best Touring Roads, John
Bartholomew & Co. London: Offices of

'Cycling', 1908. Maps 28.a.64.
'Map of the "Tubes" of London in One
Mile Squares', *Brief Guide to London.*
London: D.H. Evans & Co Ltd., 1908.
University of California Libraries.
'How the Zeppelins Came to England',
Western Daily Press, 23 January 1915.
'The Parliamentary Constituencies
of the British Isles and the Results
of the General Elections since 1885'
in 'Geographic Influences in British
Elections', *The Geographical Review.*
New York: American Geographical
Society, 1916. AC.2495/7.
The Record of the Irish Rebellion of 1916.
Dublin: Office of Irish Life, 1916.
9508.m.1.
*British Empire Exhibition, 1924: Wembley
Park April–October. Its situation described
in relation to the railways of London by
Stanley Kennedy North.* Edinburgh,
etc.: Dobson, Molle & Co, 1924. Maps
3465.(16.).
Agatha Christie, *The Murder at the
Vicarage.* London: W. Collins, Sons &
Co, 1930. NN.17328.
'Sketch Plan of Oxford (Simplified)',
Edmund Crispin, *The Moving Toyshop.*
London: Victor Gollancz, 1946.
NN.36207.
Map of the Coalfields of England and Wales,
issued by the Geological Survey of Great
Britain. Southampton: Ordnance
Survey, 1935. Maps 1180.(31.).
'Land Utilisation', Land Utilisation Survey
of Britain. Southampton: Ordnance
Survey, 1942. Maps 1135.(64.).
'City of Plymouth: New City Centre',
*A Plan for Plymouth, report prepared
for the City Council by J. Paton Watson
and Patrick Abercrombie.* Plymouth:
Underhill, 1943. 08286.m.23.
'Defence of Britain: Defences as at "D"
Day 6 June 1944'. London: Ministry of
Home Security, Key Points Intelligence
Directorate, 1945. Maps X.2931.
'Boundaries of Area Electricity Boards:
Grid Transmission Lines and Selected
Stations'. London: Electrical Press,
1947. Maps 1190.(101.)
'"Electrical Industries": Graded Supply
Map of England & Wales, Showing
Areas of Authorised Distributors,
Output of Undertakings ... and
Consumption per head of population
per annum'. London: Electrical Press,
1947. Maps 1190.(101.).
*Geographers' A to Z Street Atlas of
Birmingham and the West Midlands.*
Produced under the direction
of Alexander Gross. London:
Geographers' Map Co., Ltd., 1956.
Maps 197.a.42.

**Chapter 6 1960–Today: New Subjects,
New Techniques**
British Railways: 'Density of Passenger
Traffic', *The Reshaping of British
Railways.* London: Her Majesty's
Stationery Office, 1963. Maps
C.44.d.97.

British Railways: 'Proposed Withdrawal
of Passenger Train Services', *The
Reshaping of British Railways.* London:
Her Majesty's Stationery Office, 1963.
Maps C.44.d.97.
'Arteriosclerotic Heart Disease,
including Coronary Disease (Males)'
in *National Atlas of Disease Mortality
in the United Kingdom.* Prepared by
G. Melvyn Howe ... on behalf of the
Royal Geographical Society. London:
Thomas Nelson and Sons, 1963. Maps
62.c.38.
'Map of cherished land' published in *The
Geographical Magazine,* October 1973.
London: IPC Magazines, 1973. Maps
1080.(112.).
'Bangor', *Soil Survey of England and
Wales.* Chessington: Ordnance Survey,
1954–. Maps 1190.(116.).
'Winter Rain Acceptance Potential',
Soil Survey of England and Wales.
Chessington: Ordnance Survey, 1954–.
Maps 1190.(116.).
Weather Map of the British Isles. Compiled
and written by D.M. Houghton.
Edinburgh: John Bartholomew & Son,
1978. Maps 1101.(124.).
'ASXX EGRR MSLP Analysis DT 0600 UTC
16 Oct 1987', The Met Office.
'Upper Airedale Local Plan: Proposals
Map', Bradford: Metropolitan District
Council, 1986. Maps X.10432.
'Cornwall County Structure Plan',
Truro: Cornwall County Council, 1981.
X.525/5623.
'Relative Strength of the Principal
Parties 1950–79', *Atlas Cenedlaethol
Cymru/National Atlas of Wales.* Edited
by Harold Carter. Cardiff: University of
Wales, 1980–89. Maps 60.f.7.
Map of Liverpool, 2008–09. © Stephen
Walter.
Map of 'Scottish Land Ownership' in
'Scotland has the most inequitable
land ownership in the west. Why?'
published in *The Observer,* 10 August
2013. © Andy Wightman/Guardian
News & Media Ltd 2022.
Torquay & Dawlish. OS Explorer OL44.
Southampton: Ordnance Survey, 2015.
Maps Y.2581.
'Distribution of EU migrants in Great
Britain', 2015. © The Migration
Observatory at the University of
Oxford.
The Dis-united Kingdom (Eton Mess), mixed
media on Indian Khadi paper, 2016. ©
Iwan Bala.
*Mapping the 2019 General Election: A
cartographic look at the winning party in
each parliamentary seat,* 2019. Map by
Benjamin Henning © World Mapper.
'Then' and 'Now' Covid Tiers in the UK,
The Daily Telegraph, 27 November 2020.
© Telegraph Media Group Limited
2020.
Black History Tube Map, 2021. © Transport
for London/Black Cultural Archives.
'Offshore Activity', Crown Estates, 2022.
© Crown Copyright.